THE MERCENARIES
OF THE HELLENISTIC WORLD

THE MERCENARIES
OF THE HELLENISTIC WORLD

by

G. T. GRIFFITH

*Fellow of Gonville and Caius College,
Cambridge*

HARE PRIZE ESSAY, 1933

CAMBRIDGE
AT THE UNIVERSITY PRESS
1935

CAMBRIDGE
UNIVERSITY PRESS

University Printing House, Cambridge CB2 8BS, United Kingdom

Published in the United States of America by Cambridge University Press, New York

Cambridge University Press is part of the University of Cambridge.

It furthers the University's mission by disseminating knowledge in the pursuit of education, learning and research at the highest international levels of excellence.

www.cambridge.org
Information on this title: www.cambridge.org/9781107419308

© Cambridge University Press 1935

This publication is in copyright. Subject to statutory exception and to the provisions of relevant collective licensing agreements, no reproduction of any part may take place without the written permission of Cambridge University Press.

First published 1935
First paperback edition 2014

A catalogue record for this publication is available from the British Library

ISBN 978-1-107-41930-8 Paperback

Cambridge University Press has no responsibility for the persistence or accuracy of URLs for external or third-party internet websites referred to in this publication, and does not guarantee that any content on such websites is, or will remain, accurate or appropriate.

CONTENTS

ACKNOWLEDGMENT	page vii
BIBLIOGRAPHICAL NOTE	viii
ABBREVIATIONS	ix
INTRODUCTION	1
Chap. I. PHILIP AND ALEXANDER	8
Appendix. A note on Alexander's mercenaries	27
II. THE SUCCESSORS	33
III. MACEDONIA	57
1. Demetrius after Ipsus	57
2. Pyrrhus	60
3. The Antigonids in Macedonia 285–168 B.C.	65
IV. THE GREEK LEAGUES AND CITIES . . .	80
1. Athens and other small employers . .	80
2. Sparta	93
3. The Achaean League	99
V. THE PTOLEMIES	108
1. The Ptolemaic army before Ipsus 323–301 B.C.	109
2. Macedonians, mercenaries, and Egyptians .	111
3. Raphia: the army of Egypt at war strength	118
4. The peace strength of the army . .	125
5. Mercenary cleruchs	135
6. Conclusion	139
VI. THE SELEUCIDS	142
1. The war strength	143
2. The "Macedonians"	147
3. The mercenaries	165

CONTENTS

Chap. VII. PERGAMUM AND PONTUS . . . *page* 170
    1. Pergamum 170
    2. Bithynia, Cappadocia and Pontus . . 182

VIII. THE WEST 194
    1. Sicily 194
    2. Carthage 207
    Appendix. Mercenaries with Rome . . 234

IX. THE PROVENANCE AND RECRUITING OF MERCENARIES 236
    1. Provenance 236
    2. Recruiting 254

X. THE PAY AND MAINTENANCE OF MERCENARIES 264
    1. σῖτος (etc.) and μισθός: the process of payment in the classical period . . 264
    2. σιτώνιον (etc.) and ὀψώνιον: the process of payment in the Hellenistic period . 274
    3. Rates of pay 294
    4. The standard of life 308

CONCLUSION 317

INDEX 325

ACKNOWLEDGMENT

This essay, under the title "The Greek Soldier of Fortune", was awarded the Hare Prize for 1933. It attempted to cover the whole ground of Greek and Hellenistic history; but the publication of Mr (now Professor) H. W. Parke's admirable study, *Greek Mercenary Soldiers—from the earliest times to the Battle of Ipsus* (Oxford, 1933), made it unnecessary and undesirable for me to publish the earlier part of my own work. My first thanks are therefore due to the Awarders of the Hare Prize, for allowing this book to appear in its present form, which excludes most of what was redundant with Professor Parke's study, and includes such alterations and additions as I have thought fit to make.

I wish to thank especially Professor F. E. Adcock for his constant help to me both as a scholar and as a friend, without which this book would have been many times more imperfect than it is now: Mr B. L. Hallward, who first suggested this subject of research to me and has always shown a friendly interest in its progress: Mr N. G. L. Hammond for his great kindness and vigilance in reading the book in proof: Dr F. Heichelheim for much valuable help and advice with the Hellenistic documents: the late M. Maurice Holleaux for generously allowing me to make use of an unpublished inscription and of his own notes upon it (pp. 171, 241): and Dr W. W. Tarn for the keen and encouraging criticism which he has always placed at my disposal when I have asked for it, and which has been of more value to me than I can say.

Finally, I am most grateful to the staff of the University Press for their unfailing courtesy and efficiency.

G. T. G.

October 1934

BIBLIOGRAPHICAL NOTE

The ancient sources will everywhere be indicated as they occur.[1]
Of modern authorities, the following studies of special military topics have been of the most value:

(a) K. GROTE. Das griechische Söldnerwesen der hellenistischen Zeit. Diss. Jena, 1913.
   H. W. PARKE. Greek Mercenary Soldiers—from the earliest times to the Battle of Ipsus. Oxford, 1933.
(b) J. LESQUIER. Les institutions militaires de l'Égypte sous les Lagides. Paris, 1911.
   W. SCHUBART. Quaestiones de rebus militaribus, quales fuerint in regno Lagidarum. Diss. Breslau, 1900.
(c) A. J. REINACH. Les mercenaires et les colonies militaires de Pergame. Rev. Arch. xii, 1908, pp. 174, 364; xiii, 1909, pp. 102, 363. (This article remained unfinished.)
(d) J. KROMAYER und U. VEITH. Heerwesen und Kriegführung der Griechen und Römer. Munich, 1928.
   O. LIPPELT. Die griechische Leichtbewaffneten bis auf Alexander den Grossen. Diss. Jena, 1910.
   A. SPENDEL. Untersuchungen zum Heerwesen der Diadochen. Diss. Breslau, 1915.

[1] References to Polybius are to the edition of Büttner-Wobst.

ABBREVIATIONS

A.J.A.	American Journal of Archaeology.
Aktenstücke	U. Wilcken, Aktenstücke aus dem königlichen Bank zu Theben.
Ἀρχ. ἐφ.	Ἀρχαιολογικὴ Ἐφημερίς.
Archiv	Archiv für Papyrusforschung, etc.
B.C.H.	Bulletin de Correspondance hellénique.
B.G.U.	Ägyptische Urkunden aus den Museen zu Berlin. Griechische Urkunden.
Bull. Soc. Arch. Alex.	Bulletin de la Société archéologique d'Alexandrie.
C.A.H.	Cambridge Ancient History.
C.I.G.	Corpus Inscriptionum Graecarum.
Dikaiomata	Dikaiomata, Auszüge aus alexandrinischen Gesetzen herausgegeben von der Graeca Halensis.
Ditt. Syll.³	W. Dittenberger, Sylloge Inscriptionarum Graecarum. Ed. 3.
F.G.H.	F. Jacoby, Fragmente der griechischen Historiker.
F.H.G.	C. Müller, Fragmenta Historicorum Graecorum.
G.G.A.	Göttingische Gelehrte Anzeigen.
Head, H. N.²	B. V. Head, Historia Numorum. Ed. 2.
I.G.	Inscriptiones Graecae.
I.G.²	Inscriptiones Graecae. Editio minor.
Insch. v. Perg.	M. Fränkel, Inschriften von Pergamon.
J.E.A.	Journal of Egyptian Archaeology.
J.H.S.	Journal of Hellenic Studies.
K. Grote	K. Grote, Das griechische Söldnerwesen der hellenistischen Zeit. Diss. Jena, 1913.
Klio	Klio (Beiträge zur alten Geschichte).
L. and S.	Liddell and Scott, Greek Lexicon. Ed. 9.
Mon. ant.	Monimenti antichi pubblicati per cura della r. Accademia dei Lincei.
O.G.I.S.	Orientis Graeci Inscriptiones Selectae.
Parke	H. W. Parke, Greek Mercenary Soldiers, etc. Oxford, 1933.
P. Cairo Zen.	C. C. Edgar, Zenon Papyri. Cairo, 1925, etc.
P. Freib.	M. Gelzer, Mitteilungen aus der Freiburger Papyrussammlung, i–ii. (Sitzungsberichte Heidelberg, 1914.)
P. Grenf. I	B. P. Grenfell, An Alexandrian Erotic Fragment and other Greek Papyri chiefly Ptolemaic. Oxford, 1896.
P. Grenf. II	B. P. Grenfell and A. Hunt, New Classical Fragments and other Greek and Latin Papyri. Oxford, 1897.
P. Gurob	J. G. Smyly, Greek Papyri from Gurob. Dublin, 1921.
P. Hamb.	P. M. Meyer, Griechische Papyruskunden der Hamburger Stadtbibliothek. Leipzig, 1911, etc.
P. Lille	P. Jouguet, etc., Papyrus Grecs. Paris, 1907, etc.
P. Lond.	F. G. Kenyon and H. I. Bell, Greek Papyri in the British Museum. London, 1893, etc.
P. Mich. Zen.	C. C. Edgar, Zenon papyri in the University of Michigan Collection. Ann Arbor, 1931.

ABBREVIATIONS

P. Paris	Brunet de Presle, Notices et Extraits des Manuscrits grecs de la Bibliothèque impériale, xviii. Paris, 1865.
P. Petr.	J. P. Mahaffy and J. G. Smyly, The Flinders Petrie Papyri. Dublin, 1891, etc.
P. Rein.	Th. Reinach, Papyrus grecs et démotiques. Paris, 1905.
P.S.I.	Papiri greci e latini. (Pubbl. della Soc. Italiana per la ricerca dei papiri gr. e lat. in Egitto.) Florence, 1912, etc.
P. Strassb.	F. Preisigke, Griechische Papyrus der Universitäts- und Landesbibliothek zu Strassburg. Leipzig, 1912, etc.
P. Tebt.	P. B. Grenfell, A. Hunt and J. Goodspeed, The Tebtunis Papyri. London, 1907, etc.
P. Tor.	A. Peyron, Papyri graeci Regii Taurinensis Musaei Aegyptii. 1826-7.
P.-W.	Pauly-Wissowa-Kroll, Real-Encyclopädie der classischen Altertumswissenschaft.
R.E.A.	Revue des études anciennes.
R.E.G.	Revue des études grecques.
Rev. Arch.	Revue archéologique.
Riv. di fil.	Rivista di filologia.
S.B. Ak. Wien	Sitzungsberichte d. Akad. d. Wissenschaften in Wien.
S.E.G.	Supplementum epigraphicum Graecum.
U.P.Z.	U. Wilcken, Urkunden der Ptolemäerzeit.

INTRODUCTION

IN an age of specialists it is not easy to imagine a time when soldiers were not a special class of men who made fighting their profession. The historical tradition of modern Europe tells us that fighting is done by soldiers, and it is only comparatively recently that whole nations have been cajoled and coerced to arms. The profession is now occasionally open to almost every member of a modern state; but it is important to realize that it is only a re-opening that has recently taken place. The Greeks of the fifth century B.C. found no room in their economy for the specialist soldier. When Greek cities went to war every man did what he could, and in the two great wars which form for most people an introduction to Greek history, specialists play an insignificant part. When they do make an appearance they have little in common with the modern specialist. The professional soldier of a modern regular army is a highly respectable member of society: but the professional soldiers of the ancient world were mercenaries. The very name is equivocal, carrying with it associations romantic perhaps, but certainly shady as well.

The mercenary soldier is to be found in almost every highly organized society, and is not quite extinct from our own. To produce him three conditions are necessary: first, a war, or the prospect of a war; second, a person (or a community) willing and able to pay somebody else to fight for him; third, a man who is either so poor, or so desperate, or so adventurous, that he is willing to risk his life for a livelihood in a cause that means nothing to him. For Greek and Hellenistic history in general the first condition may be regarded as constant. The other two must clearly depend on social and economic factors which are unlikely to have remained static during a period of some hundreds of years. Poverty, despair and love of adventure are suggested as the motives most likely to induce a man to become a mercenary. The purely adventurous motive must be comparatively rare, and confined chiefly to wealthy *dilettanti* such as Antimenidas of Mytilene or Xenophon the Athenian; for, generally speaking,

HELLENISTIC MERCENARIES

Greek civilization never produced a leisured class of people who might occasionally prefer to do something dangerous rather than do nothing at all. The desperate man was perhaps more frequent; for the name should embrace most of those in every Greek city (and they seem to have been many) who were at variance with the existing government, and became exiles from their homes and possessions: and there were always, presumably, men like the lover in Theocritus who had their reasons for wishing to sleep with the brave as soon as they might. But in the case of most mercenary soldiers sheer poverty was probably the ruling motive. In a country so poor as Greece individual poverty was not a rare or strange occurrence, and it is clear from a casual reading of Greek history that it required no unexpected or extraneous influence, but merely the most ordinary sociological developments, the normal increase of population or the normal tendency of the rich to become richer and the poor to become poorer, to make the circumstances of the many unendurable. It seems to have been in such circumstances that mercenary service became most prevalent, and the study of mercenaries in the classical age of Greece is perhaps most interesting in so far as it illustrates the changes in the economic state of Greece from the lifetime of Solon to that of Isocrates.[1]

But however many poor men there might be at any given time desirous of earning their living as soldiers, they needed also somebody to employ them, and the political system of Greece as a whole was not likely, unless in exceptional circumstances, to find employment for large armies of mercenaries. The Greek city states differed from the Italian cities of the fourteenth and fifteenth centuries A.D. in two important particulars. In the first place, the citizen of a Greek city accepted it as his duty to fight in person for his city in time of war: this duty seems to have been unquestioned at least until after the Peloponnesian War, and if the rule became relaxed in the fourth century (as it certainly was at Athens in the life of Demosthenes), it is still easy to see why Greek warfare never became, as did Italian warfare, almost entirely an affair of mercenary armies. It was a question of money. Even Athens could not afford to pay large standing

[1] Cf. Parke, pp. 228 sqq. for a good summary, relating the increase in mercenary service especially to a decline in agriculture.

INTRODUCTION

armies, as we can see from the shifts made by her generals to pay the mercenaries whom she did employ; and where Athens failed it is certain that no other city could succeed. There was really only one condition under which cities could employ mercenaries copiously, namely when they happened to be under the rule of a tyrant, when the employer was in fact not the city but the tyrant himself. A tyrant often needed mercenaries for his own security; he was often a man of some private wealth originally, and he had a means of raising money which was denied to constitutional governments, by confiscating the property of his political opponents. But if the conditions generally prevailing in Greece were responsible for this limitation, there was also, outside Greece itself, another class of employer which seldom failed, the class represented by "Gyges πολύχρυσος" and his successors, the great kings who reigned in Asia and Egypt. They had the wealth of the East behind them, but the Greek infantry was better than any that the East could produce. The first certain reference to Greek mercenaries that we possess is in connection with a king of Egypt, and Greek soldiers continued to find service abroad almost continuously from the age of Psammetichus and Gyges to that of the later Seleucids and Ptolemies. With regard to employers in Greece itself, the "age of the tyrants" was an episode and nothing more; and even the tyrants were not great employers, according to later standards. The Greek cities of the fifth century fought their own battles, and it may be significant that economically the period of "the fifty years" was perhaps the nearest approach to a golden age that the Greeks ever knew. The mercenaries of the Peloponnesian War were not numerous, in fact it is to be doubted whether at any time, even during the siege of Syracuse, there were more than three or four thousand in action at one time. And if we are to accept Xenophon's own account of his comrades on the expedition of Cyrus, it becomes probable that at the turn of the century it was still not so much the economic cause as personal reasons which induced men to seek their fortune as soldiers over the sea.[1]

Speaking generally, however, there is probably nothing nearer to a single cause of the increase of mercenaries in the fourth

[1] Xen. *Anab.* vi. 4. 8.

century than the Peloponnesian War itself, which went far towards creating a demand while it certainly provided the supply. One ancient authority noticed the connection between the thirty years of almost continuous warfare and the prominence after it of mercenary soldiers.[1] The habit and discipline of war were there: and it was not long before they were reinforced by hard necessity. As early as 380 B.C. Isocrates draws a gloomy picture of the economic state of Greece, which includes "many compelled through want of daily bread to serve as mercenaries".[2] We are to conclude that the thirty years of war had served a double purpose; besides having created a population of soldiers they had undermined the prosperity of the country, such as it had been. There then is our supply. The demand may be traced, though less obviously perhaps, to the peculiar strategy of the war. The Greeks had been accustomed to settle their differences quickly with a battle in the open; but here they saw a new kind of war, a war in which the one side could not fight on sea, and the other would not fight on land. The protagonists for the most part refused to come forward on the stage to perform their parts, but confined themselves to scuffling and skirmishing in the wings—in distant theatres of war such as Acarnania, Thrace and Sicily. To warfare of this kind the citizen hoplite was not remarkably well suited, and we find Athens especially, doubtless as the richer of the two chief combatants, beginning to employ foreign auxiliaries, who showed the way to the light infantry and guerilla tactics of the fourth century. In view of the economic cause, which undoubtedly became paramount later, it may have been just as well that "Periclean strategy" came when it did, since it was probably of the highest importance in suggesting a demand for greater specialization in the art of war.

But the effect was not to make the warfare of the fourth century more decisive, or more interesting to the student. If the object of strategy is to destroy the enemy's resistance, then there can seldom have been less successful soldiers than the Greeks of the fourth century, with very few exceptions. Perhaps the best example of wastefully indecisive operations is provided by the many Athenian expeditions to Thrace and the Hellespont between 370 and 340 B.C.: little was ever accomplished, and

[1] Diod. xiv. 23. 4.   [2] Isoc. iv. 167 sqq.

INTRODUCTION

most of the details have (mercifully) not survived. It was for fighting of this kind that the mercenary was best adapted, especially as the reformed peltast of Iphicrates had become probably the model for mercenaries in general: the mistake of Diodorus—"after him hoplites were called peltasts"—has obviously some foundation in fact.[1] The surprising thing is, that in spite of the changed conditions of war, the prolonged and indecisive campaigns of foray and retreat in place of the decisive battle, no new tactical development should have appeared. The "Iphicratid" peltast by himself, no less than the hoplite by himself, reduced war to a stalemate. The lessons of the *Anabasis* were not put to use: it was forgotten how Cyrus had been ruined by his weakness in cavalry; how it had been found possible to use slingers and archers as a defence against cavalry, and to manœuvre and attack in open order as well as in phalanx; how Xenophon had experimented with the idea of a reserve.[2] More signs of the inventive spirit were shown during the one year of the adventures of the Ten Thousand than in ten years of manœuvres and fighting by the standing army of Jason or of the Phocians. Longer campaigns and professional soldiers should have meant the speedier conclusion of a war, but in fact they did not. In fairness it must be said that there is no evidence for thinking that wars were "arranged". In this period fighting still meant fighting, and not merely manœuvring for advantage with a view to the enemy's surrendering, as was the rule of Italian *condottieri*, and in a lesser degree of Greeks in the wars of the Successors. Moreover, when the real crisis arrived, the Greek city states could still put their citizen armies into the field, and it was still the citizen hoplite who won or lost the day at Leuctra, Mantinea and Chaeronea: there is nothing to suggest that any important part was played by mercenaries in the three great battles of the fourth century in Greece.

When war became a profession, it created a specialist class to follow it. Class is perhaps hardly the right word, for its specialists varied widely in character, from the theorist Dionysodorus "who professed to teach the whole duty of a general",[3] to the

---
[1] Diod. xv. 44.
[2] Xen. *Anab*. iii. 3. 16 sqq.; 4. 19 sqq.; vi. 5. 9 sqq.
[3] Xen. *Mem*. iii. 1. 1 sqq.

"Recruiting Officer" of Menander. Dionysodorus was a professor and no more, and had more in common with the sophists than with the soldiers; but we can see a practical edition of him in the Zacynthian Phalinus acting as military adviser to Tissaphernes,[1] and the next step from the lecture-room towards the battlefield is illustrated by the Theban Coeratadas, "who was going round Greece not because he was an exile, but wishing to be a general and advertising in the hope that some city or nation might need a general".[2] Such a man was a novelty in 400 B.C. What would Xenophon have said to the career of Charidemus, who began as a common slinger, and became successively pirate captain, *condottiere*, secretary of state and son-in-law to a Thracian prince, citizen and general of Athens, refugee at the court and camp of Darius III? We meet too with a professional officer of mercenaries, an Athenian called Astyphilus; and the experience of the Phliasians who found themselves without a commander and picked one up at Prasiae (an insignificant place), suggests that there were many such officers to be found.[3] As for the common soldiers, everything points to their being the poorest of the poor:[4] on one occasion some Athenian rowers deserted in order to become soldiers.[5] And though Jason might boast that, whereas each city could point to but few men in the prime of physical condition, his army contained none but the best, it may be that the average force of mercenaries, recruited from vagrants and paupers, was not nearly so well fitted to fight as the citizens who stayed at home.[6]

The effect, then, of mercenary service upon the warfare of the Greeks before Philip was to make it less stereotyped perhaps, but also less decisive; and it was reflected in no innovations worthy of the name in strategy or tactics. Its effect on the economic situation may have been more useful, in spite of the contemporary opinion that it was an unmitigated evil. Did it never occur to Isocrates, for one, that if many of the floating population had not been absorbed by mercenary service, they would either have been a burden on the resources of their cities,

---

[1] Xen. *Anab.* ii. 1. 7 sqq.
[2] *Ibid.* vii. 1. 33 sqq.
[3] Isaeus ix. 14 sqq.; Xen. *Hell.* vii. 2. 2 sqq.
[4] Isoc. ix. 76; iv. 167 sqq., 144 sqq.; *Ep.* ii. 9; Demosth. xxiii. 139, etc.
[5] Demosth. l. 14.
[6] Xen. *Hell.* vi. 1. 5 sqq.

INTRODUCTION

or else they would have starved? It is hard to compute the numbers of mercenaries serving in an average year: Diodorus' figures would make more than 50,000 take part in the wars of Artaxerxes Ochus;[1] but even if we suppose him to exaggerate greatly, and take 50,000 as the total number of mercenaries in the service of all paymasters at that time, this number must have been a useful relief to the indigent populations of Greece. That such a relief should be necessary at all was of course deplorable, and for this state of affairs Isocrates, as usual, had a remedy. A favourite dream of his was the crusade against Persia: he proposed to give Greece a fresh start by shifting the economic centre of gravity farther east, and including in the Greek world the western provinces of the Persian empire. The crusaders were to be the mercenaries, and when they had won their battles they were to found cities in the newly acquired lands and so at once form a bulwark for Greece against the barbarian and rid themselves of their own disabilities.[2] Isocrates did not live to see his dream come true, but it did, in a sense, come true with the conquests of Alexander. Had Alexander lived to give stability to the Greek empire of the East, it is possible that Isocrates' panacea would have been realized. Alexander died, but he had lived long enough to revolutionize the world of mercenaries (one of his less spectacular achievements, but real and interesting nevertheless). Mercenaries had crept into the warfare of Greece and stayed there, inglorious and perhaps unwanted. Inglorious they remain in the Hellenistic age, but after Alexander they do form part of a military system, which for want of a better name may be called the Macedonian system. The focus of interest shifts in the main from the Greek cities to Macedonia and the Graeco-Macedonian kingdoms of the Hellenistic world, and to understand the change one must begin at the beginning, with the Macedonia of Philip and Alexander.

[1] Diod. xvi. 41 sqq.; cf. Parke's table.
[2] Isoc. v. 122.

CHAPTER I

PHILIP AND ALEXANDER[1]

THE early history of the Macedonians is no more than a succession of isolated events, points of contact with Greek history, when Macedonia is drawn for a moment inside the more intimate circle of Greek politics. Such a record is, for this inquiry, of a purely negative value. It tells us that in 423 B.C. Perdiccas recruited Illyrian mercenaries for a campaign with Brasidas against the Lyncestians; that in 368 B.C. Pausanias, a pretender to the throne, captured several towns with the help of a force of Greek mercenaries, and was driven from the country by Iphicrates in the service of Queen Eurydice; that in the same year Ptolemaeus persuaded the mercenaries of Pelopidas to change sides, presumably taking them into his own service.[2] But this does not go far towards proving that mercenaries were in common use from the reign of Perdiccas onwards, especially when all the arguments from probability point in the opposite direction. For Macedonia never cut any great military figure; indeed the little that we know suggests that her wars must have been waged principally by her national army of nobles, who were the cavalry, and peasants, who were the infantry, ill equipped and untrained, incapable of permanent achievement and occasionally inadequate even for the defence of their country. Frequent dynastic troubles may have been the occasion for an ambitious candidate to the throne, such as Pausanias, to hire soldiers from abroad. But Macedonia was a backward country, and that is to say a country of peasants and landowners, with few cities, no industries, no overseas trade, none of the advantages which make for wealth. The king himself was merely the biggest landowner, and it may be taken for certainty that no king anterior to Philip, son of Amyntas, was ever rich enough to support a regular army of foreign mercenaries.

[1] In view of Parke's excellent chapters on this period, I have thought it best to condense my own to a minimum, comprising only what is necessary as an introduction to the Hellenistic system.
For Alexander's mercenaries the material is collected by H. Berve, *Das Alexanderreich*, pp. 130 sqq.
[2] Thuc. iv. 124. 4; Aeschines ii. 27 and 29; Plut. *Pel.* 27. 3.

PHILIP AND ALEXANDER

When Philip came to the throne in 359 B.C. he became the ruler of a country "enslaved to the Illyrians"; which means probably that the Illyrians were in possession of the western half of what we may call Greater Macedonia, that is, Macedonia as Philip ultimately left it. One of the natural consequences of his position was that his supply of Macedonian soldiers was circumscribed. The first known figures give him 10,000 infantry and 600 cavalry for his campaign of 358 B.C. against the Illyrians, which may well represent a full levy from the population under his control.[1] It is possible that he was too poor as yet to employ mercenaries, for earlier in the same year he had captured some mercenaries of the Athenian general Mantias, and had released them on parole instead of taking them into his own service.[2] But there is little doubt that Philip realized from the first how powerful a weapon might be forged from the native material of his country, a hardy and plentiful population, and it seems to have been in the very first year of his reign that he began to execute the military improvements which transformed his native infantry from light-armed auxiliary troops into a world-famous infantry of the line, the Macedonian phalanx.[3] The expansion of Macedonia was reflected in a phalanx more powerful numerically, and of an ever increasing effective value by reason of its constant exercise in campaigns which almost always ended in victory. Philip was creating, what no Greek city could ever begin to create, a large army which should combine a trained and specialized efficiency with the fire of national spirit and racial patriotism, at once the seasoned professional and the enthusiastic amateur of war.[4]

[1] Diod. xvi. 1. 3; 4. 4. They are called ἐπιλέκτους = perhaps all who were properly trained and armed?
[2] Ibid. 3. 6. There is a story, of slight historical value, in Carystius Pergamenus 1 (F.H.G. iv. p. 357), that Philip spent some time before his accession to the throne in 359, in living on his own lands διατρέφων δ' ἐνταῦθα δύναμιν: if there is any truth in this at all, the force that he kept must have been one of mercenaries, but it cannot have been of any great importance.
[3] Ibid. 3. 1 sqq. Diodorus lumps together these reforms, of which his description is sufficiently vague, into the year 359–358 B.C. In reality they are much more likely to have been spread over several years, beginning with the first year of his reign.
[4] It is assumed that the main divisions of the Macedonian army (phalanx, hypaspistae, "companion" cavalry, etc.) are sufficiently well known: for a résumé cf. Parke, pp. 155 sqq.

The step in Philip's advance which should, for our special purpose, perhaps be regarded as the most important of any, is his capture of Amphipolis in 357 B.C. The importance of Amphipolis lay in its position controlling the approach to the goldfields of Mount Pangaeus, where under Philip's direction the mines began to be worked more energetically than they had ever been worked before.[1] The possession of money meant that he need never be short of soldiers for the projects and enterprises to which he was prompted by the widening circle of his ambition. The nearest Greek source may have been the Chalcidice, famous for its peltasts in Xenophon's day, so that as early as 382 B.C. a Spartan general could send word to a Macedonian king to recruit mercenaries against his arrival.[2] Another possible source was Illyria, though Illyrian mercenaries are not to be found mentioned by name from the time of Perdiccas (423 B.C.) to that of Alexander. But soldiers from Greece too would not be lacking to the king with the greatest resources in Europe. The first certain notice of mercenaries in his army belongs probably to the year 352 B.C., when he captured the city of Pharcedon in Thessaly with their aid,[3] but their presence may also be suspected in the disastrous Thessalian campaign of the previous year, when Philip, severely defeated by the Phocian general Onomarchus, nearly lost control of his men, who were demoralized and ready to desert.[4] It was at this same period that the Athenian general Chares feasted the citizens in the market-place to celebrate a victory over the mercenaries of Philip.[5] They certainly provided a part if not the whole of the Macedonian army of occupation in Phocis, which the Phocians were obliged to support (perhaps finding pay as well as billets) at the end of the Sacred War (346 B.C.).[6] They appear several times in the next few years; reinforcements to Messene and Argos (344),[7] at Megara, and in Euboea, where it is possible to discover no fewer than four separate forces of mercenaries, one of them commanded by the

---

[1] Diod. xvi. 8. 6 sqq.
[2] Xen. *Hell*. v. 2. 38 (Teleutias to Amyntas).
[3] Polyaenus iv. 2. 8; cf. Diod. xvi. 35. 3. This is the commonly accepted date, but I think the capture of Pharcedon may really be some years later.
[4] Diod. *ibid*. 1.
[5] Theopomp. frag. 241 (Ox.).
[6] Demosth. xix. 81.
[7] *Id*. vi. 15.

later famous Parmenion (343–342 B.C.).¹ Later they are found in the Chersonese,² at Thermopylae (if the passage relating to them is genuine),³ and probably at Chaeronea (338).⁴

The existence, then, of Philip's mercenaries is sufficiently established: as to their relative importance we are still in the dark, nor is it altogether easy to place them in their proper light. The sixteenth book of Diodorus presents merely the barest outline of Philip's reign, devoid of most of the details, military and otherwise, which would make it of really first-rate value.⁵ The account of the battle of Chaeronea is typical: it does not say of what troops the Macedonian army consisted or how they were disposed, and it suggests that the victory was due to the personal courage of the young Alexander.⁶ Our other source is Demosthenes, and Demosthenes naturally said what it suited him to say and his hearers to hear. He has laid great stress upon Philip's dependence on his mercenaries, implying that his successes were due principally to his command of money, and even belittling the Macedonian phalanx to the advantage of the other arms: "And you hear of Philip going wherever he wants, not by virtue of commanding a phalanx of hoplites, but because he has fitted out light-armed infantry, horsemen, archers, mercenaries, and that sort of army".⁷ At other times he finds it convenient to sneer at mercenaries and Macedonians alike, and to discredit the *moral* and efficiency of Philip's Companions and mercenary officers.⁸ Evidence of this kind is practically worthless. All that it can be said to prove is that there were in Philip's army mercenaries and auxiliaries (which we knew already), and perhaps that they played a larger part in his strategic and tactical conceptions than was usual at that time in Greek warfare; which tells us, if it is true, where Alexander learnt his methods. For ourselves we can deduce that mercenaries were valuable to a general at once so active and so astute as Philip, who would wish

---

¹ Demosth. xix. 87; 295; ix. 33; 57; 58.   ² *Id*. ix. 16.
³ *Id*. ix. 32; cf. Didymus xi. 46.
⁴ Curtius viii. 1. 24 (an unlikely story, but that does not necessarily discredit the *presence* of mercenaries).
⁵ I think Parke's (p. 162) division of Philip's reign into two parts, before and after 346 B.C., is perhaps artificial. The fact is that we are much better informed for the years after 346, and almost all the information comes from Demosthenes: naturally there are more references to mercenaries.
⁶ Diod. xvi. 86.   ⁷ Demosth. iii. 49; cf. i. 32.   ⁸ *Id*. ii. 17; xi. 10.

to use indeed and exercise his best Macedonian troops but not to wear them out. Captured towns needed garrisons, and warfare on several fronts must often have required a number of small mobile forces rather than a large army capable of meeting another large army and beating it decisively. We hear of mercenaries particularly on distant enterprises, at Megara and in the Peloponnese, in Euboea and at the Hellespont; though no doubt they were included also in the field army at Chaeronea, where Philip had more than 30,000 infantry.[1] But to attempt a reconstruction of Philip's army system purely from what is known of its working under Philip himself is to look for something that is not there. A proper study for the student of Philip is Alexander. We have only to turn to Alexander's conquests to see the system exposed in detail as it works now in a more spacious setting and under an even more ingenious direction, and to appreciate with some exactitude how its various parts were co-ordinated and employed, the less spectacular (which are our province) in a sense subservient but none the less necessary to the more important; the secret, in a word, not merely of Alexander's brilliant victories in the field but also of that part of his performance which is even more remarkable, his handling of a small army during ten years of the hardest fighting and marching, in such a way that its spirit and fighting qualities remained to the end unimpaired. Philip's preparation and practice made it possible.

Alexander crossed the Hellespont with an army probably of 30,000 foot and 4500 horse, of which some 19,000 infantry and 3600 cavalry were Macedonians or Greek allies.[2] The remainder were mercenaries from Greece, Thrace or the Balkan tribes. Of the 11,000 mercenary foot soldiers, 5000 were Greeks, 5000

[1] Diod. xvi. 85. 6.
[2] Arrian, *Anab.* i. 11. 3 (=Ptolemy, frag. 4), gives 5000 cavalry; Diod. xvii. 7. 4, 4500, and enumerates their contingents. Other figures in Plut. *de fort. an virt. Alex.* 3; Callisth. frag. 33. For the evidence for Alexander's garrisons in Greece, cf. Parke, p. 187 and n. 3. I do not feel the need for explaining away the comparatively small number of Alexander's mercenaries. If an explanation is necessary, Parke's (p. 186)—shortage of money—is probably the best. But after all, Alexander, marvellous man that he was, could not read the future: he did not know in 334 B.C. that by 330 B.C. he would need nearer 50,000 Greek mercenaries than 5000. And in any case his original army of 35,000 men was not a small army: in fact as an expeditionary force it was a large army.

"Odrysians, Triballians and Illyrians", and nearly 1000 Cretan archers and Agrianian skirmishers: the only mercenary cavalry mentioned are 900 Thracian and Paeonian light horse.[1] Upon landing in the Troad this army was probably joined by that of Parmenion and Calas which was already there: Parmenion had commanded both Macedonians and mercenaries (10,000 men altogether),[2] and although this number must have been reduced by a defeat in 335 B.C., it is possible that it is this addition to Alexander's army which is responsible for some of the larger totals extant in our authorities: and this larger total would naturally imply a larger number of Greek mercenaries.[3] Such was the force which won its spurs at the Granicus (334 B.C.). From this time onwards until he left Bactria on the march to the Indus (327 B.C.), Alexander was continually receiving reinforcements which included new mercenaries, sent from Europe or recruited by his own officers in Asia. Apart from two fresh detachments of Thracian horse and some Agrianians, they were, so far as we know, all Greeks. It must not however be supposed that the mercenary part of his army increased, like a snowball, as he pursued his path farther east. He recruited partly no doubt to fill gaps left by fighting and sickness; but the principal drain were the numerous garrisons and little armies which he detached for the purpose of keeping open his communications and holding

[1] Diod. xvii. 17.
[2] *Id.* xvi. 91. 2; xvii. 7; Polyaen. v. 44.
[3] E.g. Anaximenes, frag. 15—43,000 foot, 5500 horse; Callisthenes, frag. 33—40,000 foot, 4500 horse. And they are needed to explain the numbers of mercenaries that appear in the first two years in Asia, cf. Berve, *op. cit.* p. 145, and Appendix, p. 27.

J. G. Droysen (*Kleine Schriften*, ii. pp. 211 sqq., followed by H. Droysen, *Untersuchungen*, pp. 6 sqq.) rules this theory out as impossible, partly on the ground that all the authorities evidently intend to give the numbers of *the army that crossed into Asia*. This is not an insuperable objection, but there is much weight in his insistence on the silence of Arrian—a good military historian—on the subject of this army of Calas joining Alexander. But it is difficult to see what happened to it if it did not join him in 334 B.C.: if it was recalled in 335, as has been suggested, the Persians would surely have opposed Alexander's landing in the Troad (where Calas' army is last heard of).

Droysen also discredits the "catalogue" of Diodorus, and shows from the campaign of 334 that there must have been over 7000 Greek mercenaries in Alexander's army at the time (Arrian i. 18. 1 sqq. and 5). This is undoubtedly true, but it too is explained if one can resolve to charge Arrian with omitting to mention the junction of Calas' troops with the main army. And the same explanation makes it easier to accept Arrian's own figures for Gaugamela—40,000 infantry, 7000 cavalry (iii. 12. 5).

the lately conquered and always increasing empire of the East. In fact it is doubtful if he ever had with him for more than a very short time a number of mercenaries greatly exceeding the 11,000 or so with which he left Europe.

Let us consider for a moment the organization and functions of the several mercenary contingents, with the proviso that nothing be sacrificed for the sake of arranging in a settled organization for our own satisfaction contingents which must in reality have been of a more or less fluid character. First, the Balkan mercenaries; and here it must be said that their status in the army is open to dispute. They came from peoples whose princes were more or less formally subject to the king of Macedonia, so that it is hard to say whether they were mercenaries or allies. It is probably best to avoid a splitting of hairs, and to call them all mercenaries, because if they were allies in the first place they certainly became mercenaries later, along with those of the Greek allies who volunteered to remain with the army when they were given the chance to return home.[1] How these troops were recruited is not known, whether by means of special recruiting facilities granted to Alexander by the native princes, or by direct requisitions imposed upon them as vassals. But the Agrianian king, Longarus, was an old friend of Alexander,[2] and the Odrysian Sitalces actually crossed into Asia with him in command of a contingent of his own soldiers, and never returned to his native land.[3] Of the "5000 Odrysians (Thracians), Triballians and Illyrians" mentioned by Diodorus, Sitalces' men may have been the larger part: Arrian never mentions Triballians and Illyrians, but in his army list at Gaugamela there is another contingent of Thracians in addition to that of Sitalces, and this second contingent may probably be equated with the Triballians and Illyrians of Diodorus (Arrian's nomenclature is the more likely to be accurate).[4] The Thracians were javelin-men (ἀκοντισταί), useful for operations in difficult country, and for skirmishing movements in front of or apart

---

[1] H. Berve, *op. cit.* pp. 134–9, discusses these barbarian troops in great detail: he concludes that only the Triballians and Illyrians were really mercenaries, on the ground that these peoples were less formally subject to Macedonia than the Odrysians and Agrianians.
[2] Arrian i. 5. 2.   [3] *Ibid.* 28. 4, etc.
[4] *Id.* iii. 12. 4 sqq.; Diod. xvii. 17.

PHILIP AND ALEXANDER

from the main battle line.¹ Arrian also mentions some slingers, who must certainly be included among the 5000 barbarians.² The only other barbarian infantry were Agrianians, also light-armed javelin-men.³ Their numbers are not revealed, but they and the archers together, with whom they nearly always acted in concert, were 2000 strong;⁴ but some of the archers were Macedonians, so that Diodorus' figure of "1000 archers and Agrianians" perhaps includes only the mercenary archers and is correct.⁵ The Agrianians were commanded by a Macedonian Attalus.⁶ They were perhaps the most hard-worked corps in the whole army, winning no fewer than twenty-seven separate mentions by name in Arrian's narrative. The archers were Cretans, and were commanded sometimes by a Cretan, sometimes by a Macedonian; or perhaps there were always two separate commands for the Cretan and Macedonian sections. The Agrianians and archers together went through some very hard fighting, the latter having no fewer than four commanders killed over them.⁷ At Gaugamela it fell to their lot to face the charge of the scythed chariots and prevent their interfering with the precision of the "Companion" cavalry's entry into battle, a task which they performed faithfully and well.⁸ They were favourite troops of Alexander himself, who occasionally singled them out for special favour along with the Hypaspistae and the so-called "Royal squadron" of the Companion cavalry.⁹ A new draft of Agrianians was among the first batch of reinforcements that he had sent to him from Europe.¹⁰ They are not heard of after the Indian campaign, and may have been left in garrisons or new cities on the frontiers.

The only Greek mercenaries known to have been with Alex-

---

[1] Arrian i. 28. 4.
[2] Ibid. 2. 4, etc.
[3] Ibid. 14. 1; iii. 13. 5.
[4] Id. i. 6. 6.
[5] Diod. xvii. 7. Berve, pp. 131 sqq. and 149 sqq., may however be right in taking the 1000 to include the Macedonian archers as well; because the 2000 refers to an occasion in 335 B.C., and some of them may have been left behind in Europe.
[6] Arrian ii. 9. 2; iii. 12. 2; 21. 8.
[7] Id. i. 8. 4; 22. 7; 28. 8; ii. 9. 2; iii. 5. 6; v. 14. 1. (There was also a fifth commander whose fate is unknown.) Berve's (loc. cit.) attempt to prove that the Cretan and Macedonian archers fought together always as a unit is reasonable enough, but fails from lack of evidence.
[8] Id. iii. 12. 3; 13. 5 sqq.
[9] Id. iii. 1. 4; vi. 22.
[10] Curt. iii. 9. 10; cf. Callisth. frag. 33.

ander when he left Europe are the 5000 infantry. This presents a difficulty: there ought to be some Greek mercenary cavalry as well, since they are mentioned at Halicarnassus and later at Gaugamela, and cannot be accounted for from any known reinforcements (not a certain argument, but a strong one).[1] Beloch proposed (on other grounds) to emend the text of Diodorus which relates to the Thessalian allied cavalry, altering the 1800 to 1200 ($\overline{\alpha\omega}$ to $\overline{\alpha\varsigma}$), and this would leave a spare 600 for the mercenary cavalry.[2] There is probably no need to do this. The review of the army on the Asiatic coast which supplies us with these figures of Diodorus includes only the troops who actually crossed with Alexander—οἱ μὲν οὖν μετ' Ἀλεξάνδρου διαβάντες εἰς τὴν Ἀσίαν τοσοῦτοι τὸ πλῆθος ἦσαν. But there was also the other small army which Philip had sent into Asia under Parmenion and Attalus, which, as we know, contained mercenaries, and which must presumably have joined the main army with Alexander at some time.[3] It is at least possible that the missing mercenary cavalry are to be explained in this way, and other small difficulties too (Appendix, p. 27).

Concerning the mercenary infantry H. Berve has made an interesting discovery. He believes that Arrian, following Ptolemy, preserves a terminological distinction (until after Gaugamela) between the original mercenaries of the army and mercenaries recruited or acquired after the landing in Asia, calling the one group ξένοι (ξενικόν, etc.), the other μισθοφόροι. Unfortunately this is not absolutely correct, though it is true to say that it gives a satisfactory sense in the great majority of the references. The details of this question would, if introduced here, require at the least a long and perhaps a profitless digression, and are better discussed at leisure elsewhere.[4] For the present purpose it is enough to say that the mercenary infantry accompanying the field army remained substantially the same in numbers and constitution until after Gaugamela. That is to

---

[1] Arrian i. 23. 6; iii. 12. 5. (The other of the two mercenary contingents at Gaugamela—iii. 12. 3—is known to have joined him in Egypt—iii. 5. 1.) On the other hand, no mercenaries are mentioned at Issus, but they may be concealed in τῶν ἱππέων τινές who act with the Agrianians and archers (ii. 9. 2).
[2] Diod. xvii. 17. 4; cf. Beloch, *Gr. G.* iii². 2. 324.
[3] *Ibid.* 7. 9.
[4] Berve, *op. cit.* pp. 144 sqq. See Appendix, p. 29.

PHILIP AND ALEXANDER

say, they were at least 5000 strong, possibly divided into two contingents under separate command, namely those who had crossed with Alexander and those who had crossed earlier while Philip was still alive.[1] At Gaugamela all the mercenary infantry fought together, distinguished by the name of "the Old mercenaries" (οἱ ἀρχαῖοι καλούμενοι ξένοι) in Arrian, who got it no doubt from Ptolemy or Aristobulus, who may perhaps have used it to denote soldiers who had served under Philip (Appendix, pp. 29–30). Diodorus, speaking of the same occasion, calls them τοὺς ἐκ τῆς Ἀχαΐας μισθοφόρους, which is probably nonsense, because they could hardly all have come from Achaea, as Parke rightly observes (p. 190, n. 6): with Arrian's phrase in one's mind it is difficult not to think that what Diodorus wrote (if our text is sound) is due to a misreading of ἀρχαίους in his source.[2] Of their armament we are told nothing. One would incline to believe that they were peltasts, since the innovations of Iphicrates seem to have made this the standard arm for mercenaries in the fourth century; and it is true that in the great battles they did not fight together with the picked phalanx troops of the centre. But, on the other hand, it is significant that Alexander once selected for a forced march the Macedonian infantry but not the mercenaries, who are included in the category of "those of the army who were more heavily armed";[3] the defensive armour even of the Greek peltast may have been heavier than that of the phalangite. Peltasts or hoplites, they were not among Alexander's best battle troops, not so firm a rock as the Macedonian phalanx, or so keen a spearhead as the Macedonian and Thessalian cavalry. But so far as we know they were competent soldiers, and the farther Alexander proceeded the more such soldiers he required. The tactical functions of the mercenaries have been well demonstrated by Parke (pp. 191 sqq.). In general they performed a dual function, on detached expeditions, and as garrison troops: for Alexander's high strategy the second is much the more important.[4]

This brings us to the question of reinforcements, which is

---

[1] Appendix, p. 28.
[2] Arrian iii. 12. 2; Diod. xvii. 57. 4.
[3] Arrian iii. 18. 1 sqq.
[4] Appendix, pp. 30 sqq., for a note on the "second line" of mercenaries in the three great battles.

chiefly a question of figures. There are two authorities to be considered: on the one hand Arrian, on the other Curtius Rufus, with Diodorus as an occasional supplement or variant. Now Arrian in the early part of his book seems to be scrupulous in noticing additions to the army, even when they are comparatively insignificant. Thus he tells us of 300 mercenaries, the remnant of the Persian garrison in Miletus, who joined Alexander when they surrendered.[1] They, with 4000 recruited from Greece who joined him at Sidon and were probably left behind in Egypt, are the only mercenary infantry reinforcements before Gaugamela.[2] (To these must be added 400 Greek and 500 Thracian cavalry.) That is plausible enough. But passing on to the years in the Far East we discover that Arrian only three times prior to Alexander's return from India mentions mercenary reinforcements at all, and only once gives figures—the 1500 mercenaries who had remained faithful to Darius till his death, and then were taken into Alexander's army.[3] This is far from satisfactory, for during these six years Alexander was using up soldiers all the time, on fighting and marching, and, more important still, on forming military settlements, of which more will be said presently. The man-power of Macedonia itself was limited, and could not be drained completely for fear of trouble in Greece: Alexander certainly took Asiatics with him to India,[4] but he had not as yet organized a native army, and it would have been dangerous to take too many soldiers from the newly conquered nations: and Arrian himself, in his *Indica*, accepts the figure of 120,000 men for the invasion of India.[5] Even if we regard that figure as too high, it seems that we must still look for reinforcements of mercenaries besides Arrian's, and large ones at that. These reinforcements are to be found in Curtius: the question is, how far can his figures be considered trustworthy? In common with other authorities, he admits wildly exaggerated figures into his statistics for the Persian army, but

---

[1] Arrian i. 19. 6.
[2] *Ibid.* 24. 2; ii. 20. 5; iii. 1. 3; 5. 3; Curt. iv. 8. 4; and Appendix, pp. 27 sqq.
[3] Arrian iii. 23. 8 sqq.; 24. 4 sqq.: the other two notices without figures are Arrian iii. 19. 6 (cf. Diod. xvii. 74. 4) and Arrian iv. 7. 2 (where Curt. vii. 10. 11 *does* give figures).
[4] Curt. ix. 2. 24.
[5] *Id.* viii. 5. 4; Arrian, *Indica*, 19. 5.

PHILIP AND ALEXANDER

that can be explained by the difficulty which in the nature of things even an eyewitness such as Ptolemy probably experienced in discovering the truth, and perhaps too by a conscious encouragement of high estimates after the event on the part of Alexander and his staff for the sake of their moral effect upon the army. In the case of statistics for the Greek army there is no such excuse for error. The right figures were to be had, if an historian cared to take the trouble to procure them. Did Curtius take that trouble? There is one thing that suggests that he did; the fact that when Curtius and Arrian both give a figure for the same body of men in Alexander's army, the figures sometimes agree—and Arrian, as we know, used excellent sources.[1] Examples of this agreement are the 1500 mercenaries who joined Alexander after Darius' death, and the figure of 120,000 for the Indian expedition, common to both authors (see above).[2] Moreover there are other corresponding passages in which Curtius gives a figure but Arrian does not (e.g. Curt. vii. 10. 11 = Arrian iv. 7. 2; Curt. x. 1. 1 sqq. = Arrian vi. 27. 4), suggesting that both are using the same source, whose figures Arrian discards possibly for the sake of brevity. Another point in Curtius' favour is that in dealing with a certain important mercenary reinforcement he has evidently disregarded (whether through ignorance or by design is immaterial) an impossible set of figures which is reproduced in Diodorus, and has given us a possible one (Diod. xvii. 95. 4—30,000 infantry, 6000 cavalry: Curt. ix. 3. 21—7000 infantry, 5000 cavalry). And the most pressing argument for accepting his evidence is that his figures are, taken as a whole, not impossible, and that in fact we do need some figures of that kind to fit in with what we know of Alexander's use of his army in the East. Here is a list of all the known new mercenaries added to the army:[3] it will be seen that

---

[1] It is established that Curtius did use Ptolemy or a "Ptolemaic" source for some parts of his history: cf. R. Petersdorff, *Eine neue Hauptquelle des Q. Curtius Rufus*, pp. 45 sqq.

[2] An example of a difference is the accounts of Spitamenes' ambush: Curtius says that out of 3000 infantry, 800 cavalry, 2000 infantry, 200 cavalry were killed (vii. 6. 24; 7. 39): Arrian says that out of 60 Macedonian and 800 mercenary cavalry and 1500 mercenary infantry, 820 cavalry and 1200 infantry were killed. Here different accounts are clearly being used.

[3] The list is modelled upon that of Berve (*op. cit.* p. 147); but his entry for Gordium is puzzling, and is perhaps due to a misreading of Callisthenes, frag. 33.

it comprises reinforcements of every class of troops among the original mercenaries, except the Cretan archers and the Paeonian cavalry:

At Miletus	300 infantry (Persian garrison)	Arrian i. 19. 6
At Gordium	x Agrianians (?)	Curt. iii. 9. 10 (cf. Callisth. frag. 33 ap. Pol. xii. 19. 2)
[At Chios	3000 (Persian garrison)	Curt. iv. 5. 18; cf. Arrian ii. 13. 5][1]
At Sidon	4000	Arrian ii. 20. 5
At Memphis	400 cavalry 500 Thracian cavalry	Arrian iii. 5. 1
At Susa	4000 infantry from the Peloponnese ? 980 cavalry from the Peloponnese 3500 Trallians (?) 600 Thracian cavalry	Curt. v. 1. 41; Diod. xvii. 65. 1; but cf. Arrian iii. 16. 10 sqq.
In Media	5000 infantry 1000 cavalry x infantry ⎧ (the Greek allies x cavalry ⎨ who volunteered ⎩ to remain as mercenaries) 1500 infantry (Darius' remnant)	Curt. v. 7. 12 Arrian iii. 19. 6; Diod. xviii. 74. 4 Arrian iii. 23. 8 sqq.; Curt. vi. 5. 6 sqq.[2]
At Bactra	2600 infantry 500 cavalry 3000 Illyrian cavalry 300 cavalry	Curt. vi. 6. 35
At Zariaspa	16,400 infantry 2600 cavalry	Curt. vi. 10. 11 (cf. Arrian iv. 7. 2)

---

[1] This 3000 should not be added to the total, because there is no notice in Arrian of their joining Alexander before Gaugamela, and if they joined him later they are concealed within some larger figure, so that to count them here would be to count them twice.

[2] Beloch (*op. cit.* p. 338) reckons 1000 only, because some of them were allowed to go home.

PHILIP AND ALEXANDER 21

Beginning of Indian expedition, with ? 120,000 men, Curt. viii. 5. 4; Arrian, *Ind.* 19. 5.

In India	7000 infantry, 5000 cavalry	Curt. ix. 3. 21
	[30,000 infantry, 6000 cavalry	Diod. xvii. 95. 4]
[In Carmania (return from India)	5000 infantry, 1000 cavalry	Curt. x. 1. 1 sqq. (cf. Arrian vi. 27 sqq.)][1]
At Babylon	*x*	Arrian vii. 23. 1

Total 59,180 + *x* mercenaries (say 65,000).

It may be said that this is a very high figure, and one may well ask where so many mercenaries could be found, especially if it be assumed that all mercenaries are Greek unless otherwise described. It is true that if we had met with so large an assembly fifty or even twenty years earlier, we should have had little hesitation in pronouncing the figures worthless. But the altered conditions must not be forgotten. After 331 B.C. there was only one army in the eastern Mediterranean in which Greek mercenaries could find employment, the army of Alexander: Persia, Egypt, the Greek cities, all the employers who had previously drawn upon the Greek supply, were now removed from the field. Secondly, it would be a great mistake to overlook the psychological effect of Alexander's victories. It may be supposed that any successful general was a more attractive paymaster than any unsuccessful one; but when the conqueror was Alexander and the conquered the Great King, whose power and treasure was a proverb in the mouths of Greeks, it is not hard to imagine the lure of gold at work in the minds of all poor men who could carry arms. The mercenary's calling was no longer a bare livelihood; it had become an adventure and a short cut to fortune. So many may have thought, little knowing that their return would be the return of sadder and wiser men—if they did return. But that anticipates the end of the story. One must revert for a moment to cold figures. Here is a list of all the mercenaries whom Alexander is known to have left behind in garrisons or as settlers on the track of his advance to India.

[1] Berve includes these in his list; but they may have been troops left behind with Sitalces, etc. before the Indian expedition. Cf. Arrian iii. 26. 3.

22 HELLENISTIC MERCENARIES

A comparison of the two lists will show that the figures of the first are not likely to prove too great.[1]

At Halicarnassus	3000 infantry 200 cavalry	Arrian i. 23. 6; Curt. iii. 1. 1[2]
At Side (Pamphylia)	Mercenaries not specified, but probable	Arrian i. 26. 5
At Mytilene	*x*	Arrian ii. 1. 4
In Egypt	4000	Curt. iv. 8. 4 (cf. Arrian iii. 1. 3; 5. 3)[3]
In Babylon and Babylonia	300 infantry 2000 ? infantry	Arrian iii. 16. 4; Diod. xvii. 64. 5; Curt. v. 1. 43
At Susa	3000	Curt. v. 2. 16
In Arachosia	4000 infantry 600 cavalry	Curt. vii. 3. 4
Ambushed by Spitamenes	1200 infantry 800 cavalry	Arrian iv. 5. 2 sqq.
At Maracanda	3000 infantry	Curt. vii. 10. 10
Various new cities	*x*	Arrian iii. 2. 9; iv. 3. 6; 4. 1; 16. 4 sqq.; 29. 5 sqq.; *ibid.* 6 sqq.; 22. 5; 24. 7; 30. 4; Diod. xviii. 83. 2; Curt. vii. 10. 5[4]

[1] It may be argued that if Curtius' figures are wrong in the first list they will also be wrong in the second, in which case both lists, were it possible to correct them, would produce lower figures. But the second list depends on Curtius less than the first, and the figures of Curtius which do appear in the second list are not at all improbable intrinsically.

[2] It is probable that they rejoined him later; cf. Arrian ii. 5. 7.

[3] In defence of these 4000 mercenaries, whom Parke, p. 191, will not allow to have been trusted with the serious duty of guarding the most important towns (Pelusium and Memphis), which, he says, were put under garrisons of πεζέταιροι, it should be said that his statement is based on Arrian iii. 5. 3, φρουράρχους δὲ τῶν ἑταίρων ἐν Μέμφει μὲν Πανταλέοντα κατέστησε τὸν Πυδναῖον, ἐν Πηλουσίῳ δὲ Πολέμωνα τὸν Μεγακλέους, Πελλαῖον. I think Parke's interpretation, " garrisons of πεζέταιροι", is based on a mistranslation: τῶν ἑταίρων is a partitive genitive, and means that Pantaleon and Polemon the phrourarchs were "two of the Companions". The same genitive is used of the γραμματεὺς ἐπὶ τῶν ξένων (*ibid.*), Εὔγνωστον τὸν Ξενοφάντου τῶν ἑταίρων.

[4] Mercenaries are not always specifically mentioned as settlers, but clearly they are the part of the army which he could best spare for that purpose.

PHILIP AND ALEXANDER

Army of occupation in Bactria	10,500 infantry (not all certainly mercenaries) 3500 cavalry	Arrian iv. 22. 3 sqq.
Cities in India	x	Arrian v. 8. 3; 29. 3; vi. 15. 2; 17. 1, etc.
Died in Gedrosia	x	Arrian vi. 23 sqq.
Mouth of the Euphrates	x	Arrian vii. 21. 7

Total 36,100 + x mercenaries.

It is not easy to arrive at a probable evaluation of the unknown quantity—x. The losses in battle were probably negligible (except for the ambush of Spitamenes which wins a place in our list above); but losses caused by climate and overexertion must have been considerable, especially on the dreadful return march from India through the desert of Gedrosia—Alexander's 1812. We hear of worn-out soldiers who became settlers in the new cities perforce; but we do not hear of those who were worn even to death, and calculation is really impossible. With regard to the numbers of the settlers there are two pieces of evidence that are of value. It is said that in two revolts which broke out, the one shortly before, the other shortly after, Alexander's death, no fewer than 26,000 Greeks settled in the eastern provinces took part—and some may have remained idle.[1] And after his return from India, when he had sent home 10,000 veteran Macedonians, his whole army is said to have amounted to no more than 13,000 infantry and 2000 cavalry; "he believed that he could hold Asia with a comparatively small army, since he had planted garrisons in many places, and had filled the new cities with settlers who would not revolt".[2] If these two sets of figures are correct, it must follow that Alexander used up his mercenaries almost as fast as they reached him, and that he never had any very great number attached to the field army at any one time—perhaps not more than 10,000 or so even for the Indian campaign. This conclusion would support what has been suggested previously, that these Greeks were not of the first value as battle troops (witness the small number that Alexander

---

[1] Diod. xvii. 98 (cf. Curt. ix. 7. 1 sqq.); xviii. 7. 2.
[2] Curt. x. 2. 8.

took with him to Asia in the first place), and that it was not until his great battles had been won that their real value became more and more apparent, as is reflected in the increasing numbers with which he keeps himself supplied as he moves farther and farther east. His purpose in employing them was not a tactical or even a purely strategic one. These new cities of soldier-settlers were, it is true, necessary for the pacification of the wild hill-peoples in the far-eastern satrapies; but it must be almost certain that they had a deeper significance than that. It was part of Alexander's ideal of empire that his peace should be not merely imposed from without, but should take root and grow spontaneously from within: and his conquered subjects were to be not a stubborn but a fertile and eager soil. He was to be their king, and not a king of Macedonians and Greeks exploiting the conquered. That is the meaning of his Persian clothes and his Persian wife, his encouragement of Eurasian marriages, his scheme for training the young men of his new subjects to be soldiers in his own army. And so too with his new cities. They were to be focuses of Greek life and civilization; or perhaps rather magnets of attraction for the vicinities in which they were placed. In some cases they are known to have been mixed foundations from the first, of Greeks and barbarians living side by side, and this may have been the ultimate object, if it was not the first condition, of every foundation.[1] Such was perhaps the primary function of the settlements; but incidentally Alexander was also putting into practice the cure of Isocrates for the economic problem in Greece. That the new settlers were to prove bad patients was, it may be said, no fault of Alexander. His plan was grand and simple, involving a sublime disregard of the individual that laid it open to the risk of becoming a magnificent failure. It is certain that the Greeks did not take to the new life, but the underlying causes of their revolt from it are concealed. Probably when they found themselves established in their new homes they realized that this was not what they had come forth to see. The natives may have been troublesome—we hear of friction in one city.[2] The biggest trouble may have been nostalgia: perhaps, like the Eretrians carried into captivity by

[1] Arrian iv. 4. 1; 24. 7; v. 29. 3; Diod. xvii. 83; Curt. ix. 7. 1 sqq.
[2] Curt. *ibid.*

PHILIP AND ALEXANDER 25

Darius, they missed the sea. Their effort to regain it will be described.

The organization of the field army eludes us almost completely.[1] Some figures in connection with the plunder and bonuses of the army, though probably exaggerated, transport us into the realms of high finance:[2] and indeed the pay-roll of such an army as this, involving different grades of pay extending over long periods, and for men whose terms of service did not all commence simultaneously, must in itself have engaged the attentions of a special department of officials. The traces of such a department are to be found in a passage describing Alexander's arrangements for the military administration of the province of Egypt. He appointed two governors, one at Memphis and one at Pelusium, and also a commander, a secretary (γραμματεύς) and two commissioners (ἐπίσκοποι) of mercenaries.[3] The duties of the secretary and commissioners are not defined, but were probably devoted, the former to pay and commissariat, the latter, possibly, to the questions of discipline and grievance such as were likely to arise in a garrison town: the fact that the post of secretary was filled by one of the Companions shows it to have been one of importance. The arrangement may probably be taken as a specimen of the machinery connected with the upkeep of mercenaries in all the important garrisons or seats of satraps and a skeleton of a more complicated organization which would probably be needed with the main army.

In this large and mixed army the discipline and spirit of the men was a thing of no small importance. The squabbles and differences among the members of Xenophon's expedition give an inkling of what might have occurred in a Greek army made up of officers who could not lead and men who would not follow. Then Xenophon and a few others saved the situation. With Alexander the situation did not arise. His Macedonians were attached to him by hereditary loyalty and, soon, by personal affection. The mercenaries, well led by Macedonian officers,[4]

---

[1] Much labour has been spent on reconstructing the tactical organization: the results are summarized by Berve, *op. cit.* pp. 103 sqq.
[2] Pp. 299–300.   [3] Arrian iii. 5. 3.
[4] Appendix, p. 28, also Arrian iii. 6. 8—Menander, a Companion, who at one time commanded a contingent of mercenaries, became satrap of Lydia. There is no known instance of a mercenary captain rising to high command.

seem to have shown that in ordinary circumstances they were just as trustworthy as citizen or national troops, and to have caused no trouble whatever. A first principle with the commanders must have been to prevent friction between men of different races in the army. Apart from one story of a duel between a Macedonian and an Athenian,[1] and another concerning the seduction of some mercenaries' women by two Macedonians, no trace of inter-racial enmity makes its appearance known: in the second instance the severity of Alexander's instructions, in the event of the two men being found guilty, proves him to have been alive to the importance of the principle at stake.[2]

The army never failed him in battle. The only enemy which proved too much for it was distance: and in the mutiny in the Punjaub no specific blame is attached to the mercenaries by historians who might have been well content to exonerate the Macedonians. The Macedonian Coenus, speaking on behalf of the mutineers, stresses the exhaustion and war-weariness of the remnant of soldiers who were present: his comments on the absent are of particular interest. "And of the other Greeks" (namely the mercenaries) "some are settled in the cities you have founded, though they are by no means all willing to stay there: others, and the Macedonians too, have dared and endured yet further with you; some of these have perished in battle, and some, disabled by their wounds, are now left behind scattered here and there over Asia."[3] This was part of Alexander's plan, but it was probably the whole of the mercenaries' grievance. The measures of Alexander which so estranged his Macedonians, his Persian marriage and attire and still more his enlisting and training Persian soldiers to join their ranks, probably meant little or nothing to the Greeks.[4] But when Alexander found it best for Greece and for his new conquests that the Greeks should become outposts of empire, they resented it, and when his back was turned their resentment broke out. Before Alexander had returned to Babylon he learned that some mercenaries left in

---

[1] Diod. xvii. 100.   [2] Plut. *Alex.* 22.
[3] Arrian v. 27. 5 sqq.
[4] *Id.* vii. 6. 1 sqq.; 23. 3; Curt. x. 2. 8, and x. 4; Aelian, *V.H.* ix. 3.

PHILIP AND ALEXANDER

India had killed his governor: they were overpowered by the Macedonians.[1] A rising which occurred later in Bactria was much more serious, and since it may have exercised an influence upon the Lamian War after Alexander's death it will be considered in detail in the next chapter.

APPENDIX TO CHAPTER I

A NOTE ON ALEXANDER'S MERCENARIES

On page 16 a difficulty arose over mercenary cavalry, which I tried to explain by supposing that, although Alexander brought no mercenary cavalry over with him from Europe, he acquired some very soon after landing; namely, when he was joined by the troops who had been in Asia Minor before Philip's death. It seems possible that a similar explanation may be necessary for the mercenary infantry too.[2] Alexander quitted Europe with 5000 Greek mercenaries.[3] On his advance he left behind a mercenary garrison at Mytilene,[4] another garrison at Side probably consisting of mercenaries (though we are not told so),[5] and in Caria a force of 3000 mercenary infantry.[6] That accounts for the greater part of an original force of 5000. The only new mercenaries, so far as is known, are 300 at Miletus.[7] Yet at Issus there are two contingents of mercenaries taking part in the battle. Of course it is possible that the mercenaries might have been divided into two contingents even if they were only 1000 or so strong; but it would be much more likely if they were, say, 5000 or 8000 strong. If they were 5000 strong, where had the extra 4000 come from? There are two alternatives: either Alexander had received some reinforcement of which we hear absolutely nothing from any of our authorities, or he had been reinforced by a junction with an army which we know to have been in Asia Minor previously and whose fate is otherwise quite unexplained.[8] It is clear that in either case there is an hiatus in our information; but it certainly seems better to fill it by means of troops known to have been in existence than by a reinforcement invented solely for our own convenience.

Some slight confirmation of this conclusion can be obtained by glancing at the names of the mercenary commanders mentioned up

[1] Arrian vi. 27. 3.
[2] Cf. p. 13 and n. 3 for J. G. Droysen's argument in favour of a greater number than 5000 in the campaign of 334.
[3] Diod. xvii. 17. 2.
[4] Arrian ii. 1. 4.
[5] *Id.* i. 26. 5.
[6] *Ibid.* 23. 6, cf. ii. 5. 7.
[7] *Id.* i. 19. 6.
[8] Cf. p. 13.

to and including Gaugamela. They are three: Cleander, Menander and Clearchus. The references are as follows:

CLEANDER

Arrian i. 24. 2. ἔπεμψε δὲ καὶ Κλέανδρον τὸν Πολεμοκράτου ἐπὶ ξυλλογῇ στρατιωτῶν εἰς Πελοπόννησον.

Arrian ii. 20. 5. καὶ καταλαμβάνει Κλέανδρον τὸν Π. ἐκ Πελοποννήσου ἥκοντα καὶ ξὺν αὐτῷ μισθοφόρους Ἕλληνας εἰς τετρακισχιλίους.

Arrian iii. 12. 2 (at Gaugamela). ἐχόμενοι δὲ τῶν τοξοτῶν οἱ ἀρχαῖοι καλούμενοι ξένοι καὶ ἄρχων αὐτῶν Κλέανδρος (the only mercenary infantry mentioned as having fought in the battle).

MENANDER AND CLEARCHUS

Arrian iii. 6. 7–8 (shortly *before* Gaugamela). ἐς Λυδίαν δὲ σατράπην Μένανδρον ἐκπέμπει τῶν ἑταίρων· ἐπὶ δὲ τοὺς ξένους, ὧν ἡγεῖτο Μένανδρος, Κλέαρχος αὐτῷ ἐτάχθη.

First it is to be noticed that the new mercenaries, the 4000 mentioned in the second passage, apparently were not present at Gaugamela, since they can hardly be included in οἱ ἀρχαῖοι καλούμενοι ξένοι, and are not mentioned elsewhere (their absence will be explained below). There is nothing very odd in the fact that Cleander should be separated from them, since it was not necessary for the man who recruited mercenaries also to be their commander, as Berve pointed out. What is a little odd is that Cleander should have held (apparently) the only mercenary command at Gaugamela, when we know that Clearchus received a mercenary command very shortly before. A possible explanation is this: When Cleander rejoined the army with his 4000 recruits he did not become their commander, but returned to his previous command. What that may have been we do not know, but his having been selected to recruit mercenaries suggests that he probably had experience of commanding them: let us suppose that it was a mercenary command. That gives us two mercenary commanders in the army, namely Cleander and Menander (who was superseded by Clearchus just before Gaugamela). For the battle the two contingents were combined, and Cleander's seniority naturally gave him the command over both. And supposing that there were two contingents, what is more likely than that they consisted respectively of the mercenaries who crossed with Alexander, and the mercenaries of an army already in Asia which joined him later, both equally entitled to the description οἱ ἀρχαῖοι καλούμενοι ξένοι?[1]

---

[1] It may be said that since all the mercenaries at Gaugamela were ἀρχαῖοι there was no need to distinguish them by this name. Obviously the name was an invention of some years later, when there were (or had been) with the army

PHILIP AND ALEXANDER

ξένοι and μισθοφόροι

Berve (*op. cit.* p. 144) believes that the word ξένοι (ξένοι μισθοφόροι, τὸ ξενικόν, etc.) in Arrian always refers to original mercenaries of Alexander, as opposed to mercenaries subsequently recruited, who, he says, are called μισθοφόροι alone: the distinction holds good until the year 331-330. The first thing that makes one suspicious of this theory is that the distinction is elaborate out of all proportion to the issue at stake. No other writer has employed it, and there is nothing to show that there was any difference in the meaning of the words ξένοι (in the military sense) and μισθοφόροι. It seems to have been purely a matter of taste, some writers using the one, some the other, and a few both. But since our suspicions are aroused, let us examine the question more closely, and see if the theory always works. Applied to the mercenary cavalry it works out well: thus at Gaugamela there are two lots of mercenary cavalry, those of Menidas, who, as we know, joined the army in Egypt and are called μισθοφόροι, and those of Andromachus, who are called ἡ ξενικὴ ἵππος ἡ τῶν μισθοφόρων, and are presumably cavalry who had been with Alexander from the first, since we nowhere hear of their recruiting.[1] With the infantry it is not so easy. Μισθοφόροι infantry appear in Arrian too early, at a time when, so far as is known, there were no newly recruited mercenaries to speak of. Shortly before Issus Parmenion is sent ahead with a strong advance force, consisting of the allied infantry, the Greek μισθοφόροι, the Thracians of Sitalces, and the Thessalian cavalry.[2] Now the only new mercenaries with the army at that time were 300 who had been part of the Persian garrison at Miletus: it is possible that it was they who accompanied Parmenion, but if so they form a very insignificant contingent compared with the other three contingents mentioned together with them, and it seems much more likely that the mercenaries Parmenion took were all the Greek mercenaries with the army, a force of perhaps 5000 men or more. The same difficulty occurs in the order of battle at Issus. Mercenary infantry are mentioned twice: there are μισθοφόροι ξένοι who could be explained as the original mercenaries (οἱ ἀρχαῖοι καλούμενοι ξένοι of Gaugamela); but there are also τῶν Ἑλλήνων μισθοφόρων ἐστιν οὕς.[3] The 300 of Miletus are still the only known recruits, and it seems very much less likely that our ἐστιν οὕς are *part of* so small a force (in which case what became of the others?— we are told nothing) than that they are part of the whole force of mercenary infantry present, of which the remainder are accounted many mercenaries more recently recruited: but it is very natural for a military historian (e.g. Ptolemy) to use the name retrospectively, for an occasion before the time when it was first actually used.

[1] Arrian iii. 12. 3 and 5.
[2] *Id.* ii. 5. 1.
[3] *Ibid.* 9. 4.

for under οἱ μισθοφόροι ξένοι above: thus ξένοι and μισθοφόροι would be used indiscriminately.

There is yet another difficulty. At Sidon Alexander received his first large reinforcement of mercenary infantry, 4000 strong, the only known additional recruits before Gaugamela.[1] But in the order of battle at Gaugamela they are not present: the only mercenary infantry are οἱ ἀρχαῖοι καλούμενοι ξένοι.[2] The most obvious explanation is that they have been left behind somewhere between Sidon and Gaugamela ("between" of time, not of place). There is only one place where so large a force could have been left behind, namely Egypt. Arrian, describing the army of occupation left in Egypt, mentions mercenaries and mercenaries only: their numbers were sufficiently high to require, in addition to a commander, "a secretary of the mercenaries" (γραμματεύς) who was an important man (one of the Companions), and two commissioners (ἐπίσκοποι). The word Arrian uses for the mercenaries is ξένοι. Curtius gives the number of the troops left in Egypt, and that number is, curiously enough, 4000. It seems, therefore, something more than probable that the troops left in Egypt were the newly recruited mercenaries who joined the army at Sidon. At Sidon Arrian calls them μισθοφόροι; the troops left in Egypt he calls ξένοι.

But suppose, on the other hand, that this is all quite wrong; that the mercenaries in Egypt were not the 4000 of Sidon, but part of the original mercenaries, that they really were ξένοι as Berve understands the word. Difficulties still remain. For in that case what does happen to the 4000 of Sidon? Why are they not at Gaugamela? And incidentally who are οἱ ἀρχαῖοι καλούμενοι ξένοι of Gaugamela? If 4000 of them were left in Egypt, and other garrisons elsewhere (p. 22), there could not have been very many remaining. Either Arrian has simply omitted the 4000 at Gaugamela, which is most unlikely in so minute a catalogue; or he has included them in οἱ ἀρχαῖοι καλούμενοι ξένοι, which is fatal to Berve's theory (and incidentally Arrian would be writing nonsense).

The "second line" of mercenaries in Alexander's battle-tactics

It would be difficult to say anything on this much-discussed topic that would be both new and reasonable, and I conclude that it is best to say merely what seems reasonable to me, with the warning that other views have been held by other people. On all the essential points I am in agreement with the writer in *Antike Schlachtfelder*, who discusses the matter at some length with a bibliography.[3] I can

[1] Arrian ii. 20. 5.   [2] *Id.* iii. 12. 2.
[3] *Antike Schlachtfelder*, iv. pp. 347 sqq.; esp. pp. 350, 365, and 381 sqq. Cf. W. W. Tarn, in *C.A.H.* vii. pp. 368 and 381.

see no reason for doubting that there *was* a "second line" both at Issus and at Gaugamela, and whether it is to be called a "reserve" or not is immaterial, provided that it remains clear that by a "second line" is meant something quite different from merely packing the rear ranks of the phalanx. At the Granicus the main argument in favour of a "second line" of infantry is that neither the Greek allies nor the mercenary infantry are mentioned in the line which forced the passage of the river:[1] the inference is that they were held back in reserve, but since the Granicus is much less of a "set" battle than the other two, perhaps the point should not be pressed. At Issus the terminology leaves no cause for doubt, if it is considered in connection with the terminology used to describe the "second line" at Gaugamela, which is much the clearest case of the three. At Issus Alexander drew up his best troops, the phalanx and heavy cavalry, facing the enemy (Arrian ii. 9. 1): he has a strong flank-guard (ἐς ἐπικαμπήν) of lighter troops on the right where the Persian line far overlapped his own (9. 2 and 4), and a weaker flank-guard on the left (9. 3): οἱ δὲ μισθοφόροι ξένοι πᾶσιν ἐπετάχθησαν. It is unfortunate that the word ἐπιτάσσω can mean two things, either "place *alongside*", or "place *behind*" (cf. L. and S. *s.v.*);[2] but the context in Arrian, and more especially the actual circumstances, make it almost certain that here it must mean that the mercenaries were placed *behind* everybody, for (among other things) the other interpretation would land us with the mercenaries, a medium-heavy infantry division, on the extreme left of the whole army, where it was Alexander's practice to put his lightest cavalry and skirmishers. The mercenaries at Issus then, on the evidence for Issus considered alone, almost certainly formed a second line behind the phalanx. At Gaugamela the situation is clear. Alexander again has his front line containing the best troops (ἡ ἐπὶ μετώπου τάξις—Arrian iii. 11. 8 sqq.; 12. 1): his flank-guards (ἐς ἐπικαμπήν) on the left (12. 4 sqq.), and on the right, including οἱ ἀρχαῖοι καλούμενοι ξένοι (12. 2 sqq.): and finally a second line behind the phalanx, clearly defined by the phrase ἐπέταξε δὲ καὶ δευτέραν τάξιν ὡς εἶναι τὴν φάλαγγα ἀμφίστομον. This second line must have contained the Greek allied infantry and any mercenaries who were present other than the ἀρχαῖοι, probably few in number (pp. 29 sqq.). It formed what Arrian calls διπλῆν φάλαγγα, but this does not mean that the second line extended behind the whole length of the phalanx, because in the battle the left of the phalanx broke and some Indian and Persian cavalry could ride straight through and fall upon the Thracians in charge of the baggage

---

[1] Arrian i. 14. 1 sqq. and 15.
[2] E.g. at the Granicus, of the successive τάξεις of the phalanx (i. 14. 1 sqq.), it clearly means *alongside*: the phalanx could not conceivably be in column of τάξεις.

well in the rear of the army (14. 4 sqq.). The second line evidently extended behind only the right wing of the phalanx, where there was most reason to fear an outflanking or encircling movement: that the two lines were perfectly distinct is proved by the fact that Alexander gave orders for the second line to face about and resist this encirclement should it take place (12. 1). These tactical considerations will not interest everyone. But the real point to be made—and it is made most clearly by a description of the three battles—is that the mercenaries in fact played a very secondary part in the big victories. The flank-guards were never unduly troubled, and the reserve—if it was a reserve—was never called into action either to push home a big attack that had come to a standstill, or to act as a rear-guard while the attack was finishing its work. One scholar has drawn the distinction between the field army which won the battles, and what he calls the *Occupationsarmee* which included the mercenaries, and although he made his distinction too distinct, it is useful within limits.[1] The mercenaries did not win the battles, because Alexander could manage the job without them; the most that can be said is that they might have prevented a battle from being lost had anything gone seriously wrong with the Macedonian phalanx or the charge of the Companion cavalry, and it may be a source of some academic regret that Alexander or the Macedonians never provided them with their opportunity.

[1] A. Krause, in *Hermes*, 25, pp. 68 sqq. He feels it necessary to explain why the mercenaries were so little prominent in the big battles.

CHAPTER II

THE SUCCESSORS

THE end of the war in Greece against Agis of Sparta (330 B.C.) left the Graeco-Macedonian world, now in process of being extended to the confines of India, in the dominion of one man, the sole employer in the trade of war.¹ We have already seen in what numbers Greek and Balkan soldiers went to join Alexander as he moved through Bactria and the Hindu Kush into India, and how many of them remained in those strange lands, left there to spend their lives where they had come merely to see and conquer. But nothing has been said so far of the mercenaries serving his governors in Asia, apart from casual references to forces detached from the main army. It appears that in Alexander's absence the governors, with or without his consent, recruited mercenaries as they liked: at all events one of his first acts when he returned was to issue an edict ordering them all to dismiss their mercenaries. Artaxerxes Ochus had done the same, and Alexander realized the danger of armies in the hands of men with guilty consciences.² Perhaps the guiltiest conscience was that of Harpalus. He had been left in charge of the treasure at Ecbatana, but so far from doing his duty by keeping his talents intact, he had lived like a king and supported himself and his queens at Alexander's expense. When the unlooked-for news came that Alexander would after all return, Harpalus collected 5000 talents and 6000 mercenaries and made his way to the coast. After a brief appearance at Athens where he sowed trouble for himself and greater men, he established himself with his mercenaries and ships for a time at Taenarum, and then passes out of the story, murdered on a visit to Crete.³

¹ For mercenaries with Persia against Alexander, and with Agis against Antipater, cf. Parke, pp. 179 sqq., 199 sqq.
² Diod. xvii. 106; cf. Curt. x. 1. 45.
³ Diod. xvii. 108. His mercenaries later distinguished themselves under Thibron at Cyrene—Diod. xviii. 19 sqq. For Taenarum as a recruiting centre, cf. pp. 259–60.

What Harpalus did for his mercenaries the other mercenaries were left to do for themselves. We have already noticed traces of disaffection among the soldiers who had been settled against their will in the Far East.[1] When Alexander was desperately wounded among the Malli, a false report of his death reached the mercenaries in Bactria, and 3000 of them assembled together and resolved to make a bid for freedom. According to one story they never reached Greece, but were hunted down and exterminated, though not until after Alexander's death.[2] Another and a fuller account says that their rising was not due to any feeling against Alexander but from fear of his punishment, because of a faction which had broken out between them and the native population. But they also wanted to return to their homes. Their leader was a certain Athenodorus, later murdered and supplanted by Biton, who did succeed in winning his way home with his men.[3]

But it is not certain if it was precisely the same problem that confronted the dismissed mercenaries of the governors. Did Alexander intend them to return to Greece or not? At about the same time as his edict to the governors he published another edict providing for the return of all Greek exiles to their cities, and it is hard not to see a connection between the two. Many exiles must have found a livelihood as soldiers, and probably one of Alexander's intentions in making the exiles' decree was to provide for some of the soldiers who had lost their employment with his own governors. (According to Diodorus 20,000 exiles assembled at Olympia to hear the decree proclaimed by Nicanor of Stagirus.)[4] But all the soldiers were not exiles, and Alexander may have meant also to find employment for them by adding them to the number of Greek settlers in the East.[5] If that was his intention, the soldiers had other ideas. When they received their dismissal they turned their steps homeward and streamed across Asia, gathering their livelihood from the land as they went.[6] And here we meet for the first time the interesting figure of Leosthenes the Athenian. Of his earlier life nothing is known.

---

[1] Pp. 24 and 26.
[2] Diod. xvii. 99. 5.
[3] Curt. ix. 7.
[4] Diod. xviii. 8. 2 sqq.
[5] Paus. i. 25. 5; viii. 52. 5.
[6] Diod. xvii. 111. 1 sqq.

He may have been a mercenary himself:[1] at all events he now becomes for a short time the most important personage in the world of mercenaries, the man who seems to have made it his business to take charge of these bands of unemployed soldiers when they reached the coast, to find ships for their passage to Greece, and to concentrate them at Taenarum when they arrived. Pausanias says that he was responsible for the return to Greece of no fewer than 50,000 soldiers of fortune, and that in Alexander's lifetime and in opposition to Alexander's own wishes.[2] The number is certainly an exaggeration and probably a handsome one, but there is no doubting the influence he acquired or the work he in fact achieved. But in the meantime he found himself the arbiter of the fortunes of some thousands of mercenaries waiting at Taenarum for something to turn up. His luck held and something did turn up. Alexander died in June 323 B.C.

It would be pleasant to believe that Leosthenes had from the first been working in collaboration with Hyperides and the extreme anti-Macedonian party in Athens. It is certain that from Taenarum he kept in touch with Athens. The author of the *Life* of Hyperides says of Hyperides that "he advised the people not to discharge the garrison of Taenara under Chares, because he was a friend of the general".[3] The name Chares presents some difficulty (the Athenians had no power either to disband or retain a garrison at Taenarum in 331, the date commonly assigned to this reference),[4] and to read Leosthenes instead redeems the text from sheer nonsense. It is in either case a mistake to imply that the garrison was an Athenian garrison: but it does seem possible that "the friend" of Hyperides was Leosthenes, the only man ever mentioned elsewhere as commanding at Taenarum.[5] The Athenians could retain the "garrison" of Leosthenes by paying and feeding it, and when the news of Alexander's death arrived this was precisely what they did. They gave Leosthenes money and new arms for the soldiers who lacked them, but ordered him at first to conceal his connection

---

[1] So W. W. Tarn—*C.A.H.* vi. p. 455—who suggests that Leosthenes was a captain of mercenaries under Alexander.
[2] Paus. *ibid.*
[3] [Plut.] *Vit.* x *Orat.* 18 (*Moralia*, 848 E).
[4] Cf. Parke, p. 201; Berve, No. 819.
[5] Diod. xvii. 111, etc.

with Athens so as to present the situation to Antipater in a less formidable light.[1] Finally, when all was ready Leosthenes took the field and marched north to join the Aetolians, who provided 7000 men. He received also from Athens 5000 infantry and 500 cavalry, with 2000 mercenaries in Athenian pay: his own mercenary force amounted to 8000, all veterans who had seen service in Asia, "trained athletes in warfare".[2] It was probably not to them but to the citizen troops, and more particularly to the Athenians, that Phocion referred when he said that the army of Leosthenes would "do well for the sprint".[3]

The actual operations in the war are of no great interest for us. At first Leosthenes held the advantage in numbers and initiative. He defeated a small Macedonian force in Boeotia and shut up Antipater in Lamia. Antipater had only 13,000 foot and 600 horse, probably most of them Macedonians; but there were some mercenaries in his army. The allies' great chance was to wipe out Antipater before his reinforcements arrived from Asia; but the event of the war may have been decided when Leosthenes himself was fatally wounded during the siege. The arrival of Leonnatus in Europe freed Antipater, and though Leonnatus was himself defeated and killed, his army gave Antipater an equal chance, which became a winning one when Craterus' army and Cleitus' fleet arrived to his aid. When the end of the war came it is not clear what became of the mercenaries of Leosthenes. Probably they went back to Asia to fight in the wars of the generals: employment was now assured, and now that Alexander was dead there was no longer any fear of their being sent to end their days in Bactria or on the Indian frontier.[4]

The rising engineered in Bactria by Athenodorus and Biton was a local symptom of the general dissatisfaction with which the mercenaries regarded Alexander's eastern policy as it affected themselves. In the West it finds expression in the efforts of Leosthenes with their influence on the Lamian War. In the Far East it took more time to mature, and it was not until after Alexander's death that the crisis was reached. Then within a few months the Greeks of Bactria assembled and formed an

---

[1] Diod. xvii. 111; xviii. 9. [2] *Id.* xviii. 9 and 11. 3.
[3] Plut. *Phoc.* 23. 2—καλῶς πρὸς τὸ στάδιον.
[4] Diod. xviii. 9–18; Hyperides, *Epitaphios*, 10 sqq.; Plut. *Phoc.* 25. 1.

THE SUCCESSORS

army with the object of marching to the sea and returning to their homes. They were no fewer than 23,000 men, and were not outnumbered by the army of Peithon which was sent to oppose their passage; but Peithon had an overwhelming superiority in cavalry, and the treachery of one of the Greek captains enabled him to win a victory which placed the mercenaries in his power. Although he had orders to annihilate them, he contented himself with disarming them and bidding them return to their cities, intending to use them later for his own ends: but, unfortunately for his schemes and for the Greeks, the Macedonian soldiers settled the whole affair by massacring them in their defenceless state for the sake of their spoil.[1]

Such was the end of the mercenaries' rising in the East. There has been no mention of any dominating figure who may have played the part of organizer and general-in-chief which was played by Leosthenes in the West: nor is there any evidence of collusion in the two movements. The theory of collusion is, however, advanced by W. W. Tarn, and probability is all in favour of it.[2] Alexander was perhaps trying, among other things, to utilize the surplus population of poor and unemployed Greeks which had been a growing curse to Greece in the last eighty years: his scheme of colonization might have been the means to his succeeding. Had he in fact succeeded, the losers would have been the mercenary captains, the men most likely to profit from the continuance of mercenary service. A small standing army and a system of new cities and military settlements might satisfy Alexander (p. 23), but it was not likely to satisfy them. The economic problem solved, the captains must look for a job, and that job was only too likely to be a less profitable one. Such may have been the calculations of Leosthenes and his fellows, and they were fortunate in that Alexander's solution of the problem, while it might in the end improve the soldiers' condition, failed from the very first to rouse their enthusiasm. Theirs was the dissatisfaction upon which men who wished, and who dared, might hope to play: and though it can never be proved that the leading mercenary captains of the day laid their heads together and resolved to play upon it, it cannot be denied

---
[1] Diod. xviii. 7.
[2] *C.A.H.* vi. pp. 455–6; Parke, on the contrary, p. 203, thinks it unlikely.

that it was greatly to their interest to do so. Alexander's death probably precipitated the soldiers' action[1] (it certainly precipitated the Lamian War). Had he lived he might have found the opposition a most formidable one,[2] and Asia might have witnessed the anomalous spectacle (and one which could not have failed to gladden the hearts of many ancient historians to whom anomaly was the spice of history) of the conqueror of Persia leading an army of the conquered Persians against the army of Greeks who had helped him to conquer them. The issue would probably have rested with the Macedonian soldiers. Alexander in his last years had done much that displeased them, but it is doubtful all the same whether they would ever have fought against him: "the luck of Alexander" was a potent spell, and it was as well to have it on one's own side.[3] But when Alexander died such problems were removed, though not solved. The Greeks of Bactria might still want to go home; but the professional captains must have realized at once that, with Alexander's empire as the prize to be divided among a group of able and ambitious generals, Greek soldiers need never want employment, nor they themselves fear for their profession.

The story of Alexander's life and death is surely one of the most significant in all history. The destiny of nearly the whole civilized world was identified with the fortunes of one man. For centuries kings and governments had worked and schemed to increase their portion of that world at the expense of their neighbours: kings had died and governments had fallen, and the portions of the world remained much the same. Then a new power appeared. A new king marched out of the north, and in a few years all the portions were united in one. The king must be a god. The eyes of the world are fixed upon him: what will he do next? He falls sick and dies in a few days. The civilized world, which had never before known only one master, now found itself in a second novel situation, that of knowing no master at all. But the strongest force it saw was the powerful

---

[1] Diod. xviii. 7.
[2] The mercenary population can hardly have been less than 50,000, and was probably more, cf. pp. 20 sqq.
[3] Arrian, *Anab.* vi. 16. 2.

THE SUCCESSORS

instrument its dead master had used—Alexander's military machine. The future lay in the hands of the few men who had helped to work it and understood its management, and to those men the soldiers who had fought with Alexander became persons of the first importance.

On their numbers and condition the foregoing pages have thrown some light. Probably the number of mercenaries who had seen service with Alexander himself or his governors was not far short of 100,000.[1] The condition of most of them was such as they could wish to better. The soldiers in the East wanted to return home: those who had returned home found themselves, many of them, on the losing side at the end of the Lamian War. It is certain that so many soldiers returning to Greece could not have found a livelihood by the arts of peace had they desired it. They may be counted as so much fighting material towards the redistribution of armies which was soon to take place.

In addition to these mercenaries there were the Macedonians, who were to play a somewhat equivocal part in the wars of the next twenty years. The narrative will show that they are still the most important troops in the armies of the several commanders; but henceforward they are fighting not so much for their king and country as for their general and themselves. This is true more particularly of the Macedonians who fought in Asia in the twenty years before Ipsus: those who stayed in Europe under Antipater or Polyperchon or Cassander probably retained more of the motives and spirit of a national army. But the Macedonians of Eumenes, and no doubt some of those of Antigonus, were veterans of Alexander, and to them war had become a profession and perhaps something more, a unique accomplishment. One never hears that they wanted to return to their own land or to become owners of new land in Asia: they obeyed even Eumenes, whom they disliked, when he led them hundreds of miles into the far eastern satrapies. When Antigonus and Eumenes were opposed to one another, each represented himself as the constitutionalist, partly no doubt to impress his Macedonian soldiers. But these Macedonians at Paraitacene and Gabiene show the mark of the mercenary, and the decisive event of the war is not a constitutional manifesto of either

[1] Pp. 20 sqq., and 33 sqq.

40 HELLENISTIC MERCENARIES

general, or even a crushing victory in the field, but the capture of some baggage belonging to the 3000 "Silver Shields". Parke (pp. 207 sqq.) makes a very good point when he stresses the importance of the ἀποσκευή in the military history of this short period. It is the period of large professional armies *par excellence*, and the best fighting material was the great mass of professional soldiers who lived their whole lives in the camp, carrying all their worldly possessions with them when they moved (ἀποσκευή), and preferring a change of employer to the loss of their treasure.[1] Of these professional armies the Macedonians in Asia were the flower: they are soldiers of fortune hardly less than the Greeks and others who are called mercenaries by name, and their importance entitles them to the first place in any inquiry into the armies of the Successors.

One of the first conclusions to suggest itself is that the *number* of Macedonian soldiers on active service appears excessive. There is nothing to indicate that Macedonia could, at her strongest, ever put into the field a number of heavy infantry greatly exceeding 30,000,[2] and at this time she was exhausted by the demands of Alexander upon her man-power.[3] Alexander had taken with him to Asia in the first place 12,000 Macedonian infantrymen, and his reinforcements cannot possibly have exceeded the original number, and were probably less,[4] so that at

---

[1] References to ἀποσκευή: Plut. *Eum.* 5 (Neoptolemus); Diod. xviii. 40. 8 (Eumenes 319 B.C.); Plut. *Eum.* 9; Polyaen. iv. 8. 5 (Antigonus 317 B.C.); Diod. xix. 42. 2 sqq. etc. (Eumenes at Gabiene); *id.* xix. 85. 7 (Demetrius at Gaza); *id.* xx. 47. 4 (mercenaries of Ptolemy in Cyprus); *ibid.* 111. 3 (Demetrius in Greece 302 B.C.). Cf. also Diod. xviii. 20. 6 (Thibron at Cyrene); Pol. i. 66. 7 (Mercenaries' War of Carthage).
For the later use of ἀποσκευή as the retinue of royalty or of a high official in Egypt, cf. *Dikaiomata*, pp. 86 sqq.; *U.P.Z.* i. 110. 24 and 91, and Wilcken's nn., pp. 489 and 491.

[2] The evidence is (i) the numbers for 334 B.C.—12,000 in Asia with Alexander, 12,000 at home with Antipater (and no doubt some reserve); (ii) the armies of the kings of Macedonia in the third century, which never show a phalanx exceeding 20,000; (iii) the army of Perseus (171 B.C.), which is called the greatest since Alexander's, and had only 25,000 heavy-armed Macedonians.

[3] Diod. xviii. 12. 2.

[4] Beloch (*Bevölk. d. griech.-röm. Welt*, pp. 218 sqq.) computes 8000 reinforcements, since he finds four new τάξεις in the army. The number is a likely one, but the method of reckoning by τάξεις is unsafe, because the commanders were sometimes changed, and there is a possibility that mercenaries may have fought in Macedonian τάξεις in the Indian campaign. See below.

THE SUCCESSORS

his death there were, at a liberal estimate, 20,000 Macedonian infantry in Asia, including the 10,000 who were on their way home with Craterus: and Antipater had in Europe 13,000 men, obviously the full levy.[1] Not to confuse the issue by mentioning all the minor generals who *may* have had Macedonians with them, the situation in 321 B.C. was roughly this: The allies Perdiccas and Eumenes should have had between them some 8000–10,000 in Asia. Ptolemy may have had a few in Egypt, and Antipater and Craterus perhaps 20,000 in Europe (Craterus' 10,000 being now transferred from Asia to Europe). What we find in fact is Eumenes with 20,000 infantry "of mixed origin",[2] but containing a strong nucleus of Macedonians, let us say 5000;[3] Perdiccas with a considerable "Macedonian phalanx", including the 3000 Silver Shields, certainly not less than 5000 in all (he lost 2000 men in the Nile, but we are not told they are Macedonians);[4] Craterus with "20,000 infantry, mostly Macedonians"; Antipater on his way to Egypt with another force;[5] and Polyperchon fighting the Aetolians in Thessaly "with a considerable force", sufficient in fact to defeat an army of 12,000 infantry.[6] The total number of Macedonians comprehended by these figures cannot be much less than 50,000. Are the figures, then, to be distrusted? It is possible, but this section of Diodorus is generally regarded as reliable owing to its excellent source (Hieronymus of Cardia). Far more likely the numbers are substantially correct, but the term "Macedonians" has already begun to lose its strictly national significance. The value of the Macedonian infantry had been proved for ever by Philip and Alexander, and nothing is more probable than that the Successors should have reinforced their true Macedonians with Greeks, or even with Asiatics armed and trained in the Macedonian manner, when the true supply began to fail. It will be seen that in the third century the word "Macedonians" came to denote, in Egypt especially, nothing more than a *type* of infantry, and the figures quoted above certainly lend

---

[1] Cf. Arrian, *Anab.* vii. 12; Diod. xviii. 12. 2.
[2] Diod. xviii. 30. 5; cf. 29. 4.
[3] *Ibid.* 29. 4 sqq.
[4] *Ibid.* 36. 1 sqq.; Arrian, τὰ μετὰ ᾽Αλεξ. 38.
[5] Diod. *ibid.* 30. 4; 29. 7.
[6] *Ibid.* 38. 1 sqq.

colour to the suggestion of K. Grote, that the period of transition began very shortly after Alexander's death.[1] But it should be insisted that there is still, in the army of Perdiccas, a strong body of real Macedonians, veterans of Alexander, of whom the Silver Shields were the *corps d'élite*.[2] Nor can any trace be found of a strong Persian element in the phalanx, which would point to a successful completion of Alexander's scheme for equipping a mixed infantry to take the place of the disbanded troops:[3] the jealousy of the veterans was probably too strong. Any strengthening of the phalanx that may have occurred must have been in the form of an infiltration of seasoned troops, that is to say Greek mercenaries. It has been suggested that during Alexander's lifetime the mercenary infantry in his field army, or part of it, was incorporated in certain of the Macedonian τάξεις, but there is no satisfactory evidence in the history of his campaigns proving that this was so.[4] There is one piece of confirmation, however, if not a particularly important one. In one account of the dissension after Alexander's death between the infantry and the cavalry of the army, three envoys are chosen to negotiate for the infantry, and of these three one is a Thessalian and another a Megalopolitan: the infantry as a whole are called *Macedones*.[5]

Apart from Macedonians, the armies of the Successors were composed of mercenaries or Asiatics or both. The Asiatics were probably not mercenaries, but troops levied by the generals in their capacity of governors of provinces: the adjective παντοδαποί sometimes denotes Asiatics, and in Antigonus' army at Paraitacene, they are mentioned separately from the ξένοι, the Greek mercenaries.[6] And Eumenes' strong Cappadocian horse which defeated and killed Craterus was plainly the levy from a province which was famous for its cavalry.[7] But Asiatics, unless they were cavalry, or infantry armed in the Macedonian style, were of little value as battle troops (e.g. Eumenes was compelled to beat Craterus with his cavalry; his infantry was equal in

[1] K. Grote, p. 38.
[2] Arrian, τὰ μετὰ 'Αλεξ. 32 and 38: cf. their subsequent career with Eumenes.
[3] For Alexander's scheme, cf. Arrian, *Anab.* vii. 6. 1 sqq.; 23. 3.
[4] J. G. Droysen, *Gesch. d. Alex.* p. 137; *Kleine Schriften*, p. 233; Berve, p. 148.   [5] Curt. x. 8. 15.
[6] Diod. xix. 29. 3. K. Grote, p. 37, takes them for mercenaries here and often.
[7] *Id.* xviii. 30. 5; Plut. *Eum.* 4 and 7.

THE SUCCESSORS

numbers to that of Craterus, but not in quality); the Greek infantry was still the only possible substitute for Macedonians. It follows, therefore, that the demand for mercenaries in the wars both in Greece and Asia was very great indeed, and it is not altogether easy to understand how the supply kept pace with it, as it undoubtedly did. Probably there was a considerable number of Asiatics in the mercenary bands which followed the generals in Asia. But the flow of mercenaries from East to West, which began in 324 B.C. (pp. 33 sqq.), the overthrow of Alexander's peace in Greece and Western Asia in the next year, and the troubled state of Greece following the Lamian War, released great numbers of unemployed soldiers or homeless citizens to fill the ranks of the armies.[1]

We have seen how the Lamian War found employers for mercenaries on both sides. At about the same time or very shortly afterwards, there began a movement on the part of several other employers to strengthen their armies for the coming wars. Thibron, who succeeded Harpalus in the command of his 6000 mercenaries brought from Asia, recruited in Crete before selling his services to Cyrenean exiles: and he later obtained a further reinforcement of 2500 men by sending officers from Cyrene to the recruiting centre at Taenarum in the Peloponnese.[2] In Asia, Ariarathes, the dynast of Cappadocia, knowing that he must fight for his land against Perdiccas and Eumenes, called out the native levies and recruited mercenaries till he could finally put 30,000 infantry into the field (322 B.C.).[3] Eumenes himself, after taking possession of Cappadocia, must have strengthened himself with mercenaries, since we hear of ξεναγοί in his army: he may well have taken over those of Ariarathes after he had defeated him, as well as the power of enlisting the Cappadocians to his need.[4] When he was isolated by the death of Perdiccas and deprived of the use of the royal treasuries by the ensuing decree of outlawry passed upon him in his absence, he tried to solve his financial difficulties by the novel method of parcelling Antigonus' province of Phrygia into

[1] Cf. *I.G.*² ii. 1. 398, for Athenians serving in Asia before 320 B.C.
[2] Diod. xviii. 19-21: Arrian, τὰ μετὰ Ἀλεξ. 16 sqq.
[3] Diod. xviii. 16. 1.
[4] Plut. *Eum.* 8. 5. Perdiccas and Eumenes took prisoner 5000 of Ariarathes' army—probably mercenaries who changed sides.

lots which he sold to his officers for their men to plunder;[1] but it may have been lack of money that ruined him in the end, since his defeat by Antigonus shortly afterwards (320 B.C.) was due to the defection of one of his cavalry officers with his men.[2]

Meanwhile other enemies of Antigonus were in a position to give trouble. Alcetas, the brother of Perdiccas, had spent the years 322–320 B.C. in Pisidia, trying to establish his rule by cultivating the affections of his subjects. His army of 17,000 men contained 6000 Pisidian infantry, but the fact that after his defeat by Antigonus the whole of his army except the Pisidians changed sides and continued to serve under the victor, makes it almost certain that these others were mercenaries.[3] In the north too Arrhidaeus, the governor of Hellespontine Phrygia, had collected a formidable force of over 10,000 mercenaries, with 1000 Macedonians, a few Persians and some cavalry, which enabled him to resist Antigonus for over two years before going the way of Alcetas and other less important commanders (320–318 B.C.).[4] But the greatest employer of all was Antigonus himself. He owed the beginnings of his bid for greatness to his old friend Antipater the Regent, who had allowed him to take the remainder of Perdiccas' army (itself including mercenaries), and himself added an invaluable 8500 Macedonians.[5] Then his victories over Eumenes and Alcetas enabled him to incorporate the greater part of their armies, so that at the time of Antipater's death (319 B.C.), he commanded no fewer than 60,000 infantry and 10,000 horse.[6] That he had mercenaries we are told,[7] and they must have been numerous in view of the wide extent of his increasing empire, which needed many garrisons to make it secure: how numerous it is impossible to say, but they may have provided half or nearly half of his infantry, "since the land of Asia could support them without stint".[8] It must be

[1] Plut. *Eum.* 8. 5. [2] Diod. xviii. 40. 8.
[3] *Ibid.* 45. 1. [4] *Ibid.* 51. 1.
[5] Arrian, τὰ μετὰ ᾽Αλεξ. 38 and 43. Little is heard of the mercenaries of Perdiccas, but that they existed is proved by the small expedition to Cyprus of Medius the Thessalian with 800. Medius later became an officer of Antigonus.
[6] Diod. xviii. 50. 3 (cf. too *ibid.* 44 and 45. 1) for the growth of Antigonus' army.
[7] *Ibid.* 52. 7.
[8] *Ibid.* 50. 3. Cf. *ibid.* 52. 7 for a consignment of gold on its way to Macedonia commandeered by Antigonus "for his mercenaries".

THE SUCCESSORS

remembered that after Antipater died no fresh Macedonians came over into Asia to help Antigonus, since Polyperchon the new Regent was hostile, and Cassander, who was friendly, could fight for his own hand only with Antigonus' help.

Meanwhile, in Greece, the military situation had resolved itself into a struggle between Polyperchon and Cassander. The Regent, by virtue of his office, had the right to call out the Macedonian levy, which in 318 B.C. amounted to 20,000 infantry and 1000 horse, an unduly large figure when we bear in mind the Macedonians who were still fighting in Asia.[1] Moreover he was nominally in control of the garrisons which Antipater had left in many Greek cities, comprising probably some thousands of mercenaries all told; but it may well have happened that these troops, engaged by Antipater's officers, now considered themselves Cassander's men. At all events one of Polyperchon's first acts was to make a bid for popularity with the Greeks by means of a manifesto providing for the withdrawal of garrisons and the overthrow of oligarchies: and one of the clauses which says "the Greeks are to agree that no one is to fight or to act against us" (i.e. Polyperchon's party),[2] may have been inserted with the object of making mercenary service with Cassander illegal, and perhaps of hindering the flow of soldiers eastward to join Antigonus. (It can have been only a feeble hindrance at best, and the words may easily apply to the Greek states rather than to individual Greeks.) Cassander in the meantime was at the outset no more than a commander of mercenaries: he had 4000 from Antigonus and a very strong mercenary garrison at Athens.[3] But the struggle was not to be decided by any great display of force on Greek soil: it was really a civil war between two Macedonian factions, in which Polyperchon's mistakes in policy, his defeat at sea by Antigonus, and his failure to crush Cassander in Greece, brought about a rapid reversal of fortunes. By 316 B.C. it was Cassander who was ruler of Macedonia, while Polyperchon had lost his national following, and could do no more than maintain himself with an army, no doubt largely of mercenaries, at Corinth and in the Peloponnese.[4]

[1] Diod. xviii. 68. 3.
[2] Ibid. 56, esp. 4 and 5.
[3] Ibid. 68. 1; 64. 4; Polyaen. iv. 11. 1.
[4] Diod. xix. 54. 3 sqq.; 52. 6.

Cassander, on the other hand, was now in a position to enlist the Macedonian levies, and the scale of his operations on three or four fronts points to his having in the field an army of not less than 20,000 men.[1] Moreover the continuous and often indecisive nature of his campaigns during the next six years must have made it impossible for him to rely on more than a nucleus of Macedonians in the army: a standing army was essential to him, and the more so since he made a return to the garrison policy of his father Antipater. There is abundant evidence for this policy at work in northern, central and western Greece, and later in the Peloponnese also; and the garrisons can have consisted only of mercenaries, as we know was the case at Athens.[2]

Polyperchon too was at large during all this period, but the only figures for his army relate to an exceptional year. In 310 B.C. he made a bid to regain Macedonia by identifying his interests with those of Alexander's illegitimate son Heracles, a move which probably rallied a number of Macedonians to his side: he was also allied with the Aetolians, so that his army of over 20,000 cannot be held to represent the number of his permanent force of mercenaries. It was his last effort, and ended ignobly, for he betrayed and murdered Heracles and consented to become Cassander's general in the Peloponnese, receiving from him 4000 Macedonians, very likely those whom he commanded already.[3] In these wars in Greece, the fact that Macedonians are found with either leader does not really make them mercenaries, since each represented opposite currents of national opinion, namely that which remained loyal to the house of Alexander and that which supported the policy and party of Antipater, the late Regent. Polyperchon's son Alexander, who had previously received mercenaries from Antigonus, had deserted to Cassander some time before: when he died his

---

[1] Diod. xix. 35. 4; 36. 1 sqq.; 52. 5; 53. 1 sqq.; 54; 60. 2; 68. 2; 74. 2.
[2] Paus. i. 15. 1. Garrisons of Cassander are found at the following places (the list does not pretend to be complete): Patrae, Aegae, Dymae (Diod. xix. 66); in Acarnania and Epidamnus (*ibid.* 67); Athens (68. 2); Chalcis (76. 5); Oropus and Thebes (xix. 78 and xx. 110. 4); in Phocis (xix. 78. 5); at Leucas—commanded by an Athenian (88. 5; 89. 3); Corinth (xx. 103. 1 sqq.); in Achaea (103. 4); in Arcadia (103. 7); Larissa and Pherae (110. 3 sqq.); Megara (46. 3); three garrisons in Peloponnese (xix. 66. 3 sqq.); Argos, Sicyon, and Corinth (Plut. *Dem.* 25. 1).
[3] Diod. xx. 20. 3 sqq.; 28. 1 sqq.

THE SUCCESSORS

mercenaries were kept together by his widow Cratesipolis, who seems to have been a most engaging character.[1]

It is now time to return to Asia and the last great struggle between Eumenes and Antigonus, much the most interesting episode of any, from the military standpoint, in all the Successors' wars. Early in 319 B.C., after his defeat by Antigonus, Eumenes was a penniless fugitive shut up in Nora with a few faithful adherents. But he escaped by a trick, and at once began to collect a new army. The process was at first a slow one: he did not dare to leave the hinterland of Cappadocia, and could do no more than pick up such of his old soldiers as remained "wandering over the countryside" (they had probably split up into bands and turned brigand); but he was helped by his "great popularity" with the men.[2] Then came a letter from Polyperchon with offers of alliance, which meant the use of the royal treasure and of the 3000 Silver Shields who had become detached from Perdiccas' army some time previously and had never served under Antigonus.[3] Now he could recruit in earnest. "He engaged in the business the ablest of his friends, gave them plenty of money for the recruiting, fixed a high rate of pay and so sent them out. They immediately passed into Pisidia and Lycia and the neighbouring land and began to recruit diligently: others went to Cilicia or to Coele-Syria and Phoenicia or to the cities in Cyprus. The recruiting was soon widely bruited and the pay offered was high, so that great numbers of soldiers from the cities of Greece as well came of their own accord and enlisted. Very soon there were assembled more than 10,000 infantry and 2000 horse, apart from the Silver Shields and Eumenes' original force" (over 2000 in number).[4] This bald statement of fact evokes a lively picture of the bustle and activity of an intensive recruiting campaign. The recruiting officers could not enter the great cities of Lydia and Ionia, of which Antigonus was master; but they spread southward to the ports where a floating population was likely to congregate, and whence the news would quickly travel by merchant ships bound for Greece; the high pay did the rest.

---

[1] Diod. xix. 61. 5; 64. 4; 67; xx. 37. 1; cf. Polyaen. viii. 58.
[2] Diod. xviii. 53. 6 sqq.; Plut. *Eum.* 12. 3.
[3] Diod. *ibid.* 57. 3; 58. 1.   [4] *Ibid.* 61. 4 sqq.; 53. 7.

Eumenes had an army again, but he was not yet strong enough to face Antigonus, and accordingly turned his face to the East in the hope of raising the Macedonian governors against him. In this he was mainly successful. Peithon indeed, the satrap of Media, supported Antigonus, and Seleucus at Babylon ultimately followed his lead. But the rest joined Eumenes with valuable reinforcements. The strongest was Peucestas, the satrap of Persis, who brought, in addition to some Persian cavalry and a vast throng of archers and slingers, 3000 Asiatics (παντοδαποί) armed in the Macedonian style, and 600 Thracian and Greek horse, old mercenaries and settlers of Alexander.[1] The other five governors brought each a small force, varying in numbers from 800 to 2500, with a very large proportion of cavalry:[2] this makes it almost certain that the cavalry was native, which is supported by the story of the Indian cavalry commander Keteus and his wives.[3] On the other hand the infantry statistics make it seem probable that the eastern governors had a few Macedonians, and had begun to put into practice Alexander's idea of a mixed Macedonian-Asiatic phalanx: Eumenes, however, rightly judged that for his purposes a solid pure-Macedonian kernel was more valuable, and we therefore find the Asiatic phalanx separate at Paraitacene.[4] Eumenes was now ready for Antigonus.

Antigonus for his part had not been idle. When he heard of Eumenes' escape, he set out with a picked force of 20,000 infantry and 4000 horse, intending to crush him before he became strong; but he was not quick enough and was obliged

[1] Diod. xix. 14. 5; 27. 5.
[2] *Ibid.* 14. 6 sqq.   [3] *Ibid.* 33–34.
[4] The infantry from the eastern satrapies comprises Peucestas' 3000 παντοδαποί εἰς τὴν Μακεδονικὴν τάξιν καθωπλισμένοι + 5500 (indeterminate) from the other governors. *Total* 8500. At Paraitacene we get 5000 παντοδαποὶ καθωπλισμένοι εἰς τὰ Μακεδονικά + more than 3000 οἱ ἐκ τῶν ὑπασπιστῶν, who have not been previously mentioned, but now appear under the same command as the Silver Shields, the "crack" Macedonian corps. *Total, more than* 8000.

It thus seems almost certain that Eumenes must have separated the Asiatics from the Macedonians out of the 8500 infantry from the East.

Cf. too the Alexander festival at Persis (Diod. xix. 22). The outer ring was allotted to "the mercenaries and the mass of the allies" (i.e. the Asiatics); in the second ring were "the Silver Shields and *the Companions who had served with Alexander*." These latter must have been *foot* companions, because the cavalry were in the third ring.

to follow Eumenes to the East.[1] He was in Mesopotamia when the news reached him that the eastern satraps had declared against him, news which made it plain that he had underrated his task. We hear that "he rested his army and enlisted more soldiers":[2] obviously he did not find mercenaries in Mesopotamia, and the meaning must be that he sent back officers to recruit. He also got reinforcements from Seleucus and Peithon when he had reached Babylon.[3] But in the pursuit of Eumenes his army suffered terribly from the climate and at the hands of the wild mountaineers, and there was nearly a great disaster at the crossing of the river Coprates, when many soldiers were drowned and 4000 were ambushed and captured by Eumenes' men.[4] The efficiency of his cavalry in particular was greatly impaired, so that Peithon's reinforcement of Medians, and the supply of remounts and baggage animals furnished by his satrapy, was especially valuable. But for that he would have found himself with a fatal inferiority in cavalry. As it was he had fewer infantry than Eumenes, but his phalanx was more numerous and contained more Macedonians (8000). When the two armies met at Paraitacene Antigonus had 28,000 infantry with 8500 horse;[5] and about one-third of the infantry and one-half of the cavalry were mercenaries. The cavalry mercenaries were 2200 "Tarentine" horse "who had accompanied him from the coast", 800 of the cavalry called "amphippoi" and of the (Thracian?) settlers, 500 mercenary horse of all nations (παντοδαποί) distinct from the other larger Asiatic contingents, and 1000 Thracians possibly from Bithynia.[6] The mercenary infantry are called simply "9000 ξένοι"; their armament is not specified, nor is it stated whether they were phalanx troops or not, whereas the "8000 mixed infantry (παντοδαποί) armed in the Macedonian style" were clearly intended to fight with the Macedonians.[7]

Eumenes took the field with 35,000 infantry, 6100 horse.[8] In the cavalry numbers here there is a deficiency of 1200 as compared with the numbers which, as we know, joined him from

[1] Diod. xviii. 73. 1.
[2] Id. xix. 15. 6.
[3] Ibid. 17. 2; 20. 3.
[4] Ibid. 18. 2; 19.
[5] Ibid. 27. 1.
[6] Ibid. 29. 2 and 4; the "Tarentines" are discussed on pp. 246 sqq.
[7] Ibid. 29. 3.
[8] Ibid. 28. 4.

time to time,[1] nor is there any body of cavalry which can be identified with the 2000 who were enlisted at the time of the big recruiting: perhaps some of them were now to be found in the "agemata" or picked squadrons commanded by the several governors. The only other mercenary cavalry were the Thracian settlers mentioned above.[2] The mercenary infantry too have dwindled from 10,000 or more to 6000, but these 6000 definitely belong to the phalanx,[3] and it is possible that the remainder were included in the cloud of light infantry which was thrown out in front of the army along with the elephants:[4] or they may be accounted for by losses and garrison duties. In the battle it cannot be said that the mercenaries of either side decided the day. The cavalry of Eumenes' strong right defeated Antigonus' left, and after a desperate struggle his phalanx won the mastery, thanks to the Silver Shields; but Antigonus then struck with his strong right so that Eumenes could not pursue for fear of being taken in rear.[5] Antigonus' losses were far the heavier, especially in infantry,[6] and it seems that the burden of them must have fallen on his mercenaries, since they were on the left of his phalanx and opposed to the Silver Shields and the other Macedonians: he probably feared to oppose his own Macedonians to the men who had fought with Alexander, and hoped to win the battle elsewhere.

In the next year, at Gabiene, the tactics were rather different. The two commanders joined issue personally with their strong cavalry wings, and Antigonus' proved the stronger: in the centre, however, the magnificent fighting of the Silver Shields drove his infantry off the field. But meanwhile he had won the fruits of the two years' campaign behind Eumenes' back. In the heat of the fray he despatched his Median cavalry and some of the "Tarentines" to circle the battle unperceived and take possession of Eumenes' camp. The Silver Shields were furious at losing their women and their treasure. They had always been difficult to manage, and had disliked having Eumenes as their

---

[1] Diod. xviii. 61. 4; xix. 14. 5 sqq.
[2] *Id*. xix. 27. 5.
[3] *Ibid*. 27. 6.
[4] *Ibid*. 27. 5; 28. 2.
[5] *Ibid*. 30.
[6] *Ibid*. 31. 5.

THE SUCCESSORS

general because he was a Greek, and now they resolved to make him their prisoner and barter him to Antigonus in return for their possessions.[1] Antigonus profited by the trick, but the Silver Shields did not: the truculent old men ended their days in Arachosia, at the limits of Antigonus' empire.[2] What happened to the rest of Eumenes' army is not clear. Most of his generals were allowed to return to their satrapies and no doubt took sufficient troops with them.[3] Eumenes' mercenaries presumably now became Antigonus' mercenaries. It may have been these new soldiers whom Peithon tried to corrupt during the winter:[4] another account says that he recruited mercenaries, which may be merely a different way of saying the same thing.[5] When Antigonus departed after settling the affairs of the East, he left a new governor of Media in place of Peithon with 3500 mercenary infantry and an uncertain number of cavalry.[6]

At the end of 316 B.C. Antigonus was by far the most powerful of the dynasts. His extensive territories made it essential to maintain a huge army, but the great wealth derived from the Persian treasuries, and a large annual income from his tax-paying subjects, made it possible for him to do so.[7] Its precise numbers and constituents are never revealed. At its greatest it must have numbered at least 100,000, for his great expedition against Egypt in 306 B.C. included more than 80,000 infantry and about 8000 cavalry; and mercenary garrisons, if not an army of defence, must have been left in his northern territories.[8] After his defeat of Eumenes he had something over 10,000 Macedonians; but there was no means of replenishing the stock except by a fortunate accident. His Asiatic subjects could provide him with sufficient cavalry and light infantry, and were, moreover, as we have seen, being trained to fight in the phalanx with Macedonian arms and methods. But the Macedonians could not be everywhere at once and must be carefully preserved, and it would have been suicidal at this point to entrust the defence of Asia to Asiatics. The brunt of the defence must have been borne, year in and year out, by Greek mercenary

[1] Diod. xix. 40. 1 sqq.; Polyaen. iv. 6. 13.
[2] Diod. xix. 48. 3 sqq.; cf. 41. 2.
[3] *Ibid.* 48.
[4] *Ibid.* 46. 1 sqq.
[5] Polyaen. iv. 6. 14.
[6] Diod. xix. 46. 5.
[7] *Ibid.* 48. 8; 56. 5.
[8] *Id.* xx. 73. 2.

4-2

infantry, as is confirmed by such evidence as we have relating to the armies commanded by Antigonus, or more often by his son Demetrius, in the years 316–301 B.C. Unfortunately it does not enable us to reconstruct the organization of Antigonus' standing army. Recruiting was probably an easy matter and regulated by the needs of the moment. We hear of an agreement with Sparta which enabled a general of Antigonus to recruit at will.[1] The thousands of Athenians who fought among Demetrius' mercenaries at Ipsus make it seem likely that there was a similar agreement with Athens after Demetrius had freed her.[2] Pirates assisted Demetrius at the siege of Rhodes, selling their swords probably for the duration of that single campaign against the maritime power which was their special enemy.[3] Mercenaries were plentiful, and the years of fighting for a reliable paymaster and under the same commanders must have made of them an excellent fighting machine.

Our evidence, insufficient though it is, does at least illustrate the copious supplies upon which Antigonus and his captains could draw. Aristodemus, the general just mentioned, recruited 8000 mercenaries in the Peloponnese with the assistance of Sparta (perhaps from the *depôt* at Taenarum).[4] Other expeditions were sent to Greece under Telesphorus and Polemaeus, the latter of 5500 men: Telesphorus seized Elis and ruled there for a short time on his own account with such of his mercenaries as were willing to repudiate their contracts with Antigonus.[5] Polemaeus too deserted Antigonus, first for Cassander and later for Ptolemy.[6] The armies under Demetrius seem always to have consisted partly, if not mainly, of mercenaries. In the disastrous

---

[1] Diod. xix. 60. 1.
[2] *I.G.*² ii. 1. 657, ll. 17 sqq., a decree in honour of the comic poet Philippides (284 B.C.), then living at the court of Lysimachus: καὶ νικήσαντος Λυσιμάχου τοῦ βασιλέως τὴν μάχην τὴν Ἴψωι γενομένην πρὸς Ἀντίγονον καὶ Δημήτριον, τοὺς μὲν τελευτήσαντας ἐν τῶι κινδύνωι τῶν πολιτῶν ἔθαψε τοῖς ἑαυτοῦ ἀναλώμασιν, ὅσοι δὲ αἰχμάλωτοι ἐγένοντο, ἐμφανίσας τῶι βασιλεῖ καὶ λαβὼν αὐτοῖς ἄφεσιν, τοὺς μὲν βουλομένους στρατεύεσθαι διώικησεν ὅπως ἂν καταχωρισθεῖεν ἐν ἡγεμονίαις, τοὺς δὲ προαιρουμένους ἀπιέναι ἀμφιέσας καὶ ἐφόδια δοὺς παρ' ἑαυτοῦ ἀπέστειλεν οὗ ἕκαστοι ἠβούλοντο, πλείους ὄντας ἢ τρισχιλίους. Cf. *S.E.G.* i. 358 for a similar decree respecting Samians serving under Hipparchus, Antigonus' general in Caria.
[3] Diod. xix. 82. 4.   [4] *Ibid.* 57. 5; 60. 1.
[5] *Ibid.* 74. 1; 77. 2; 87. 1 sqq.
[6] *Id.* xx. 19. 2; 27. 3; cf. *I.G.*² ii. 1. 469 for a garrison of Polemaeus on the Euripus.

THE SUCCESSORS 53

battle of Gaza (312 B.C.), the "Tarentine" horse reappear, and mercenaries provided 8000 of his phalanx of 11,000, a fact which may explain the very large number of prisoners taken by Ptolemy.[1] Yet within six months Demetrius was marching to Babylon with 10,000 mercenaries in his army.[2] "Tarentines" are again mentioned in connection with the siege of Athens.[3] Later in Cyprus the wonderful successes of Demetrius led to the surrender of the entire army of Egyptian mercenaries in the island, to the number of 16,000 infantry and 600 cavalry, an acquisition which more than doubled his army.[4] At the siege of Rhodes he was helped by the pirates, and used Cretan archers for shooting from his floating engines of war: Cretans were adepts both at piracy and at mercenary service as bowmen.[5] In the Peloponnese (303 B.C.) he captured Cassander's garrison in Orchomenus, 2000 mercenaries, and added them to his army.[6] Plutarch's story that in the previous year 6000 Macedonians had deserted to him does not sound likely on the face of it; yet Diodorus' figures for his army when he invaded Thessaly (302 B.C.) give him "no fewer than 8000 Macedonians", and at that date Antigonus can hardly have had more than that number altogether. The other troops in Thessaly were 15,000 mercenary infantry, 25,000 allies, 1500 cavalry and 8000 light-armed, including pirates; a grand total of 57,500.[7] This was the army which would have conquered Macedonia; but meanwhile Seleucus and Lysimachus were converging upon Antigonus in Asia Minor, and Demetrius was recalled. The issue was to be fought out not in Thessaly but at Ipsus.

Before coming to the battle itself it will be well to examine the resources of the coalition against Antigonus: Cassander, Lysimachus, Seleucus and Ptolemy. Cassander's strength has

---

[1] Diod.xx.82.2sqq.;85.3; cf.Plut.*Dem.*5.2. The prisoners numbered 8000, out of an army of 18,300.
[2] Diod. xx. 100. 4. [3] Polyaen. iii. 7. 1.
[4] Diod. xx. 47. 1; 52. 6; 53. 1.
[5] *Ibid.* 85. 3. There is an incomprehensible reference to μάχιμοι, *ibid.* 98. 4—ἐπέλεξε τῶν τε μαχίμων τοὺς κρατίστους καὶ τῶν ἄλλων τοὺς εὐθέτους. This seems to be nonsense, for μάχιμοι is never used as a technical name for soldiers except in the case of the warrior class in Egypt. Μακεδόνων would make sense, and may be right.
[6] *Ibid.* 103. 5.
[7] *Ibid.* 110. 4; Plut. *Dem.* 23. 1 sqq.

already been considered. In 302 B.C. he opposed Demetrius in Thessaly with 29,000 infantry and 2000 horse, and had already sent probably 6000 foot and 1000 horse to the help of Lysimachus[1]: at least one-third of the total must have consisted of mercenaries, since it is unlikely that an exhausted Macedonia could put into the field many more than 20,000 men. For Lysimachus we are never given any figures. He cannot have had many Macedonians; but the account of a brilliant campaign in 313 B.C. makes it clear that his army was a fairly strong one.[2] No doubt he recruited mercenaries with a view to the final struggle with Antigonus, and his recruiting ground may have been among the Thracian tribes as well as the Greeks. When Demetrius left Europe, Cassander sent him a further reinforcement of 12,000 foot and 500 horse, of which force at least one-third perished *en route*.[3] Lysimachus seems to have been short of money, for some of his mercenaries deserted to Antigonus because they were not paid: they were 2000 Thracians (Autariatae, whom Lysimachus may have recruited by permission of Cassander, cf. W. W. Tarn, *C.A.H.* vi. p. 502), and 800 Lycians and Pamphylians.[4] The army of Seleucus at Ipsus was over 30,000 strong (20,000 infantry and 12,000 horse).[5] In 312–311 B.C. he had won Babylon and the eastern satrapies by a swift dash from Palestine and a single battle at the head of a few mercenaries and some Macedonian settlers. He may ultimately have incorporated into his army 6000 mercenaries of Demetrius, who are not heard of again after Demetrius' return from Babylon to the coast.[6] But the provinces of Media and Persia were his most copious recruiting grounds: Greek mercenaries were probably not easy to acquire, since he was cut off from the sea; and though he may have pressed into service the remnants of the mercenary settlers, the bulk of his army at Ipsus and especially of the cavalry, must have been Asiatic. Finally, of Ptolemy the fourth member of the coalition, we are told nothing save that he invaded Syria "with a respectable army":[7] but evidence for the

---

[1] Diod. xx. 110. 4; 107. 1 sqq.
[2] *Id.* xix. 73. 1 sqq.
[3] *Id.* xx. 112. 1 sqq.
[4] *Ibid.* 113. 3.
[5] *Ibid.* 113. 4. But in Plut. *Dem.* 28. 3 the *combined* total of the cavalry is only 10,500.
[6] Diod. xix. 90. 1; 91. 1 sqq.; 92. 1 sqq.
[7] *Id.* xx. 113. 1 sqq.

previous years shows clearly that he was a great employer of mercenaries (pp. 109 sqq.). The total for the army of the allies at Ipsus may have been something like 64,000 infantry and over 10,000 cavalry.[1]

The army of Antigonus and Demetrius numbered 70,000 foot and 10,000 horse:[2] probably half or more of the infantry were mercenaries—we know that Demetrius brought 15,000 from Greece. But the greatest battle of the age was not a battle of infantry; it was not even a soldiers' battle. It was lost and won by the wasted energy of Demetrius and the superior wits of Seleucus. When Antigonus' phalanx was left denuded of cavalry and outflanked, the greater part of it surrendered without a blow, and the remainder was cut to pieces.[3] It would be pleasant to know that the Macedonians at least sold their lives dearly and that it was only the mercenaries who knew when they were beaten: but as to this we are utterly in the dark, though it appears that the majority of the Athenians serving under the liberator of their city chose the discreeter part.[4]

And here the story ends abruptly, where the consecutive narrative of Diodorus ends. It has shown us already how for more than twenty years the Hellenistic world was convulsed by the struggles of half-a-dozen able and ambitious men for dominion based upon military power, struggles in which mercenary soldiers achieved a prominence and an importance which had never been theirs in the past. It has shown how narrowly one man—Antigonus—had failed in an attempt to concentrate in his own person the power which Alexander had formerly wielded in Asia. The death of Antigonus made possible the partition of his empire by the members of the victorious coalition; but, if the fruits of such an empire—the land and its revenues—could be so divided, was it possible also to divide the instrument by which these fruits had been won and held— the greatest army in existence at that date? Although there is no ancient evidence describing the fate of the mercenaries of Antigonus, it is perhaps legitimate to infer that such instruments

---

[1] The figures are Plutarch's; *Dem.* 28. 3. The infantry total is plausible, but the cavalry must have numbered nearer 15,000 if Diod. is right in saying Seleucus brought 12,500 (see above). Diod. gives no figures for the combined army.

[2] Plut. *ibid.*   [3] *Ibid.* 29.   [4] *I.G.*² ii. 1. 657.

as these were not wasted by the victorious generals: Lysimachus and Seleucus, to say nothing of Cassander and Ptolemy, had need of them, and it can hardly be doubted that the twenty years after Ipsus, had their history survived, would show scarcely any diminution in the activities of mercenaries in the East. This inference must remain an inference for the moment, but it is necessary to add that a study of the military institutions of the Seleucids at a later date will suggest that the soldiers of Ipsus did not cease to be important at the moment when Antigonus met his death and the battle was decided: a more important function still remained for them to perform.[1]

[1] Pp. 149 sqq.

CHAPTER III

MACEDONIA

1. Demetrius after Ipsus

THE defeat of Ipsus killed the great Antigonus and wrecked his power, but it did not utterly annihilate it. Defeat was not annihilation so long as Demetrius survived, for Demetrius could make poor tools do more and better work than any man then living: even when he later became a king, he remained the adventurer *par excellence*, and he was by temperament probably the greatest leader of mercenaries who ever commanded Greek soldiers. This was the man who escaped from Ipsus at the head of 9000 men, of whom 4000 were the victorious cavalry whose valour had been wasted. He had lost his father's great kingdom in Asia, but he still retained a footing on the coast, and notably at Ephesus, his first rallying-point after the disaster. Plutarch tells us that everyone expected him to rob the famous temple, for he was destitute, and a rich plunder would have been the finest tonic for dispirited soldiers: but it is typical of this extraordinary man that he refrained from the impious act, whether from motives of honour or policy—it is significant that very soon afterwards he obtained money by legitimate means, the 1500 talents which remained of Antigonus' treasure at Kyinda.[1] With money in his chests and the Aegean Sea his lake, he sailed to Greece, where the news of Ipsus had turned his friends into enemies and his garrisons of mercenaries into wanderers. These he probably now reassembled; at all events, he could soon leave the young Pyrrhus to look after his interests in Greece while he himself sailed to the Chersonese against Lysimachus. This expedition not only did great harm to his enemy, but restored the strength and *moral* of his own army, which "began to be once more by no means contemptible", from which we may perhaps infer that he had been recruiting steadily in Greece and elsewhere.[2] But a leader of mercenaries, even with the command of the sea, could not hope

---

[1] Plut. *Dem.* 30. 1 sqq.; 32. 1.   [2] *Ibid.* 31. 1 sqq.

to win a kingdom by fighting alone, and for Demetrius the seven years after Ipsus were a time of struggle in which he could do little more than maintain his footing in Greece and Asia while he waited for something to turn up. When it did turn up, it was several slices of luck, and a little intrigue, which presented him with his throne.

Demetrius' reign of six years in Macedonia is a record of constant military activity. His first object was to subdue all Greece, but he had always Pyrrhus with whom to reckon on his flank, and Lysimachus as a perpetual menace to his rear. Thus in a typical year we find Demetrius himself operating against Pyrrhus in Thessaly with 11,000 men, and his son Antigonus besieging Thebes, and there must have been an army of defence left in Macedonia; this argues a total force of at least 25,000 men in the field at one time.[1] Nor were his enterprises invariably successful, for on another occasion one of his armies was routed by Pyrrhus in Aetolia and lost 5000 prisoners.[2] It is quite certain that the man-power of Macedonia alone, impaired as it must have been, could not keep pace with the annual drain of incessant warfare. Demetrius must have had a field army of mercenaries as well, though we have no particulars of his army list. A still greater necessity was that of mercenaries for garrison duty in the Greek cities. At Athens alone the garrison in the Piraeus, probably the largest of any, may have amounted to 2000 men, and it is interesting that in addition to a governor, probably a Macedonian, in supreme charge of the city, there is also a Carian captain of mercenaries in command of the garrison.[3] Within the city itself was a fort containing a garrison on the Museum hill, which was stormed by the Athenians in or after 288 B.C. with the help of Strombichus, a mercenary captain of Demetrius who seems to have deserted to the Athenians with some of the mercenaries inside the city, and helped to expel his former comrades: he may have entered the Athenian service permanently, and was certainly honoured by them with the citizenship.[4]

The only other garrison of Demetrius of which particulars

---

[1] Plut. *Dem.* 40.
[2] *Ibid.* 41; *Pyrrhus* 6. 3 sqq.
[3] Polyaen. v. 17; Paus. i. 29. 10. Cf. P.-W. *s.v.* Heraclides Macedon.
[4] *I.G.*² ii. 1. 666–7 (Ditt. *Syll.*³ i. 386–7); Paus. i. 26. 1 sqq.

survive was a much more modest affair. In an inscription of Megara the inhabitants of Aegosthena in the Megarid recommend to the Megarian government Zoilus a Boeotian, who commanded the soldiers of Demetrius among them: Zoilus has behaved well, and has seen to it that his men behaved well, and is rewarded with a crown, with citizenship of Megara, and with a front seat in the theatre.[1] Many other small cities and villages of Greece must have been profoundly affected by the behaviour of their Macedonian garrisons, but the organization of this important instrument of Demetrius is hidden from us except in these isolated cases; nor do we know more of the mercenaries, if any, whom he kept ready to hand for his annual campaigns. One of his captains, Diodorus, perhaps the man who is earlier mentioned as commanding the mercenaries at the capture of Sicyon, became governor of the important garrison town of Ephesus, where he was put to death for treachery.[2] And the story is that Ephesus ultimately fell into the hands of Lysimachus through the greed of the pirate king Andron, who was in the employ of Demetrius, and who accepted a price for changing sides: the new master of Ephesus had the good sense to dismiss the pirates with their pay as soon as his purpose was served.[3]

But all Demetrius' activities were directed by his ambition to reconquer Asia. Plutarch says that he had prepared a fleet of 500 ships and an army of 110,000 men.[4] The number seems at first glance an incredible one; but it has been argued that if it be taken as a paper total of all the troops really or nominally at his disposal (Macedonians, Greek subjects, mercenaries, and pirates), it may be found to be not excessive.[5] The only check upon the figures is the number of mercenaries whom Demetrius could take to Asia after he had lost his kingdom—11,000:[6] it may be taken for granted that he then took every man he could command with the exception of the force, certainly a small one, left with Antigonus in Greece. A possible total of 20,000 mercenaries perhaps means a *real* grand total of some 50,000 for his army before he lost Macedonia: the Greek subjects never

[1] Ditt. *Syll.*³ i. 331.   [2] Polyaen. iv. 7. 3 and 4.
[3] *Id.* v. 19.
[4] Plut. *Dem.* 43. 1 sqq.; *Pyrrhus* 10. 3 (100,000).
[5] Cf. W. W. Tarn in *C.A.H.* vii. p. 85.
[6] Plut. *Dem.* 46. 2.

appear in actual fact. One of the most searching commentaries upon Demetrius' character as a man and as a king is to be found in the behaviour of his soldiers when the end came in Europe. Lysimachus and Pyrrhus had invaded Macedonia simultaneously from opposite sides, and Demetrius hastily collected the Macedonian levy to meet them. The temper of the Macedonians was not equal to the hopeless position: they first began to desert to Lysimachus, and finally went over in a body to Pyrrhus.[1] But if the virtues of Demetrius were not of the solid kind to appeal to the nation, they could still command his army of mercenaries, with which he hastened south to besiege Athens which had rebelled.[2] And when he landed in Asia for the last time at the head of his faithful 11,000, he displayed all the qualities which were so sorely needed. Assuming the offensive, he won over by force or persuasion a number of cities including Sardis, and induced some of Lysimachus' commanders to join him with recruits of money and men. He refused battle with the main army of Lysimachus in Asia, but turned his face to the east, hoping to reach Armenia, and perhaps to create trouble in the rear of Seleucus. But the difficulties were too great. The soldiers lost heart as they retreated from the sea, and when food became scarce, they died by famine and disease to the number of 8000. The army was forced to turn south and maintain itself in the Taurus range of Cilicia, cut off from the north by Lysimachus, and attacked from the east by Seleucus. Even so all was not lost, had not Demetrius himself fallen ill. Then the soldiers began to desert, and though Demetrius recovered and took the field at their head, in the end they surrendered in a body when Seleucus displayed himself to them in person. They had shown that mercenaries can be heroes, and had endured far more than any commander has a right to demand of his men for pay alone.[3]

2. Pyrrhus

The other great adventurer king, contemporary with Demetrius, was Pyrrhus the Epirote. Pyrrhus learnt his fighting trade in the school of the Successors, and turned his natural abilities to good

---

[1] Plut. *Dem.* 44. 2 sqq.; *Pyrrhus* 11.   [2] Plut. *Dem.* 46. 1 sqq.
[3] *Ibid.* 46. 3 sqq.; 47–49.

MACEDONIA

account by making himself king of a united Epirus: he even ruled in Macedonia too for a short time after the fall of Demetrius. Little is known of his administration of his own kingdom: and that part of it in particular which is our present concern, the Epirote army, remains a complete mystery. The best that can be done is to open the story of Pyrrhus at the beginning of his greatest adventure, the expedition to Italy, in the hope of relating the few certain facts to some probable conjecture.

In 278 B.C., Pyrrhus, already well established in a reputation for daring and generalship, accepted the invitation of Tarentum to help her to maintain herself against Rome. His advance guard consisted of 3000 men under his general Cineas, and was soon followed by Pyrrhus himself with the main army, 20,000 strong in infantry, and with subsidiary arms of 3000 cavalry, 2000 archers, and 500 slingers.[1] This was a very great force to quit the peninsula at such a time, hardly less in fact than that which had landed in Asia with Alexander; and Pyrrhus was not, like Alexander, the ruler of all Macedonia and Greece, but only of Greater Epirus, as we may call the newly established kingdom. How much of this army was purely Epirote? Beloch, considering the same question, computes from a passage in Polybius, that the total population of Epirus may have been about 300,000, yielding roughly 100,000 men of military age; but he insists that Epirus was a backward country, which meant that the proportion of the fighting men who were equipped for fighting in phalanx was probably very slight, and he concludes that even so small (relatively) a figure as Pyrrhus' 20,000 infantry must have included mercenaries.[2] Support for his theory can be found in the list of Pyrrhus' army at the battle of Asculum (which Beloch seems to have overlooked). In addition to the Tarentine citizen levy, the mercenaries in Tarentine pay, and the Italian allies, he had a Macedonian phalanx and some Thessalian horse lent to him for two years by Ptolemy Keraunos, the king of Macedonia; mercenary infantry from Aetolia, Acarnania, and Athamania; and a body of Greek mercenary

---

[1] Plut. *Pyrrhus* 15. 1 sqq.
[2] Beloch, *Bevölkerung*, pp. 195 sqq., using Pol. xxx. 15, the passage which describes the enslavement of 150,000 Epirotes by Aemilius Paullus in 168 B.C.

cavalry, Acarnanians, Aetolians and Athamanians. His recruiting was done in northern Greece, as was to be expected; but the only troops from his own kingdom were Ambraciots, Thesprotians and Chaonians.[1] Asculum was decided by the steadiness of the Macedonians, as Heraclea had been decided by the charge of the Thessalian horse.[2] The purse of Tarentum and the name of Pyrrhus would not fail to attract recruits, and the presence of Macedonians and Thessalians is not surprising in view of his intimate connection with the kingdom of Macedonia in the past: the Macedonian soldiers of Demetrius had once deserted to Pyrrhus (above), as those of Demetrius' son were again to desert to him not many years later.

It does not appear that Pyrrhus recruited more mercenaries after he had landed in Italy, though he was of course supported by Tarentum with her citizens, mercenaries, and allies; but the victories of Heraclea and Asculum were terribly expensive, and it may well have happened that the losses (nearly 8000 in the two battles) fell principally upon the seasoned troops of Pyrrhus himself. After Asculum he ruefully said: "Another such victory over the Romans, and we are ruined!"[3] So far as accomplishing anything permanent against Rome was concerned, he was ruined already, and the interlude in Sicily reveals the high price which he had had to pay for his fame. No more than 10,000 soldiers accompanied him to Sicily, and though his army was there swelled by local support to a size of over 30,000,[4] and he actually returned to Tarentum with more than double the force with which he had left it (20,000 foot, 3000 horse),[5] the defeat at Beneventum made his position in Italy impossible. Probably the soldiers whom he had brought from Sicily were mercenaries

---

[1] Dion. Hal. 20. 1. For the loan of the Macedonians and Thessalians, cf. Justin, 17. 2. 3 sqq., who gives 5000 Macedonians and 4000 cavalry (race unspecified: the number seems excessive).
C. Klotzsch (*Epirot. Gesch. b. z. Jahre* 280 *v. Chr.* pp. 172 sqq.) has argued that the Acarnanians were not mercenaries but allies. The question turns upon the political status of Acarnania at the time. W. W. Tarn (*Antigonus Gonatas*, p. 120 and n. 20) gives the evidence, and believes that they were mercenaries.
[2] Dion. Hal. 20. 2. 4; Plut. *Pyrrhus* 17. 3.
[3] Plut. *Pyrrhus* 17. 4; 21. 8 sqq.
[4] *Ibid.* 22. 4 sqq.; Diod. xxii. 2; 7 sqq.; 10.
[5] Plut. *Pyrrhus* 24. 4.

MACEDONIA

recruited in the name of Tarentum[1]: they must now have been dismissed or left behind in the city, for he sailed from Italy and set foot again in Epirus with no more than 8500 men out of the original army of 30,000 (275 B.C.).[2]

But Pyrrhus, the great general and the blind statesman, did not know when he was beaten, or could quickly forget the knowledge. His sword irked him when it was not in his hand, and perhaps he could not afford to put up his sword if he would, because his purse was empty and nothing but more fighting could fill it. Plutarch in fact says that he at once plunged into a war with Macedonia purely as an expedient for keeping his army paid; but a modern historian reads into the apparently unconsidered act an understanding with Arsinoe, the ambitious queen of Egypt, who laid claim to the throne of Macedonia for her son, and concludes that Pyrrhus was paying for his war with Egyptian gold.[3] However that may be, he recruited Gauls, invaded Macedonia, captured cities, won over 2000 soldiers of Antigonus, and finally defeated Antigonus himself in an important battle which throws a somewhat curious light upon the behaviour of the different sections of the Macedonian army: Antigonus' Gauls, perhaps new to the game, fought bravely and were massacred, while his "infantry" (which can only mean the Macedonians themselves) deserted to Pyrrhus. Once again the Epirote was master of a great part of Macedonia, and again he quickly lost what he had won. One of his more indiscreet acts was to allow some of his Gallic mercenaries to plunder the tombs of the Macedonian kings at Aegae. His supremacy in Macedonia lasted little more than a year, and when the ground began to slip from beneath his feet he made his next, and last, leap, this time to the Peloponnese, where he hoped to make his Spartan friend Cleonymus king of Sparta.[4] It is problematical how far his short-lived success in Macedonia affected the army at his command. The Macedonians who deserted Antigonus probably did so not because they disliked fighting for him but

---

[1] It is unlikely that they were Sicilian *allies* of his own; the latter were not likely to undertake to fight his battles abroad, and had moreover reason to complain of their treatment at his hands (Plut. *Pyrrhus* 23. 3).
[2] Plut. *Pyrrhus* 26. 2.
[3] *Ibid.* Cf. W. W. Tarn, *C.A.H.* vii. p. 213.
[4] Plut. *Pyrrhus* 26.

because they no longer cared to fight at all. Pyrrhus invaded the Peloponnese with 27,000 men,[1] but it is unlikely that the increase in his army was due to the presence of the Macedonian levy: no doubt he had collected Macedonian volunteers, as well as Greeks, and perhaps a levy from Epirus. The Gauls remained with him, and a picked force of 2000 mixed Gauls and Epirotes under the leadership of Pyrrhus' son Ptolemaeus played a prominent part in the assault upon Sparta.[2] The whole army seems to have surrendered to Antigonus when it was left leaderless by the death of Pyrrhus at Argos (272 B.C.).[3] What became of it does not appear: very likely Antigonus generously allowed the Epirotes to return home (as he allowed Helenus, the heir to the throne), and incorporated the mercenaries into his own army.

The whole career of Pyrrhus in these last six eventful years of his life resembles that of a captain of fortune rather than of a responsible monarch: Professor Tenney Frank well describes him—"When he left his native mountains his behaviour at times suggests that of some viking chieftain running amuck in a Renaissance city".[4] The utter lack of policy that accompanies his warlike exploits makes it almost incredible that the Epirote nation would have borne with him as it seems to have done, if he were really imposing those heavy sacrifices upon his own subjects. The Italian expedition alone, with its dead loss of 20,000 men, would surely have sufficed to make the reunion of the king and his people an awkward one, to say the least. The truth perhaps is that Epirus could not provide Pyrrhus with the right kind of troops in sufficient numbers: there is no evidence for any great military strength in the country either before or after Pyrrhus' reign. Epirotes may have served with him as light infantry, and perhaps as cavalry; but it is most probable that by far the greatest part of his army, and in particular the heavy infantry which was a match for the Roman legions, consisted of Graeco-Macedonian soldiers armed and trained to fight as a phalanx, and that Pyrrhus was a general of mercenaries in reality as well as by temperament.

[1] Plut. *Pyrrhus* 26. 9.
[2] *Ibid.* 28. 1; 30. 2; 32. 1 sqq.
[3] *Ibid.* 34. 6.
[4] In *C.A.H.* vii. p. 643.

MACEDONIA

3. THE ANTIGONIDS IN MACEDONIA, 285-168 B.C.

With the accession of Antigonus Gonatas (276 B.C.) Macedonia began once again to enjoy a period of settled rule, the effects of which must certainly have reacted upon the military affairs of the kingdom. While it is true that Gonatas and his successors were seldom at peace with *all* their neighbours and rivals, it is also true that for nearly eighty years—until the war of Philip V with Rome—they were never engaged in a life-and-death struggle for existence. In the beginning a quiet policy was the policy of necessity, and it is certain that Antigonus was at some pains to give peace to his war-weary people. Macedonia was indeed weary of war, as is proved by the action of the Macedonian army on two occasions already described, when first Demetrius and again Antigonus were deserted by the soldiers of their own people, eager to end the fighting at the expense of their own military honour.[1] As a consequence we might expect to find the king sparing his subjects (wherever possible) the unwelcome labour of military service, and relying instead upon soldiers who made fighting their profession, and in fact there can be little doubt that this is what happened. Unfortunately, the evidence for the early part of this period is so extremely scanty that it is impossible to reconstruct an army system. With regard to the Macedonians themselves, it has been said that "the day of the professional long-service Macedonian army was over, and that army was again a levy of farmers called up when needed":[2] the best illustration of this is to be found in the story of the campaign which culminated in the battle of Sellasia (222 B.C.), when Antigonus Doson wintered in Argos "with a few mercenaries, the Macedonians having been dispersed to their winter quarters by cities".[3] Whatever *standing* army the king of Macedonia could maintain must have been an army of mercenaries, but it is impossible to determine its size, though it may be said that it was probably kept down to a minimum, because the kingdom was, comparatively speaking, a poor one.

But after the fall of Demetrius a space of ten years passed before Antigonus Gonatas could establish himself on the throne.

---

[1] Pp. 60 and 63. [2] W. W. Tarn, in *C.A.H.* vii. p. 201.
[3] Pol. ii. 55. 1; cf. Plut. *Cleom.* 25. 4.

In those years of waiting, Antigonus found himself in a very similar position to that of Demetrius himself after Ipsus: he could do no more than cling to what he held in Greece with a small army of mercenaries.¹ All particulars of his forces are wanting. But it is known that in 285 B.C. he sent soldiers (who can only have been mercenaries) to help Pyrrhus against Lysimachus, and his military weakness is perhaps reflected in the loss of the forts at Athens, which may have occurred after the reinforcement to Pyrrhus.² Financial difficulties (his only source of revenue being direct taxation of the Greek cities) would also help to keep his army small. And though he was able to hold the Piraeus until 280 B.C.,³ his possessions in that year can have amounted to no more than the fortresses of Demetrias, Corinth and the Piraeus, the island of Euboea, and some small towns in the eastern Peloponnese,⁴ a "kingdom" which probably required fewer than 10,000 men for its defence.

But at length, after ten years of waiting, something happened. It was the famous invasion of the Gauls, which left Macedonia kingless and helpless, and ready to the hand of any man who could show himself a man. In resisting the Gallic irruption into Greece, Antigonus seems to have played an insignificant part; his contingent at Thermopylae was only 500 strong.⁵ But a little later (277 B.C.) he met a Gallic army of 18,000 near Lysimacheia in Thrace, and defeated it handsomely, the first occasion on which Greek or Macedonian arms proved victorious over Gauls in a pitched battle.⁶ Macedonia was now Antigonus' obvious goal, and, with a view to expelling the pretender Antipater, he engaged some or all of the beaten Gauls who survived, for a short campaign which ended in victory.⁷ The final

¹ Cf. Pol. ii. 41 for garrisons and tyrannies in small towns of the Peloponnese.
² Plut. *Pyrrhus* 12: for the most probable date of the expulsion of the Athenian garrisons (*I.G.*² ii. 1. 666–7), cf. W. W. Tarn, *Antigonos Gonatas*, p. 118, and in *J.H.S.* 54 (1934), pp. 30 sqq.
³ Plut. *Moral.* 754 B, cf. Tarn, *ibid.*
⁴ Cf. Tarn, *A.G.* p. 137.
⁵ Paus. x. 20. Tarn, *A.G.* p. 150 n. 50, supposed that Pausanias'"Athenian" fleet must have been manned by Antigonus' mercenaries as marines; but his latest word on this subject (*J.H.S., ibid.*) makes this impossible.
⁶ *I.G.*² ii. 1. 677; Diog. Laert. ii. 141; Justin 25. 2; Trogus, *Prol.* 25.
⁷ Polyaen. iv. 6. 17. Gauls were at this moment perhaps the cheapest, certainly the most plentiful, soldiers in northern Greece.

MACEDONIA

step was to win the powerful city of Cassandreia, now for some years separated from the kingdom of Macedonia and governed by the tyrant Apollodorus, who had won his tyranny by playing the demagogue and conciliating the mercenaries of Lachares,[1] and maintained it by enlisting Gauls and a strong force of mercenaries at a high rate of pay.[2] Cassandreia was a hard nut for Antigonus to crack, but he cracked it with the aid of Ameinias, the Phocian pirate king: in a night attack a storming party of 2000 mercenaries with some pirates (headed by ten Aetolians) ended the long siege successfully.[3] Antigonus could now sit back and pause for breath. He owed his throne and his fortune to the army of mercenaries who had learnt their discipline and steadiness in years of watchful tedium as garrison troops, and had not forgotten it in face of an unknown unconquered enemy at Lysimacheia.

The strength of the new kingdom was very soon tried by Pyrrhus when he returned from Italy (p. 63). To meet his invasion, Antigonus seems to have led an army in which the only mercenaries were Gauls, who died fighting when the Macedonians deserted or surrendered.[4] This state of affairs argues that he had sufficient regular mercenaries only for the garrisons in Greece and probably on the Macedonian coast; but his speedy recovery of the territories captured by Pyrrhus must have been accomplished with what mercenaries he had, and such as he could quickly recruit. Again in the Peloponnese, in 272 B.C., the relief of Sparta was undertaken by Ameinias the ex-pirate, now Antigonus' general commanding the mercenaries at Corinth:[5] and it seems unlikely that the army of Antigonus himself at Argos can have contained a national levy, in view of his recent experience. It was undoubtedly politic not to call out the Macedonians except in absolute necessity, so that anything approaching the standing army of Philip and Alexander was out of the question. Indeed the Antigonid kings appear to have kept about them no more than a guard of Macedonians, namely the "agema"

---

[1] Whoever he may have been. P.-W. (s.v.) supposes him to be identical with the Lachares who had been expelled from Athens by Demetrius. He may have been the minister or general of Eurydice, the real ruler of Cassandreia before Apollodorus.
[2] Polyaen. vi. 7. 2; Diod. xxii. 5. 2.
[3] Polyaen. iv. 6. 18.
[4] Plut. *Pyrrhus* 26. 3; cf. Justin 25. 3. 2.
[5] Plut. *Pyrrhus* 29. 6.

of infantry, 2000 strong, and a survival of the "Companion" cavalry which in the reign of Philip V remained at some figure higher than 400.[1] The only other permanent soldiers of whom we know were the mercenaries in garrisons: but recruiting was always quick and easy among the numerous barbarian populations on the confines of the kingdom. There is in fact evidence for believing that the use of barbarian soldiers by Macedonian kings was on the increase. A reference in Plutarch's *Life* of Aratus deprecates the possibility in 226 B.C. of the Peloponnese *again* becoming "barbarized" with Macedonian garrisons and the citadel of Corinth filled with Gauls and Illyrians, which implies that the earlier garrisons (i.e. those of Gonatas) were recruited at least in part from the barbarian fighting stocks.[2] No direct evidence has survived from Athens or Corinth, the two biggest garrison cities, though in Corinth at the time of its capture by Aratus there were at least 400 Syrians for whose presence it is not easy to account.[3] It is possible, too, that the tyrants of the Peloponnese, who owed their position to Macedonian support,[4] terrorized their subjects with half-savage soldiers as Dionysius II had done at Syracuse: a case in point is that of Aristotimus of Elis, who lost his tyranny because he was unable to restrain the brutality of the "mixed barbarians" who were his mercenaries.[5] This introduction of Illyrians, Gauls and the like into Greece raises the question of how they compared as soldiers with the Greek mercenaries whom they displaced. Were they armed and trained to fight like Greeks or Macedonians? Aristotimus' barbarian officer would incline us to answer that they were not. Were they paid as much as Greeks? Again the answer is probably No: a soldier of the line probably always received more than a light- or half-armed warrior.[6] For their entry into the Macedonian armies and garrisons several reasons may be sug-

[1] Pol. iv. 67. 6; Livy 42. 51. 4.
[2] Plut. *Arat.* 38. 4. Cf. Justin 26. 2. 1 sqq. for the mutiny of Gauls (265 B.C.).
[3] *Ibid.* 18. 2 sqq.; 24. 1. I know of no Syrian mercenaries elsewhere, but I can suggest no remedy, unless it be to read Μυσοί and Μυσούς for Σύροι and Σύρους in these two passages.
[4] Pol. ii. 41; 44. 3 sqq.
[5] Plut. *Moral.* 251 sqq. (confirmed in outline by Pausanias and Justin). Even the officers were barbarians, if we are to judge by the ξεναγός Leukios who was guilty of the outrage upon Mikka.
[6] P. 302.

gested. In the first place, if they *were* cheaper that fact in itself would recommend them. Then again Macedonia possessed in her national levy sufficient material for winning any pitched battle in Greece: the comparatively peaceful period which Gonatas gave to his people soon provided a new generation of fighting men, and towards the end of the century we shall see the Macedonian phalanx restored to something like its old strength both in numbers and in quality. Finally, the supply of Greek mercenaries was not unlimited. Since the accession of Alexander they had been in constant request, and in particular the new demand created by the rise of the Achaean League and the dictators in Sparta may well have meant that there were not enough Greek mercenaries in Greece to go round. It is significant, too, that Antigonus Doson took steps to open up a supply of soldiers from Crete. Two treaties survive which he concluded with the Cretan cities of Eleuthernae and Hierapytna, and, though both are fragmentary, they do give us information of a reinforcement of citizen troops which the two cities were bound under certain conditions to send to Doson, and of the pay which Doson undertook to provide.[1] But the interesting thing is that another treaty survives, between Hierapytna and Rhodes at the end of this century, in which Hierapytna promises in almost the same words to send help to Rhodes if necessary, and there is an additional clause guaranteeing facilities to Rhodian recruiting officers in Crete.[2] It seems at least possible that, if we had the whole of Doson's treaty, we should find a similar clause at the end of that too. Cretans had always been good mercenaries, and in the second century B.C. they were to become more active than ever before.

The first Antigonid army of which particulars exist is that of Doson in the Peloponnese in 223–222 B.C. He appeared at the head of 20,000 Macedonian infantry and 1300 horse, which must have been nearly a full levy; but the Macedonians were sent home for the winter, which Doson spent at Argos with no more than "a few" mercenaries.[3] Plutarch's evidence is con-

---

[1] *B.C.H.* xiii. (1889), pp. 47 sqq. and 51 sqq.—there ascribed to Gonatas; but Tarn, *A.G.* p. 471, gives it to Doson, regarding the description ('Ἀντίγονον καὶ Μακεδόνας, not 'A. βασιλέα) as conclusive.
[2] Ditt. *Syll.*³ ii. 581.
[3] Plut. *Arat.* 42. 1; *Cleom.* 25. 4; cf. Pol. ii. 55. 1.

firmed by Polybius' account of the battle of Sellasia in 222 B.C. The army there consisted of about 28,000 infantry and 1600 horse, and of the infantry 13,000 were Macedonians, 9600 allies and 5000 mercenaries. Of the mercenaries 1000 were Agrianians and 1000 Gauls: the remaining 3000 are called simply μισθοφόροι, which may be taken to mean Greek or Greek-armed troops, and they seem to have included some Cretans who are mentioned by name in the description of the battle. There were also 300 mercenary cavalry, presumably Greeks too since they are coupled with the 3000 infantry. The proportion of mercenaries is smaller than might have been expected, little more than one-sixth of the whole; but Doson was well supported by allies, and just as he did not call out the whole strength of Macedonia in this year, so he may not have thought fit to denude his garrisons, much less to recruit new mercenaries specially for the occasion.[1] Still, the early campaigns of Philip V do not show any greater numbers of mercenaries in the field. In 220 B.C., Philip moved from Macedonia against Aetolia with an army in which only Macedonians are mentioned.[2] In 219 B.C. his army included the full levy of Epirus as well as of Macedonia, the only other troops mentioned by name being 300 Achaean slingers and "the 500 Cretans sent by the Polyrhenians", the latter a citizen contingent despatched in accordance with a treaty similar to that between Doson and the two Cretan cities (above).[3] But in the same year the Dardanians, who were planning an invasion of Macedonia in Philip's absence, heard of his unexpected return through some Thracian deserters, which means that there were Thracian mercenaries in Macedonia, probably on garrison duty.[4] In 218 B.C. Philip's army against Lycurgus of Sparta is described as consisting of 6000 Macedonians and 1200 mercenaries: contingents

---

[1] Pol. ii. 65. 2. In these figures a contingent of 1600 Illyrians is included among the 9600 allied infantry, as Polybius seems to intend (they were commanded by Demetrius of Pharos). But Tarn, *A.G.* pp. 425–6, puts them among the mercenaries, whose number is accordingly raised from 5300 to 6900.
[2] Pol. iv. 37. 7.
[3] *Ibid.* 61. 1 sqq. The Achaean slingers *may* have been sent officially by the League. On the other hand, the League had a great deal of fighting on its own hands at the time, and had indeed actually asked Philip for help (*ibid.* 60. 2; and again 64. 1). The Cretans were sent in payment for an earlier reinforcement sent by Philip and the League to the Polyrhenians: it had included 400 Illyrians—*ibid.* 55. 1 and 5.
[4] *Ibid.* 66. 6.

MACEDONIA 71

which are distinguished incidentally by name are 300 Cretans, some Gallic cavalry, Thracians, and Illyrians; but the Illyrians are mentioned as separate from the "mercenaries" and may not have been mercenaries at all.[1] On the other hand the Cretans, Gauls and Thracians are more likely to have been mercenaries than anything else, though whether they are to be included in Polybius' original 1200 "mercenaries", or whether these, as at Sellasia, represent the Greeks only, it is impossible to say for certain: perhaps the fact of their being called upon to undertake some rough work in the hills, along with the Illyrians and the Macedonian peltasts (as Polybius calls them), means that they were light-armed, and hence perhaps mostly Thracians and Cretans.[2]

In Philip's great war against Rome (199–197 B.C.) his defensive policy with its system of garrisoned fortresses made the upkeep of a large establishment of mercenaries essential. Niese (vol. ii. p. 600 and note) has collected the names of such garrison towns as are known, and has reckoned that at least twenty to thirty thousand men were needed to maintain them.[3] His figures are perhaps too high, and may be based upon our knowledge concerning the garrison at Corinth in the last year of the war. At that time, the citadel contained no fewer than 6000 men. But we are told that this figure includes a special reinforcement of 3000 men from Philip (1000 Macedonians, 1200 Illyrians and Thracians and 800 Cretans) and contingents of his allies and of the Corinthians themselves, and that the normal strength of the garrison was only 1300 (500 Macedonians and 800 mercenaries).[4] Corinth was the most important and probably the largest of all

[1] Pol. v. 2. 11; iv. 67. 6; v. 3. 2; 7. 11; 22. 9.
[2] *Id.* v. 22. 9; 23. 1 sqq.; 27. 5 sqq. The εὔζωνοι mentioned in 23. 6 are probably identifiable with the mercenaries, since the Illyrians and the peltasts are mentioned separately as different corps. Other references to "the mercenaries of Philip" in this army are v. 13. 1; 14. 5; but they provide no further information.
[3] Corinth, Orchomenus, Demetrias and other Thessalian towns, Chalcis, Eretria, Oreus, Carystus, Andros and Cythnos, Cassandreia, Thessalonice, Amphipolis, Abdera, Aenus, Maroneia, Thasos, Lysimacheia, Perinthus, Abydus, Myrina, and in Caria.
[4] Livy 33. 14. 3 sqq. Livy's phrase for the mercenaries is *mixtos ex omni genere auxiliorum octingentos*, i.e. probably Greek mercenaries as opposed to the Illyrians, Thracians and Cretans who are mentioned by name in the reinforcement.

the garrisons; perhaps, too, the only one which always contained a force of Macedonians. We do hear of 500 Macedonians in a small army of 3000 under Deinocrates in the Rhodian Peraea in the same year, but they too must have been a special reinforcement with a view to the attack by sea which actually did come: the remaining strength of this force included Agrianians and Carians in addition to Cretan and Thracian mercenaries.[1] The garrisons as a whole may have occupied at least 15,000 mercenaries, and of course Philip had others with him in his field army, who appear usually to have operated under the same Macedonian commander Athenagoras.[2] Philip had trained his mercenaries as well as the Macedonians in preparation for the war, which implies that he either had some permanent mercenaries, or had recruited some at least a year before the fighting began.[3] Nevertheless, they can have been no more than auxiliaries to the main Macedonian fighting force, upon which he chiefly depended, as is shown by his ruthless recruiting campaign in the winter 198–197 B.C., when he "pressed" boys and veterans from the exhausted population.[4] Mercenaries could probably have been recruited in their stead, but they might have cost more, and it is very likely that Philip could not afford to do more than maintain the soldiers who were absolutely essential for his garrisons. Certainly the mercenaries in the field army are surprisingly few. We hear of small bodies of 400 Trallian Thracians and 300 Cretans early in the war,[5] but even at the great battle of Cynoscephalae the Macedonian army of 25,500 men contained only 5500 who were not native Macedonians or Thessalians. The mercenaries were 2000 Thracians, 2000 Illyrians, and 1500 Greeks or men of different nations,[6] who were probably light-armed.[7] The Trallians fought in the battle under Philip himself, and many of them escaped with him from the general slaughter.[8] They may have been favourite troops of his: it was a force of Thracians whom he employed for the massacre at Maroneia in 185 B.C.[9]

[1] Livy 33. 18. 9 sqq.
[2] *Id.* 33. 35. 1 sqq.; 32. 5. 9 sqq.; 7. 11 sqq.; Pol. xviii. 22. 2.
[3] Livy 32. 5. 9 sqq. [4] *Id.* 33. 3. 1 sqq.
[5] *Id.* 31. 35. 1 sqq. [6] *Id.* 33. 4. 4 sqq.
[7] They operated with Thessalian cavalry—Pol. xviii. 22. 2.
[8] *Id.* xviii. 26. 8. [9] *Id.* xxii. 13. 6.

MACEDONIA

In the twenty-five years of peace which settled upon Macedonia after Cynoscephalae, the country was free to recruit its strength, and certainly the later years were employed in preparation for the next war.[1] The old king Philip had reason to complain of his treatment at the hands of Rome. He worked for vengeance himself and left the task as a legacy to his son Perseus. Since the way to expansion was closed in the south and west, Philip's last years were spent in subjugating the restless barbarians on his northern frontiers. He is said to have acted with capricious extravagance in transplanting barbarians into Macedonian cities and removing Macedonians from the cities into Paeonia to replace them. But he may in fact have had an excellent military purpose in mind, the dual one of bringing a supply of barbarian soldiers within his own territory, and of safeguarding his frontiers with settlements of Macedonians to act as a check upon his neighbours in the north.[2] He may also have established a protectorate over some of the Thracian and Illyrian princes, and it seems certain that his energy in this direction was not wasted, but was reflected to some extent in the military strength of Perseus, just as the Thracian conquests of the great Philip had been reflected in the army of Alexander. Perseus himself was no less zealous than his father. He spent the first years of his reign in making the final preparations for war with Rome, including negotiations with powerful and independent Balkan kings, which were particularly disquieting to his enemies.[3] The fears of Rome's clients in the East are voiced in a speech put into the mouth of Eumenes II of Pergamum addressing the Roman senate: his facts may not be greatly exaggerated (his figures at least are confirmed by those which appear later in connection with the army of Perseus)—"30,000 infantry, 5000 cavalry; hoards of grain to last him ten years and enable him to leave untouched both his own and his enemies' territory for provisioning his army; enough money to keep 10,000 mercenaries, apart from his Macedonians, for 10 years, as well as his annual revenue from the mines; arms for three such

---

[1] Cf. Livy 42. 51.
[2] Pol. xxiii. 8 and 10, esp. 10. 4 sqq. For military settlements in Macedonia, cf. pp. 77 sqq.
[3] *Id.* xxv. 6. 2 sqq.; Livy 42. 11.

armies stored in his armouries; conquered Thrace, a fountain to yield him a perennial supply of warriors should Macedonia run dry".[1]

In 171 B.C., when war was imminent, Perseus held a review of his army, of which the particulars have been preserved.[2] He assembled at Pella 43,000 men, of whom 4000 were cavalry. Of the 39,000 infantry, 26,000 were Macedonians; the remaining 13,000 are described by Livy as *auxilia*, a word which often means "mercenaries" pure and simple, and means that here in some cases, but not in all, as will be seen. These 13,000 *auxilia* were made up as follows: (1) 3000 Thracians and Agrianians—*Paeones et ex Paroraea et Parstrymonia (sunt autem ea loca subiecta Thraciae) et Agrianes, admixtis etiam Thraciis incolis, tria millia ferme et ipsi expleverunt numerum. Armaverat contraxeratque eos Didas Paeon*. These people came from districts which were almost certainly subject to Perseus, so that it is doubtful whether they can strictly be called mercenaries, particularly as they included "Thracian settlers", that is, Thracians who had been allotted land in Macedonia. On the other hand, they were recruited, not levied (*contraxerat*); and were armed and trained by an officer of Perseus. Perhaps in truth they were a *picked* levy from the subject peoples. (2) 2000 Gauls commanded by Asclepiodorus—Gallic mercenaries certainly, with a Greek or Macedonian officer. (3) 3000 free Thracians with their own commander. These Thracians no doubt *were* mercenaries, recruited from one tribe (the Sintii) probably through diplomatic exchanges between Perseus and their king. (4) 3000 Cretans commanded by two Cretan officers, Susus of Phalasarnae and Syllus of Cnossus—plainly mercenaries too. (5) 500 mixed Greek mercenaries under Leonidas a Spartan. (6) 500 Aetolians and Boeotians under Lycon an Achaean. The Aetolians were *socii et amici* to Perseus,[3] but the presence of an Achaean commander makes it impossible for this to be an official contingent from Aetolia and Boeotia. Very likely they were volunteers serving under an officer of Perseus, and may be counted as mercenaries. (7) Finally, Cotys, king of the Odrysians, brought in person 1000 infantry and 1000 cavalry. It appears later that Perseus had contracted to pay a year's wages for the cavalry, but

[1] Livy 42. 12. 7 sqq. [2] *Id.* 42. 51. [3] *Id.* 42. 12. 7.

Cotys was clearly an equal and an ally, and not a hired captain of Perseus. Of the *auxilia* at the review then, 9000 may be called mercenaries with some certainty; and the army as a whole was the largest that any Macedonian king had put into the field since Alexander. But besides this field army there must also have been a smaller force in the line of garrisons which held the important cities of the Macedonian coast. The three greatest, Cassandreia, Amphipolis and Thessalonice,[1] contained at least 7000 men, Macedonians and barbarians, and smaller towns such as Antigoneia and Torone were also held in force.[2] In Thessaly too the small town of Larissa Cremaste had its own garrison,[3] and Demetrias cannot have been of less importance than the three great Macedonian cities.[4] Kromayer estimates Perseus' garrison army at 15,000–20,000 men,[5] and if the lower figure be adopted we can be sure of having erred on the right side. All the garrison troops were not mercenaries (e.g. those in Thessalonice and Antigoneia), but the majority probably were, perhaps two-thirds of the total. With 9000 mercenaries in the field army, and at least as many in garrisons, Perseus was far stronger in this branch than any of his predecessors.

Mention has already been made of negotiations between Perseus and Balkan kings before the outbreak of war. They are referred to in vague terms by Polybius (followed by Livy), but it is not until the war has actually been in progress for two years or more that anything definite is produced. An alliance with Genthius, an Illyrian king, seems to have been no more than an agreement to the effect that Genthius is to attack the Roman possessions on the Illyrian coast in return for 300 talents from Perseus.[6] But another bargain struck with the king of the Bastarnae is much more interesting in its possibilities, being no less than a project for defeating the Romans with the help of a huge reinforcement of barbarian arms. The Bastarnae were probably

---

[1] Cassandreia—2000 Illyrians sent by Pleuratus, 800 Agrianians (Livy 44. 11. 7), +Gauls (in 10 *lembi*) (*ibid*. 12. 6).
Amphipolis—2000 Thracians (*ibid*. 44. 4).
Thessalonice—2000 peltasts = Macedonians? (*ibid*. 32. 6).
[2] Antigoneia—included Macedonians and cavalry (*ibid*. 10. 9 sqq.).
Torone—*valida manu* (*ibid*. 12. 8).
[3] *Id*. 42. 67. 11. [4] *Id*. 44. 12. 8—*repleta armis*.
[5] J. Kromayer, *Antike Schlachtfelder*, iii. pp. 339–40.
[6] Appian, *Mac*. 18. 1 sqq.; Livy 44. 26; Plut. *Aemil*. 13. 1 sqq.

a wandering tribe of Gauls, but their numbers were so great that they may better be called a nation than a tribe.¹ In reply to the approaches of Perseus their king Clondicus or Cloelius marched to his aid at the head of a vast army of 10,000 cavalry and 10,000 infantry, the latter accustomed, as Livy tells us, to keep pace with the horsemen on the march. Perseus undertook to pay 10 golden staters to each cavalryman, 5 to each foot-soldier, and 1000 to their leader (151,000 staters altogether),² a gigantic outlay which must mean that Perseus was prepared to gamble heavily on the chance of the Bastarnae winning the war for him against Rome. But in the end he did not gamble at all. Clondicus was met by envoys with only a small sum of money. He was furious, and demanded cash in advance. Perseus sent word that he did not want so large an army, but only 5000 cavalry, whereupon Clondicus went away in disgust. Perseus' motive for going back upon his declared purpose will never be known for certain. Livy attributes it to his avarice, which had previously defrauded Genthius of his due reward. But more probably when it came to the point Perseus' nerve failed him. He probably decided that even a victory over the Romans would be bought too dearly, at the price of admitting a great army of barbarians into his own kingdom. And so there were no Bastarnae at Pydna in 168 B.C.

The army at Pydna was very much the same, to all appearances, as that at the review three years before. No great engagement having taken place, the war had cost Perseus very little in casualties, certainly no more than could be replaced by local recruiting or a slight weakening of the garrisons. There were 4000 cavalry and nearly 40,000 infantry, of whom at least 10,000 were mercenaries, including Cretans and Thracians as before.³ The victory of the Romans meant that Perseus' army

¹ For the origin of the Bastarnae, cf. A. J. Reinach, *B.C.H.* 1900, p. 295. The sources are: Livy 44. 26 sqq.; Appian, *Mac.* 18. 4; Plut. *Aemil.* 12 sqq.; Diod. xxx. 24.
² Obviously a fixed payment for a definite term of service; cf. p. 306, n. 1.
³ Plut. *Aemil.* 13. 3; 16. 1 sqq.; 18. 1 sqq.; Pol. xxix. 6. 1; 15. 2. Plut. *Aemil.* 18 speaks of a contingent of Thracians in a uniform white equipment worn over black tunics. Next to them, he says, οἱ μισθοφόροι παρενέβαλλον, ὧν σκευαί τε παντοδαποί καὶ μεμιγμένοι Παίονες ἦσαν. The last three words seem to be nonsense due to a corruption of the text. The mercenaries are probably mixed Greeks, or perhaps Cretans; the Thracians may be the tribe of Sintii mentioned above.

was destroyed, as an army, utterly and permanently. Perseus escaped from the battlefield with three officers, as Plutarch says, a Cretan, an Aetolian, and a Boeotian; or, as Livy says, with 500 Cretans who followed him in the rôle of creditors (*spem pecuniae secuti*).[1]

With the fall of Perseus, the Macedonian army disappeared for ever. Since the days of Philip and Alexander it had remained the best army in the Hellenistic world, and it had always owed its supremacy to its national character. Although the auxiliaries played an important part, they never became the protagonist: the prestige of Macedonia depended upon the phalanx of 20,000 men or more which remained always in the background as a potential force, and her great victories depended upon the same phalanx when it did, in actual fact, appear. One final point remains for discussion. In Egypt and Asia are to be found traces of a system of military settlements by which the government hoped to found and to maintain a constant supply of soldiers of the Graeco-Macedonian type; not indeed a standing army, but a population of reservists to fill the place of the ordinary population who in Macedonia and Greece could be called to the colours in time of war. Is any such system to be found in Macedonia itself? The evidence is unsatisfactory. There does exist one inscription of Cassandreia which records a gift of land made by the great Philip to one of his nobles, and renewed by Cassander, in terms which enable us to see that the conditions of the gift were in many respects identical with those which prevailed later in the Hellenistic kingdoms.[2] From this inscription W. W. Tarn has reconstructed, with probability, a system according to which the kings of Macedonia disposed of the considerable "Royal Demesnes" which they possessed.[3] But it does not seem possible to argue from one example of an allotment made by a king to a noble, that it was the practice of the kings to make such allotments to common soldiers, as was the case in Egypt and elsewhere; still less that they habitually made them to their mercenaries. The only evidence for soldier cleruchs is to be found in two statements of Livy. In his description of Macedonia in

---

[1] Plut. *Aemil.* 23. 3; Livy 44. 43. 8; and 45.
[2] Ditt. *Syll.*³ i. 332 (306–297 B.C.).   [3] *A.G.* pp. 190 sqq.

167 B.C. he says that there were numerous Gauls and Illyrians settled in the "third region" of Macedonia—*incolas quoque permultos Gallos et Illyrios, impigros cultores*:[1] and "Thracian settlers" are present at Perseus' army review in 171 B.C.[2] Tarn says of the Gauls and Illyrians that "the object of their settlement was doubtless military service";[3] but this is to some extent stultified, as he himself sees, by Livy's *impigros cultores*, and it may be significant that the "Thracian settlers" in Perseus' army were only part of a contingent of 3000 which embraced also Paeonians and Agrianians. Perhaps the likeliest explanation is that the Gauls and Illyrians were settled in Macedonia not with a view to military service but as a reward for military service after it was completed. Barbarian mercenaries have appeared constantly in all the Macedonian armies since the time of Antigonus Gonatas, and they may in time have become sophisticated enough to expect grants of land upon their discharge, as other mercenaries did elsewhere:[4] in that case the communities which they formed would no doubt be liable to provide their men of military age for service in the same way as other Macedonian subjects. Certainly it seems most improbable that *active* mercenaries should have been given land. The whole purpose of a mercenary force was that it constituted the permanent and standing army which a rural population could not supply. There were Macedonians enough for short annual campaigns (provided that they did not follow one another too frequently); but the duties which demanded the constant presence of soldiers who were not obliged to winter at home, those duties were the mercenaries' sphere, and to settle mercenaries on the soil with the power of becoming "diligent farmers" would have been to defeat the purpose for which mercenaries were employed.[5]

The most important development of mercenary service in Macedonia in the third century and after is the great increase of barbarian soldiers. It was accompanied by a decline in the numbers of Greek mercenaries in Macedonian pay. In Alexander's army the proportion of Greek to barbarian mercenaries

[1] Livy 45. 30.
[2] *Id.* 42. 51.
[3] *Op. cit.* p. 192.
[4] Pp. 313 sqq.
[5] In Egypt there do appear people called μισθοφόροι κληροῦχοι (cf. pp. 135 sqq.); but they are comparatively rare, and in any event the circumstances in Egypt were not those of Macedonia.

MACEDONIA

was perhaps as high as 10:1 (pp. 20–21): in the army of Perseus, the ratio of Greeks (including Cretans) to barbarians was roughly 4:5, and of Greeks of Greece proper to other nationalities 1:8. The apparent decline in the number of Greeks at this period will be discussed in more detail in the chapter devoted to Provenance. But the reasons for the increase of barbarian mercenaries are evident enough. The barbarian nations were more numerous, nearer of access and hence easier to recruit, and perhaps cheaper into the bargain. The greatest acquisition was the Gauls. From the time when Antigonus Gonatas used Gauls to help him to conquer his kingdom, to the time when Perseus came within an ace of employing a whole Gallic nation in arms against Rome, the kings of Macedonia were probably never without some of these brave new soldiers in their pay. Greek statesmen sometimes attempted to justify to each other the existence of Macedonia by saying that she was a useful buffer between Greece and the barbarians: it was an ironical justice that Macedonia should employ those same barbarians as tools in her consistent policy of extending her influence over the Greeks.

CHAPTER IV

THE GREEK LEAGUES AND CITIES

1. ATHENS AND OTHER SMALL EMPLOYERS

ALTHOUGH Greek history is sometimes supposed to have come to an end with the battle of Chaeronea, yet in reality the Greeks of the third century were no less active politically than their ancestors, and political activity in Greece had only one ending—war. Wars were quite as common in the third century as they had been in the fourth or the fifth: it is only that the power of making war is now in different hands. Sparta alone of the military "employers" of the fourth century retains a position of some importance in the third. Athens is definitely a second-rate power, when she is not actually in the hands of a Macedonian garrison. Macedonia herself, whose military affairs have just been considered, has become the greatest European employer. The other most important military powers are the two new Leagues of Aetolia and Achaea. Achaea and Sparta share the military history of the Peloponnese in this period, and it is to them that the greater part of the evidence of mercenaries must relate, since the Aetolian League, for reasons which will be discussed presently, remains for the most part outside the discussion. But many of the smaller governments too must have fought with mercenaries, although we possess no more than casual references embracing quite a small proportion of the whole. It will be the present plan to write a short general essay covering the smaller Greek employers of mercenaries, before devoting more special attention to the mercenaries of Sparta and of the Achaean League.

It is first necessary to account for the backwardness of the Aetolians in taking advantage of the method of warfare which had become so congenial to contemporary Greeks. The principal reason is probably to be found in their general backwardness in other respects. The Aetolian League made a late entry into Greek politics, and did not in fact begin to play any important part until after Alexander's death. The Aetolia of

Thucydides' day was a wild and barren country inhabited by a semi-barbarous race of fighters. In the third century the country remained a poor one, and the inhabitants, though they had advanced politically, and from being mere warlike villagers had formed the cities which were the component parts of their federation, had yet never caught up with the rest of Greece in the refinements of culture. Above all they were still fighters. Since the soil of their country would never make them rich, the barest necessity combined with their native vigour to suggest the pursuit of arms as the most profitable profession open to them, with the result that they were readier to fight for themselves or for others than to employ others to fight for them. The Aetolian League could perhaps put into the field an army of 20,000 men at its maximum. It was not a great army, as armies went in the third century; but the national spirit of the soldiers, and the natural defences of the Aetolian mountains, made it very nearly an unbeatable proposition. In actual practice, the Aetolians hardly ever needed so large a force, and could better afford to let some proportion of their fighting men go out on their own account as mercenaries or pirates—as a nursery of pirates Aetolia was second only to Crete itself.[1] Curiously enough, on the only occasion when it is possible to suspect the Aetolians of using mercenaries, there is evidence of an understanding between their League and a Cretan city. At a time when Cnossus was beset by a confederation of several other cities, she obtained a reinforcement of 1000 men from Aetolia "in accordance with her alliance", and repaid the loan in kind soon afterwards when Aetolia in turn was at war with Macedonia and the Achaeans (218 B.C.).[2] The 1000 Cnossians are mentioned in Polybius' account of the operations in that year: they are in two detachments of 500 each, the one in Elis fighting against the Achaeans, the other in Aetolia, and the latter are called definitely "mercenaries".[3] Mercenaries they no doubt were in effect, and it is tempting to find here an early example of a kind of trade "cartel", effecting that two states, which each made a profitable business of freebooting, should place their resources at each other's disposal if the demands upon one partner's strength

---

[1] For man-power and armies of Aetolia, see Beloch, *Bevölkerung*, pp. 186 sqq.
[2] Pol. iv. 53. 8; 55. 5.   [3] *Id.* v. 3. 1; 14. 1.

proved greater than his own resources. But other similar treaties are known which can be endowed with no such special significance;[1] all that can be said for certain is that Aetolia followed a fashion in establishing a connection with one of the best sources of supply.

At about the same date (219 B.C.) we find Elis, an ally of the Aetolians, employing "mercenaries and pirates" most of whom were probably Aetolians. The officer in command was an Aetolian Euripidas, who was not officially recognized by his government: the mercenaries were originally at least 700 in number, and were increased considerably by recruiting.[2] In this connection Polybius allows himself an odd digression, in which he gives a brief history of Elis and condemns the folly of the Eleans for not having made capital of the sacrosanctity of Olympia, in order to withdraw themselves completely from the rivalry with their neighbours the Arcadians which had been their ruin: the Greeks, he says, would have respected their property for the sake of Olympia, or alternatively their fertile land would have made them amply rich enough to support an army of mercenaries for their protection.[3] This is one of the very few examples of an ancient author advocating the use of mercenaries;[4] and it is especially interesting in that it depicts as a possible condition for Elis that which was the actual condition of Athens in the third century and later. This we will next examine.

It is quite certain that during the greater part of the fourth century Athens had used mercenaries more freely than any other Greek city. The intrigues of Leosthenes and the Lamian War have been discussed already (pp. 34 sqq.); but there also is evidence from a much earlier date which ought perhaps to be mentioned here. Isocrates devoted a long passage in his "Peace" pamphlet to illustrating the reliance placed by Athens on hired troops, and the inefficiency of the native Athenian soldiers. "We are ambitious", he wrote, "to rule all Greece, but we ourselves refuse to fight: we engage in war almost, it might be said, against the

[1] E.g. the Hierapytna treaties, pp. 69 and 91 sqq.
[2] Pol. iv. 68. 1; 71. 7; 75. 6; 77. 7; 80. 4; v. 3. 1; 30. 2.
[3] Id. iv. 73 and 74.
[4] Cf. Diod. xxix. 6 for praise of the Carthaginian military system, and the advantages in general of a mercenary army.

whole human race, but it is not ourselves we train with a view to the war, but men who are exiles, or deserters, the conglomerate scum of the criminal world, men who, if someone will only give them higher pay, will fight with him against us.... Such is the extent of our degeneration from the virtues of our ancestors that ...though we are so poor, and ourselves so numerous, we yet employ mercenary armies with the prodigality of the Great King himself. Our ancestors, if they manned a fleet, put the foreigners and slaves aboard as sailors, and sent out as soldiers Athenian citizens. We use the foreigners as soldiers, and make our citizens pull at the oar; when an expedition goes out to a hostile country, the aspirant rulers of Greece disembark with their rowing-pads, and it is they, the scoundrels I have just described, who play a soldier's part."[1] This is rhetoric, but it cannot be completely false. Demosthenes[2] in his political speeches frequently spoke against the apathy of the Athenian citizen, which allowed wars to be waged by mercenaries in the city's pay, an apathy produced no doubt by a combination of causes connected with the political experience of the Athenian people. But there is also a very obvious external cause that ought not to be ignored. The military history of Athens throughout the fourth century was undistinguished, and the truth is that its one really brilliant page was provided by the exploits of Iphicrates in the Corinthian War. The first army that Athens sent out after the disaster of 405 B.C. was the force which went to Corinth in 394, and in this force the mercenaries of Iphicrates became famous, while the citizen troops remained obscure. It seems highly probable that this turn of events may have exercised a great influence on the later policy of the Athenians, and may help to explain why Athens took so readily to the practice of fighting with mercenaries whenever and wherever it was possible. The fact itself is not in doubt, and there are traces in the period before Chaeronea of an organization for dealing with the new branch of the army. The "commissioners for the mercenaries" had probably the same duties as the ἀποστολεῖς who accompanied all Athenian expeditions abroad, the maintenance of a proper

---

[1] Isoc. viii. 44 sqq.; cf. 24; and vii. 9.
[2] Demosth. iv. 46; xiii. 16; xxiii. 139; iii. 35; iv. 19 and 24 sqq., etc.

standard of efficiency:[1] and it is possible that the office of ξενολόγος became a recognized λειτουργία.[2] But the epigraphic evidence relating to the mercenary garrisons at Athens in the Hellenistic period throws a better light upon the organization which became necessary for their upkeep.

The earliest relevant inscription dates from 321 or 318 B.C., and reveals the presence of a force of mercenaries at Athens (τὸ ξενικόν) and of an administrative officer (στρατηγὸς ἐπὶ τῶν ξένων) to look after it.[3] This official reappears in the third century, and since a certain Phaedrus is known to have held the office three times, it seems possible that it was a permanent one.[4] It would follow from this that Athens always had a force of mercenaries in her service, and that is likely enough, since it was necessary to keep several small garrisons at Eleusis, Sunium and various other forts of Attica. Two inscriptions of the end of the fourth century or soon after are in effect lists of mercenary soldiers, which will be of value later when the question of provenance is to be discussed.[5] Nevertheless it seems that some scholars have overstated the case for Athens' dependence on mercenaries in the third century, and in particular the statement that the word στρατιῶται in Attic inscriptions of that period always means mercenaries[6], is not corroborated by an examination of the inscriptions themselves. It is true that in several inscriptions στρατιῶται certainly does mean mercenaries;[7] but it is also true that in others the meaning is dubious,[8] and that in one inscription at least στρατιῶται is used collectively of people who have been described previously as τοὺς στρατευομένους...τῶν πολιτῶν καὶ τοὺς ξένους.[9] In actual fact there is no doubt that

[1] Aeschines i. 118—Timarchus was ἐξεταστὴς τῶν ἐν Ἐρετρίᾳ ξένων, in which capacity he admitted to having been bribed: for the functions of ἐξετασταί in general, cf. P.-W. s.v. [2] Demosth. xl. 36.
[3] I.G.² ii. 379. 10 sqq. The active commander was the ξεναγός or ἡγεμών; ibid. 1313; 1299. 42 and 94 sqq.; cf. Livy 31. 24. 6 (Dioxippus).
[4] Ibid. 682, esp. l. 25. Cf. the Aristophanes στρατηγός of ibid. 1299, who may be στρατηγὸς ἐπὶ τῶν ξένων as is suggested by Ditt. Syll.³ i. 485.
[5] Ibid. 1956 and 1957. Cf. pp. 240 sqq.
[6] Cf. note on I.G. ii. 3. 1349 VII; W. S. Ferguson, Hellenistic Athens, p. 128 n. 2.
[7] I.G.² ii. 682. 25 sqq. (ca. 290 B.C.); 1286 (ca. 256–243 B.C.); 1299, 20 sqq., 40 sqq., 93 sqq. (ca. 235 B.C.); 1313 (end of third century).
[8] Ibid. 1287 (middle of third century); 1310 (end of third century).
[9] Ibid. 1270, 5 sqq. and 10 (298 B.C.); cf. probably 1302 (222 B.C.); 1954 (306 B.C.); 1958 (second half of third century).

GREEK LEAGUES AND CITIES 85

Athenian citizens served as soldiers in these garrisons throughout the third century, since there are at least sixteen inscriptions mentioning them explicitly, usually in the formula Ἀθηναίων οἱ τεταγμένοι (e.g.) Ἐλευσῖνι.[1] They received their maintenance from the State, and since there is a case on record of a στρατηγός issuing what was known as a πρόδομα (an advance of pay, in this case εἰς ἐσθῆτα), it seems likely that these garrisons of Athenians consisted of poor citizens, and that this was a useful means of employing them in the public service.[2] These soldiers were στρατιῶται no less than the mercenaries, and there is no need to assume, when we find a list of στρατιῶται most of whom are Athenian citizens, that therefore Athenian citizens must have served Athens as mercenaries.[3]

What is less easy to find out, is the proportion of mercenaries to citizens, and our only clues are two of the lists of soldiers that have been mentioned.[4] In a list that is to be dated about 235 B.C., when Athens was in a state of war, there appear the names of soldiers at Eleusis who subscribed money towards erecting a statue of their general Aristophanes: only 11 are the names of citizens, 23 are the names of mercenaries with their provenance, and 25 additional names which survive in their first two or three letters only, appear to belong to mercenaries too.[5] The second list (though not certainly second in point of time, since it can be dated only approximately to the second half of the third century) contains 63 names also from Eleusis, of which only 9 belong to foreigners, and the rest to citizens: and since the 9 foreigners appear at random among the citizens it is quite possible that they are really metics, and not mercenaries at all.[6] It is dangerous to argue from these two pieces of evidence alone,

---

[1] E.g. *I.G.*² ii. 1191 (321 B.C.); 500. 14 sqq. (302 B.C.); 1217 (263 B.C.); and thirteen others between 1272 and 1311, varying in date from the beginning to the end of the century.

[2] *Ibid.* 1304. 34 sqq. (about 210 B.C.)—προδιδοὺς ἀργύριον εἰς ἐσθῆτα; cf. pp. 278, 292–3, for other examples of πρόδομα. For σῖτος paid to Athenian garrisons, *I.G.*² ii. 1264. 5 sqq.; 1272. 9 sqq.; 1281. 3 sqq.

[3] *Ibid.* 1958; cf. Ferguson, *op. cit.* p. 251.

[4] It is not legitimate to argue from the fact that we have in the inscriptions about three times as many notices of the citizen soldiers as of the mercenaries; because one would expect the citizens to be much the more prominent in records of that kind, many of which are decrees by the soldiers in honour of their general, himself an Athenian citizen.

[5] *I.G.*² ii. 1299. 81 sqq.   [6] *Ibid.* 1958.

which may be the result of pure chance; but it is at least possible that they reflect the state of the Athenian garrisons first in war time and second in time of peace;[1] or again it is possible that the second inscription really dates from the period after 229 B.C., when Athens had almost ceased to be an active force in politics, and one might expect a decline in her mercenary forces. But there was such a force in Athens again at the time of the war with Philip V (200 B.C.), though probably not a large one.[2] The second century yields no information whatever.

A small matter with a possible bearing upon the mercenary garrisons at Athens is the existence in the second century of a torch race for "Tarentines" as one of the events in the Theseian games. This does not mean that "Tarentine" mercenaries took part in the games, since the contest was on a tribal basis.[3] But it may mean that this peculiar cavalry style had been copied from mercenaries stationed in Athens at an earlier date (e.g. those of Demetrius, p. 53). There exists also a dedication of spoils by "the Tarentines", probably early in the third century; but there is no indication as to whether these "Tarentines" are citizen or mercenary soldiers.[4] The evolution of the "Tarentine" style will be discussed at greater length elsewhere (pp. 246 sqq.).[5]

Finally there is the question of the Athenian περίπολοι, a force for the defence of Attica. Some scholars have assumed from statements of Aeschines and Aristotle, that the περίπολοι were Athenian ephebes, but this theory is not free from difficulties.[6] The oligarch Phrynichus in the year 411 B.C. was killed

---

[1] Cf. Ditt. *Syll.*³ i. 491, an appeal for funds by a ταμίας τῶν στρατιωτικῶν in war time (*ca.* 232 B.C.), perhaps to meet a temporary increase in the number of the mercenaries.

[2] Livy, 31. 24. 6, calls Dioxippus "prefect of a mercenary cohort", which may mean that his force was approximately 600 strong (e.g. between 400 and 800).

[3] *I.G.*² ii. 958. 56 sqq.; 960. 33; 961. 34.

[4] *I.G.* ii. 3. 1218.

[5] In some ways the history of the "Tarentines" at Athens may be analogous to that of the ἐπίλεκτοι, though the latter were always citizen troops. The ἐπίλεκτοι were a fighting force—early in the third century (*I.G.*² ii. 680. 12; 1209. 3); but reappear in the Theseian games in the second century (*ibid.* 956–61).

[6] Aeschines ii. 167—'Εκ παίδων μὲν γὰρ ἀπαλλαγεὶς περίπολος τῆς χώρας ταύτης ἐγενόμην δύ' ἔτη, καὶ τούτων ὑμῖν τοὺς συνεφήβους καὶ τοὺς ἄρχοντας ἡμῶν μάρτυρας παρέξομαι. *F.H.G.* ii. 112—'Αριστοτέλης δὲ ἐν 'Αθηναίων πολιτείᾳ περὶ τῶν ἐβήβων λέγων φησὶν οὕτως· τὸν δεύτερον ἐνιαυτὸν ἐκκλησίας ἐν τῷ θεάτρῳ γενομένης, ἀποδει-

GREEK LEAGUES AND CITIES 87

by one of the περίπολοι: the murderer was Thrasybulus of Calydon; his accomplice was an Argive; and all the other persons concerned were foreigners.[1] So much for the περίπολοι being ephebes, in the fifth century at least. One must try to discover their origin. Thucydides outlines the military resources of Athens at the beginning of the Peloponnesian War: ὁπλίτας δὲ τρισχιλίους καὶ μυρίους εἶναι ἄνευ τῶν ἐν τοῖς φρούροις καὶ τῶν παρ' ἔπαλξιν ἑξακισχιλίων καὶ μυρίων. τοσοῦτοι γὰρ ἐφύλασσον τὸ πρῶτον ὁπότε οἱ πολέμιοι ἐσβάλοιεν, ἀπό τε τῶν πρεσβυτάτων καὶ τῶν νεωτάτων καὶ μετοίκων ὅσοι ὁπλῖται ἦσαν.[2] He does not mention περίπολοι by name, though he does later mention quite small details such as the horse and foot archers; but it will be noticed that the functions of the defence force described by Thucydides are identical with those of the περίπολοι described by Aristotle (above). The first specific mention of περίπολοι by name comes under the year 425 B.C. in connection with an expedition against Megara: οἱ δὲ μετὰ τοῦ Δημοσθένους τοῦ ἑτέρου στρατηγοῦ Πλαταιῆς τε ψιλοὶ καὶ ἕτεροι περίπολοι ἐνήδρευσαν ἐς τὸ Ἐνυάλιον·[3] they may, then, have been foreigners. They come again in the *Birds* of Aristophanes (413 B.C.), but the reference is not helpful, except that it proves them to be quite distinct from the archers.[4] Finally, the murder of Phrynichus is by a foreign περίπολος with foreign accomplices.

So much for the evidence: how is it to be used? It is possible that the περίπολοι were an innovation of the early years of the war, when the Athenians chafed under the annual inconvenience and mortification of seeing a Peloponnesian army devastate Attica. That they could not prevent. But they may have decided to form a small force for home defence, more mobile and manageable than the force of 16,000 old men, boys and metics, for the purpose of preventing minor incursions from Boeotia after the

ξάμενοι τῷ δήμῳ περὶ τὰς τάξεις καὶ λαβόντες ἀσπίδα καὶ δόρυ παρὰ τοῦ δήμου περιπολοῦσι τὴν χώραν καὶ διατρίβουσιν ἐν τοῖς φυλακτηρίοις. Παρατηρητέον οὖν ὅτι μὲν ὁ Ἀριστοτέλης ἕνα φησὶν ἐνιαυτὸν ἐν τοῖς περιπόλοις γένεσθαι τοὺς ἐφήβους, ὁ δὲ Αἰσχίνης δύο.

[1] *I.G.*[2] i. 110; Thuc. viii. 92. 2 sqq.; Lysias, *Agoratus* 71.
[2] Thuc. ii. 13. 6 sqq; cf. Aristotle, *Ath. Pol.* 24.
[3] Thuc. iv. 67. 2.
[4] Aristoph. *Aves* 1177 sqq.

οὐκοῦν δῆτα περιπόλους ἔχρην
πέμψαι κατ' αὐτὸν εὐθύς;
          ἀλλ' ἐπέμψαμεν
τρισμυρίους ἱέρακας ἱπποτοξότας.

main invasion was over, and into such a force the Plataean refugees may well have been incorporated. Thus the περίπολοι may have been at this time a kind of foreign legion of which the Plataeans were the nucleus; or they may have consisted of citizens and mercenaries together. But the foreigners involved in the murder of Phrynichus make it distinctly probable that by 411 B.C. the περίπολοι were a corps of mercenaries. That they were still soldiers (and not merely ephebes) at the end of the fourth century is certain from two inscriptions in which a peripolarch commands στρατιῶται.[1] A somewhat earlier inscription (352 B.C.) proves that there was more than one peripolarch, so that there were probably several companies of περίπολοι assigned to the several forts and districts of Attica.[2] The final conclusion is that there seems to be no essential difference between the περίπολοι at Eleusis at the end of the fourth century and the garrisons of citizens and mercenaries at Eleusis about the same date: indeed it seems possible that they were in fact the same people, and that the name περίπολοι may have gone out of use though the peripolarch still survived.[3] To return to Aeschines and Aristotle, the statements that ephebes served as περίπολοι cannot be ignored; but they can be explained if we suppose that part of the youth's training was to go into garrison duty for a year (or two years) to be "licked into shape" by a professional sergeant-major.

The organization which has been seen at work in Athens may perhaps be taken as typical of any self-governing Greek city in the third century, though the smaller communities no doubt employed fewer soldiers. But the tyrants who flourished in several cities of the Peloponnese must have been considerable employers. The most powerful were the socialist dictators at Sparta, to whom a separate section will be allotted. But we have noticed how Aristotimus maintained a cruel hand over Elis by means of a large force of mercenaries (some of them barbarians), upon whom he was so greatly dependent that he was really as much in their power as the citizens were in his own.[4] An *impasse*

[1] *I.G.*² ii. 1193 and *I.G.* ii. 5. 1219 (*b*).
[2] *I.G.*² ii. 204. 20.
[3] Compare *I.G.*² ii. 1193 (peripolarch with στρατιῶται, end of fourth century), with *ibid.* 1191 (citizens in garrison at Eleusis, 321 B.C.).
[4] P. 68. Plut. *Moral.* 251 sqq.

GREEK LEAGUES AND CITIES 89

of this kind was one of the most serious dangers of tyranny. The tyrant knew that if ever he became short of money his soldiers might turn against him: to avoid being short of money he must tax his subjects the more severely: the more severely he taxed his subjects the more discontented they became, and the more soldiers he must employ for his own safety—and so the vicious circle revolved. The tyrants of the Peloponnese were fortunate to find a friend in Macedonia, whose kings, hoping by this means to secure control of southern Greece, were always ready to push a tyrant into his seat, and help him to keep it when he was there.[1] When Macedonian influence weakened, there was a general collapse of the tyrant system.[2] But while it lasted it must have maintained some thousands of soldiers in permanent employment, though unfortunately there is no evidence for the numbers or conditions of the tyrants' armies in most instances. It is no more than common sense to assume that they all *had* mercenary armies, of greater or smaller size to suit their station, and the assumption is supported by casual references to the mercenaries of Cratesipolis[3] and Nicaea at Corinth,[4] of Nicocles at Sicyon,[5] of Aristotimus at Elis, and of Aristippus and Aristomachus at Argos. The tyranny at Argos was probably the most powerful of all, except those at Sparta. In the battle of Cleonae in which Aristippus lost his life, the casualties on the Argive side amounted to 1500:[6] and when Aristomachus compounded with the Achaean League and laid down his tyranny, he received from the League 50 talents to enable him to "settle" with his mercenaries.[7] Neither of these pieces of information is valuable as a clue to the size of their armies, because in the first case there may have been Argive citizens in the ranks as well, and in the second we do not know if the 50 talents were for arrears of pay, and if so for how long, or whether they were merely intended as a bonus to the soldiers on the termination of their contract.

[1] Pol. ii. 41. 10; ix. 29, from which passages K. Grote, p. 68, concludes that the tyrants were often Macedonian officers commanding garrisons, who had become tyrants with the consent and support of their king. So much cannot be extorted from the words of Polybius: it is obviously untrue of (e.g.) Aristomachus of Argos, Lydiades of Megalopolis, Xenon of Hermione, Cleonymus of Phlius—Pol. ii. 44. 5 sqq.
[2] Pol. ii. 44.
[3] Diod. xix. 67. 1 sqq.; Polyaen. viii. 58.
[4] Plut. *Arat.* 17. 2 sqq.
[5] *Ibid.* 8. 4.
[6] *Ibid.* 26. 1; 29. 4.
[7] *Ibid.* 35. 2.

If we turn to the outskirts of the Greek world, we do not fail to find scattered references which show that the mercenary system was as prevalent here as in the armies of Greece proper or of the great monarchies. A most interesting inscription of the island of Cos (*ca.* 200 B.C.) records the voluntary subscriptions of "citizens, citizenesses, bastards, and aliens" to a fund for military expenses.[1] Its importance relative to the question of pay and maintenance will be discussed later,[2] and it is sufficient to say here that there was certainly a standing army of mercenaries in Cos at the end of the third century. An equally interesting inscription of Priene (*ca.* 275 B.C.) is of a more particular character.[3] It refers to the events following the first coming of the Gauls into Asia Minor (277 B.C.). The brutality and impiety of the strange warriors inspired the Greeks of Asia with an almost universal panic. The government of Priene was no braver or cooler than anyone else, and the citizens shrank from leaving their walls to face the enemy. It was then that a man named Sotas took the lead in organizing a defence force which beat off the invaders and restored security to the city. The force seems at first to have consisted of mercenaries and slaves, and hindered the Gauls in their depredations; but it was later increased by volunteers of the citizens and neighbouring countryfolk who assisted in the final repulse of the Gauls. The important fact is that it was Sotas, and not the government, who was responsible for it all. It may be surmised that he was a wealthy merchant or landowner whose profits were vanishing while the authorities prepared to do many things: he may have paid and equipped the impromptu army, and have recruited mercenaries, or added to the number of those already in the employ of the city. He was apparently not an ambitious man, since he did not take advantage of his military success to make himself tyrant of Priene.

It is to be expected that Rhodes, the great Greek merchant state of the time, should have kept a permanent army of defence. Traders are not very often good fighters, and especially they do not like to interrupt their business with active service in the

---

[1] W. R. Paton and E. L. Hicks, *Inscriptions of Cos*, 10. D. 64 sqq.
[2] See below, pp. 283-4.
[3] *O.G.I.S.* ii. 765.

GREEK LEAGUES AND CITIES 91

field. Rhodes was wealthy enough to support a standing army of paid soldiers, though there is no absolute proof that she did so. But an army of about 3000 men which acted against the troops of Philip V in Asia Minor (197 B.C.) seems to have contained few if any Rhodian citizens, and at least 1800 mercenaries.[1] An inscription of uncertain date records some details of a naval expedition, and mentions several officers by name. Rhodian citizens are an artillery expert (καταπαλταφέτας), two naval officers (?), and a συνταγματάρχης ἐπὶ τῶν ξένων; but five λοχαγοὶ τῶν ξένων τῶμ μισθοφόρων are foreigners, two from Cos, and one each from Calymnus and Carystus (for the fifth the provenance is missing). This is a valuable confirmation of the evidence from Athens, for it is certain that the συνταγματάρχης is the superior officer of the λοχαγοί, just as the στρατηγὸς ἐπὶ τῶν ξένων at Athens was the superior of the ἡγεμών or ξεναγός: though the probability is that this Rhodian officer was a real soldier and not a mere administrator, and his own position may in fact have been equivalent to that of a ἡγεμών.[2] It is to the end of the third century that the well-known inscription of the treaty between Rhodes and the Cretan city of Hierapytna is to be assigned. Hierapytna is to send 200 men to help Rhodes whenever necessary, and details of their pay are settled; but the important part of the treaty, for our present purpose, is the clause safeguarding Rhodian recruiting officers in Hierapytna and its neighbourhood, allowing Rhodes a monopoly of the recruiting there, and forbidding any citizen of Hierapytna to take service as a mercenary against Rhodes.[3] It is probably permissible to argue that Rhodes would not have troubled to enforce a strict agreement of this kind had she not considered it likely to be useful to her, and to be really useful it would have to exist along with similar agreements with other cities opening to her an extensive recruiting field in Crete. Rhodes was not the state to require a really large standing army; but it seems almost certain that she maintained a moderate one which may have become larger when

---
[1] Livy 33. 18. 1 sqq. The Achaeans mentioned in this passage are probably not mercenaries.
[2] G. Jacopi, *Clara Rhodos*, ii. p. 169; and M. Segre in *Riv. di fil.* 1932, pp. 452 sqq.
[3] Ditt. *Syll.*³ ii. 581, esp. ll. 18 sqq., 26 sqq., 40 sqq. For the pay, see below, p. 303.

she became a power on the mainland after 188 B.C., though as a military power she can never have equalled Carthage, the great mercantile employer of mercenaries in the West.

It might be thought that foreign mercenaries landing in Crete must have found themselves in a false position, since the Cretans themselves were famous mercenaries. And yet in this same treaty of Rhodes with Hierapytna the Cretan city is guaranteed the same facilities for recruiting in Asia that she herself guarantees to Rhodes in her own sphere of influence.[1] Moreover, we have seen that when Aetolia was at war with Philip V (218–217 B.C.) both parties sent reinforcements of troops to opposing groups of Cretan cities, apparently on identically the same terms as those on which the Cretans later repaid them in kind.[2] Philopoemen, in his youth, served as a mercenary leader in Crete, and the Gortynians thought it worth while to ask him to pay a second visit as their general, which he did.[3] It can have been seldom enough that perfect peace reigned in the island, so that the cities may sometimes have found themselves short of men, particularly if they made no attempt to restrain their nationals from entering foreign service just as they pleased. That this was very likely the case appears from a Cretan embassy to Rome at the time of the third Macedonian War. It was the purpose of the ambassadors to conciliate the Senate, and they reminded it that they had never failed to send archers to the Roman consul in Macedonia when he wanted them. The reply was that more Cretan archers were serving with Perseus than with the Romans, and that if the Cretans seriously desired the friendship of Rome they must recall all their soldiers from Perseus' garrisons.[4] This must mean that, though the Cretan governments had *sent* mercenaries to the Roman general, they had also at least done nothing to prevent other mercenaries from leaving Crete to serve with Perseus; that is to say, they did not control the exodus of their subjects into service abroad. Their *laisser faire* brought them into trouble on this occasion, and it may sometimes have produced the situation that when they needed their own soldiers for defending their own cities, they found that there were not enough of them at home, and were thus compelled to recruit

[1] Ditt. *Syll.*³ ii. 581, ll. 76 sqq.; 82 sqq.
[2] Pp. 70 and 81.
[3] Pp. 103 and 105.
[4] Livy 43. 7. 1 sqq.

GREEK LEAGUES AND CITIES

foreign mercenaries. Another possible reason for such recruiting is that they needed a different kind of soldier as well as their own, for the Cretans were famous chiefly as archers and experts in the tactics of the guerilla.[1]

2. SPARTA

In the first half of the third century it is only occasionally that Sparta, isolated in her Laconian backwater, emerges to play an important part in the history of the time. As a natural consequence her own history is for the most part lost, entirely lost indeed so far as the subject of this inquiry is concerned. Times were bad at Sparta. Money and land were concentrated into the control of a few powerful citizens: the State and the people alike were poor. How this may have affected the military arrangements of the city cannot be laid down with any certainty. The fact that full Spartan citizens were now few in number does not mean that the population as a whole was smaller: there were still men enough to guard the State, as is proved by the heroic defence against Pyrrhus in 272 B.C.[2] But the social disturbances which came later must mean that the largest part of the community was disaffected and perhaps not to be trusted with arms except in a national emergency, while the poverty of the State probably made it impossible to maintain a sufficient standing army of mercenaries: the two facts combined doubtless account for the unambitious policy of Sparta in this period. Twice only did she commit herself to any serious fighting; on the first occasion Pyrrhus forced her into action by his attack, and on the second her traditional hostility to Macedonia induced her to participate in the Chremonidean War in an effort to break the Macedonian control in the Peloponnese and restore her own. Of her armies in the Chremonidean War nothing to the purpose is known, and from her struggle with Pyrrhus none but negative conclusions can be drawn. One of her kings, Areus, was away at the time fighting in Crete, and certainly the city contained barely enough soldiers to keep Pyrrhus out until help came. There can have been few mercenaries; but Pyrrhus' horse was killed "by a Cretan shot", and Areus' relief force of

[1] Cf. (e.g.) Pol. iv. 8. 11.   [2] Plut. *Pyrrhus* 27 sqq.

2000 men probably contained Cretans whom he had hired when he heard of the danger.[1] At all events, there were 1000 Cretans in the army with which Areus carried the war into the enemy's camp at Argos.[2]

Some information about the social revolution attempted by Agis and temporarily achieved by Cleomenes has survived in Plutarch's two *Lives*. Agis' popular programme gave him the whole-hearted support of the poor of Sparta, and it is evident that the only military operations upon which he embarked, a campaign against Aetolia in alliance with the Achaean League, was undertaken with an army of young and enthusiastic devotees of social reform.[3] There is no evidence of his having attempted to support his position by hiring foreign soldiers, indeed he was content to lose it, and with it his life, rather than incur the responsibility of shedding Spartan blood; sufficient proof that he had no mercenaries, whom he could have sacrificed without compunction. But Leonidas, the exiled king and his enemy, returned to Sparta at the head of a large force of mercenaries (perhaps mostly Peloponnesians, since his headquarters had been at Tegea), which gave back to him the control of the State (244–240 B.C.).[4] There can be little doubt that till his death in 237 B.C. he relied upon his soldiers to keep him in power, since his policy was reactionary and he ruled unconstitutionally without a colleague. His son Cleomenes was another social reformer, but he realized that the reforms of Agis had failed mainly because they had had no backing of military force. It seems that Cleomenes too in the early part of his reign was poorly supported in this respect. He lay low for eight years, and his first two campaigns of which we have knowledge were undertaken with armies of less than 5000 men.[5] But in the end he made his foreign war with the Achaean League the means to fulfilling his purpose at home. In 226 B.C., with a larger army than before, he defeated Aratus and Lydiades near Megalopolis, and it is plain that he had been able to recruit more mercenaries, since "Tarentines" and Cretans appear in the account of the battle.[6]

---

[1] Plut. *Pyrrhus* 29. 4 and 6.   [2] *Ibid.* 32. 2.
[3] *Id. Agis* 14.   [4] *Ibid.* 16. 2 and 19. 3.
[5] *Id. Cleom.* 4. 5.
[6] *Ibid.* 6. 3; *id. Arat.* 36 sqq. For Cretans again, *id. Cleom.* 21. 3.

He then astutely wore out his citizen soldiers with unnecessary and exhausting marches, left them encamped in Arcadia, and rushed to seize Sparta with his mercenaries.[1] Like Agis he soon had an army of poor Spartans who were well-disposed to him; but he was more of a soldier than Agis had been. His army was intended for fighting: he formed a corps of 4000 *Perioeci* and another of 2000 helots, arming them both in Macedonian style. The two together may have become a standing army, for it is this precise number of 6000 Lacedaemonians which fought later in his phalanx at Sellasia.[2] But the figures for his army at Sellasia prove that he had at least as large a force of mercenaries as well, large enough to embarrass him financially even though he received subsidies from Egypt.[3] The Spartan army against Antigonus Doson numbered 20,000, of whom the "phalanx" of 6000 with 5000 mercenaries faced the Macedonians: there were other mercenaries operating with the cavalry, and the remainder were *Perioeci* and Peloponnesian allies.[4] The honours of the day were carried off by the Spartan heavy infantry, who died almost to a man, but the mercenaries too fought well and suffered heavily in the defeat:[5] it is probable from the description of the battle that they were lightly armed soldiers, more akin to the Greek peltast than to the Macedonian phalangite.[6]

From this time on Sparta becomes, as never before in her history, a power relying mainly upon mercenary soldiers. In the war of the Allies (220–217 B.C.) the king Lycurgus is twice to be found on campaigns "with the mercenaries and some of the citizen troops",[7] but no particulars are forthcoming except that he had at least 200 Cretans.[8] The tyrant Machanidas maintained a large standing army and was evidently at some pains to make it good as well as large. At the battle of Mantinea (207 B.C.) Sparta and the Achaean League came to grips at full strength, each side sending out a full citizen levy as well as a big force of mercenaries.[9] Machanidas commanded his mercenaries himself, and not the Spartan heavy infantry, which is sufficient comment on the value he attached to the former: in

[1] Plut. *Cleom.* 7. 3 sqq.
[2] *Ibid.* 11. 2; 23. 1 sqq.; 28. 5.
[3] *Ibid.* 27. 2; 22. 3.
[4] Pol. ii. 65. 10; 69. 3.
[5] Plut. *Cleom.* 28. 1 sqq.
[6] Cf. esp. Pol. ii. 69. 3 sqq.
[7] *Id.* iv. 36. 4, ἀναλαβὼν τοὺς στρατιώτας καί τινας τῶν πολιτικῶν; cf. v. 20. 6.
[8] *Id.* iv. 80. 4 and 6.
[9] Plut. *Phil.* 10 sqq.

fact there is the curious spectacle of the two rival commanders each commanding his mercenaries in preference to the citizen troops. Machanidas' mercenaries did all that soldiers could do. They were both more numerous and more efficient than those of Philopoemen, which, as Polybius points out, was only to be expected in the mercenaries of a tyrant as compared with those of a democracy:[1] they seem to have been mostly mobile troops, if not strictly light-armed infantry, but they included also some "Tarentine" horse. In the battle they swept the League mercenaries off the field, but Machanidas turned his victory into defeat just as Demetrius had done at Ipsus, and Antiochus at Raphia. He pursued too far, allowed his Spartans to be isolated and defeated by the Achaeans, and then found his retreat barred. His soldiers stood by him in a desperate attempt to cut his way through to safety, and it was not until they saw that it was hopeless that they scattered and tried every man to save himself. Obviously they hoped that Philopoemen, when he saw them no longer dangerous, would accept their surrender, and perhaps their service in his own army. But Philopoemen too failed them: rightly believing that the danger of the Spartan tyrannies had lain in their mercenary armies, he gave orders that not one of the fugitives should be spared.[2]

The last of the socialist tyrants at Sparta was Nabis (206–192 B.C.), and he was also perhaps the most thorough. He advanced so far towards communistic ideals as to deprive the rich of their money, property and wives, in order to give them to the more outstanding of his own supporters and to his mercenaries. The latter are described by Polybius, with a bourgeois bias perhaps, and not less vividly on that account. "They were murderers and housebreakers, footpads, robbers. He collected all such fry with diligence from every land, men to whom their mother country was a forbidden land, because of their impiety and crime. These were the men of whom he proclaimed himself leader and king and whom he employed as his spearmen and bodyguards, clearly intending to win a lasting reputation for impiety, and a lasting power."[3] It will not be doubted that

---

[1] Pol. v. 13. 1 sqq.
[2] *Ibid.* 13. 1 sqq.; 17. 4 sqq.; 18. 1.
[3] *Id.* xiii. 6. 3 sqq.; cf. Diod. xxvii. 1.

Polybius presents an exaggerated picture of the numbers as well as of the infamy of these warriors. Nabis announced that his military strength was the merest precaution of prudence against the animosity of the Achaean League, and there is probably much truth in what he said.[1] Moreover, the very nature of the state which he ruled perhaps prevented any great accumulation of wealth into the hands even of the ruler himself, so that we hear of his acquiring an interest in the profession of brigandage in order to make money. He was the friend of the Cretan pirates by sea, and in the Peloponnese he employed gangs of highwaymen and brigands whose booty he shared in return for a convenient base in Sparta and a safe refuge should they be hard pressed.[2] No doubt they served also as soldiers in his field army when he had need of them. He found employment for Cretans in other directions. His policy included the merciless hunting and slaying of the many Spartans who had fled from Sparta in the hope of starting a new life in some other city of the Peloponnese. It was Nabis' custom, when he heard of a likely victim, to recruit Cretans through secret agents (so that his own official mercenaries might not be seen and recognized), and despatch them to the city in question, where they would kill the wretched exile by breaking holes in the walls of his house and shooting him like a rat in a trap.[3] In these practices he seems to have been ahead of his time.

Despite these many and varied activities, his army was no bigger than that of Cleomenes at Sellasia, and contained about the same proportion of mercenaries. To meet the attack of Flamininus in 195 B.C., he had 2000 Cretans (1000 picked soldiers specially recruited from Crete for the occasion) and 3000 other mercenaries: the citizens numbered 10,000.[4] But some of the citizens were raw peasants, and Livy adds that all Nabis' confidence was reposed in the mercenaries.[5] We know that

---

[1] Pol. xiii. 7. 4. It is worth noting that once when Philopoemen was planning a raid into Laconia, he gave instructions as to what was to be done "if *the mercenaries* should come to the rescue and prove troublesome," with no mention of the Spartans (*id.* xvi. 37. 3).
[2] *Id.* xiii. 8. 2.   [3] *Ibid.* 6. 7 sqq.
[4] Livy 34. 27. 2. For Cretans again, cf. *id.* 32. 40. 4, where Nabis, at that time friendly to Rome, gave or lent at least 600 to Flamininus.
[5] *Id.* 34. 27. 2; 28. 8; cf. 35. 27. 15. For Nabis' bodyguard, cf. *id.* 34. 20 (no particulars).

he had garrisons in Gythium and Argos (1000), possibly in other places also; so that his total strength in mercenaries may be estimated at about 7000-8000 men.¹ In 192 B.C. "Tarentine" horse appear in his army against Philopoemen, as well as Cretans and other mercenaries.² Philopoemen had known upon what foundation the structure of Machanidas' tyranny had been based, and that Flamininus realized that the same held true for Nabis is shown by the terms of a peace treaty which he offered, but which Nabis refused. "The mercenaries of Nabis who have either returned to their own cities or have joined Flamininus are to receive their property entire: Nabis is to hold no city in Crete, and to deliver to Rome those that he actually does hold: he is to make no alliance with any Cretans, or with anyone else, and is not to go to war."³ Finally, when, after the death of Nabis, Sparta was coerced into joining the Achaean League, she ceased to be an independent military power. Her walls were razed, and "all foreign mercenaries who had served under the tyrants" were forced to quit Laconian soil.⁴ They had been for years her second wall of defence, and Livy's paraphrase of the agreement indicates that some of them were veterans of many years' service. One such veteran is still remembered to-day by his tombstone which has been recovered from the ruins of Sparta. He was Botrichus, an Arcadian captain of mercenaries who lived in the country of his profession with his wife Timo, and it is hard to believe that the six simple lines of his epitaph can conceal a ruffian of the type Polybius described:

> Τὸν δὲ ποτὲ Σπάρτα Βότριχον, ξένε, πολλὸν ἄριστον
> ἀνδρῶν αἰχματᾶν ἔτρεφεν ἀγεμόνα,
> κυδαίνοντ' ἀρετὰν Λακεδαίμονος, ἄν ποτ' ἐτίμα
> ἀλκαῖς Ἑλλάνων ἔξοχα ῥυόμενος.
> Νῦν δέ νιν Ἀρκαδίας ἀπὸ πατρίδος ὧδε θανόντος
> κουριδία Τιμὼ τύμβῳ ἔκρυψε ἄλοχος.⁵

¹ Livy 34. 29. 14.   ² Id. 35. 29. 1 sqq.
³ Id. 34. 35. 8.   ⁴ Id. 38. 34. 1.
⁵ I.G. v. 1. 724.

GREEK LEAGUES AND CITIES

3. THE ACHAEAN LEAGUE

The military importance of the Achaean League coincides almost exactly with the careers of its two great generals Aratus and Philopoemen (*ca.* 245–183 B.C.). Aratus virtually made the League into a military power of the first class. He was not even a member of it by birth, but became one of its leading figures by virtue of one startling feat of arms through which he obtained control of his native city Sicyon and was able to offer it to the League as a new member. The incident is typical both of the small acts of war which must have played a conspicuous part in the story of the more insignificant Greek states, and also of the coolness and resource of its young protagonist. Aratus lived as a boy in Argos, an exile from Sicyon and an enemy of the successive tyrants by whom Sicyon was controlled. He cannot have been much more than twenty years old when he decided to free his city and repatriate himself, and the way in which he set to work was to get into touch with one Xenophilus, "the foremost of the pirate (or brigand) chiefs", through whom he hired a few soldiers, spreading the report that he was meditating a raid into the territory of Sicyon in order to steal some horses of the tyrant. On the appointed day, before it was light, Aratus led his men along the road to Sicyon. It was not until they were on the march that he told them the real object of the expedition: he had practised upon his handful of cut-throats the same stratagem which Cyrus had practised upon the "Ten Thousand", and, like Cyrus, he promised that the broken contract should be amply compensated by the fruits of victory. The soldiers bore the deception well, followed Aratus over the deserted walls of Sicyon, surprised the tyrant's mercenaries and forced them to surrender without a blow, and within an hour were masters of the town. Whether they received their promised rewards is not related: the probability is that they were installed as the guardians of Sicyon instead of, or perhaps together with, the captured soldiers of Nicocles, and so became mercenaries of the Achaean League.[1]

The military resources of the League in the year 250 B.C. cannot have been very impressive. Achaeans had always indeed

[1] Plut. *Arat.* 6 sqq.

been good fighters, but there had never been an Achaean national army. They lived for the most part in small cities, and enjoyed no natural aids of soil or climate to bring them wealth. The door of commerce was closed to them, since their coastline included no really good harbour. Consequently the Achaeans were poor and weak, their combined strength being, as Plutarch says, less than that of one considerable city.[1] In Aratus' first year of office as general of the League (245 B.C.) he commanded an army of 10,000 men, which may represent nearly a full citizen levy with a force of mercenaries. For fully fifteen years after this date the League was constantly working and fighting against Macedonian supremacy in the Peloponnese. No army figures are obtainable for the years during the struggle, but its happy result for the Achaeans is reflected later in the fighting against Cleomenes of Sparta. The League had won from Macedonia (or her clients) the big cities of Corinth (243 B.C.), Megalopolis (235 B.C.) and Argos (229 B.C.), and had enlisted them as willing members. This meant a vast increase in military strength. On the one hand a greater population meant a greater citizen army, and on the other hand more wealth meant more mercenaries. Thus in 228 B.C. the Achaean army led by Aristomachus against Cleomenes numbered 20,000 infantry and 1000 cavalry.[2] It is clear that there were mercenaries among them, and indeed that it had become the practice of the League to employ them in its armies, for in the next year, after Aratus had been defeated by Cleomenes near Megalopolis, the angry citizens voted that his supplies of money should be stopped and the mercenaries left unpaid: if Aratus wanted to make war, he must provide for himself.[3] This was no more than a passing mood of defeatism, for mercenaries appear again in the army in 225 B.C.[4] At Sellasia three years later the Achaean reinforcement with Antigonus consisted of a picked force of citizens only:[5] this may have been in accordance with the wishes of Antigonus himself, or perhaps the League may have been too much exhausted to support mercenaries, having been very hard hit by Cleomenes.

The "War of the Allies" (220–217 B.C.) reveals the League

[1] Plut. *Arat.* 9. 4 sqq.
[2] *Id. Cleom.* 4. 4.
[3] *Id. Arat.* 37. 3.
[4] *Id. Cleom.* 17. 4.
[5] Pol. ii. 65. 3.

GREEK LEAGUES AND CITIES

restored to its old size and vigour, and throws further light upon the army question. The Achaeans recruited vigorously both cavalry and infantry mercenaries;[1] but they had in addition mercenaries who had fought for them against Cleomenes, and whose wages were still unpaid. There seems to have been some kind of strike on the part of the soldiers, for Aratus had difficulty in getting them into the field, and a later general suffered much from their undisciplined behaviour, which was aggravated by his own incompetence. In the end the mercenaries were disbanded, but upon what terms it is not possible to say. It is to be presumed that their employers, who had previously been unwilling to make the sacrifices necessary for retaining them, finally concluded that no price was too high that would ensure their departure.[2] The enemy had not failed to take advantage of this embarrassment. In particular the outlying western districts of Achaea had been exposed to the raids of the Aetolians using Elis as their base. In these circumstances three small Achaean communities—the Dymaeans, Pharaeans and Tritaeans—despaired of the central government and, resolving to take their own measures to protect themselves, recruited in common a mercenary force of 300 infantry and 50 horsemen.[3] It is curious to realize how small an army was large enough to protect a little Greek city in this type of guerilla warfare. The citizens themselves were probably competent to hold the small circumference of their city walls against raiders without a siege-train; but the presence of a small but mobile force of trained soldiers might save their farms from being plundered, or by harassing the enemy on their retreat compel them to abandon their booty.

But in the meantime Aratus had begun to set the affairs of the League as a whole upon a better footing. When he entered upon his year of office in 217 B.C. he found the mercenary army hopelessly reduced (κατειλήφει τὸ ξενικὸν κατεφθαρμένον); but he roused the Achaeans to a great effort, persuading them to vote a standing army of 8000 mercenary infantry and 500 horse, as well as the "guards" (ἐπίλεκτοι, 3000 foot, 300 horse) who represented the pick of the citizen troops.[4] In effect, what was probably the usual composition of the Achaean field army is

[1] Pol. iv. 37. 6.
[2] Ibid. 60. 2; v. 30. 5 sqq.
[3] Id. iv. 60. 4 sqq.
[4] Id. v. 91. 4.

here, for the time at least, crystallized into an army system. There were three distinct classes of soldiers. First, the mercenary, who was now to be maintained on a long-service contract; second, the picked citizen soldier who was to remain in arms for the duration of the war (this may have been an established practice already, witness the Achaeans at Sellasia, 3300 strong, and the same number earlier in this war—Polybius iv. 11. 16); finally the full citizen levy which could be called out in case of emergency, but was in fact called out only very rarely, and perhaps with increasing difficulty. The flaw in the system was that too much depended on the mercenaries. The ἐπίλεκτοι were probably very good, but they were very few for the purposes of so large a state: and the great force of mercenaries was a serious problem for the exchequer. It is almost ludicrous to think of a government embarking upon a war when it could pay its soldiers only if it were fortunate enough to win important spoils in the course of the fighting; but that is precisely what the Achaeans did here. Luckily for them, they did meet with success, and as a result the soldiers fought all the better for being certain of their pay, while the citizens heaved sighs of relief at the prospect of lighter taxation.[1] We can only conclude that the men in authority had grown to learn by experience that it was better to risk becoming defaulters towards their own mercenaries than to risk losing a war without mercenaries. There were certain things that citizen soldiers could not tolerate, and the chief of them was any kind of military service which kept them for long periods absent from their homes. Garrison duty was particularly distasteful. In 227 B.C. the Achaean League had been invited by the Mantineans to install a garrison in their city as a protection against Cleomenes. The affair was one of importance, for it would have been a great gain to win Mantinea as a permanent member of the League. Yet of the 500 soldiers who were sent, 200 were mercenaries—and the 300 citizens had to be chosen by lot.[2]

The rise of Philopoemen to the head of affairs in Achaea may have done something to reawaken popular enthusiasm for the art of war. Philopoemen had won his spurs with the cavalry at Sellasia under the critical eye of Antigonus Doson. He was a

[1] Pol. v. 94. 9.   [2] *Id.* ii. 58. 1 sqq.

GREEK LEAGUES AND CITIES

born soldier and his first taste of battle and victory may have caused him to chafe under the restraint of older and more cautious leaders. At all events he went to Crete soon after the battle, to gain experience in perhaps the hardest and toughest school of rough-and-ready fighting that the ancient world could afford. He was probably a captain of mercenaries.[1] When he returned to his native country he was just the man the Achaeans needed. Himself a cavalryman *par excellence*, he first devoted his attention to the citizen cavalry. This branch of the army was in a disgraceful condition. It was recruited from the wealthiest and most aristocratic citizens of Achaea, but that is not to say that he found it a "crack" corps or even a serviceable body of troops. The "knights" were in the habit, when a campaign was announced, of mounting themselves with any miserable "screw" that offered (φαύλοις ἱππαρίοις ἐκ τοῦ προστυχόντος), or more often than not they would send a substitute in their own place; this probably does not mean that they hired mercenaries privately, but that the rich man paid some poor dependent to run his risks and fight his battles for him. Philopoemen altered all that.[2] He also effected reforms in the citizen infantry, transforming it from some kind of light skirmishing troops into a force armed and trained to fight like Macedonians.[3] An even more important reform, which came later, was that by a system of special messengers he made possible a rapid mobilization in case of necessity, each city simultaneously sending out its quota to a prearranged point of concentration.[4] These innovations must have done much to restore the balance between citizen and mercenary service which had been destroyed by the successful proposals of Aratus in 217 B.C. But it must not be supposed that mercenaries were no longer employed. They are to be found constantly in the Achaean armies after Philopoemen no less than before him, a fact which lends point to the jeer of Flamininus: "O Philopoemen, what fine arms and legs you have —but you have no belly!" It was a home thrust, for Philopoemen, though he had excellent infantry and cavalry soldiers, was often short of money.[5]

[1] Plut. *Phil.* 7. 1 sqq.; Paus. viii. 49. 7. [2] Plut. *ibid.*
[3] *Ibid.* 7. 1 sqq.; Paus. viii. 50. 1; Polyaen. vi. 4. 3.
[4] Pol. xvi. 36. 3 sqq. For the system at work, cf. Livy 33. 14. 9 sqq.
[5] Plut. *Phil.* 2. 3.

In spite of the attention which he gave to the cavalry and the heavy infantry of the League, Philopoemen probably acquired in Crete a wholesome respect for Cretan methods of fighting with light armour and missiles, and it seems to have been to this department of the army that the mercenaries are to be assigned. At the battle of Mantinea (207 B.C.), the Achaean army was in three divisions, of which two consisted entirely of citizens, cavalry on the right wing and the phalanx in the centre. The third division was made up as follows: (1) Illyrians, (2) θωρακῖται, (3) εὔζωνοι, (4) mercenaries, (5) mercenary cavalry (extreme left).[1] Two interesting features are the first recorded appearance of barbarians with a League army, and the fact that Philopoemen himself chose to command the mercenary cavalry, who were probably light horse ("Tarentines").[2] Although Polybius calls only one of the four contingents of infantry making up the left wing by the specific name of mercenaries, yet his later account of the fighting makes it obvious that the εὔζωνοι are mercenaries too,[3] and possibly his original phrase—τὸ ξενικὸν ἅπαν καὶ τοὺς εὐζώνους—is loose writing for "the mercenary light infantry":[4] a similar criticism may apply to τοὺς Ἰλλυρίους καὶ θωρακίτας, for θωρακίτας by themselves must remain a mystery. The Illyrians can only be mercenaries, so that (if Polybius is convicted of inaccuracy) the whole of the left wing was in reality composed of mercenaries, which is very likely, since the citizen troops are accounted for elsewhere. In the battle the left wing retreated before Machanidas' mercenaries, but the probability is that Philopoemen withdrew it purposely: certainly he retained control of his men, so that at the critical moment, when Machanidas had pursued far enough and his own centre and right were victorious, he could stand his ground and force the enemy mercenaries to fight between two converging lines.[5] Such an interpretation best accounts for Philopoemen's commanding the mercenaries, and not the Achaean cavalry, or the Achaean phalanx: he could trust no one else to see that the left wing retreated in good order and retreated far enough, but not too far.

The influx of foreign mercenaries into the Peloponnese con-

---

[1] Pol. xi. 11. 4 sqq. (no figures).   [2] *Ibid.* 12. 6; Plut. *Phil.* 10. 1 sqq.
[3] Pol. xi. 11. 5; 13. 1.   [4] Plut. *Phil.* 10. 2 mentions ἀκοντισταί.
[5] Pol. xi. 12 sqq.

tinued in the early part of the second century. Philopoemen's second visit to Crete (204 B.C.), when he was employed as general by the city of Gortynia, probably established a close connection with one of the most prolific recruiting grounds:[1] soon after his return a Cretan *condottiere* is to be found fighting with the Achaeans against Sparta (201 B.C.).[2] In 197 B.C. a small League army (2000 foot, 100 horse) posted at Sicyon to watch the Macedonian garrison at Corinth, included Thracian cavalry, and probably consisted entirely of mercenaries.[3] The army of 192 B.C. acting against Nabis contained 500 Cretans and some "Tarentine" horse,[4] and Cretans appear again in the contingent of Mantinea to the League army in this campaign.[5] There were both Cretans and Thracians present in the Messenian expedition which cost Philopoemen his life (183 B.C.).[6] And the most striking testimony to the influence of Crete in particular upon the warfare of the Peloponnese at this time, is Livy's description (if accurate) of a small Achaean force which fought with the Romans in 171 B.C.: "the Achaeans provided 1000 of their own youth, *armed for the most part in the Cretan manner*".[7] It is a curious accident that the man who had so enthusiastically converted the Achaean infantry into a heavy-armed phalanx, should himself have become the indirect cause of its relapsing after his death into something which was the very antithesis of what he had intended.

The last war of the Achaean League was against Rome (146 B.C.). It was a hopeless enterprise, badly led and backed by no adequate reserves of money or men. In all probability few if any mercenaries can have been employed, though the anti-Roman demagogue Critolaus apparently had some sort of bodyguard.[8] But his successor was reduced to freeing and arming 12,000 slaves, and the shifts to which he was put to raise

[1] Plut. *Phil.* 13. 1 sqq. for Philopoemen in Crete.
[2] Pol. xvi. 37. 3.
[3] Livy 33. 14. 6 sqq.; 15. 3 sqq.
[4] *Id.* 35. 28. 8 sqq.; 29. 1 sqq.; cf. Pol. xxxiii. 16. 6. The Cretan officer was called Telemnastus, and his valour on this occasion was the cause of his son's later being favourably received by the Achaeans when he visited them as an envoy.
[5] Ditt. *Syll.*³ ii. 600.   [6] Livy 39. 49. 2.
[7] *Id.* 42. 55. 10.
[8] Pol. xxxviii. 13. 1, περισπασάμενος τοὺς στρατιώτας.

money hardly allow of his possessing any organized professional army requiring regular payment.[1] The Achaeans failed, as they would have failed against a less powerful antagonist than Rome. It is easy to generalize about decadence and a decline in civic virtue, but the story of the League leaves the reader in no doubt that these were contributory causes of its eclipse. Beloch saw that the Achaeans never fought at full strength:[2] even in the palmiest days of Aratus their largest army was little more than 20,000 strong, including mercenaries. In the fifth century a power controlling more than half of the Peloponnese would have fought without mercenaries, and at the end of the fourth century Megalopolis alone could arm 15,000 men, including slaves, to defend her walls against Polyperchon.[3] But the League was never without mercenaries: the luxury was accepted as a necessity from the very first. The inefficiency of the Achaean cavalry as Philopoemen found it was probably typical of the citizen army as a whole, with the possible exception of the ἐπίλεκτοι who were almost regular soldiers. There is even evidence for believing that in Philopoemen's lifetime it had become permissible for a city to include mercenaries in place of citizens in its contingent for the League army. An inscription of Mantinea (193–192 B.C.) preserves the names of some soldiers who left the city under the Mantinean contingent-commander (ἀποτελεῖος) to fight under Philopoemen against Nabis: the names are those of 13 Mantinean infantrymen, 7 Mantinean cavalrymen, and 7 Cretans.[4] What was the place of Cretans in a Mantinean citizen contingent? If they were not substitutes for citizen soldiers, they must at least have been members of a garrison employed by Mantinea because the citizens had ceased to guard their own city. If the practice of Mantinea here had been the practice of the Achaean cities in common,[5] there is little cause for surprise at the League's poor showing against Rome in 146 B.C., when few mercenaries were employed. There may, too, have been a decline in the population of the Peloponnese in the second century B.C., which

---

[1] Pol. xxxviii. 15. 6 sqq. [2] Beloch, *Bevölkerung*, p. 157.
[3] Diod. xviii. 70. 1 sqq. [4] Ditt. *Syll.*³ ii. 600 and nn. 1 and 5.
[5] There is no other evidence to prove that it was so; though in 218 B.C. in an Achaean force of 3300 (=the ἐπίλεκτοί?) under Aratus, the cavalry and light infantry (εὔζωνοι) were detached to act under the orders of an *Acarnanian* Epistratus, who was probably a mercenary officer (Pol. iv. 11. 16).

would account for the frequency with which foreign mercenaries, especially Cretans and Thracians, are to be found with Achaean armies. The evidence of Polybius is that in 170 B.C. the League *could* raise 30,000–40,000 fighting men; but of course it never did, and the figures themselves are not remarkably high considering that the League at that time embraced everything south of Corinth.[1] In a later passage Polybius admits that there was a decline in the latter half of the century, but he ascribes it not to the ravages of warfare or of pestilence, but to the psychological temper of the age. Money, he says, was considered the touchstone of happiness. There was a general aversion from marriage, and of the children born few were reared: a small family living in comfort or affluence was preferred to a large one with the likelihood of poverty.[2] The condition of mind which he describes will easily be understood by the modern reader. An age distinguished by a sophisticated materialism will naturally prefer the comfort of the individual to the safety or the glory of the State. The Greeks of the fifth century had regarded a campaign as no more than a part of their year's work: the Greeks of Polybius' day were content to resign that part of their work to specialists or professionals. And it is significant that of the professionals themselves an increasing proportion seems to have been recruited from the peoples which were less civilized than the Greeks. The supremacy of Greek mercenaries, even in Greece, was on the wane long before the final collapse of the Achaean League.

[1] Pol. xxix. 24. 8. [2] *Id.* xxxvi. 17. 4 sqq.

CHAPTER V

THE PTOLEMIES

OF the Hellenistic kingdoms Egypt has left by far the richest store of information concerning its machinery of government, including the affairs of its army. The army of Egypt as a whole has been reconstructed by more than one modern scholar, and notably by Jean Lesquier, whose book is the best and fullest work upon a military subject in this period.[1] Since we are concerned only with the mercenaries in the service of the Ptolemies, constituting no more than a part of the whole system as presented by Lesquier, the conclusions which he has reached upon the more general subjects will sometimes be quoted here without the tedium of retracing the steps by which he reached them. If his book has a fault, it is that it does not devote enough space to the mercenaries, being more interested in the "regular" army drawn from the military settlements, of which more will be said later. It is to this regular army that most of the papyrological evidence relates. The evidence which is the strict concern of this essay is more limited, though it is hoped that it will yet provide sufficient material from which to demonstrate the very great importance to the kings of Egypt of their mercenary soldiers. Our literary evidence deals mainly with two short periods of Egyptian history, the first from Alexander's death to the battle of Ipsus, the second covering a generation or so almost exactly a century later: the years in between are years of silence. Nevertheless, knowing something as we do of the Egyptian army in its infancy, and again of the same army after the experience of a century should have introduced a settled military system, it is possible in some way to trace the course of mercenary service throughout the whole period, and to supply missing information with more or less probable conjecture.

[1] J. Lesquier, *Les institutions militaires de l'Égypte sous les Lagides*, Paris 1911. Other shorter works are: P. M. Meyer, *Das Heerwesen der Griechen u. d. Römer in Ägypten*, Leipzig 1900; W. Schubart, *Quaestiones de rebus militaribus, quales fuerint in regno Lagidarum*, Diss. Breslau 1900. Of these two essays, which appeared simultaneously and independently, that of Meyer is of little value, but Schubart's is excellent as far as it goes.

THE PTOLEMIES

1. THE PTOLEMAIC ARMY BEFORE IPSUS, 323–301 B.C.

When Alexander died Egypt was still under the government of Cleomenes, the finance minister who had been installed nearly ten years previously at the time of the first settlement of the conquered land. This settlement had provided also for two "generals" in charge of the defence of the country, and mercenaries had been left behind when Alexander himself returned to Syria (p. 22, etc.).[1] But their numbers were insufficient for a force of defence, more especially as Cleomenes was an unpopular governor, and they were probably substantially increased. In 323 B.C. Ptolemy the son of Lagus received Egypt as his share of Alexander's empire. As far as we know, he went there without an army. But finding the finances in a flourishing condition, he at once "recruited mercenaries and made ready an army", and "his nobility caused a host of friends to flock to him"; an important addition this, since it would give him a supply of good officers.[2] He very soon had need of his new troops. In 322 B.C. a fortunate chain of events enabled him to win Cyrene, and in the next year he was called upon to resist an invasion of Egypt by the Regent Perdiccas. There are no figures either for the invading or for the defending army, but Ptolemy was quite strong enough to hold the line of the Nile at Pelusium. Moreover, deserters soon began to make their way from Perdiccas' camp to his, and when Perdiccas was finally murdered, a number of Macedonians joined the Egyptian army before they could be prevented.[3] But it is not until 315 B.C. that we meet with any figures for Ptolemy's army. In that year he sent out 13,000 mercenaries, under his brother Menelaus and an Athenian officer Myrmidon, as an expeditionary force working partly in Cyprus, partly in Caria; and at the same time he had in Palestine a considerable army of defence, which was forced to join Antigonus.[4] At the battle of Gaza (312 B.C.) Ptolemy commanded 18,000 infantry, 4000 cavalry, exclusive of native Egyptians. These figures represent "Macedonians and mercenaries", but it seems impossible that more than one-quarter, at the very most,

---

[1] Arrian, *Anab.* iii. 5. [2] Diod. xviii. 14. 1.
[3] *Ibid.* 19–21; 33–36.
[4] *Id.* xix. 62. 3 sqq.; 59. 2; 61. 5.

of the army was Macedonian.¹ The force at Gaza was the field army, and cannot have represented the full military strength of Egypt: although Diodorus does say that Ptolemy set out from Egypt "after collecting his forces from everywhere", it stands to reason that Cyprus and Cyrene could not be left denuded of soldiers, and the more so as disaffection in both these provinces had had to be put down by force earlier in this very year.² A minimum strength for the garrisons of the two would be 10,000 mercenaries, which would give Ptolemy a total strength, not counting Egyptians, of at least 32,000 men.³ It may be added that he took 8000 prisoners in the battle, mostly mercenary infantry.⁴

In the ten years after Gaza Ptolemy was an active member of the coalition against Antigonus and Demetrius. In the first place he was in a position to take the offensive, so that his expeditionary forces are to be found in southern Asia Minor, where he won over some of Antigonus' soldiers to his own army,⁵ and in Greece, where he captured, and for a time held, the fortresses of Corinth and Sicyon.⁶ But he had to maintain in addition the burden of guarding his frontiers against possible attack from the north, and in particular of defending Cyprus and Palestine, upon which an invasion of Antigonus must first fall: the importance of Cyprus is shown by the fact that Ptolemy's own brother Menelaus continued to be its governor.⁷ Demetrius' capture of the island in 307 B.C. must have been a terrible blow, involving as it did the loss of perhaps half the Egyptian army. The original garrison army of Menelaus was 12,000 infantry and 800 horse, plainly no match for Demetrius.⁸ Ptolemy himself brought from Egypt a reinforcement of 10,000 men. But the fate of the reinforcement, and of the island, was decided by the naval battle of Salamis, for after the Egyptian war-fleet had been beaten, many of the transports, containing nearly 8000 soldiers, fell into the

---

¹ Diod. xix. 80. 4, ἔχων πεζούς μὲν 18,000 ἱππεῖς δὲ 4000, ὧν ἦσαν οἱ μὲν Μακεδόνες, οἱ δὲ μισθοφόροι. This sentence can mean several things, but it is almost certainly correct to take the ὧν as referring back to both πεζούς and ἱππεῖς, and not to ἱππεῖς alone: nor can οἱ μὲν refer to πεζούς, οἱ δὲ to ἱππεῖς.
² Ibid. 79.
³ Ptolemy no doubt had *all* his Macedonians with him at Gaza.
⁴ Diod. xix. 85. 3; cf. 82. 4 and 84. ⁵ Id. xx. 19. 4 sqq.; 27. 1 sqq.
⁶ Ibid. 37. 1 sqq. ⁷ Ibid. 21. 1.
⁸ Ibid. 47. 3 sqq.

THE PTOLEMIES

hands of Demetrius, whereupon Menelaus, despairing of relief, abandoned Cyprus and his own army, the total number of Demetrius' prisoners exceeding 16,000.[1] And in the next year Ptolemy may have suffered similar losses in his other frontier province of Palestine, which was invaded by Antigonus at the head of a vast army of over 80,000 men. Resistance was out of the question. Ptolemy let Palestine go, but he held carefully prepared positions on the Nile, with his fleet to prevent a turning movement by sea; and above all he realized the victories to be won with a well-filled purse. When the two armies lay face to face, he offered high rewards to any of Antigonus' soldiers who would change sides. It was a successful move: Antigonus ended by posting slingers so as to shoot down deserters as they left the ranks, but he lost many men nevertheless, while Ptolemy was all the time making good his own losses of the previous year in Cyprus.[2] Antigonus' huge army was stopped by an army of little more, perhaps, than a quarter its size, backed with plenty of money. Ptolemy easily obtained new mercenaries, and sent 2000 to help Rhodes against Demetrius within the year.[3] Money was in fact at the root of the highly artificial military system which so early reveals itself in Egypt, and which must now be considered in some detail.

2. Macedonians, Mercenaries, and Egyptians

It will be found that the army of Egypt is to be divided into three classes of troops, classes which have already made their appearance in the army which fought at the battle of Gaza: (1) the Macedonians, (2) the mercenaries, (3) the Egyptians.[4] A century later, in the army at Raphia, precisely the same three classes are to be distinguished;[5] and they emerge also from the great mass of papyrological evidence relating to the army.[6] The fact is conclusively proved. What is harder is to determine the precise limits of class 2, the mercenaries, and to draw if possible a line of demarcation between it and class 1, the Macedonians.

---

[1] Diod. xx. 49. 1 sqq.; 52. 6; 53. 1; Plut. *Dem.* 16–17.
[2] Diod. xx. 75. 1 sqq.; 76. 7.   [3] *Ibid.* 88. 9; 98. 2.
[4] *Id.* xix. 80. 4.   [5] On the Raphia army, cf. pp. 118 sqq.
[6] E.g. in P. Petr. ii. 31 (*a*), cf. iii. 53 (*d*), ll. 5–6, are mentioned soldiers of each of the three classes.

But it will perhaps be best to dispose first of the Egyptians. At Gaza there was present "a mass of Egyptians", some of whom were used for the transport and commissariat, while others were armed combatants (πρὸς μάχην χρήσιμον).¹ At Raphia the Egyptians were a much more important part of the army, 20,000 heavy infantry.² It is thus probable that in the first place the Ptolemies had simply continued to use the military class of the Egypt of the Pharaohs, distinguished by this very name of μάχιμοι.³ Shortly before Raphia there was a revolutionary reform in the Egyptian part of the army, which accounts for the important part played by the Egyptian infantry in the battle. With a view to the coming struggle they were trained by Greek officers, armed in the Macedonian style, and recruited probably from the Egyptian population in general, and not merely from a closed class or order. And this reform, as Polybius points out, gave to the native population a power which it had hitherto lacked, and which is illustrated by the series of dangerous revolts which occurred at the end of the third century and later.⁴ The case for the Egyptian μάχιμοι is admirably put by Lesquier, and leaves no room for doubt that they were entirely separate from the Graeco-Macedonian divisions of the army.⁵ Nevertheless, it should perhaps be mentioned that P. M. Meyer had previously advanced the view that it was only the *name* μάχιμοι which survived from the Pharaohs' army system into that of the Ptolemies; that this name was now applied to the Macedonians and mercenaries indiscriminately (Meyer himself never discriminated between the two); and that there were in reality no Egyptian soldiers under the Ptolemies.⁶ The theory, which completely ignores the evidence of the papyri, is demolished by Lesquier with a thoroughness which makes it unnecessary ever to demolish it again.⁷ There are only two other points in connec-

---

¹ Diod. xix. 80. 4.   ² Pol. v. 65. 9.
³ Cf. A. Bouché-Leclercq, *Histoire des Lagides*, iv. pp. 2-4.
⁴ Pol. v. 65. 9; 82. 6; 107. 1 sqq.; cf. Lesquier, *op. cit.* p. 7.
⁵ Lesquier, pp. 5-10; 19-21; cf. 298; 310; 311 sqq.
⁶ Meyer, *op. cit.* p. 64 and n. 217; p. 82.
⁷ Lesquier, p. 8. The more important references proving the μάχιμοι to be Egyptians are: *C.I.G.* 4697, ll. 19 sqq. (the famous Rosetta stone); P. Tebt. App. I, pp. 546 sqq. (esp. 551 sqq.); *C.I.G.* ii. 2623; *B.C.H.* 1896, pp. 177 sqq. and 1897, p. 166 (inscription of Hermoupolis Magna); *U.P.Z.* i. 110; Pol. xv. 29. 1 sqq.; 25. 16; v. 36. 4.

THE PTOLEMIES

tion with the Egyptians which need detain us, namely the meaning of two slightly mysterious phrases occurring in papyri. The first is οἱ ἐν τῷ στρατιωτικῷ φερόμενοι, who are known from a document which deals with grievances of the Egyptians, both civilians (λαοί) and soldiers (μάχιμοι); between the two classes comes this third class of οἱ ἐν τῷ στρατιωτικῷ φερόμενοι. Lesquier submits that they were Egyptians who were soldiers but not cleruchs (it is clear from the document that they were in receipt of pay from the royal treasuries): it is sufficient for our purpose that they were certainly Egyptians here, and not hired foreign soldiers.[1] The other phrase which needs explaining is Ἕλλησι μαχ(ίμοις), which comes twice in the Tebtunis papyri, both documents dating from the first century B.C.[2] Lesquier admits that they may be our only clue to a new phase in the development of the army which otherwise escapes us completely; but it is far more probable, as he suggests, that the introduction into the μάχιμοι of Greeks and of other races, perhaps Arabs or negroes, is really a reflection of the fusion which must have taken place between the natives and the lower orders of the Greek population.[3]

It is now possible to ignore the Egyptian μάχιμοι entirely, since by no stretch of the imagination can they be represented as mercenaries. It remains to consider the Macedonians, and the mercenaries so called. Are they really two separate divisions of the army, as they appear to be, or are the Macedonians mercenaries in disguise? The evidence falls into three groups: (1) the literary evidence relating to the first twenty years of Ptolemy Soter's rule in Egypt, and especially the details of the army at Gaza, (2) the evidence of Polybius as to the army at Raphia a century later, (3) the evidence of papyri. The first of these groups we have already examined (above). It amounts, in brief, to this: Ptolemy comes to Egypt with no soldiers of whom we know; he finds there a garrison army of unknown strength, of which very few can be Macedonians, the rest being mercenaries; he recruits mercenaries in great numbers, so that it is

[1] *U.P.Z.* i. 110, esp. col. iv, ll. 100 sqq.; cf. Lesquier, pp. 19 sqq. For some further comments on this phrase, see below, p. 125.
[2] P. Tebt. i. 120, Introd. (97 or 64 B.C.); and *ibid.* 139 descr. (beginning of first century B.C.).
[3] Lesquier, p. 10.

possible for him within a few years to send abroad an expeditionary force of 13,000 mercenaries; he wins over numerous Macedonians (perhaps even several thousands) from the invading army of Perdiccas; he takes the field at Gaza with 18,000 infantry, 4000 cavalry, Macedonians and mercenaries; he captures 8000 prisoners in the battle, of whom less than 2000 are Macedonians;[1] he loses 16,000 prisoners in Cyprus, perhaps all mercenaries; he wins over deserters (number and kind unknown) from the invading army of Antigonus. From this it may be concluded that in 305 B.C., after the departure of Antigonus, Ptolemy's army, whatever its size exclusive of Egyptians, cannot have contained more than 5000 Macedonians at the very outside, and that the remainder were mercenaries. And it is important to stress the fact that, so far as can be seen, no king of Egypt, either before or after this date, could ever recruit from Macedonia direct.

Next, the Raphia evidence (217 B.C.). Polybius is at some pains to describe the different contingents or divisions of the army. He never uses the word "Macedonian" in respect of any division (or indeed in any sense whatever). It is therefore our duty to pick out such divisions as *could* be Macedonian. They are four in number: the 700 "household" cavalry, the 3000 royal guards, the 2000 peltasts, and the "phalanx".[2] All others are impossible.

Finally, the papyri contain abundant evidence for the existence in Egypt in the third and second centuries B.C. of a class of military settlers, and Lesquier has proved conclusively that these people were not merely discharged veterans, but active soldiers up to this point at least, that they were all *liable* to active service in the army if they were required. They were organized in military divisions (hipparchies and chiliarchies) and received *kleroi* of varying sizes, from 100 acres downwards. The majority of them was of Greek or Macedonian origin, though there was a strong representation of Thracians, and other barbarian settlers are known also.[3]

[1] The infantry of Demetrius which opposed him (the cavalry apparently either escaped or fell) amounted to 11,000 men—2000 Macedonians, 1000 Pisidians, 8000 mercenaries. There is no reason why *all* the Macedonians should have been among the 8000 prisoners: it is even possible that they all escaped, and that the mercenaries surrendered *en bloc*.
[2] Pol. v. 65. 2–4; cf. pp. 118 sqq.
[3] Cf. pp. 242 sqq. For the settlers in general, cf. Lesquier, especially pp. 42 sqq., 110 sqq., 291 sqq. (Appendix I). A certain amount of new evi-

THE PTOLEMIES

One may be convinced, therefore, of the existence in Egypt in the third century of a Graeco-Macedonian population of military settlers, who remain within a military organization and are not, nominally at least, mere pensioned veterans. The final link in the chain of evidence is the existence of a class known as οἱ ἐπίγονοι, the children of military settlers who receive a military training and (at least during that training) a payment from the State.[1] They are the young men who are destined to succeed their fathers in the ranks when they should become too old for military service, and in the tenure of their land when they died. Their military purpose is precisely the same as was that of Alexander's ἐπίγονοι in Asia,[2] so that the Ptolemaic system should now be plain enough. It was, to allot pieces of land to Greek and Macedonian soldiers on condition of their continued military service should they be required, and the training of their sons to succeed them both as soldiers and as cultivators of the soil. To examine the cleruch system in its legal and social aspect would require a separate essay, and is not relevant to this inquiry.[3] Its military purpose and effect is our field, and this purpose plainly was to found in Egypt a community capable of supplying the reliable army upon which a military monarchy must depend. In the Greek city states the citizens were the soldiers: the same was true of Macedonia. But in Egypt the Ptolemies could draw upon no such supply, since the native Egyptians were in the position of a conquered people. The cleruch system was introduced as an attempt to meet the need, to fill the vacant place of a citizen population whose well-being and existence was bound up in the well-being and existence of the State. The cleruch soldier in Egypt had thus more in common with the citizen soldier in Greece than with the mercenary, and that this distinction was admitted by the Ptolemaic

---

dence has come to light since the publication of Lesquier's book, but it concerns only matters of detail, and never affects his main conclusions.

[1] U.P.Z. i. 14. The ἐπίγονοι and οἱ τῆς ἐπιγονῆς are really not one class but two, but the difference between them (a matter of dispute) does not concern us. The question is discussed by Lesquier, pp. 52 sqq.; and cf. F. Heichelheim, *Die auswärtige Bevölkerung im Ptolemäerreich*, pp. 45 sqq., for Πέρσαι τῆς ἐπιγονῆς in the second century B.C. and later.

[2] Cf. Justin xii. 4. 8.

[3] Cf. Lesquier, pp. 202–54; Bouché-Leclercq, iv. pp. 13 sqq.; M. Rostovtzeff, *Studien z. Gesch. d. röm. Kolonates*, pp. 6 sqq.

authorities themselves may be taken as proved by the appearance (though rarely) of a different class of cleruch described in documents as μισθοφόροι (κληροῦχοι). The precise standing of the "mercenary cleruch" is one of the difficult questions to which some answer must be attempted;[1] but for the moment let us return to our "regular" cleruchs in an effort to trace them from their beginnings down to the army at Raphia, our original starting-point.

There appears to be no support for the assertion of Meyer that there were three "deductions" of cleruchs in Egypt, and no more than three.[2] It is far more likely that the process of colonization was a gradual one, carried on by successive kings according as they found themselves with soldiers and land to spare. There is quite good ground for believing that it was begun by Ptolemy I himself, and early in his reign. When he found himself after the battle of Gaza (312 B.C.) with 8000 of Demetrius' soldiers as his prisoners, he sent them to Egypt and ordered them to be dispersed about the several regions or districts—ὁ δὲ Πτολεμαῖος τοὺς μὲν ἁλόντας στρατιώτας ἀποστείλας εἰς Αἴγυπτον προσέταξεν ἐπὶ τὰς νομαρχίας διελεῖν.[3] It is possible that this sentence conceals the first stage in the cleruch system. Ptolemy may have felt himself unable to trust so large a force of prisoners should he take them into his own service as mercenaries, or he may have felt that they were more than he needed; or again, he may have thought that by making cleruchs of them he would gain so many loyal soldiers in case of need, and may already have had in mind the creation of a cleruch population to take the place of a population of citizen soldiers which he lacked. Whatever his motives may have been, one piece of evidence can be adduced in support of the view that he made cleruchs of his prisoners. In a certain papyrus mention is made of a cleruch who was "one of the prisoners of war from Asia":[4] the document is dated in the third year of an unnamed king, "probably Euergetes I" (editor's note *ad loc.*), which would make the date 244 B.C. If that is the correct date, clearly this man could not be a prisoner of Gaza; but the fact of his being both a prisoner and a cleruch proves that there *can* have

---

[1] Pp. 135 sqq.
[2] P. M. Meyer, *op. cit.* p. 32.
[3] Diod. xix. 85. 5.
[4] P. Petr. iii. 104.

THE PTOLEMIES

been prisoner-cleruchs under Soter—and indeed it would be a striking coincidence if this case of 244 B.C., the only case on record, was the very first case that ever existed. But there is no reason to think that all or even most of the cleruchs were prisoners of war. Ptolemy Soter's original Macedonians, comparatively few though they can have been, may have formed the nucleus of a cleruch system, and it is likely enough that Greek mercenaries were added from time to time to the list of cleruchs, who were to become Egypt's "regular" army as well as cultivators of her soil. It would not be surprising if, in the unbroken peace enjoyed by Egypt during the last twenty years of Ptolemy III (241–221 B.C.), the cleruchs became better and better farmers, but worse and worse as soldiers. Some such process would explain Polybius' comment to the effect that shortly before Raphia (217 B.C.) the military resources of Egypt were so weak that she could not protect herself from injury.[1] If the regular army had ceased to be a real force, it is easy to understand the elaborate preparations for the approaching war, the recruiting of mercenaries from Greece, the procuring of experienced Greek commanders, the training of the Egyptians to fight like Macedonians.[2] And if the military experts took these steps to renovate the army of Egypt, is it possible that they ignored the most obvious material that lay ready to their hand, the cleruch population, which needed only practice to make it a useful fighting unit once more? Finally, where did the Raphia "phalanx" come from, if not from the cleruch population? Although mercenaries were recruited for the occasion, and although the phalanx was drilled and trained along with the Greek mercenaries, the wording of Polybius shows very clearly that they were two distinct corps.[3] The men of the phalanx were not mercenaries. They can only have been the

[1] Pol. v. 62. 7–8, οἱ δὲ περὶ τὸν Πτολεμαῖον τοῦ μὲν ἐκ χειρὸς βοηθεῖν τοῖς σφετέροις πράγμασιν, ὅπερ ἦν καθῆκον, οὕτως παρεσπονδημένοι προφάνως, οὐδ' ἐπιβολὴν εἶχον διὰ τὴν ἀδυναμίαν· ἐπὶ τοσοῦτον γὰρ αὑτοῖς ὠλιγώρητο πάντα τὰ εἰς τὰς πολεμικὰς παρασκευάς.
[2] Ibid. 63. 8 sqq.; 64; 65.
[3] Ibid. 65. 3–4, ὁ δὲ Ἀχαιὸς Φοξίδας, καὶ Πτολεμαῖος ὁ Θρασέου, σὺν δὲ τούτοις Ἀνδρόμαχος ὁ Ἀσπένδιος, συνεγύμναζον μὲν ἐπὶ τὸ αὐτὸ τὴν φάλαγγα καὶ τοὺς μισθοφόρους Ἕλληνας· ἡγοῦντο δὲ τῆς μὲν φάλαγγος Ἀνδρόμαχος καὶ Πτολεμαῖος, τῶν δὲ μισθοφόρων Φοξίδας, οὔσης τῆς μὲν φάλαγγος εἰς 25,000, τῶν δὲ μισθοφόρων εἰς 8000. The 25,000 includes the Egyptian phalanx, cf. pp. 122–3.

118   HELLENISTIC MERCENARIES

military settlers, the representatives of the old Macedonian tradition of warfare going back through Gaza and Ptolemy Soter to the phalanx of Alexander and Philip.

3. Raphia: the army of Egypt at war strength

The two preceding sections have accounted for the presence at Raphia of Egyptian μάχιμοι, specially trained for the emergency to fight in a phalanx, and of the phalanx proper consisting of Graeco-Macedonian settlers. But in order to review the whole army at its war strength, and especially to discover the importance of mercenaries in Egyptian warfare, it is necessary to examine also the other contingents who make their appearance in the battle. They are:

1. 3000 royal guards (τὸ ἄγημα) — Pol. v. 65. 2
2. 2000 peltasts — Ibid.
3. 8000 Greek mercenaries — Ibid. 3–4
4.[1]
   - 700 Household cavalry (τοὺς περὶ τὴν αὐλήν)
   - — Libyan cavalry
   - — Egyptian cavalry

   Total 3000   Ibid. 5

5.
   - — Cavalry from Greece (τοὺς ἀπὸ τῆς Ἑλλάδος)
   - — Mercenary cavalry (πᾶν τὸ τῶν μισθοφόρων ἱππέων πλῆθος)

   Total 2000   Ibid. 6

6. 3000 Cretans (including 1000 "Neocretans") — Ibid. 7
7. 3000 Libyans armed in Macedonian style — Ibid. 8
8. 6000 Gauls and Thracians — Ibid. 10
   (4000 ἐκ τῶν κατοίκων καὶ ἐπιγόνων, 2000 newly recruited)

Grand total, adding the two "phalanxes" (25,000, cf. pp. 122 sqq.), 50,000 infantry, 5000 cavalry.

---

[1] No household cavalry cleruchs have come to light. And on the other hand, Polybius does not mention the cavalry of the "numbered" hipparchies or of the "racial" hipparchies (Lesquier, pp. 12 sqq.) who are known to have existed as cleruchs before this date. Polybius may have included both the numbered and the racial hipparchies in his mercenary cavalry—πᾶν τὸ τῶν μισθοφόρων ἱππέων πλῆθος. But if he has, it is impossible to reconcile his version with P. Petr. iii. 112, where "numbered" cavalry and μισθοφόροι ἱππεῖς appear, and are obviously distinct classes. See below, pp. 135 sqq.

THE PTOLEMIES 119

Taking the items in order, numbers 1, 4 and 7 are to be accounted for under the "regular" or Egyptian sections of the army; the guards were cleruchs of the highest class (100 acres), and the Libyans were probably recruited from subject peoples and trained along with the Egyptians. Of the items which remain, 3 and 5 are plain mercenaries. As for 2, the 2000 peltasts, there is absolutely nothing to show whether they were "regulars" (i.e. cleruchs) or mercenaries; Meyer thinks the latter. It may be suggested, on the other hand, that when Polybius says "peltasts" he means "hypaspists", in which case these people are a "crack" infantry corps, perhaps part of the Royal Guard. "Hypaspists" are mentioned by Polybius when he is speaking of the guard at Alexandria some years later (the only place where the word occurs in Polybius at all),[1] and it may be significant that these peltasts are put next in the list to the ἄγημα. Moreover, there are passages in Polybius relating to warfare in Greece, where he speaks of Macedonian "peltasts" when he may really mean "hypaspists".[2] The point is a small one, and must be left doubtful. Passing on to item 6, the Cretans are almost certainly mercenaries, and the "Neocretans" among them may be Cretans fighting in a new style.[3] Finally the 6000 Gauls and Thracians (8) explain themselves: 2000 of them are newly recruited mercenaries, the remainder cleruchs, and the fact that some of them are ἐπίγονοι shows that they are sons of long-established settlers, and hence members of the "regular" army.[4]

The mercenaries of Raphia are, then, as follows: 2000 peltasts (?), 8000 Greek infantry, 2000 cavalry, probably 3000 Cretans, 2000 Gauls and Thracians. The total is 13,000 (or 15,000) infantry, 2000 cavalry: that is to say, two-fifths of the cavalry in the battle were mercenaries, and rather more than a quarter of the infantry. This is the result of the elaborate preparations, the concentration of mercenaries from the garrisons, and the

---
[1] Pol. xv. 25. 3, συνεκάλεσαν τοὺς ὑπασπιστὰς καὶ τὴν θεραπείαν, where ὑπασπιστάς might = the peltasts of Raphia, τὴν θεραπείαν might = τὸ ἄγημα of Raphia. On the other hand, the whole phrase may be a paraphrase of τὸ ἄγημα.
[2] Id. v. 21. 3 sqq.; cf. Livy 33. 4. 4.
[3] P. 144 and n. 2, for the question of Neocretans.
[4] Cf. P. Edgar i. 3, from which it seems certain that already in the reign of Ptolemy II the village of Pitos, south of Memphis, contained numerous Thracian settlers.

recruiting of new ones from Greece.[1] In relation to the large numbers for the whole Egyptian army, the result may not appear particularly impressive. But it must be remembered that *some* mercenaries must still have remained in the garrisons, which, though they may have been weakened to strengthen the field army, cannot have been withdrawn altogether: and also if only half of the mercenaries in the battle were recruited from Europe as Polybius says, yet that number (about 8000) is at least as high as can reasonably be expected.[2] Including the garrison troops, there must have been at least 25,000 mercenaries in Egyptian pay in the year 217 B.C.[3]

The year of Raphia gives us our only opportunity of inspecting the war strength of Egypt on land while the military system of the Ptolemies was still flourishing. The army at Raphia was the outcome of exceptional efforts on the part of the government, though it is true that those efforts were made necessary by the exceptional conditions produced by the twenty years of peace which preceded this war. As far as the mercenaries in the army are concerned, it is easy to see that there were already mercenaries before the great effort was made, namely those who were called up from the garrisons to fight in the battle; and in addition there were the new mercenaries who were recruited especially with a view to this war. The implication is that the soldiers from the cleruchies, even when they were here reinforced with an up-to-date Egyptian phalanx, still left something to be desired. Assurance was made doubly sure if mercenaries were recruited from the north. This principle is to be suspected even before Raphia, in the period of the great Syrian wars, which have, unfortunately, no literary history for our purposes. The solitary piece of evidence relates to the reign of Ptolemy II. In 274 B.C., his half-brother Magas, whom he had made governor of Cyrene, declared himself independent, and Egypt was in

[1] Pol. v. 63. 8–9, ἀνεκαλοῦντο δὲ καὶ συνήθροιζον εἰς τὴν Ἀλεξανδρείαν τοὺς μισθοφόρους τοὺς ἐν ταῖς ἔξω πόλεσιν ὑπ' αὐτῶν μισθοδοτουμένους. ἐξαπέστελλον δὲ καὶ ξενολόγους καὶ παρεσκεύαζον τοῖς προϋπάρχουσι καὶ τοῖς παραγιγνομένοις τὰς σιταρχίας.
[2] Polybius does not specifically say from Europe, but it must have been so —e.g. 2000 Gauls and Thracians, some Cretans (?), and some cavalry from Greece: how many of the 8000 Greek infantry were newly recruited it is impossible to say.
[3] Mercenaries in the garrisons will be discussed in the next section.

THE PTOLEMIES

danger. Ptolemy, "making ready to resist the attack of Magas, engaged, amongst other mercenaries, 4000 Gauls".[1] After Raphia, however, several cases are known of recruiting for an emergency. In 203 B.C. the Aetolian Scopas, who held a high position at the court, was sent to Greece to recruit soldiers with a view to the war with Antiochus the Great. This was the occasion of his enlisting 6500 of the Aetolian youth, and he was prevented from draining the country completely only by the expostulation of the general of the League.[2] In 190 B.C., when Ptolemy V was campaigning in Egypt against the rebel chieftains, he received a reinforcement of mercenaries who had been recruited in Greece by his warlike eunuch Aristonicus.[3] Again, in 168 B.C. the brother-kings, Philometor and Euergetes II, at the mercy of Antiochus IV, tried to protect themselves by sending for a reinforcement from their ally the Achaean League, and also for a mercenary force of 1000 men.[4] The last case on record is hardly parallel. Ptolemy Philometor had quarrelled with his brother and fled to Rome for redress. Rome divided the kingdom between the two, and Philometor promptly went to Greece and raised an army (ξενολόγιον ἐμβριθές). He was persuaded to disband it and return to Egypt in peace, and contented himself with recruiting 1000 mercenaries in Crete on his journey, presumably to serve him as a bodyguard when he landed (163 B.C.).[5]

These scraps of information are not really very helpful, because there is no means of regaining touch with the Ptolemaic field army as a whole in this period. One knows that the victory of Raphia was said to be chiefly due to the new phalanx of Egyptians; but one knows also that this development was eventually a source of trouble to the government, and it may be suspected that the new phalanx can scarcely have proved a permanent source of strength to the kingdom. More probably the government soon looked for greater strength in the mercenaries and

---

[1] Paus. i. 7. 2. As it turned out they did him no good. Magas' invasion was frustrated by a revolt in his rear which forced him to return: Ptolemy was then prevented from pursuing him by the disaffection of the Gauls, whom "he took to a desert island in the river, where they perished by hunger and each other's swords".
[2] Pol. xv. 25. 16 sqq.; Livy 31. 43. 5 sqq.   [3] Pol. xxii. 17.
[4] Id. xxix. 23. 5 sqq.   [5] Id. xxxi. 17.

the old phalanx of cleruchs, as a means of coercing the disaffected Egyptians.[1] And this brings us to the question of the importance of the recruited mercenaries relative to that of the cleruch soldiers in the army; or (simplifying the issue still further) how strong really was the "regular" phalanx? The only means of answering this question is by deciding how strong the "regular" phalanx was at Raphia—the only occasion for which there is any information. The answer ought to be simple, because Polybius describes the army in detail; but unfortunately it is by no means certain if Polybius knew exactly what he meant when he was writing about the phalanxes, or if he did know he has at least succeeded in obscuring his meaning from the casual reader. First, when he enumerates the separate contingents of the army, he mentions "the phalanx" under Andromachus and Ptolemaeus, 25,000 strong; and later, in the course of the same enumeration, he mentions "the Egyptian phalanx" of 20,000 under Sosibius. This gives the impression that the combined phalanx numbered 45,000, and this was undoubtedly Polybius' own opinion, because his total for the army is 70,000 infantry, which is just right with a combined phalanx of this size.[2] But next, in his order of battle he seems to omit the Graeco-Macedonian phalanx altogether, perhaps because it was in the very centre of the army, and he enumerated the contingents by working inwards from each wing in turn.[3] In the battle itself he leaves no doubt that both phalanxes were there, fighting together in the centre, because the *two* generals Andromachus and Sosibius are twice mentioned as the commanders of the combined phalanx, which ultimately won the battle for Ptolemy.[4] And finally, Raphia was regarded as primarily an "Egyptian" victory.[5] It was Mahaffy who first saw that if the Ptolemaic phalanx were really 45,000 strong as Polybius says, and the Egyptians comprised less than half of it, Raphia could not be called an Egyptian victory.[6] This was a strong argument, and

[1] Cf. Pol. v. 107. 1 sqq. (a generalization); it is implicit in the internal history of Egypt subsequently.
[2] *Ibid.* 65. 3 and 9; 79. 2.   [3] *Ibid.* 82. 1–6.
[4] *Ibid.* 83. 3; 85. 9; 86. 1.   [5] *Ibid.* 107. 1 sqq.
[6] *Hermathena*, x. (1899), pp. 140 sqq., followed by W. W. Tarn in *C.A.H.* vii. p. 730, and M. Cary, *History of the Greek World, etc.* p. 405. Mahaffy himself however did not accept an Egyptian phalanx of 20,000, and proposed to expunge it from the text of Polybius (v. 63. 9): I do not see the necessity for this.

THE PTOLEMIES

becomes conclusive when one considers that a superiority in phalanx of 45,000 to Antiochus' 20,000 must certainly have been reflected in the Ptolemaic tactics. Raphia, as it was actually fought, was at one time a lost battle for Ptolemy: had Antiochus, instead of pursuing too far, used his victorious cavalry to take the phalanx in flank and rear, he could have destroyed it while it was still waiting for the command to engage. Why had this command not been given earlier? Perhaps because the Ptolemaic generals were doubtful about the new Egyptian phalanx. But if the Egyptians were less than half of the whole phalanx, and the cleruch phalanx alone outnumbered that of Antiochus, why should they hesitate? Clearly, in those circumstances they would have thrown their overwhelmingly superior phalanx into the battle at the earliest possible moment, and would not have risked losing everything by being defeated on one wing while the phalanx stood inactive. Undoubtedly the right conclusion must be that Polybius muddled the two Ptolemaic phalanxes when he was getting out his figures: the *combined* phalanx was 25,000, of which 20,000 were the new Egyptians.

This conclusion is of real importance to us. If the Graeco-Macedonian phalanx at Raphia numbered only 5000, then the whole number of military settlers in the army of 50,000 cannot possibly have exceeded 15,000:[1] and this only as the result of an extraordinary period of training by which the "regular" army had been rescued from perfect inefficiency and decay.[2] This is a poor recommendation for the cleruch system in the third century, and one must conclude that very much must have depended on the other sections of the army and especially on the mercenaries. The attempt to create a substitute for a national army must be judged a failure: and when the real national army, the Egyptians, came into existence, it served its immediate purpose indeed of repelling Antiochus, but soon became an embarrassment.

In these circumstances what can have been the later history

---

[1] I.e. the phalanx proper (5000), the ἄγημα (3000), perhaps the peltasts (2000), the cavalry περὶ τὴν αὐλήν (700), and two-thirds of the Gauls and Thracians (4000); cf. p. 118.
[2] Pol. v. 62. 7 sqq. and 63. 11 sqq. Admittedly these passages must refer partly to the new Egyptian phalanx; but 64. 1 sqq. refers definitely to a previously existing army now reorganized.

of the Graeco-Macedonian "regulars"? We do not know, but we may guess that for a short time at least after Raphia they remained an army in fact as well as in name; they must have been used freely during the great Egyptian rebellion which broke out almost immediately, and very likely they were strengthened by the admission of new cleruchs from among the mercenaries newly recruited from Greece. This new lease of life may be reflected in the composition of the Royal Guard at Alexandria, which certainly seems to be different in 202 B.C. from what it had been in 221 B.C. (pp. 126 sqq.). But after 202 B.C. there is very little positive evidence. The existence of cleruch soldiers in the second century is perfectly well established—but so it is for the period before Raphia, when in effect the system, as a military system, had broken down. One would perhaps have suspected that in the second century it might have relapsed again rather rapidly, and this time beyond recovery, were it not for some new evidence published only last year. Two documents of about the middle of the second century contain references to troops whom one may suppose to have been none other than the "regular" infantry and cavalry, and these troops seem to have been engaged in active service, in the one case apparently on garrison duty, in the other as a reinforcement to the police in a time of unrest.[1] But since the same set of documents contains also references to μισθοφόροι,[2] it is evident that the old policy of employing mercenaries still persisted, and that the ideal of a purely "national" army was no nearer to being realized. The loss of the empire overseas to Philip V, the collapse before Antiochus IV in 170 B.C., and the subsequent dependence upon Rome in questions of foreign policy, all argue a military weakness that could not be overcome. One is perhaps to conclude that the army of Raphia was the last real army that Egypt ever put into the field. As we have seen, there are occasional notices of the later Ptolemies hiring mercenaries for this purpose or that, and these notices may really represent the true policy of

---

[1] P. Tebt. iii. i. 722. 10 sqq., τοῖς ἐν τῷ νομῷ πεζοῖς ὑπαίθροις τοῖς ἐκ τοῦ Μακεδονικοῦ... (*ca.* 157 B.C.); *ibid.* 736. 47 sqq., (100) τῶν κατοίκων ἱππέων called out to reinforce the police (143 B.C.); cf. *ibid.* 729. 2 sqq., a cleruch absent from his *kleros* κατὰ βασιλικὴν χρείαν (154/3 or 144/3 B.C.); this is perhaps to say that he is on military service?

[2] *Ibid.* 736. 11 and 723. 3 (137 B.C.).

THE PTOLEMIES

the time—to keep out of trouble whenever it was possible, and when it was not possible, to hire some soldiers to fight until the trouble was over.

4. THE PEACE STRENGTH OF THE ARMY

In time of peace many, perhaps most, of the cleruch soldiers must have ceased to be active members of the army, but there is no means of telling to what extent they were used for duty in garrisons at home and abroad, though there is some evidence for their activity in the Royal Guard at Alexandria (below). It seems possible that the peace strength of the army might become clearer if one could know for certain what is the meaning of the obscure phrase οἱ ἐν τῷ στρατιωτικῷ φερόμενοι. Lesquier's interpretation based on a document of the second century— "Egyptian soldiers on active service but not cleruchs"[1]—became impossible in the light of a more recently published document dating from about 250 B.C.,[2] supported by another reference (156 B.C.) which Lesquier had missed.[3] It is now certain that the phrase includes Greeks as well as Egyptians, and probably Schubart's interpretation of it is generally accepted—military people in the widest sense, as opposed to civilians:[4] it certainly includes ἐπίγονοι, who were probably not full soldiers, but undoubtedly were military people in some sense.[5] Nevertheless, it seems possible that, though Lesquier's interpretation was too narrow, Schubart's may perhaps be too wide. Of the three qualifications proposed by Lesquier (Egyptian—active—non-cleruch), only one has so far been proved wrong: οἱ ἐν τῷ στρατιωτικῷ φερόμενοι were not necessarily Egyptians. On the other hand there is every reason to think that the second qualification is right, for in two of the three documents which comprise our evidence, the phrase is applied to persons whom we know to have been in receipt of pay from the royal treasury.[6]

[1] Lesquier, pp. 19 sqq., using *U.P.Z.* i. 110, ll. 103, 162, 175, and cf. Wilcken's notes (=P. Paris 63).
[2] *Dikaiomata* i. 161 and p. 94, τῶν ἐν τῷ στρατιωτικῷ τεταγμένων.
[3] *U.P.Z.* i. 15. 9–10 (=P. Vat. E), ὅπως φέρηται ἐν τῷ στρατιωτικῷ.
[4] *G.G.A.* 1913, p. 614 (review of Lesquier), accepted by Wilcken, *U.P.Z.* i. p. 492.   [5] *U.P.Z.* i. 15 and 14.
[6] *U.P.Z.* i. 14. 24 sqq. and 15. 9 sqq. (the ἐπίγονος Apollonius); *ibid.* 110. 103 sqq., καὶ ὀλίους (*sic*) δὲ καὶ τῶν ἐν τῶι στρατιωτικῶι φερομένων καὶ τὴν ἀναγκαίαν τροφὴν μόλις ἐχόντων ἀπὸ τῶν ἐκ τοῦ βασιλικοῦ τιθεμένων...

It is very unlikely that any "military person" was paid for doing nothing, and in the case of the ἐπίγονος it is known that he was not merely the holder of a title: these two considerations make it at least very probable that the class of οἱ ἐν τῷ στρατιωτικῷ φερόμενοι in general included only *active* military persons. With regard to Lesquier's third qualification, it is difficult to reach a certain decision without more evidence; but since the cleruchs were certainly intended to become active soldiers when required, it seems impossible to exclude them altogether from this category. Moreover, the words στρατιώτης, στρατεία, στρατεύεσθαι in Ptolemaic documents appear always to refer to people in active service, and there is one certain case where στρατιῶται are cleruchs.[1]

The proposed translation, therefore, of οἱ ἐν τῷ στρατιωτικῷ φερόμενοι is "people on the active army list", or something like it. If this is correct, it must include the whole of the standing army of the Ptolemies,[2] and we have seen already that it includes both Graeco-Macedonian cleruchs and (in the second century) Egyptians. With regard to the mercenaries it has given us no explicit information, and for them one must turn to the scattered evidence referring to the army in time of peace. This will be considered in two sections, first the evidence for the troops at Alexandria, where the Royal Guard had its quarters, and secondly for the numerous garrisons both in Egypt and overseas.

i. *The troops at Alexandria.*

The Royal Guard was perhaps originally no more than a body of "Companion" cavalry and a corresponding body of infantry, each derived from the "Companions" of Philip and Alexander.

---

[1] P. Cairo Zen. ii. 59242. 2, τῆς καταμεμετρημένης γῆς τοῖς στρατιώταις (252 B.C.).
[2] Since it included the ἐπίγονοι, it may also have included other classes of a doubtful status, such as the φυλακῖται and κυνηγοί. The latter were certainly used for the elephant hunt in the south, but the evidence quoted by P. Roussel, *R.E.G.* 43 (1930), pp. 364 sqq., makes it seem very likely that they were also used by the Ptolemies for work in garrisons; cf. especially Aen. Tact. 22. 14; Plut. *Arat.* 8 and 24, for examples of such work in the Peloponnese, and *O.G.I.S.* i. 20, for κυνηγοί in conjunction with a φρούραρχος at Citium in Cyprus, where the obvious inference is that they formed part of the Ptolemaic garrison. I think the balance of probabilities is in favour of their belonging to the Ptolemaic army (so Lesquier, p. 353; Wilcken, *Grundzüge*, p. 387; for a different view cf. M. Rostovtzeff, *Archiv*, iv. p. 304; v. p. 181).

THE PTOLEMIES

These two corps both appear in the Raphia army, under the names τὸ ἄγημα (3000 strong), and τοὺς περὶ τὴν αὐλὴν ἱππεῖς (700).[1] But at some later date, perhaps after the army reforms of 218 B.C., Egyptian soldiers too were included in the guard. The full title of these Egyptian guards was περὶ τὴν αὐλὴν ἐπίλεκτοι μάχιμοι;[2] the word ἐπίλεκτοι in this connection can apply to the Egyptian guards only, and is not the name for the guard as a whole, as Meyer took it to be.[3] Thirdly, there were mercenaries in the guard. But it is probably misleading to give the impression that the guard was permanently composed of these three classes, "regulars", Egyptians, and mercenaries.[4] The literary evidence on the subject shows that it varied considerably from time to time, and the variations follow the lines which we should expect them to follow.

In 221 B.C., the mercenaries seem to have been the most important part of the guard. The royal minister Sosibius wishes to make the throne safe for the new king Ptolemy Philopator, and to that end plans to murder Philopator's mother and brother. But he is afraid of the soldiers, τοὺς ξένους καὶ μισθοφόρους—no others are mentioned. Cleomenes, the exiled Spartan king, who is in the plot, reassures him by saying that the mercenaries will not hurt him, but will in fact help him. Sosibius is surprised. "Do you not see", says Cleomenes, "that nearly 3000 are mercenaries from the Peloponnese, and 1000 are Cretans? I (ἡμεῖς) have only to give them the sign, and they will all obey. If they get together, whom do you fear? The soldiers (στρατιώτας) from Syria and Caria, I suppose?"[5] The picture evoked by Cleomenes' words is of a mercenary force in Alexandria, of whom 4000 are Peloponnesians and Cretans, and strong enough to carry the day against the opposition of the others (i.e. perhaps a half of the whole force?). Cleomenes' reference to the soldiers from Syria and Caria—τίνας ἀγωνίας; ἢ δῆλον τοὺς ἀπὸ Συρίας καὶ Καρίας στρατιώτας;—is contemptuous: it may imply that Peloponnesians and Cretans will soon

---

[1] See above, p. 118.   [2] *Bull. Soc. Arch. Alex.* iv. 1902, p. 94.
[3] P. M. Meyer, *op. cit.* p. 64, and note 214; cf. *U.P.Z.* i. 110, l. 21; Pol. (v. 82. 2) uses ἐπιλέκτους to denote apparently the whole Egyptian phalanx, but probably wrongly.
[4] Lesquier does give this impression, pp. 21–4.
[5] Pol. v. 36. 1 sqq.

settle with a pack of Asiatics; or, more probably, it refers to the Ptolemaic garrisons in Asia. The fact remains that the people to be reckoned with were other mercenaries: Cleomenes does not say "Whom do you fear? The ἄγημα, I suppose?", or "the soldiers from the cleruchies", or "the Egyptian guards". The Egyptian guards did not exist at this time, if they were, as they may have been, a product of the preparations before Raphia. But we know of the existence of the ἄγημα in 236–235 B.C.:[1] that is to say, we know of two soldiers who belonged to it, but we do not know that it was equal to the ἄγημα of Raphia in size or efficiency. A likely explanation of Cleomenes' confidence in the mercenaries from Crete and the Peloponnese, is that the ἄγημα had fallen upon evil days, just as had the phalanx before Raphia, and may have become small and inefficient, or even non-existent. However that may be, this conversation of the two conspirators proves that in 221 B.C. the important soldiers at Alexandria were the mercenaries.

The next piece of evidence concerns the events which followed the death of Ptolemy Philopator (204–203 B.C.). The minister Agathocles wishes to ensure the succession of the young Epiphanes by winning the support of the soldiers. He accordingly sends Scopas the Aetolian to Greece as a recruiting officer on a grand scale: he wants mercenaries for the coming war with Antiochus, but he has a plan also for ridding himself of the mercenaries already at Alexandria and refurnishing the guard with soldiers of his own recruiting upon whom he can rely.[2] But events move too fast for him, and when the mercenaries of Scopas arrive Agathocles is already in need of them. The story that follows is exciting enough, and the struggle for supremacy between the two parties, that of Agathocles and that of his rival Tlepolemus (and Moiragenes), turns on the temper of the soldiers of the guard. But its importance for us lies in the minor details of Polybius' thrilling narrative. In the first place, there is more than one class of soldier in the guard, but one of the classes predominates in importance. Agathocles summons to an

[1] P. Petr. i. 11 = iii. 12, l. 19.
[2] Pol. xv. 25. 16 sqq., ... τοὺς ἀρχαίους καὶ προϋπάρχοντας ξένους ἐπὶ τὰ κατὰ τὴν χώραν φρούρια καὶ τὰς κατοικίας ἀποστεῖλαι, τοῖς δὲ παραγενομένοις ἀναπληρῶσαι καὶ καινοποιῆσαι τὴν θεραπείαν καὶ τὰ περὶ τὴν αὐλὴν φυλακεῖα, παραπλησίως δὲ κατὰ τὴν ἄλλην πόλιν....

THE PTOLEMIES

assembly "the hypaspists and the bodyguard (θεραπείαν), and along with them the officers of the foot and horse":[1] that is to say, the hypaspists and the bodyguard are more important here than the foot and the horse, who are represented by their officers only. And Polybius always in this story calls them "Macedonians".[2] Again, it is to the camp of the "Macedonians" that Moiragenes first goes when he incites the soldiers against Agathocles: when a band of the "Macedonians" is won over, the movement spreads first through the rest of their camp, and then to the camp (or camps) "of the other soldiers".[3] Who were the "Macedonians"? Obviously they were not born in Macedonia. Equally obviously there is some reason for their name, something which connects them with the Macedonians who fought with Alexander and the first Ptolemy. It can scarcely be doubted that they were the ἄγημα of Raphia still surviving after fifteen years, "regular" soldiers whom we meet in papyri with cleruchies of 100 acres to their name.[4] And "the other soldiers"? Possibly the phrase includes the Egyptian guards (see above). Quite certainly it must include the mercenaries for whom Agathocles had been anxious to substitute his own recruits from Greece. It follows that the guard of 202 B.C. differed materially from that of 221 B.C. In the latter mercenaries were predominant, if indeed they were not the whole guard in themselves: here the ἄγημα of "regulars" is the most important part of the guard, although there were certainly mercenary members of the guard as well.

We never have the chance of observing the guard in action after 202 B.C. But there is reason to think that in the second century the pendulum reverted to its pre-Raphia position, and that most or all of the soldiers at Alexandria were mercenaries.

[1] Pol. xv. 25. 3.   [2] Ibid. 26 sqq., passim.
[3] Ibid. 28. 4 sqq., καὶ μετὰ ταῦτα διελθὼν τὴν αὐλὴν ἀνελπίστως παρέπεσε γυμνὸς εἴς τινα σκήνην τῶν Μακεδόνων, σύνεγγυς κειμένην τῆς αὐλῆς. Ibid. 29. 1–2, οἱ δὲ Μακεδόνες ἀκούσαντες τούτων παροξύνονται, καὶ πέρας ἐπείσθησαν τῷ Μ., καὶ πρώτας εὐθέως ἐπήεσαν τὰς τῶν Μακεδόνων σκηνάς, μετὰ δὲ ταῦτα τὰς τῶν ἄλλων στρατιωτῶν· εἰσὶ δὲ αὗται συνεχεῖς, πρὸς ἓν μέρος ἀπονενευκυῖαι τῆς πόλεως.
[4] The only soldier of the ἄγημα whose provenance is known is an Arcadian (a cleruch). But "Macedonians" is an obvious name for a corps patently modelled upon the foot-guards of Alexander: and it is probable that originally the ἄγημα was recruited mainly from Macedonian settlers. But see Lesquier, pp. 120 sqq., on the unreliability of "race" names, especially in the second century.

According to Strabo, Polybius deplored the condition of the city in his own time (under Euergetes II); it was inhabited by three classes or races (γένη): (1) the Egyptians; (2) the soldiers (τὸ μισθοφορικόν)—"for according to their ancient custom the soldiers whom they kept were mercenaries (or foreigners?—ξένους ἔτρεφον τοὺς τὰ ὅπλα ἔχοντας), who had learnt to rule rather than be ruled, because the kings were nonentities"; (3) the Alexandrians, "they too possessing no real political ability, for the same reasons, but they were better than the others all the same, for they were Greeks in the first place, if mixed, and had some recollection of the Greek code".[1] This would suggest that in the latter half of the second century the Alexandrian army was all mercenaries, and mostly foreigners. Certainly it is true of the army in 48 B.C., when Julius Caesar was in Alexandria. Its commander Achillas had under him 20,000 men, ? including 2000 cavalry. Some of them were "the Gabinian soldiers", Roman legionaries who had been long enough in Alexandria to assume the vices of their environment. But the rest were pirates and bandits from Syria and Cilicia, outlaws, exiles, and fugitive slaves. "These men had been accustomed to demand the heads of the kings' friends, to plunder the property of the rich, to besiege the royal palace for a rise in wages, to expel (kings) from the kingdom and to summon others in their stead: this was a kind of immemorial privilege of the army of Alexandria."[2] Nothing is said of a cleruch army, nor can it be admitted that the men whom Caesar describes may have been cleruchs. They are mercenaries receiving wages, and their behaviour is that of mercenaries who have been allowed to get out of hand, not of cleruchs who owe their land to the king. It was certainly a mercenary army to which Caesar found himself opposed, and there is no reason to doubt his word when he says that such had been the army of Alexandria for years. Probability in fact lies all in that direction. It needed a great effort to renew the cleruch army, as an army, for the Raphia war. The effects of that effort are still visible fifteen years later at the time of the fall of Agathocles. But if no similar effort was made during a century and a half after that time (and we know of none),

[1] Pol. xxxiv. 14 (apud Strabo 797 sqq.).
[2] Caesar, *Bell. Civ.* iii. 110.

THE PTOLEMIES

it would be most surprising that the cleruch army *should* survive, even to form part of the Royal Guard; so that there is not the slightest reason for hesitating to accept the evidence of Polybius and Caesar, and to conclude that the Ptolemies came to rely for their army of Alexandria upon mercenaries alone.[1]

ii. *The garrisons.*

The largest and most important Egyptian garrison was the permanent army stationed at Alexandria for the defence of the king and his court. But there were also very many smaller garrisons placed at strategic points within the Ptolemaic empire both at home and abroad. Notices of these garrisons are to be found as early as the wars of the Successors, at Tyre (315 B.C.),[2] Aspendus (*ca.* 310–306 B.C.),[3] Cyrene (probably 308–7 B.C.),[4] and Sicyon (303 B.C.).[5] At Aspendus and Cyrene the garrison is known to have consisted of mercenaries, but it must certainly be true of the others also, since Ptolemy would never have risked his precious Macedonians so far afield, and was in fact one of the great employers of mercenaries in this period (pp. 109 sqq.). And many of the Ptolemaic possessions (such as Cyrene) must have been garrisoned continuously for more than 100 years. In 172 B.C. the approach to Egypt itself was guarded by a military camp at Pelusium in the east.[6] In the south there were the military stations on the Red Sea whence the supply of African war-elephants was drawn, and there must have been many small garrisons within the borders of Egypt of which only one or two are now known. Even more important was the garrison system by which the foreign empire of the Ptolemies was held. According to Theocritus Ptolemy II ruled over "parts

---

[1] P. M. Meyer, *op. cit.* pp. 82 sqq., reached the same conclusion, but by a false line of reasoning, based on the phrase οἱ Πτολεμαίου καὶ τῶν υἱῶν (P. Grenf. ii. 15. 3; P. Lond. ii. 219—doubtful reading). He concluded that this must refer to the Royal Guard, which (he said) after the death of Philometor consisted merely of this regiment of mercenaries. Meyer was ignorant at that time of the fact that these so-called "eponymous commanders" are comparatively numerous (cf. Lesquier, pp. 292 sqq.).
[2] Diod. xix. 61. 5.
[3] A. Wilhelm, *S.B. Ak. Wien*, 1915 (179), p. 60 = *Mon. Ant.* pp. 116 sqq.
[4] S. Ferri, *Alcune Inscrizione di Cirene* (Abh. preuss. Akad. 1925), p. 5; cf. F. Heichelheim, *Klio*, xxi. (1927), pp. 175 sqq.
[5] Diod. xx. 102. 2.
[6] Pol. xv. 25. 26 sqq.

of Phoenicia and Arabia, Syria, Libya, and the black Ethiopians: all the Pamphylians and warrior Cilicians, the Lycians, the warlike Carians and the islands of the Cyclades".[1] Allowance is to be made for the enthusiasm of a court poet, but the empire at its greatest did really embrace many of the islands, Palestine and Coele-Syria, the coast of southern Asia Minor, and a footing in Thrace. All this was to be defended: who were the soldiers who defended it?

In Egypt itself the work may have been shared by the cleruch soldiers and the mercenaries, if the documents quoted above (p. 124) are to be taken as representative of the general rule. If the cleruchs could be used at all they could be used for this purpose most easily, but even so one hears of mercenary cavalry on duty at Diospolis Magna,[2] and at Diospolis Parva and Ptolemais.[3] A late inscription from Hermoupolis Magna (probably later than 69 B.C.) contains more than 250 names, most of which must belong to soldiers on garrison duty there (οἱ παρεφεδρεύοντες): most of the names are Greek, but at this date it is unsafe to deduce a Greek soldier from a Greek name, since there are many cases on record of Egyptians and others with Greek names.[4] The στρατιώτης of a garrison at Syene is not necessarily a mercenary soldier, since the meaning of the word in papyri generally cannot be defined more closely than "a soldier on active service", and this would apply equally to a cleruch soldier on garrison duty.[5] It is when one moves farther afield that one may be more confident of seeing mercenaries in garrisons (even when they are not so described). Thus it is known for certain that in 238 B.C. the outposts on the Red Sea, the centres for the famous elephant hunt, were held by μισθοφόροι,[6] and it is perhaps a legitimate inference that the στρατιῶται of a later inscription (ca. 208 B.C.) were mercenaries too.[7] Another inscription (254 B.C.) gives us

[1] Theoc. xvii. 85 sqq.   [2] *Aktenstücke*, v–vii.   [3] P. Grenf. i. 42.
[4] O.G.I.S. i. 182 (cf. B.C.H. 1896, pp. 177 sqq., and 1897, p. 166; also *Archiv*, i. p. 207).
[5] B.G.U. vi. 1247. 5 sqq. For στρατιώτης cf. especially P. Cair. Zen. iii. 59245. 2; Mich. Zen. 32. 5; Gurob 19. 5; Tebt. iii. i. 767. 1; P.S.I. v. 495. 13 sqq.
[6] P. Grenf. i. 9. 1 sqq.
[7] O.G.I.S. i. 86; cf. Strabo xvi. 769 and 774, for the names of several commanders, στρατηγοὶ ἐπὶ τὴν θήραν, including Charimortus, a *condottiere* "savage and intemperate" who was later the friend and accomplice of Scopas the Aetolian at Alexandria (Pol. xviii. 55. 2).

THE PTOLEMIES

the names of soldiers (all Greek) who guarded a cistern on the route from Apollonopolis to the emerald mines and the Red Sea.[1] As to the garrisons overseas there is little information, but one hears of mercenaries in the Ptolemaic garrison at Erythrae about 275 B.C., and of Thracians at Ephesus a little later.[2] In an inscription of Thera (229 B.C.) the στρατιῶται are more likely *a priori* to be mercenaries than "regulars": the names of more than 200 of them are preserved, and nearly all are Greek.[3] Other notices of these island garrisons have survived, but they tell us little of the soldiers themselves: in one of them the phrase οἱ...στρατιῶται καὶ μάχιμοι must refer to Greek and Egyptian soldiers respectively, but who the Greeks were there is no means of telling.[4]

But most of our information comes from Cyprus, which remained the most important possession overseas, commanding the flank of the Phoenician province and the coast of Egypt itself. It was in Cyprus that in the time of Ptolemy I 16,000 of his mercenaries were taken prisoners by Demetrius.[5] It is interesting to find that Demetrius could not use them against Ptolemy because their baggage and possessions were in Egypt, a fact from which it might be tempting to conclude that they were *cleruch* soldiers and not mercenaries at all. But the conjecture is probably wrong, for it is unlikely that Ptolemy I had at that date 16,000 military settlers altogether, and there is moreover a parallel case in the mercenaries of Carthage in Sicily during the first Punic War, whose baggage remained at Carthage while they themselves were abroad.[6] There are abundant traces of Greek soldiery in the island under the Ptolemaic *régime*. Most of them date from the second century, but there is one gravestone of a Cretan infantry officer of Ptolemy Soter.[7] Later inscriptions give us an Aetolian cavalry officer,[8] an Aspendian,[9] some

---

[1] *O.G.I.S.* i. 38. [2] Ditt. *Syll.*³ 410; cf. 285; Athenaeus xiii. 593 *a*.
[3] *I.G.* xii. 3. 327 (= *O.G.I.S.* i. 59).
[4] *Ibid.* 466 (= *O.G.I.S.* i. 102: "Crete, Thera, and Arsinoe in the Peloponnese"), and *ibid.* iii. 1. 854 (a garrison of Ptolemy VI at Methana).
[5] Diod. xx. 53. 1. The inscription of Citium (*O.G.I.S.* i. 20) which gives us the name of a "phrourarch" most probably belongs to the later years of Ptolemy I, after Ipsus, if indeed it belongs to the reign of Ptolemy I at all (cf. note *ad loc.*).
[6] P. 218. [7] *C.I.G.* ii. 2613.
[8] *O.G.I.S.* i. 134. [9] *B.C.H.* xx. p. 353 n. 5.

Cyrenaeans,[1] and some soldiers who are called definitely mercenaries (ξενολογηθέντων).[2] And in the reign of Ptolemy VIII we meet with an interesting development, in the national "clubs" (κοινά) of foreign soldiers on service in Cyprus. Those which are known are the club of the Cilicians (τὸ κοινὸν τῶν ἐν τῇ νήσῳ τασσομένων Κιλίκων),[3] of the Thracians,[4] Ionians,[5] Cretans,[6] Lycians,[7] and "Achaeans and other Greeks" (οἱ ἐν Κύπρῳ στρατευόμενοι Ἀχαιοὶ καὶ οἱ ἄλλοι Ἕλληνες);[8] but there is also one inscription of a club embracing apparently all the soldiers in the island, which makes one wonder what precisely is the meaning of the word κοινόν here (τὸ κοινὸν τῶν ἐν τῇ νήσῳ τασσομένων δυνάμεων).[9] It is also doubtful as to what value is to be set upon these ethnic names, since it is established that "ethnics" occurring in papyri of this period are to be viewed with suspicion.

The weight of this evidence should be sufficient to prove that the island of Cyprus was garrisoned by mercenaries, and there is no reason to suppose that what is true of Cyprus is false of the other Egyptian garrisons abroad. But it must certainly be mentioned that an inscription of about 209 B.C. informs us of an individual who was "secretary" (γραμματεύς) of the "mercenaries (?) and Egyptians in Crete, Thera, and Arsinoe in the Peloponnese" (τῶν κατὰ Κρήτην, etc., στρατιωτῶν καὶ μαχίμων).[10] How large a share of the garrison duties may have been allotted to Egyptians it is quite impossible to say, but it may be argued that people whose loyalty was not to be trusted in Egypt can never have been trusted very highly with the defence of foreign possessions.[11] When it is added that the cleruch soldiers were obviously not intended for continuous spells of distant service on the frontiers or abroad, it must follow that the garrisons were held chiefly by mercenaries, as is to be expected. Confirmatory

---

[1] *B.C.H.* xx. p. 338 n. 4; cf. *ibid.* no. 3—a Thessalian, a Carystian, a Thracian, and an Aspendian.
[2] *C.I.G.* ii. 2623.
[3] *O.G.I.S.* i. 148 and 157.
[4] *Ibid.* 143.
[5] *Ibid.* 145.
[6] *Ibid.* 153.
[7] *Ibid.* 146, 147 and 162.
[8] *Ibid.* 151.
[9] M. L. Strack, *Die Dynastie der Ptolemäer*, no. 112, p. 258.
[10] *I.G.* xii. 3. 466, ll. 10 sqq.
[11] Cf. *O.G.I.S.* i. 90. 19 (the Rosetta stone of Ptolemy V), for the disloyalty of the Egyptian μάχιμοι at the time of the great rebellion.

THE PTOLEMIES 135

evidence is forthcoming from Polybius. When the Egyptian government decided on a concentration of the army at Alexandria in the year before Raphia, they "collected the mercenaries from the cities abroad"—τῶν ἔξω πόλεων—a phrase which could refer to garrisons both in Egypt and farther afield.[1] And in 203 B.C. Agathocles wished to disperse the mercenaries on duty at Alexandria "to the settlements and garrisons", where the same interpretation is possible.[2] In time of peace this service in the garrisons was probably much the most important function of the mercenaries in the Egyptian army, more important even than the guard duty at Alexandria, since a king might be changed at Alexandria without great inconvenience to the nation as a whole, but a province lost meant a loss for ever or an expensive war for its recovery.[3]

5. "MERCENARY CLERUCHS"

The purpose and the performance of the military settlers in Egypt has already been noticed. They were intended to serve two useful purposes, as farmers and as soldiers, but we have seen that on the military side the system was in fact a failure. And in so far as they remained soldiers in anything at all but the name, the settlers can no more be called mercenaries than the citizen troops of Athens or Sparta in the fifth century can be called mercenaries. They could accordingly be dismissed from this inquiry without further consideration were it not that a certain class from among them must by its very name arrest and hold our attention. They are, namely, the settlers who are described in our records as "mercenary cleruchs" (μισθοφόροι κληροῦχοι).

[1] Pol. v. 63. 8; cf. ibid. 36. 5, a probable reference to the garrisons in Caria and Syria.
[2] Id. xv. 25. 16. For the settlements, see next section.
[3] There is no evidence dealing specifically with the tactical organization of mercenaries in the standing army of the Ptolemies. There is however plenty of evidence for the military organization of the cleruchs, and this is treated so fully by Lesquier (pp. 80 sqq.) that it is unnecessary to do more than refer the reader to him. Two small points remain unelucidated, namely the significance of (1) the "eponymous" officers (Lesquier, pp. 77 sqq.), and (2) the τακτόμισθοι (Lesquier, pp. 99 sqq.). New references to these officials have come to light since Lesquier's book was published, but since I can still find nothing that connects them with the mercenaries, I have thought it best to omit them from this discussion, although I feel that the last word about them has not yet been said.

Before we look at the evidence relating to them it should not be forgotten that the mere existence of a class bearing this name proves two things: first, that the other settlers from whom they are distinguished were not regarded as mercenaries; second, that there must have been some real difference between them and the others, which made the distinction necessary. The task is to consider what exactly the difference may have been. Mahaffy, in his introduction to the Flinders Petrie papyri, seems in the first place to have ignored the difference, and though he admits it later he never explains it.[1] Lesquier, too, sees that there must be a difference. But he explains the existence of the mercenary cleruchs by supposing that they were settled in Egypt in order to facilitate quick recruiting in case of war.[2] The explanation is good sense, but it is not in itself sufficient, for it makes the *raison d'être* of the mercenary cleruchs precisely the same as that of the other cleruchs who are not called mercenaries, and does not explain the difference in the name. If there was in reality some good reason for this difference—and it is hard to see why it should appear in official documents if there was not—some better explanation than Lesquier's is still to be found.

Our first notice of mercenary cleruchs is in a papyrus of 243–242 B.C., and relates to the property of a Greek cavalry mercenary (an officer) from Selymbria, one of an unknown number who had been granted lots of land in Egypt; but it can tell us nothing further to our purpose.[3] A document of 220–219 B.C. illustrates the different classes of cleruch. It mentions separately "regular" cavalry of two kinds, "regular" infantry, and finally mercenary cavalry.[4] Smyly, in his note on the passage, suggests that their holding was one of 80 acres; but he admits that the abbreviation which he is interpreting "differs considerably from that employed elsewhere in this papyrus for ἄρουρα, and it may be thought too that 80 acres is too high, since the highest class of 'regular' cavalry received only 100 acres". The distinction between mercenary cleruchs, and "Macedonians" (="regulars"), and "the others" (=natives?), is made again in a frag-

[1] P. Petr. i. pp. 20 sqq., 40 sqq. (1891); ii. p. 14 (1892). Also J. G. Smyly, note on P. Petr. iii. 112.
[2] Lesquier, pp. 46–7. [3] P. Lille 14; cf. perhaps *ibid.* 10.
[4] P. Petr. iii. 112; the sections referring to mercenary cleruchs are (*f*) l. 19; (*g*) ll. 16 sqq., and notes.

THE PTOLEMIES 137

ment belonging to the years between 260 and 224 B.C.[1] The existence of the mercenary cleruch before Raphia is thus already established. It is also made clear by literary evidence of the Raphia period. In connection with the 6000 Gauls and Thracians who fought for Egypt in the great battle, Polybius says that 4000 were "from the settlers and their descendants (ἐπιγόνων)", and although this may mean that they had become "regular" soldiers, it is clear that the original Gauls and Thracians came to Egypt as mercenaries.[2] And in 203 B.C. Agathocles was anxious to procure new mercenaries for the army at Alexandria, and to send away the old ones "to the garrisons and settlements".[3]

Are we then to infer that mercenaries received land only when their service was completed; that as veteran settlers they became part of the "regular" military class, and could hand on its privileges and its duties to their children, the ἐπίγονοι? Not necessarily, it seems, at all events in the second century. For we know with certainty of a mercenary, who possessed land at Hermoupolis, and who was on active service in the garrison at Acoris,[4] and there are other cases of mercenaries who are probably both cleruchs and active soldiers at the same time.[5]

This second-century mercenary cleruch, with his three or four supporters of more doubtful value, may provide the key to the riddle. Let us suppose that the mercenary cleruch could *only* be a soldier upon active service: that is to say, he received his piece of land not at the end of his service as a reward, but at the beginning of, or at some period within, his term of service and as part of his pay. There is nothing intrinsically impossible in the idea, for it is known that ordinary settlers were allowed to sublet their holdings and draw rent for them.[6] In such a case the procedure was perhaps something like this: a Greek mercenary would land in Egypt to join the army, and would enter into a contract to serve a certain number of years. He would agree to receive a piece of land instead of money as part of his pay; or

[1] P. Petr. ii. 31 (*a*), cf. iii. 53 (*d*), l. 6.
[2] Pol. v. 65. 10.   [3] *Id.* xv. 25. 17.
[4] P. Rein. 7, ll. 3 sqq.
[5] P. Tor. iii. ll. 2 sqq. (=Part ii. p. 1); P. Rein. 17, ll. 1 sqq.; 13, ll. 2 sqq.; 31, ll. 3 sqq.
[6] E.g. P. Petr. iii. 104, 105 and 106.

perhaps the land was added as a bonus after so many years of service. If he had a family he could support it with the produce of the land; if he had none he could draw the rent from the cultivator while he was himself upon active service. And when he retired at the end of his service he was perhaps allowed to remain in possession of the land and become an ordinary settler. If this theory is right every mercenary cleruch should be a soldier recruited from abroad, but from what we have seen already of Egyptian recruiting it can hardly be possible that every soldier from abroad became a cleruch while he served. The privilege was probably reserved for long-service mercenaries who had no intention of ever quitting Egypt to take service elsewhere, and may have been an inducement to soldiers to remain in the country in which they had received a vested interest. It may be of some significance that of the four cases of mercenary cleruchs known in the third century, two refer to cavalry officers, and in the other two the status cannot be deduced.[1] (But Agathocles' scheme to send the soldiers at Alexandria "to the garrisons and the settlements" obviously does not refer to cavalry alone.) As to the size of the lots given to mercenaries nothing better than guesswork is possible. Smyly's estimate of 80 acres may not be too high for a cavalry *officer*. And Lesquier suggests 25 (or 24) acres for mercenary infantry, but admittedly on insufficient evidence and with the warning that the figure seems to him to be too high.[2]

It is impossible to say with confidence that this explanation puts the obscure μισθοφόρος κληροῦχος in his proper place; but it is to be hoped that at least it is not beyond the bounds of common sense. There is no reason why a paid soldier should not hold land. There is every reason why a landholder should not be paid unless he does something to earn his money. The ordinary settler apparently did nothing except in a crisis such as the Raphia campaign, and as far as we know for doing nothing he received no pay, but merely a piece of land to preserve him in case he should be needed. Egyptian officials thought it worth their while to show in their reports that there was a difference between ordinary landholders and the paid landholders. What

---

[1] P. Lille 14; P. Petr. iii. 112; ii. 31 (*a*).
[2] Lesquier, pp. 175 and 176.

THE PTOLEMIES

is suggested here is that the reason why the paid landholders were paid, was that they earned their money as active soldiers in the standing army, and that this was the position of the mercenary cleruch.

6. CONCLUSION

A survey of the military history of Egypt under the Ptolemies leaves us with the following picture. In the years after Alexander's death the first Ptolemy made it his business to keep his allotted possessions and to acquire more, by building up a strong army out of the materials which came to his hand. The greatest part of the army was the product of mercenary recruiting, but he had a valuable body of real Macedonians, and at Gaza he was able to use Egyptians also as soldiers. But the continual recruiting of new mercenaries was likely to prove both expensive and inconvenient, and accordingly he introduced the system of military settlements; or rather he revived the old system used by the Pharaohs to create and preserve a permanent military class in their kingdom. The military class of the Ptolemies, however, must be primarily Macedonian, since the Macedonians had proved themselves the best fighters of the eastern Mediterranean. Although Ptolemy Soter and his successors had few Macedonians and could never renew the supply, the best substitute for a Macedonian army was an army of Greeks accustomed to warfare as their means of winning a livelihood. It can only have been the Greek mercenaries who received land in Egypt, and became the class, handing down its profession from father to son, from which the regular army was to be formed in time of war. Such a class, however efficient in its origin, had obvious limitations. Its members, like the citizen soldiers of the Greek states, could not be expected to serve as soldiers all the year round, and in an era of peace its military discipline could not fail to be neglected and forgotten. Thus it happens that the use of mercenaries could never be entirely abandoned, as is very clear from the texts quoted above. The great Ptolemaic empire required a peace strength of professional soldiers for its provinces and garrisons, and in times of unexpected danger new mercenaries were still constantly recruited from Greece and elsewhere.

The story of Raphia is the most important piece of evidence in our hands. In its introduction it shows the military strength of Egypt reduced to insignificance. It goes on to describe how by a very great effort the regular army of military settlers was re-trained, re-equipped, and placed in the field again as an efficient fighting force, though even so it constituted less than one-third of the whole army. The regular phalanx was now supported by an entirely new Egyptian phalanx armed and trained for the first time to fight in the Macedonian style. And even this army was not complete without a very considerable force of mercenaries, some of whom were freshly recruited for the occasion. At Raphia the army of Egypt was born again, but the promising child was destined never to reach maturity. It had been an error of policy to arm the Egyptians, and the internal struggles in the beginning of the second century, the result of having taught a subject people that they could fight as well as their masters, were the death-blow to all hopes of a truly national army. The military settlers too towards the end of the second century probably counted for less and less as active soldiers, although there is ample evidence for their having continued to exist under the old forms of organization: "the Macedonians had become Egyptians".[1] A hand-to-mouth military policy became the order of the day. Mercenaries were recruited as they were needed, but they could never fill the place of a regular army imbued with a national discipline and spirit. When Egypt ceased to be a great power, and was relieved of the dangers as well as of the advantages of empire, it is probable that the mercenary army concentrated round the court of Alexandria became in effect the army of Egypt. In the decline of the Ptolemaic *régime* Alexandria was at the mercy of an overbearing and ill-disciplined soldiery just as Rome and her weaker emperors were later to be at the mercy of their praetorian guards. The history of Egypt plainly shows the weakness as well as the strength of the Hellenistic military monarchy. The army was all-important, and the army was most reliable when it could be recruited from

---

[1] Livy 38. 17. 5, "Macedones, qui Alexandriam in Aegypto, qui Seleuciam ac Babyloniam, quique alias sparsas per orbem terrarum colonias habent, in Syros Parthos Aegyptios degenerarunt", a piece of rhetoric put into the mouth of the Roman consul Manlius addressing his troops on the campaign against the Galatians in 189 B.C.

a "Greek" population within the kingdom. But this population was bound to be comparatively slender, and constantly required reinforcement from outside. The reinforcements were the mercenaries, who could supply a momentary need, and could also perhaps be turned to permanent advantage, if they remained in the country as military settlers: their recruiting was at once a source of strength and a sign of weakness.

CHAPTER VI

THE SELEUCIDS

ALMOST the whole history of the Seleucid empire is fragmentary and obscure. From the time when Seleucus Nicator borrowed 1000 mercenaries from Ptolemy I and made his spectacular dash from Egypt through Syria and Mesopotamia to seize Babylon,[1] we are conscious indeed of the existence and growth of a new power in the East, but we are quite unable to follow its development at all closely, especially in the early stages. The third century, too, is, most of it, a particularly bare period. The Seleucid empire becomes known to us usually when it is at war, and the best that can be said is that it was at war reasonably often. But even these wars, wars with Lysimachus, wars with Egypt, with the Gauls, with Pergamum, in the East, all these have scarcely any historical background at all. It is known that they happened but not how they happened: the fact of their having happened at all proves that the early Seleucids had an army and probably a strong one; but there is no literature describing what the army was like or what it did. In these circumstances a chronological account of mercenary service in the Seleucid armies is impossible. There is, however, one period about which the information is better. The account by Polybius of the battle of Raphia gives us a start: Livy's account of Magnesia, though not above suspicion, is still valuable: and finally Polybius again describes the army of Antiochus IV at his great military review at Daphne. These three pictures of the army at three separate points within a period of some fifty years (217-165 B.C.) are at least a starting-point, and it will be best to begin with this "clear" period before trying to rescue stray facts or inferences from the obscurity before and after.

[1] Diod. xix. 90. 1 sqq.

THE SELEUCIDS

1. THE WAR STRENGTH (217–165 B.C.)

i. *Raphia.*

When Antiochus III ascended the throne his whole kingdom seems to have been under arms. One's first feeling is one of amazement at the very numbers of the soldiers who must have been involved. The king's uncle Achaeus was master of Asia Minor at the head of an army.[1] Molon, the viceroy of the eastern provinces, was soon in open rebellion and ready to defend himself. A royal army under Xenoetas, an Arcadian officer, was sent to reduce him and was cut to pieces.[2] And finally Antiochus himself took the field and marched against Molon with a fourth army. In the decisive battle which settled Molon's pretensions we do not know the size of the armies, but we do know their constituents. The rebel army seems to have been recruited principally in Media and the East: it contained cavalry (probably native), heavy infantry including Gauls, and light infantry (archers, slingers, etc.).[3] The Gauls must have been mercenaries, but the light infantry may have been native subjects; the heavy infantry (apart from the Gauls) were certainly Greeks and Macedonians from the eastern settlements.[4] In the king's army there was a "phalanx" and a body of "Companion" cavalry, some native lancers, and some Cretan "allies"; the mercenaries were Gauls and "the mercenaries from Greece".[5]

The army at Raphia was certainly greater, for it contained troops from the East who had formerly been with Molon (but Achaeus was still at large in Asia Minor). It numbered 62,000 infantry and 6000 cavalry. Of the composition of the cavalry we are told nothing: the contingents of infantry were as follows:

1. 5000 Dahae, Carmanians and Cilicians, light armed.
2. 10,000 armed in Macedonian style, "mostly argyraspids, picked from the whole kingdom".
3. 20,000 τὸ τῆς φάλαγγος πλῆθος.

[1] No figures; but Achaeus' general Garsyeris was later in Pisidia with 6500 men, before Achaeus himself joined him with the main army, including Mysians (Pol. v. 72. 3; 76. 7).
[2] Pol. v. 46. 6 sqq.   [3] *Ibid.* 53. 8 sqq.
[4] For the settlements in general, see section 2 of this chapter. For the deduction that there were Graeco-Macedonian settlers in Molon's army (as in that of Achaeus in Asia Minor), cf. p. 168 n. 2.
[5] Pol. v. 53. 2 sqq.

144   HELLENISTIC MERCENARIES

4. {2000 Agrianian and Persian archers and slingers.
   {1000 Thracians.
5. 5000 Medes, Cissians, Cadusians and Carmanians.
6. 10,000 Arabs.
7. 5000 mercenaries from Greece.
8. 2500 Cretans.
9. {500 Lydian ἀκοντισταί.
   {1000 Cardaces.[1]

The native contingents need not trouble us. The Scythian Dahae and the Arabs were probably mercenaries, since the Seleucid power did not reach north to the Caspian or south into the Syrian desert. The certain mercenaries are the Thracians and the 5000 Greeks, and perhaps the Cretans too.[2] The Greeks fought well, breaking the section of the Egyptian line which was opposed to them. For some unknown reason, the Gauls, who had fought previously with Molon and Antiochus, are missing from the army at Raphia.

ii. *Magnesia.*

Livy's figures for Antiochus' army at Magnesia are 70,000 infantry, and more than 20,000 cavalry. It appears that the numbers of the cavalry in particular must be greatly exaggerated, and it will be seen from the following table that the high figures may be due in part to some confusion in connection with the Gallic and "cataphract" horse.

The army was as follows:

1. The centre—the phalanx, 16,000 strong.
2. The right wing (working outwards from the centre):
   (i) 1500 equites Gallograecorum ⎱ Appian, Γαλάται τε κατά-
   (ii) 3000 cataphracti equites ⎰ φρακτοι (a mistake?);
   (iii) 1000 equitum agema;

[1] Pol. v. 79. 3 sqq.; cf. 82. 8 sqq.
[2] 1000 of them are called "Neocretans", i.e. newly recruited (the usual interpretation)? Cf. in the Ptolemaic army in the same battle, p. 118; also in Antiochus' army at Magnesia (below), again 1000 of them: and with the Aetolians in 218 B.C. I hardly think that "newly-recruited Cretans" can be the right translation of Neocretes. Dr Tarn suggests to me that it may be a question of a new kind of *armament*, quoting my list p. 145 (viii)—3, and (ix)— ex eodem *armatu*: this is much more plausible, but I know of no further evidence to develop the theory, unless it be the Κρῆτας ἀσπιδιώτας of Pol. x. 29. 6.

THE SELEUCIDS

(iv) argyraspides;
(v) 1200 Dahae equites sagittarii;
(vi) 3000 levis armatura, pari ferme numero pars Cretenses pars Tralles;
(vii) 2500 Mysians;
(viii) 4000 misti Cyrtaei funditores et Elymii sagittarii.

3. The left wing (working from the centre):

(i) 1500 Gallograeci equites ⎱ Appian, Γαλατῶν τ'
(ii) 2000 Cappadocum ab Ariarathe missi rege ⎰ ἔθνη Τεκτοσάγαι τε καὶ Τρόκμοι καὶ Τολίστοβοι, καὶ Καππαδόκες τινες...?
(iii) 2700 auxiliares misti omnium generum ⎱ Appian, μιγάδες ἄλλοι ξένοι;
(iv) 3000 cataphractorum equitum;
(v) alii equites, Lydians, Phrygians and "Arabes sagittarii";
(vi) Tarentines;
(vii) Gallograecorum equitum 2500;
(viii) 1000 Neocretes;
(ix) 1500 ex eodem armatu Cares et Cilices;
(x) 1500 Tralles;
(xi) 3000 cetratorum, Pisidae, Pamphyli, Lycii.[1]

As at Raphia and in the battle against Molon, there is a phalanx and a force of "Companion" cavalry. The mercenary contingents of Dahae, Cretans, Thracians (Trallians) and Arabs are repeated at Magnesia, though at varying strengths. The 2700 "mixed mercenaries" of Magnesia are perhaps parallel to the "5000 mercenaries from Greece" of Raphia. In the case of some Asiatic contingents, such as the Mysians and Pisidians, it is impossible to say whether they came as mercenaries, allies or subjects; most probably as mercenaries, since such peoples were practically free and independent, though they may have been nominally subjects of the king. The most surprising thing is that there were so few, if any, Greek mercenaries. The disaster in Greece which preceded Magnesia may have had some effect upon recruiting.[2] On the other hand, there is a considerable

---
[1] Livy 37. 40; Appian, *Syriaca* 32. 1 sqq.
[2] Antiochus had certainly had mercenaries with him in Greece, as well as "Macedonians", but their nationality remains hidden (Livy 36. 14; 18. 2 sqq.; Pol. xx. 3. 7).

accession of Galatians, even if Livy's 5500 cavalry is an exaggeration. Livy's third contingent of Galatians, 2500 strong, is missing in Appian; but perhaps one of the two contingents of 1500 is a doublet, and a total of 4000 is right, since Livy says that Antiochus had given orders earlier in the winter for Galatians to be recruited, and as a result sent 4000 to ravage the territory of Pergamum. If this is wrong it is at least consistently wrong.[1]

iii. *Daphne.*

In the review of 165 B.C. we find eight separate contingents:
1. 5000 infantry armed in the Roman style.
2. 5000 Mysians.
3. 3000 light-armed Cilicians.
4. 3000 Thracians and 5000 Gauls.
5. 20,000 Macedonians, 5000 Bronze Shields, and some Silver Shields.
6. 1000 Nisaean cavalry and 3000 cavalry "from the cities" (πολιτικοί).
7. 4000 picked cavalry, including the Companions.
8. 1500 cataphract cavalry.[2]

By the treaty of Apameia the kings of Syria had been forbidden to recruit mercenaries from the Roman sphere of influence, or even to receive them if they came to them of their own accord.[3] They were thus cut off from all supplies of soldiers from Greece, from the Thracians and Gauls of Europe, from Crete, and from the Greeks or natives of much of Asia Minor. It is interesting to notice the effects of the interdict upon the personnel of the army. The most obvious change is the great increase of the "Macedonians", the phalanx and the footguards, who jump from 16,000 at Magnesia to over 25,000 at Daphne (over 30,000 if the Roman-armed infantry are "Macedonians"). The increase extends to the cavalry as well, though the picked cavalry may really be of Asiatic origin at least in part: the cavalry "from the cities" is a mystery.[4] In the mercenary con-

---
[1] Livy 37. 8. 4; 18. 7.   [2] Pol. xxx. 25. 3 sqq.
[3] *Id.* xxi. 43. 15; Livy 38. 38. 10; Appian, *Syr.* 39.
[4] They could conceivably be "cavalry from the military settlements" (see below, esp. p. 153 for Antiochus IV's settlements).

THE SELEUCIDS

tingents, Greeks and Cretans have quite disappeared, the latter being replaced probably by the Cilicians, who had fought *ex eodem armatu* at Magnesia. The Gauls and Thracians here are probably recruited from the Asiatic stocks. The Mysians too are something of a surprise, for one would have thought that they came from the Roman sphere of influence, being adjacent to, if not within, the boundaries of Pergamum. Apparently the independent north of Asia Minor was regarded as a no-man's-land, and Syrian recruiting officers were allowed to work among the Mysians as well as among the Thracians and Gauls. The Mysians must certainly be mercenaries here, and cannot possibly have been a subject contingent.

2. The "Macedonians"

A modern historian of the Seleucids has said: "Nous ignorons même si ces rois toujours en guerre disposaient d'une armée regulière, dont le recrutement fût assuré par d'autres moyens que par la levée de soldats improvisés ou l'enrôlement de mercenaires à chaque campagne. On ne rencontre chez eux rien qui ressemble à ce qu'on pourrait appeler l'armée territoriale des Lagides" (referring to the "regular" cleruch army of Egypt).[1] Let us see what justification can be found in our sources for this dispiriting confession.

In the first place, then, the three army lists above have revealed in each case a "phalanx" of heavy infantry, which appears to correspond exactly with the Egyptian phalanx of cleruch soldiers, the Ptolemaic substitute for Alexander's Macedonians. This correspondence is especially well illustrated by Appian's description of the Seleucid phalanx at Magnesia. "The whole army was 70,000 strong, and the strongest part of it was *the phalanx of Macedonians*, 16,000 men, still equipped in the style of Philip and Alexander": and again: "*the phalanx of Macedonians*, well trained and well manned then as never before, and possessing an invincible and formidable reputation".[2] Of the review at Daphne Polybius writes: "Next came 20,000 Mace-

---
[1] A. Bouché-Leclercq, *Histoire des Séleucides*, i. p. 476.
[2] Appian, *Syr.* 32. 1 sqq.; 37. 1 sqq.

donians and 5000 Brazen Shields and Silver Shields in addition".[1] In the face of this evidence alone, it is hard to see how the complete ignorance professed by Bouché-Leclercq is to be justified. The traditional style of Philip and Alexander is not to be expected from Asiatic levies or mercenaries recruited at random. The literary texts by themselves make it probable that that style must have been fostered of set purpose, and the next step is to discover by what methods. Nor are the methods beyond discovery.

Bouché-Leclercq was not ignorant of the fact that there existed in the kingdom of the Seleucids, as in that of the Ptolemies, a system of military settlements (in this case called κατοικίαι). But he will not concede that there is any real similarity between the two systems, believing that the Seleucid military colonies were filled merely with veterans who had no further obligation to serve as soldiers; though he does concede that the military spirit was likely to endure for several generations even in the absence of such an obligation.[2] At the time when he passed this judgment there was no evidence either one way or the other, apart from considerations of probability. We have seen that in Egypt a period of 20 years' peace was sufficient to make a cleruch army, under definite obligations to fight if required, nearly useless as a practical military weapon.[3] What, may we suppose, was likely to happen to the Seleucid cleruchs, if they were bound by no such obligations, during the lapse of one and a half centuries between the beginning of the *régime* and the Daphne review? Clearly they would, in the military sense, have ceased to exist. We are faced therefore with two alternatives. Either the Seleucid military colonists had no obligations, in which case they have no connection with the Seleucid phalanx at Daphne: or they must be assumed to have had obligations, in which case the endurance of a "Macedonian" phalanx for a century and a half is, partly at least, explained. The second alternative seems the more likely.

It is probable from the first, then, that the military settlements are relevant to this inquiry. They are far too wide and complicated a subject to be discussed at leisure, though there is a real

---

[1] Pol. xxx. 25. 3 sqq.
[2] *Loc. cit., ibid.*
[3] See above, pp. 117 sqq.

THE SELEUCIDS

need for a special study of them in detail; but the bulk of the evidence is contained incidentally in V. Tscherikower's admirable book, which, though it is concerned primarily with the Graeco-Macedonian *polis* foundations, rightly does not ignore the evidence for military settlements: the two classes are indeed often indistinct.[1] All that can be done here is to summarize and condense the material, reserving for discussion one or two points which are irrelevant to Tscherikower's purpose, but to us are of the first importance.

The Seleucid system of settlements was not of course an invention of Seleucus I or of one of his successors. The idea was first put into practice by Alexander, and perhaps later by Antigonus, and it is to be remembered that the empire of Seleucus I was really carved out of the territories first won and held by these two great soldiers and statesmen. The influence of the Antigonid empire, especially, on that of Seleucus is not generally appreciated. To take a very obvious and concrete example, the field army of Seleucus at Ipsus is supposed to have been 32,000 strong:[2] in the years before Ipsus Antigonus must have had an army of at least 100,000 men:[3] when Antigonus was killed at Ipsus Seleucus annexed a very large part of his empire, and it seems certain that he must also have taken over a very large part of the army, and that it is from this time (301 B.C.) that the great military strength of the Seleucids must date. Before 301 Seleucus must have found it difficult to get Greeks or Macedonians for his army at all;[4] whereas Antigonus' army for years had contained some Macedonians and vast numbers of Greek mercenaries: and the victory of Ipsus re-opened to Seleucus the Mediterranean coast, whence the supply could be renewed at will.

There is sufficient evidence for Antigonus himself as a founder of cities, some of which had certainly a military function. The sites of Antigoneia on the Orontes and of a group of four

---

[1] V. Tscherikower, *Die Hellenistischen Stadtbegründungen von Alexander dem Grossen bis auf der Römerzeit*, Leipzig 1927. Cf. M. Rostovtzeff, in *C.A.H.* vii. pp. 157 sqq.: and P.-W. *s.v.* κάτοικοι.
[2] Diod. xx. 113. 4.   [3] Pp. 51 sqq.
[4] He probably had *some*, the remainder of Antigonus' troops in the East, e.g. the defeated army of Antigonus' general Nicanor; and it is believed that the "Macedonian" fortress of Doura-Europos was founded before Ipsus (p. 156). But the supply can never have been renewed except with great difficulty and expense.

150 HELLENISTIC MERCENARIES

cities near the Hellespont were clearly chosen for strategic reasons, being intended as permanent points of garrison (Stephanus calls Antigoneia near Cyzicus simply φρούριον).[1] Eight new cities of Antigonus are known in all; but the one piece of information most interesting for our purpose is inconclusive. Diodorus says that after Antigonus' final victory over Eumenes in the East he himself spent the winter near Ecbatana, τοὺς δὲ στρατιώτας ἐπιδιεῖλεν εἰς ἅπασαν τὴν σατραπείαν, καὶ μάλιστα εἰς τὴν ἐπαρχίαν τὴν προσαγορευομένην Ῥάγας. The actual words of Diodorus must be interpreted as meaning that Antigonus scattered his men about the province and especially near Rhagai for the winter only.[2] But it is very significant that this same neighbourhood later contains a group of the new cities (Rhagai-Europos, Heraclea, Apameia, Laodicea); and Tscherikower suggests that these cities probably began as military settlements of Antigonus' invalid or veteran soldiers after this campaign of 316 B.C.[3] The names Europos, Apameia and Laodicea all suggest Seleucid foundations (cf. Doura-Europos: Europos was Seleucus' birthplace in Macedonia); but this does not invalidate Tscherikower's suggestion. Seleucus I's great city Apameia on the Orontes was originally called Pella, ὑπὸ τῶν πρώτων Μακεδόνων διὰ τὸ τοὺς πλείστους τῶν Μακεδόνων ἐνταῦθα οἰκῆσαι τῶν στρατευομένων, and was apparently still called Pella as late as 286 B.C.[4] "The first Macedonians" are much more likely to have been Antigonus' Macedonians before 301 than those of Seleucus after 301, and the probability is that a foundation of Antigonus (Pella) was re-founded and enlarged by Seleucus I. The same thing seems to have happened in a modified form to Antigoneia on the Orontes, which was largely depopulated for the founding of the great Antioch, the capital of the Seleucid empire.[5] And very likely the four cities near Rhagai have the same history: the important thing is that, if the Diodorus passage is really the beginning of that history, we have

[1] On the strategic purpose of Antigoneia on the Orontes, Diod. xx. 47. 5. The Hellespontine cities are obviously a weapon against Lysimachus, whether offensive or defensive, cf. Tscherikower, *op. cit.* p. 156 and n. 471.
[2] Diod. xix. 44. 4; 46. 1 and 5.
[3] *Op. cit.* pp. 159 sqq.
[4] Strabo xvi. 752; Diod. xxi. 20.
[5] For the evidence, cf. Tscherikower, pp. 60 sqq. and 124, with n. 427.

THE SELEUCIDS 151

a proof that these cities began as purely military foundations, whatever they may have become later.[1] There are other reasons too for thinking that some of the new Hellenistic cities were founded as military settlements, or at least with a military settlement attached to the new foundation. First, there were certain cities of Asia Minor whose inhabitants still called themselves "Macedonians" centuries after the cities themselves were first founded.[2] Generally speaking, all Macedonians who crossed from Europe into Asia were originally soldiers, so that new "Macedonian" foundations must almost certainly have been composed of soldiers too.[3] When we hear of them these foundations are in most cases certainly πόλεις, but that is not to say that they were always πόλεις, and the probability is that they began as "Macedonian" κατοικίαι. That it was possible and feasible for κάτοικοι to become πολῖται is proved by two inscriptions describing the process, at Smyrna in 240 B.C. and at Pergamum in 133 B.C.[4] (The Smyrna inscription is particularly valuable, and will be considered later.) The same process is also possible in another class of cities: cities where it is not known indeed that the inhabitants were "Macedonians", but the fact is perhaps to be inferred from the placenames, which are the names of cities of Macedonia. Such names are Pella, Edessa, Beroia, Europos. They are very numerous, over thirty in all. But in only one case (Larissa in Syria) can the

[1] Diodorus was transcribing and abridging Hieronymus of Cardia, who may well have set down some valuable information which Diodorus has omitted, as Tscherikower points out.
[2] E.g. Nakrasa (*O.G.I.S.* i. 268; *C.I.G.* 3522); Doidye (*O.G.I.S.* i. 314); a city in Hyrcanis (Mostene?) (*B.C.H.* xi. 1887, p. 91; Tac. *Ann.* ii. 47); Peltae (Head, *H.N.*[2] 682); Blaundos (*ibid.* 649; *C.I.G.* 3866); Kadoi (Pliny v. 29. 11); Otros? (Ramsay, *Cities and Bishoprics of Phrygia*, ii. p. 702; Tscherikower, *op. cit.* p. 35); Dokimion (Head, *H.N.*[2] 672).
[3] Even if the "Macedonians" are not real Macedonians, they must still be soldiers.
[4] *O.G.I.S.* i. 229; 338. A clear case too seems to be Nakrasa, a κατοικία early in the reign of Eumenes II of Pergamum (*ibid.* 290), but a πόλις in the reign of Attalus II (*ibid.* 268; Dittenberger, *ad loc.*, gives this inscription to Attalus I, but this seems impossible in view of this change from κατοικία to πόλις (a change from πόλις to κατοικία being out of the question); the Eumenes inscription is dated roughly through Menogenes νομοφύλαξ, who recurs *later* as ἐπὶ τῶν πραγμάτων—a promotion, *ibid.* 293. I owe this information to Dr Tarn.) Unfortunately the case of Nakrasa loses in point because the change did not take place under the Seleucid *régime*; but it is still valuable evidence.

theory be tested by literary or archaeological evidence: Larissa in Syria, according to Diodorus, was inhabited by descendants of people from the Thessalian Larissa.[1] This particular confirmation is weak, but the presumption is in general a reasonably strong one. The "dynastic" names (e.g. Apameia, Seleuceia, Antiocheia) are clearly no help at all.

This excursus on the military settlements was begun on the assumption that they are relevant to the question of the Seleucid field army (p. 148), and it has now been shown that the city foundations may in turn be relevant to the settlements. The Seleucids in the first place took over a number of new cities founded by Alexander or Antigonus. They themselves persevered with the policy, and their activities as founders of cities seem to fall into two main periods, the early part of the third century B.C. (Seleucus I and Antiochus I) and the early-middle part of the second century (Antiochus IV). There is nothing in the early period that is at all unexpected. Over forty cities are known as foundations of the first two Seleucid kings, and it is to be supposed that some of them, but not necessarily all, were founded as fortresses and military settlements for soldiers of the phalanx, a double weapon of defence for the new empire.[2] It may at first sight seem surprising that there should have been a kind of recrudescence of this policy under Antiochus IV, at a time when Syria had already ceased to be a great power in the politics of the Mediterranean. But it becomes less surprising when one considers that the Seleucids had always two fronts to advance or to defend, and that the reverse in the West may have provided all the more reason for activity in the East. There at least all was not yet lost, and the probability is that Antiochus IV, a sanguine and energetic king, by his new foundations was trying to make a last stand against the forces which showed signs of overpowering his kingdom. Fifteen new cities of Antiochus IV are known,[3] and their association with the increased phalanx of

[1] Diod. xxxiii. 4 a. For a list of these cities, Appian, *Syr.* 57 (not accurate). I count Thessaly as part of Macedonia. Greek place-names are rare—only 4: Megara in Syria; Anthedon in Palestine (cf. Tscherikower, p. 201); Methone in Persis (G. Herzfeld, *Klio*, viii. 14 and W. W. Tarn, *J.E.A.* 1929, p. 11 n. 4); and Achais in Aria (which cannot possibly be connected with Achaeus, as Tscherikower, p. 102, supposed).
[2] For the lists, Tscherikower, *op. cit.* pp. 174 sqq.
[3] *Ibid.* p. 176.

THE SELEUCIDS

Antiochus' review at Daphne (25,000 or 30,000, as against 20,000 at Raphia and 16,000 at Magnesia, pp. 143 sqq.) is too obvious to be ignored. It is difficult not to speak of the two sets of facts in terms of cause and effect. Whether it is right to do so is another matter, for there is no means of proving or disproving the suggestion. It remains a probability merely, but perhaps a strong one.

This completes a very brief abstract of the history of Seleucid colonization in so far as it can possibly affect the army. There remain many questions to be resolved as to the organization and practical working of the system, and a few pieces of evidence that may be of use towards resolving them; but anything like a complete or even a coherent account is still impossible. All that we have established so far is that the Seleucids followed the lead of Antigonus in founding many new cities, that the presence of "Macedonians" in some of the cities argues a military connection of some sort, and that in these cases at least the new foundation probably consisted originally, whether exclusively or in part, of a κατοικία of military settlers. Some previous writers have insisted on the distinction between κατοικία and πόλις as if it were fast and unalterable.[1] It is now clear that this view is not correct.[2] In the first place there are the "Macedonians" who strike coins and are therefore certainly citizens of a πόλις; but this is not conclusive because we cannot tell for certain that they were ever originally κάτοικοι without being πολῖται. The case of Thyatira too does not really prove anything.[3] Strabo calls Thyatira κατοικία Μακεδόνων, and Stephanus derives the name from θυγατήρ and says that the city was founded by Seleucus I. The false derivation does not stultify the history, which is proved by two inscriptions of Macedonians at Thyatira, one as early as 275–274 B.C.[4] The other, of uncertain date,

---

[1] E.g. A. Schulten, *Hermes*, xxxiii. (1897), pp. 523 sqq. and 533, following to some extent G. Radet, *De coloniis a Macedonibus in Asiam cis Taurum deductis* (Paris 1892). Both these writers have valuable information on the κατοικίαι in Asia Minor.
[2] Cf. F. Oertel in P.-W. *s.v.* κάτοικοι, p. 12, and W. W. Tarn, *Hellenistic Civilisation*, pp. 134–5.
[3] Schulten, p. 528, seems to use it to prove that κάτοικοι cannot be πολῖται. Of similar value to the numismatic evidence is the inscription Βλαυνδέων Μακεδόνων ἡ βουλή καί ὁ δῆμος, *C.I.G.* 3866.
[4] J. Keil u. A. v. Premerstein, *Reise in Lydien*, ii. No. 19.

is a dedication—Βασιλεῖ Σελεύκωι τῶν ἐν Θυατείροις Μακεδόνων οἱ ἡγεμόνες καὶ οἱ στρατιῶται. Here the military organization is apparent, differing from the Μακεδόνων ἡ βουλὴ καὶ ὁ δῆμος of Blaundos. But, first, a military organization does not absolutely exclude a concurrent political organization; and also Thyatira was most probably an old Lydian city existing before the Seleucid κατοικία,[1] and is not a fair test of a system concerned mainly with new Hellenistic foundations. And the Blaundos inscription is of imperial date, which leaves several centuries for a possible change from κατοικία to πόλις status.

Finally there is the case of Magnesia ad Sipylum near Smyrna. We possess a long and extremely complicated inscription (ca. 244 B.C.) by which the δῆμος of Smyrna confers its citizenship upon military settlers at Magnesia and a neighbouring fort (χωρίον) called Palaimagnesia.[2] The circumstances are peculiar, because this grant of citizenship is made at a time shortly after the accession of Seleucus II, when he had not yet disposed of Berenice's rival claimant to the throne. It is evident that Smyrna is acting on behalf of Seleucus (no doubt instructed by him), and that an effort is being made to confirm the loyalty of the military settlers and other soldiers at Magnesia and Palaimagnesia. The salient points in the inscription are these: (1) Magnesia is itself a πόλις (l. 56 and elsewhere). Its inhabitants are divided into two classes: (i) Military, (a) κάτοικοι οἱ κατὰ πόλιν ἱππεῖς καὶ πεζοί (35 and passim, with variants in phraseology, but never in sense); (b) κάτοικοι οἱ ἐν τοῖς ὑπαίθροις ἱππεῖς καὶ πεζοί (35 and passim, with variants in phraseology, but never in sense); (ii) Civilian, οἱ ἄλλοι οἰκηταί (35 and passim, with variants). (2) All the κάτοικοι now become πολῖται of Smyrna (35–36 and elsewhere).[3] (3) The κάτοικοι do not on that account cease to owe allegiance to Seleucus. They keep their land and with it their obligations. (This must be the interpretation of the phrase ὅσα παρείληφαν παρὰ τοῦ βασιλέως Σελεύκου φυλάξαντες εἰς δύναμιν εἶναι τὴν αὐτῶν ἀποδώσουσιν τῶι βασιλεῖ Σελεύκωι (38–39).)

In the case of the fort Palaimagnesia the situation is even

[1] Cf. Tscherikower, p. 22.   [2] O.G.I.S. i. 229.
[3] This being so it is immaterial for the present argument whether the κάτοικοι were already πολῖται of Magnesia or not: Oertel (P.-W. loc. cit. p. 6) thinks not.

clearer. Not only all the κάτοικοι become citizens of Smyrna (98 sqq.), but also some soldiers on active service at that moment who are on garrison duty there. (*a*) Infantry of the phalanx— Τίμωνι καὶ τοῖς πεζοῖς τοῖς τεταγμένοις ὑπὸ Τίμωνα τοῖς ἀποταχθεῖσιν ἀπὸ τῆς φάλαγγος ἐπὶ τὴν φυλακὴν τοῦ χωρίου (103–4). (*b*) Persians (cavalry?) under Omanes. ((*c*) Mercenaries in the pay of Smyrna sent there as a garrison.) Here too by receiving πολιτεία the κάτοικοι do not cease to be κάτοικοι nor the soldiers to be soldiers. In this case the inscription says specifically that the κάτοικοι are to keep "the land (κλήρους) which Antiochus I gave to them" (100); and the garrison troops are to continue "to receive *from the Royal Treasury* the allowances and pay (τά τε μετρήματα καὶ τὰ ὀψώνια τἄλλα) which they have previously received from the Royal Treasury" (106 sqq.).

This inscription is of the first importance, because it proves that the Seleucid system differed from the Ptolemaic system, in that its military settlers could be attached to a πόλις; could be, in fact, πολῖται as well as κάτοικοι (or perhaps *become* πολῖται instead of κάτοικοι). The possible significance of this discovery will be shown later (pp. 162 sqq.).

In the meantime the inscription has also some importance on the purely military side. It shows a military organization of the κάτοικοι at Magnesia, parallel to the organization at Thyatira (above—τῶν ἐν Θ. Μακεδόνων οἱ ἡγεμόνες καὶ οἱ στρατιῶται). It may be said that a military organization does not necessarily prove anything, because it has been shown already that the elaborate organization in Egypt became at one time a pure formality, and was in fact a failure. Moreover the presence at Palaimagnesia of a garrison of soldiers who are not themselves settlers does not speak highly for the military efficiency of the settlers themselves: can it be that the guardians require guarding? This last question is not quite as awkward as it sounds, because the circumstances at Magnesia are exceptional: the settlers may have been perfectly willing and able to serve as active soldiers, but there were at the time two claimants to the throne, and it was important that they should serve the right man; this may explain the garrison from Seleucus' phalanx and Persians, as it certainly explains the whole transaction between the city of Smyrna and the settlers at Magnesia. With regard to the more general criticism, that a military organization may mean little or nothing, the reply is not so easy. Perhaps the most convincing reply is merely to point to the Seleucid phalanx in action (pp. 143 sqq.). But there remain several other documents to examine, which throw some light on the condition of the settlers, though the light does not always reveal the kind of thing that we would most wish to see.

Perhaps the most interesting new discoveries in Seleucid history are the result of the excavations at Doura-Europos on the Euphrates. But it must be confessed that, for the present purpose, Doura is a sad disappointment. It is not that there is no evidence, but that the evidence is disquieting. Up to a point indeed the finds tell us what we want to know; that is to say, they confirm what we had been told already by various literary sources.[1] The earliest walls of fortification (the so-called "redoute") date from the late fourth century (Νικάνορος κτίσμα, note 1); but the city walls are perhaps a century later, dating from Antiochus III.[2] Finally, the settlement long outlives the Seleucids; it continues to exist under the Parthian kings, and becomes an outpost of the Roman empire. Doura was in fact a strategic point of importance, on the eastern route from Palmyra and Antioch near the place where it crossed the Euphrates: the foundation should be a military settlement in the first place, and one might expect to find traces of a military organization like that at Magnesia and Thyatira. The actual finds are disappointing. Traces of occupation in the Seleucid period (apart from the walls themselves) are extraordinarily few.[3] But among the valuable parchments discovered there are two which ought to serve our purpose. The first is a deed of mortgage, by which a certain Aristonax mortgages land lying ἐν τῇ Ἀρύββου ἑκάδι ἐν

[1] These sources are to be found collected in *Fouilles de Doura-Europos* (F. Cumont), Paris 1926, pp. lxv sqq. The most important are Pol. v. 48. 16 (cf. *op. cit.* p. xxv), and Isidore of Charax (*Geogr. Graeci Minores*, i. p. 248). ἔνθεν Δοῦρα, Νικάνορος πόλις, κτίσμα Μακεδόνων, ὑπὸ δὲ Ἑλλήνων Εὔρωπος καλεῖται.

[2] *Excavations at Dura-Europos*, (P. V. C. Baur, etc.), i. pp. 50 sqq.; ii. p. 151 and n. 1. Other relevant pieces of evidence from the American excavations are the early inscription "Seleucus ?Nicator" (iii. pp. 54 sqq.), and the coin of Seleucus Nicator (iii. pp. 1 and 149 sqq.) and other Seleucid coins.

[3] Inscriptions of the Parthian era are of value, however, because they retain Seleucid titles, etc., e.g. στρατηγὸς τῆς πόλεως (*Fouilles*, Inscriptions, Nos. 52, 116, 134); ἐπιστάτης τῆς πόλεως (Nos. 53 and 134); βουλή and βουλευτής, etc. (Nos. 9 and 50).

THE SELEUCIDS

τῶι Κόνωνος κλήρωι.[1] The meaning of "hekas" is uncertain, but "the lot of Conon" is thought to be a piece of land retaining the name of its original settler and now in the possession of Aristonax.[2] If the original Conon was a military settler, Aristonax ought to have inherited military obligations along with his κλῆρος, and it is surprising to find that he can apparently mortgage part of the κλῆρος at will. One would have thought that the first principle of the system must be for the settler to "keep safe what he received from King Seleucus" (the Magnesia inscription, above), if indeed he is to continue to be an *active* military settler, serving in the field army when required.[3] And the date of this parchment is 195 B.C., when the "phalanx" of Antiochus III was in its prime.

This is discouraging enough, but there is worse to come. The second relevant parchment appears to be a fragment of the original *lex coloniae* (not the original document indeed, but a copy of much later date).[4] The surviving fragment contains the *lex ab intestato*, prescribing the order of succession to κλῆροι becoming vacant by the death of the first possessors: τῶν δὲ τελευτησάντω[ν τ]ὰς κληρονο|μείας ἀποδίδοσ[θ]ε τοῖς [ἄγ]χιστα γένους· ἀγχιστεῖς δὲ οἶδε. ((1) children or adopted children; (2) father; (3) mother, if not married again; (4) brother consanguineous; (5) sister consanguineous;[5] (6) paternal grandfather; (7) paternal grandmother; (8) paternal cousin german;

---
[1] *Fouilles*, Parchment No. I, ll. 1–2 (pp. 287 sqq.).
[2] *Ibid.* p. 290.
[3] One naturally compares this mortgage with the mortgage of the Sardis inscription (W. H. Buckler and D. M. Robinson in *A.J.A.* xvi. (1912), pp. 12 sqq.). There Mnesimachus mortgages his estate which includes two κλῆροι. But there is really no analogy between the two cases, for Mnesimachus was certainly not an ordinary military settler with two κλῆροι (like some of the Magnesia settlers, *O.G.I.S.* i. 229, ll. 100 sqq.); he was the possessor of a large estate including several villages, of which the two κλῆροι form an insignificant part. He was probably a high officer of Antigonus, and received the estate as a gift to himself and his heirs, subject to a φόρος payable to the Royal Treasury. The military obligation would not enter into this case.
[4] *Fouilles*, Parchment V (pp. 309 sqq.); it is impossible to fix a precise date; but it is certainly later than 100 B.C., and probably very much later.
[5] The parchment itself gives (ll. 6–8):

ἐὰν δὲ μηθείς, τοῦ νόνου·
ἀδελφοὶ ὁμοπάτριοι· ἐὰν δὲ μηδὲ
οὗτοι ὦσιν, ἀδελφοὶ ὁμοπάτριοι·

which makes the order of succession (see text above) (4) paternal uncle; (5) brother consanguineous. But line 6 was suspect from the first (*Fouilles*,

(9) failing all these, the property to return to the king.) From the legal standpoint this document has two main peculiarities. First, there is no provision at all for the disposal of the κλῆρος by testament. Second, the ascendant line of succession is extremely prominent, the descendant line extending in fact no further than first cousins by the father's side: this prominence in the ascendant is unique in Greek law, so far as is known.[1] Neither of these legal peculiarities is surprising to us, in view of the historical peculiarity of Doura. The king is legislating for a new colony of Graeco-Macedonian settlers to whom he has made grants of land. He wishes the land to remain in their families, and hence the gift of land is not accompanied by freedom of testamentary disposal. Perhaps he also wishes the land to be held by settlers as purely Graeco-Macedonian as possible, and hence the ascendant line in the order of succession. The adherence throughout to the paternal side will have the same tendency; but it is not peculiar to Doura, κρατεῖν τοὺς ἄρρενας καὶ τοὺς ἐκ τῶν ἀρρένων being a principle of the Solonian law.

It is not these peculiarities in the Doura law which cause perplexity to the historian, but rather the fact that there are not more of them. The great obstacle is, that females can inherit a κλῆρος. If it is assumed that the original settler is a military settler with an obligation to go on active service when required, it is difficult to see what is to be done with his mother (if not married again), his sister, or his paternal grandmother, should she inherit his κλῆρος when he dies, as she is entitled to do. Two alternatives are possible. Either these κλῆροι at Doura are not military κλῆροι at all, a conclusion most damaging to the whole reconstruction of the military settlement system, Doura

loc. cit.), and this order was unsatisfactory to the lawyers. The passage has been emended as follows:

ἐὰν δὲ μηθεὶς τούτων ᾖ,
ἀδελφοὶ ὁμοπάτριοι· ἐὰν δὲ μηδὲ
οὗτοι ὦσιν, ἀδελφαὶ ὁμοπάτριοι.

Demetrios Pappulias, Συμβολὴ εἰς τὴν ἱστορίαν τῆς ἐξ ἀδιαθέτου κληρονομικῆς διαθήκης ἐν τῷ Ἑλληνικῷ δικαίῳ. Ἀκαδημία Ἀθηνῶν, 1929. Cf. L. Wenger in *Archiv*, x. (1932), p. 131. Pappulias' emendation is certainly right.

[1] But it is only fair to say that very little is known at all. The situation is well summarized by M. Bernard Haussoullier in *Rev. hist. de droit français et étranger*, 1923, esp. pp. 530 sqq., where it is considered in relation to Athenian law and the law of Gortyn.

THE SELEUCIDS 159

being one of the places *par excellence* which *ought* to have military κλῆροι—κτίσμα Μακεδόνων according to Isidore, and having the Macedonian place-name Europos. Or else (the other alternative) the possibility of inheritance by females was not so preposterous in practice as it sounds. After all, a settler had only to get or adopt a single son for the whole remaining order of succession to become superfluous as applied to his κλῆρος, and probably most of the settlers had sons. No doubt if the king had had a free choice, he might have excluded females from inheriting κλῆροι. But the break from the traditional Greek law would have been abrupt and stern, and the settlers could have had little sense of security had there been the possibility of a mother or a daughter being left destitute. The maker of the law was legislating for a real and not for an ideal state of affairs, and he may have had no choice but to follow the main lines of the Greek law of inheritance, and to submit to the military loss it involved, which may in practice have been comparatively slight. There is the possibility in addition that this law is concerned mainly with fixing the point at which succession by ἀγχιστεία was to be interrupted by the king's right of escheat. And if we possessed the whole *lex coloniae* (which may have filled the remaining part of our parchment—for only part survives)[1] we might find in it some solution to this problem of female succession. It is possible that provision was made by which the κλῆρος was responsible for providing a soldier, who need not necessarily be its owner; and this would explain the mortgaged κλῆρος also. In brief, although this law seems at first sight to exclude any possibility of the κλῆροι at Doura being military κλῆροι, a second consideration leaves the issue at least open: and the *a priori* probability, that Doura *was* founded for military settlers, still remains.[2]

[1] Cf. esp. P. Koschaker, in *Zeitschrift d. Savigny-Stiftung f. Rechts-Geschichte*, 46. ii. (1926), p. 302.
[2] Throughout this discussion I have taken a somewhat strict view of the settler's obligations in Asia with regard to his *kleros*, believing that the stricter the obligations the more likely the settler to be of military value. In Egypt, however, the obligations were not particularly strict in practice (cf. Lesquier, pp. 202 sqq., on "Les biens clérouquiques", etc.; and M. Rostovtzeff, *Gesch. d. röm. Kolonates*, pp. 23 sqq.); but I know of only one case of female inheritance (E. Sachau, *Aramäische Pap. u. Ost.* No. 30: 494 B.C., under the Persian administration).

An interesting parallel to this Doura fragment of a *lex coloniae* is perhaps to be found in the παλαιά συγγραφή of the Avroman parchments.[1] Here the settlement system is seen flourishing in Media under a Parthian king long after the Seleucid empire has passed away (the dates of the two parchments are 88 or 24 B.C. and 22 B.C. or A.D. 42).[2] It is well known that the Parthian kings took readily to Greek culture and set a high value on their Greek population. The Greek cities in the East were left in enjoyment of their native organization, and the same must have been true of the military settlers, who may have been regarded as especially desirable and useful subjects. In this connection two Greek inscriptions of Susa are extremely significant: their dates are respectively 98 B.C. and A.D. 2.[3] The first of them shows Greeks (or descendants of Greeks) on garrison duty at Susa.[4] The second is even more illuminating: it is a short elegiac poem composed for Zamaspes the "stratiarch" of Susa in gratitude for a successful scheme of irrigation. The last four lines are worth quoting:

ἀνθ' ὧν μιν μεγάλης ἄκρας φρουροὶ ναετῆρες
ἕστασαν μνήμαις ἄφθιτον ἐσσομένοις,
τῶν κλήρους ἀνέσωσε πάλαι λειφθέντας ἀνύδρους
νάμασι Γονδείσου καρποφόρους θέμενος.

This is perhaps the most important piece of evidence of all that

[1] E. H. Minns, *J.H.S.* 35, 1915, pp. 22 sqq.; esp. Parchment I, l. 18; II, l. 9, and p. 52. Doubt has been cast on this interpretation of παλαιά συγγραφή, by Haussoullier, *loc. cit.* p. 539: Haussoullier believes that this συγγραφή may be merely an earlier legal transaction, now being used as the basis of these later transactions; I think this less probable.
[2] The earlier dates are those of Minns, *loc. cit.*; the later of Rostovtzeff, *Excavations at Dura-Europos*, ii. p. 206, and Yale Classical Studies, ii. pp. 39 sqq. It is a question as to whether the dates in the parchments are to be reckoned as of Seleucid or Parthian era. A decision is difficult, and (luckily) unnecessary here, as it cannot affect my argument.
[3] F. Cumont, *Comptes rendus de l'académie des inscriptions et belles lettres*, 1931, pp. 233 sqq.
[4] Οἱ ἐκ τῆς μέσης ἐφημερίας Λυσίμαχον Ἀπολλοφάνου τῶν σωματοφυλάκων τὸν ἐξ αὐτῶν εὐχρηστίας ἕνεκεν...etc. I think M. Cumont is wrong in inferring (pp. 236 sqq.) that there is a *corps* of Greek σωματοφύλακες on duty here. Under the Seleucids σωματοφύλαξ was simply an honorary title, as he himself points out; and the text itself does not really support his inference. Lysimachus is probably an officer of the garrison, who has in some way received the title σωματοφύλαξ, and is now honoured by his men; but there is nothing to imply that they are all σωματοφύλακες too, and it would in fact be very odd if they were.

THE SELEUCIDS

we have considered, and fortunately it speaks for itself. These settlers are still called φρουροί, at least 150 years after the settlement can possibly have been founded: their military duties have not fallen completely into abeyance even under a new, foreign government. If they remained "resident guards of the great citadel" for a Parthian king, they were certainly as much for the Seleucids. And it may not be too bold to infer that they were more, that it was in fact from them and the other military settlers like them that the Seleucids recruited the phalanx of their field army for Raphia and the other great battles.

This digression on the military settlements and settlers is not really irrelevant though it may appear so. In the first place many of the earlier settlers must have been Greek mercenaries before they became settlers. But the real object was to try to clear up the question of the Seleucid phalanx, to find out what it really was and why it lasted so well. To prove that the phalanx of Antiochus the Great was *not* an army of recruited mercenaries is one stage, and it is hoped that implicit proof of this will have been found in most of the evidence for military settlers that has been discussed. But there is explicit evidence too, which becomes all the stronger from the fact that it relates to the declining years of the dynasty, when the phalanx might reasonably be expected to have fallen into decay. The phalanx at Daphne (165 B.C.) was more numerous than that at Magnesia. And the conflict of interests in the time of Demetrius II (*ca.* 145 B.C.) between the foreign mercenaries and the "Macedonians" proves, first, that the latter were not yet a spent force, and second, that they were not themselves mercenaries recently recruited, or anything like it. They are called by Justin *milites paterni*, and by the author of 1 Maccabees "the forces of his father" as opposed to "certain bands of strangers, whom he (Demetrius) had collected from the isles of the heathen".[1] The preference shown by Demetrius for his mercenaries at the expense of the "Macedonians", a preference quite alien to the hereditary policy of the Seleucids, is well described by Josephus: "Seeing that there was peace and no danger or fear of war, he dismissed his army and reduced the pay: even so he gave it only to the mercenaries who came with him from Crete and the other islands. For this

[1] Justin 35. 2; 1 Macc. 11. 38.

reason he became very unpopular with the soldiers, to whom he no longer gave anything, though the previous kings had continued to pay (or maintain, χορηγοῦντες) them even in time of peace, in order to ensure their loyalty when the need for them in war did arise".[1] In 1 Maccabees this dismissal of the army is called sending them away "every one to his own place", which is particularly appropriate to soldiers from military settlements.[2] Finally, one may suspect that the "phalanx" still survived about 95 B.C., when we have a notice of communal dining *al fresco* introduced by Heracleon the minister of Antiochus Grypus.[3]

This is one stage reached: the phalanx was not an army of mercenaries. The second stage is to show what it was. And in spite of one or two awkwardnesses in the evidence (the mortgaged κλῆρος and the inheritance of κλῆροι by women, pp. 156 sqq.) there can be little doubt as to the direction in which the evidence points in general: the military settlers were the material from which the phalanx was made. Their function was the same as that of the cleruchs in Egypt. The third stage is to show why the two systems in Egypt and in Syria, introduced from the same motives and using the same material, produced such widely differing results: for the plain fact is that whereas in Egypt the cleruch system was, comparatively speaking, a failure, in Syria the system seems to have been a great success and even outlived the dynasty that introduced it. This third stage is certainly outside the province of this work, and ought to be treated in a special study of the κατοικίαι of the Seleucid empire. But certain suggestions may be helpful. First, there seems to have been no difference in the human material used by the Ptolemies and the Seleucids adequate to explain the different results: Seleucus I may have had a few thousand more Macedonians than Ptolemy I, but in both cases the greater part of the cleruchs or κάτοικοι must have been originally mercenaries. Contributory causes of the difference may have been the strategic position of the two empires, and perhaps even the character of the two ruling houses. Egypt itself was almost, for strategical

---

[1] Joseph. *Ant.* xiii. 129 sqq.   [2] 1 Macc. 11. 38.
[3] Posidonius 24 (*F.G.H.* ii. A. p. 232), ἐποιεῖτο δὲ τῶν στρατιωτῶν τὰς κατακλίσεις ἐπὶ τοῦ ἐδάφους ἐν ὑπαίθρῳ ἀνὰ χιλίους δειπνίζων. τὸ δὲ δεῖπνον ἦν ἄρτος μέγας καὶ κρέας, τὸ δὲ πότον κεκραμένος οἶνος οἷος δήποτε ὕδατι ψυχρῷ. διηκόνουν δὲ ἄνδρες μαχαιροφόροι καὶ σιωπὴ ἦν εὔτακτος.

THE SELEUCIDS

purposes, an island, and Egyptian strategy the strategy of an insular power with foreign possessions to defend; Seleucid strategy was "continental" and probably kept larger armies in more continuous employment. But the truest cause (to use a discredited phrase) is internal, a difference inherent in the two systems themselves, for though the material was much the same in each case, the method of using it was different. The difference is, in a word, that whereas in Egypt the system was based on a rural organization, in Asia it was based on the *polis*.[1] In Egypt the cleruchies were scattered over the country and superimposed on a very ancient rural civilization; and there were only two true Greek cities, Alexandria and Ptolemais.[2] In Asia the κατοικίαι were far more widely scattered, and an ancient civilization was equally there before them; but in Asia new Greek cities were founded simultaneously, and the connection between them and the κατοικίαι has been hinted at above. One is not concerned here with the social and economic aspect of the settlements, but from the purely military point of view this difference is of the deepest significance, and may well explain by itself the long life and vigour of the Seleucid military system, and the comparatively rapid decay of the cleruchies in Egypt as a military asset. And the idea is illuminating not merely for the military historian but for the history of Greek politics and civilization in general.

There is only one other point that can be mentioned here. It is true, as Bouché-Leclercq pointed out, that there is no evidence for a system of ἐπίγονοι in Asia analogous to the systems of

---

[1] This cause was proposed to me by Dr Tarn, who read this work in its earlier stages. I was convinced at the time that he must be right, and am more certain of it now that I have gone into the question of the Seleucid κατοικίαι more closely. It is probably one of those things that can never be definitely proved; but I believe it is also a thing that, once suggested, is so obviously right as not to require proving.

[2] It is true that in the third century soldiers in Egypt could become citizens of Alexandria (cf. *Dikaiomata*, I. iv. 159 sqq., τῶν ἐν τῷ στρατιωτικῷ τεταγμένων ὅσοι ἂν ἐν ᾿Αλεξανδρείᾳ πεπολιτογραφημένοι...). But in the first place one does not know how freely this citizenship was given (W. Schubart, in *G.G.A.* 1913, pp. 613 sqq., perhaps overestimates the importance of this passage). And secondly, even if it were given freely, citizenship of Alexandria, the great metropolis, would be a very different thing from citizenship of (e.g.) Doura-Europos: in a small city the Greek political life and traditions would be far more likely to survive than in Alexandria with its great mixed population and royal court.

Alexander and of the Ptolemies.[1] But the objection is not decisive, as Bouché-Leclercq supposed. Apart from the fact that the evidence for Asia is far scantier than that for Egypt, it is also quite possible that the mere act of living in a κατοικία was sufficient to make any man of military age liable for service, just as if he had been a real Macedonian citizen living in Macedonia; that the network of settlements was in effect the Seleucids' "Macedonia", upon which it was their purpose to draw for a constant supply of Graeco-Macedonian soldiery born and bred in the traditions of the phalanx of Philip and Alexander. Moreover, the constant warfare in which they were involved may have made them something very like a standing army.[2] Certainly they came nearer to it than the "Macedonians" of Egypt, nearer perhaps even than the real Macedonians of Europe under the Antigonids. It was a matter for comment when Demetrius II dismissed them "every one to his own place" in time of peace; and Josephus would seem to imply that they had been kept together *and paid* by earlier kings even when there was no immediate fighting to be done (which is not as remarkable as it sounds, because the contingency was rare enough). This makes them out to be the nearest approach to a standing army, such as our own, that occurs in ancient history between the army of Philip and Alexander and that of the Roman empire. Certainly they have nothing in common with the ordinary mercenary army, except in so far as recruited mercenaries may have been added to the settlers from time to time to fill up gaps or infuse new blood. The Seleucid phalanx was an army of nationals, and cannot be placed in the same category as the mercenary contingents who are often to be observed fighting as auxiliaries by its side.

[1] See above, p. 115. For Alexander's ἐπίγονοι, Justin xii. 4. 8.

[2] Bouché-Leclercq, pp. 478 sqq., acutely points out the important intrusions of the army into politics, and especially in questions of the *succession*, in which they behave like direct descendants of the real Macedonian armies. E.g. on the death of Seleucus III it is the army that summons his brother Antiochus (III) from Babylon (Eusebius i. 253 Sch., exercitu a Babelone eum revocante; Hieron. in Daniel 11. 10, exercitus qui erat in Syria Antiochum fratrem eius de Babylone vocavit ad regnum).

THE SELEUCIDS

3. THE MERCENARIES

The army list at Raphia shows that Greek mercenary infantry was still in demand, and obtainable, in Asia towards the end of the third century (pp. 143 sqq.); and it is hardly to be doubted that it is only the poor information that prevents our tracing their service with the Seleucid armies throughout the century. There was of course always the regular "phalanx"; but obviously the phalanx could not be everywhere in the immense area covered by the empire, and, especially, recruited mercenaries, well led and regularly paid, are likely to have been more efficient than military settlers whose mobilization in itself must have caused wasteful delays and whose fighting qualities were liable to decay in periods of inactivity.[1] It may be guessed that the government was always anxious to procure as many Greek mercenaries as it could, if only in the hope of adding them eventually to the Graeco-Macedonian population within its frontiers. And the reason why there were not more Greek mercenaries at Raphia and at Magnesia is probably that there were no more to be had. The Miles Gloriosus of Plautus, a recruiting officer of Antiochus visiting Ephesus, was probably a common enough figure in the cities of the coast;[2] but there were other employers nearer home, and it can never have been possible to make up the whole of the required army strength with Greeks. Nevertheless, even in the second century, Rome thought it worth while to prohibit Seleucid recruiting west of Mt. Taurus. In addition to the clause to that effect in the treaty of Apameia, there is a proposed agreement with the Aetolians just before Magnesia, according to which no Aetolian is to cross over to Asia "either independently or by official command".[3] Probably the severest loss to Seleucid recruiting was the island of Crete, which was closed to it after 188 B.C. Cretans are missing from the Daphne review, though they have been present previously in all the great enterprises of Antiochus III; against Molon, at Raphia, against Arsaces, at Magnesia, and probably before that in

---
[1] Such periods were, however, rarities to the Seleucids.
[2] Plautus, *M.G.* 72 sqq., etc.
[3] Pol. xx. 10. 4, μήτε κατ' ἰδίαν μήτε μετὰ κοίνου δόγματος.

Greece.[1] They do appear again in the service of Demetrius II, of whom more will be said later.

Of the barbarian mercenaries the most interesting are the Asiatic Gauls, the Galatians. The story of these warrior peoples after the time of their crossing into Asia in 278 B.C. is one of incessant fighting, now for private gain, now in the service of one or other of the monarchs. Their first service was with Nicomedes of Bithynia, at whose invitation they first landed in Asia.[2] They are found later with Mithridates I of Pontus and with his successor Ariobarzanes,[3] and they helped Antiochus Hierax against Seleucus II at the battle of Ancyra.[4] Their first dealings with the Seleucids were hostile, and they were defeated in a great battle by Antiochus II in 275 B.C.[5] The first notice of them as Seleucid mercenaries is shortly after the accession of Seleucus II: it was a bodyguard of Gauls that murdered Berenice the mother of the rival claimant to the throne.[6] The Gauls were certainly chief among the mercenaries of Antiochus Hierax, as is proved by the Pergamene inscriptions recording Attalus' victories over both.[7] From that time on they were probably always to be found in the royal army also.[8] Under Antiochus the Great they appear in the army of 220 B.C. (though they are absent from Raphia), and at Magnesia; and there were 5000 Gauls at Antiochus IV's review (pp. 143 sqq.). After that they are not heard of again, but that is not surprising in view of our ignorance in general. Along with the Gauls go the Thracians, who like them were included in all three of the great armies which have been described above. We hear of his employing Thracian mercenaries in one of his Thracian campaigns (196–194 B.C.), this being the only certain instance of his recruiting European Thracians.[9] It was at this time too that he entered into friendly relations with some

---

[1] Against Arsaces, 2000 Κρῆτας ἀσπιδιώτας (Pol. x. 29. 6). In Greece, a Cretan officer (id. xx. 3. 7). The other references will be found above under Raphia and Magnesia.
[2] Livy 38. 16. 6 sqq.; Memnon 19 (F.H.G. iii. p. 535).
[3] Apollonius 13 (F.H.G. ii. p. 312).
[4] Justin 27. 2. 10; Eusebius i. 251. 23; Plut. Moral. 489 A.
[5] Appian, Syr. 65 (Lucian, Zeuxis 8).
[6] Polyaen. vii. 50; Justin 27. 1.
[7] Insch. v. Perg. i. 23, etc.; cf. Justin 27. 2.
[8] E.g. Seleucus III murdered by a Gaul called Apaturius (Pol. iv. 48; Trog. Prol. 27).
[9] Polyaen. iv. 16.

THE SELEUCIDS

of the Gauls of Thrace, whose fine physique attracted his favourable notice, and who may have swelled the numbers of his Gauls at Magnesia.[1] But in the main it must have been the Galatians who came in the greatest numbers to fight for him; and in particular after the area open to his recruiting became circumscribed by the Roman treaty, Galatia and other barbarian strongholds of Asia must have become, next to the Graeco-Macedonian settlements, his greatest military assets.

Other barbarian nations too were called upon to supply cavalry and light troops generally to the army. Such were the Mysians at Magnesia and Daphne,[2] the Scythian Dahae and the Arabs at Raphia and Magnesia, and perhaps the Cilicians at Raphia, Magnesia and Daphne. In general it is hard to say whether the kings had any but a nominal right to their services (in the case of the Arabs and Scythians not even that), and they probably regarded them as mercenaries pure and simple. The experience of the Jews in the second century illustrates the methods of recruiting. Shortly after Alexander Balas had granted independence to the Jews he wrote to Jonathan, the popular leader and High Priest, intending to use the new friendship to the end of obtaining new soldiers: "I will further, that there be enrolled among the king's forces about thirty thousand men of the Jews, unto whom pay shall be given, as belongeth to all the king's forces. And of them some shall be placed in the king's strongholds, of whom also some shall be set over the affairs of the kingdom, which are of trust: and I will that their overseers and governors be of themselves, and that they live after their own laws, even as the king hath commanded in the land of Judea".[3] The danger of such an arrangement is obvious. The Jews were to be commanded by their own officers, and their usefulness depended entirely upon friendly relations being

[1] Appian, *Syr.* 6. 1 sqq.
[2] It is just possible that Mysians may have come to denote a *kind* of troops, like the "racial" hipparchies in Egypt. One hears of κατοικίαι τῶν Μυσῶν in 216 B.C. (Pol. v. 77. 7), which may mean that Mysians were included in the "regular" army, whether in the phalanx or the cavalry. But after 188 B.C. the κατοικίαι τῶν Μυσῶν were included in the kingdom of Pergamum, so that the Mysians of the Daphne review were either mercenaries, or were not Mysians at all but merely people who fought like Mysians (however Mysians did fight).
[3] 1 Macc. 10. 36 sqq.

maintained between the two governments: if they ceased to be friendly, then the mercenaries ceased to be useful and became dangerous.[1] In the unsettled state of the Seleucid kingdom during most of the second century kings and pretenders probably recruited foreign soldiers desperately in their shortsighted efforts to meet the needs of the moment, and in consequence the real strength and discipline of the army must have deteriorated from the standard of Antiochus the Great and his predecessors.

As far as numbers went, indeed, the armies that fought in the civil wars of the two Demetrii and Alexander Balas can have been little inferior to those of earlier kings. It is interesting to see that the "Macedonians" usually remained true to the king by rightful succession.[2] When Demetrius I, who had been kept a prisoner in Rome, escaped with a few friends and landed in Syria, he was very soon in command of an army. We are told that he recruited mercenaries at Tripolis, but the immediate collapse of the opposition makes it almost certain that the "Macedonians" had chosen to fight for him and to desert Antiochus. In the same way Alexander Balas, the pretender supported by Rome, had to win his kingdom with a mercenary army and with the help of the kings of Pergamum, Cappadocia and Egypt. The Roman Senate rescinded in his favour the ban on recruiting in their sphere of influence, and it seems that his officer Heraclides recruited soldiers on his way to Asia (i.e. in Greece?), and also in Asia with Ephesus as his centre: the friendship of Pergamum would be of help there.[3] Alexander probably never won the whole-hearted support of the "Macedonians", which perhaps explains his efforts to get fresh soldiers from Judaea: he finally lost his kingdom through the desertion of the "Macedonians" in battle to Demetrius II (as he then became).[4] This young son of Demetrius I had landed in Asia with a great army of mer-

[1] Antiochus VI would not take 2000 Jewish soldiers sent to him by the High Priest Simon (1 Macc. 15. 26).
[2] Two earlier examples of the same loyalty early in the reign of Antiochus III: (1) the revolt of Achaeus: Achaeus' troops mutinied and would not march against τὸν κατὰ φύσιν αὐτῶν ἐξ ἀρχῆς ὑπάρχοντα βασιλέα (Pol. v. 57)—this *must* be the Graeco-Macedonian κάτοικοι. (2) Molon's revolt (*ibid.* 54): Molon's troops refused to fight when they saw Antiochus.
[3] Pol. xxxiii. 18. 14; Joseph. *Ant.* xiii. 58 sqq.
[4] Justin 35. 2.

THE SELEUCIDS

cenaries recruited from Crete. This was of course a flagrant breach of the Roman interdict, for it cannot be supposed that the Romans granted the favour to the son of the king whom they had caused to be deposed, and against the interests of the ruling king their protégé: Demetrius must have acted without permission, and, as he himself was only fourteen, the army was collected and commanded by a Cretan *condottiere* called Lasthenes.[1] It was this man who now directed the policy of the kingdom, turning government into piracy, reducing the army from a weapon of war to an instrument of oppression, and introducing into Antioch the worst excesses of Alexandria. He was foolish enough to disband the "regular" army altogether, so that none but the Cretan and Greek mercenaries remained on the pay list. Naturally the regular soldiers were furious. The Antiochenes too were made furious by their sufferings, and actually dared to assault the royal palace. There was a desperate battle in the city, but the Cretans, with the help of 3000 Jewish mercenaries, succeeded in repelling the attack, and then the town was given over to havoc (the Jews returned home laden with spoil and good stories of the massacre; they alone killed 100,000 civilians, according to the Jewish historians!).[2] But of course the reckoning with the "Macedonians" was to come. As soon as a rival for the throne appeared they joined him in a body, and Demetrius and his mercenaries were not strong enough to withstand them.[3]

This episode in the history of the later Seleucids proves two things. The "regular" army (as we have seen) was preserved through nearly two centuries in the most remarkable way; and mercenary service did not necessarily decline with the weakening of the empire. As the empire became a kingdom, and the kingdom became more and more circumscribed by the encroaching powers in the north and west, and less and less secure within itself, the drain of warfare did not cease, but rather became greater by the frequent civil wars of king against pretender. But

---

[1] Justin 35. 2; Joseph. *Ant.* xiii. 86; 1 Macc. 10. 67.
[2] Diod. xxxiii. 4; Joseph. *ibid.* 129 sqq.; 1 Macc. 11. 38 and 44 sqq. The influence of the mercenary captain Lasthenes upon the young Demetrius is shown by a letter in which the king addresses him as "father"—βασιλεύς Δημήτριος Λασθένει τῷ πατρὶ χαίρειν (Joseph. *ibid.* 127).
[3] Joseph. *ibid.* 144.

the "Cretan Tyranny", as Bevan well describes it, was a terrible lesson, teaching that a purely mercenary army was an impossibility, so deeply rooted was the military tradition in the Graeco-Macedonian regular soldiers. The early Seleucids had fashioned a good weapon. They clearly intended it to be their main weapon, though they could and did reinforce it with auxiliaries in the shape of hired soldiers of different types and races. These latter, however, never usurped the functions of the regulars, as did the mercenaries of Egypt in the later years of the Ptolemies. The reason for this is merely that the Seleucid regular army lasted much better than the cleruch army of Egypt, and the reason for that has been discussed already (above). The Seleucids needed mercenaries, no doubt, as our evidence has shown; but they did not, even in their declining years, need an army of mercenaries, and their use of mercenaries reveals them as having preserved the original Macedonian idea of an army with much more success than might have been expected. Their mercenaries often proved good servants; but except for Lasthenes and his Cretans, they were never allowed to become bad masters.

CHAPTER VII

PERGAMUM AND PONTUS

1. PERGAMUM[1]

IT is even more difficult to reconstruct the army of Pergamum than that of the Seleucids. The information is scanty, and what there is of it is to be used with care. If one uses every piece of evidence indiscriminately, it may be possible to reconstruct for the Attalids a system on the same principles as those we have noticed in the two previous chapters. Nevertheless, one would be making a great mistake, for while the reconstruction might seem coherent, it would certainly be false. The mistake would lie in the unhistorical method of approach: for the history of Pergamum in general comprises two distinct periods—before and after the peace treaty of 188 B.C.—and this qualification is especially true of the evidence relating to the army.

In approaching the earlier period a start is to be made from the Lilaea inscriptions, concerning a small detachment from the army of Attalus I, which may perhaps be representative of the whole. The inscriptions are in honour of the garrison of the small city of Lilaea, and this garrison had been sent by Attalus I, then an ally of the Aetolian League (probably 209–208 B.C.). The garrison consists of six tactical units called ἡγεμονίαι, of which one is of Pergamene citizens only, three are of Mysians, and the remaining two of Greek mercenaries.[2] This tells us what we may expect of the Attalid army in this period (though

---

[1] By far the best general account of the army of Pergamum is that of M. Rostovtzeff, in *C.A.H.* viii. pp. 594 sqq. G. Cardinali, *Il regno di Pergamo*, Rome 1906, pp. 211 sqq., ignores the citizen troops of Pergamum; but he was writing before the discovery of the Lilaea inscriptions, when the existence of these troops must have been highly problematical. A. J. Reinach, "Les mercenaires et les colonies militaires de Pergamon", *Rev. Arch.* 1908, pp. 176–218, 364–89; *ibid.* 1909, pp. 102 sqq., 363 sqq. (an unfinished article), discusses the evidence for mercenaries in detail and with great care, but with special reference to the well-known inscription, *O.G.I.S.* i. 266.

[2] I rely upon the description in *C.A.H.* vii. p. 594 n. 3, since three of the four inscriptions are not yet published. I owe my warmest thanks to the late M. Maurice Holleaux, who sent me particulars of the mercenaries, which are used in chapter IX (p. 241).

not necessarily *all* that we may expect). The most important thing that it establishes is that Pergamene citizens served as soldiers in the field army: and in the field army operating nearer home one would probably look for a higher proportion of citizens than the one-sixth found in this expeditionary force overseas. The position of the Mysians is not perfectly clear. The fact that they have ξεναγοί as well as ἡγεμόνες does not make them mercenaries, for the Pergamene citizens have a ξεναγός too. And the fact that Mysians appear in the army of Attalus III (133 B.C.) as military settlers may also be a false clue (p. 177). The truth is that we do not know the exact relationship of Mysia to the kingdom of Pergamum at this date, so that it is impossible to say whether these Mysians are subject levies or mercenaries.[1] The Greek mercenaries themselves yield no further information. There is no reason, on the face of it, why they should not be part of the standing army of Pergamum: of the 73 or 74 soldiers whose provenance is known, 17 come from Lysimacheia and 12 from Asia and the islands; the remainder from Greece, or the West (9).

Whatever the truth may be about the Lilaea mercenaries, there is no doubt at all that Pergamum employed mercenaries in the standing army at a very early date. The very first notice of mercenaries in the history of Pergamum is contained in a text which is one of the most important pieces of evidence in our possession not only for Pergamum but for the whole condition of mercenary service. This is a Pergamene inscription, probably of the year 260 B.C., recounting the details of a reconciliatory agreement between Eumenes I and some mercenaries who had evidently mutinied.[2] It settles numerous details about the pay and maintenance of the soldiers, and in fact constitutes a very hard and fast contract between the employer and his servants. (This contract has been very fully discussed by A. J. Reinach in an (unfinished) essay specially devoted to it, which will be used later.)[3] It is sufficient to say here that it establishes beyond all doubt that Eumenes had at this time an army of mercenaries

---

[1] Pol. v. 77. 7—κατοικίαι τῶν Μυσῶν—does not help us here, for if these κατοικίαι are military settlements at all, they are Seleucid settlements, as is clear from the context.
[2] M. Fränkel, *Insch. v. Perg.* i. 13 = *O.G.I.S.* i. 266.
[3] A. J. Reinach, *loc. cit.*; cf. pp. 282 sqq.

PERGAMUM AND PONTUS 173

in active service and apparently engaged on a long-service contract. The soldiers here in question are the garrisons of Philetaireia on the N.E. frontier of his kingdom, and of Attaleia on the river Lycus, very close to the Seleucid frontier. The troops of Philetaireia form a στρατηγία, and the στρατηγός was Paramonus, who seems to have been himself a mercenary commander, since it is obvious that he is on the side of the soldiers and not of the king. A similar command (though it is not expressly called a στρατηγία) is held at Attaleia by Polylaus, who has under him a commander of cavalry (ἵππαρχος) Attinas and his horsemen, and a Thracian (?) Oloichus with his Trallians (Paramonus may have infantry only). And there is a third commander Arces who may be in control of a smaller garrison or garrisons (Ἀρκητι καὶ τοῖς ὑφ' αὐτὸν φρούροις).[1] The inscription establishes that about the year 260 B.C. the king of Pergamum possessed a considerable mercenary force of all arms. Although it is known that he was not at that time on good terms with the Seleucid monarchy,[2] it also seems certain that this was not an army recruited merely with a view to a short campaign or a special crisis. Had that been so, Eumenes would surely have rid himself of his mutinous soldiers on the best terms possible (as Attalus I later rid himself of some Gauls who turned awkward), instead of concluding this agreement, in which he makes important concessions to soldiers who are evidently part of a permanent army. And from the same tone of concession in the agreement it may perhaps be argued that the mercenaries were too powerful to be coerced, or that they were, to put the matter crudely, more than one-half of the whole army of Pergamum.

The literary evidence for the history of Pergamum in general is so very slight, that it is only natural that it should contain very few references to the military establishment, and those mostly relating to the period when Pergamum was involved in the wars of Rome in the East. But, earlier still, we hear of an army of Gauls recruited by Attalus I for his war against Achaeus. They were of the tribe of Aegosagae, Gauls settled in Europe,

[1] *Loc. cit.* ll. 20 sqq., 54 sqq.
[2] Strabo xiii. 624 speaks of a battle at Sardis, in which king Eumenes defeated Antiochus the son of Seleucus: Eumenes became king in July 262 B.C., and Antiochus I died in July 261 B.C., so that the battle of Sardis was probably early in 261.

and it may be thought a little discreditable to the power which had done perhaps the most to quell the Gallic peril of some fifty years before, that it should now introduce a fresh instalment of the same trouble into Asia Minor. Attalus may have found himself in urgent need of a strong reinforcement for his standing army, whatever that may have been. But as it happened the Aegosagae were a reinforcement of doubtful value, for though they were brave, they were too superstitious (an eclipse of the moon threw them into a panic), too intolerant of the tedium and discipline of a prolonged campaign, and too much encumbered with their families which accompanied them, to be really good soldiers. Attalus may have intended to add them to his standing army, since he promised them land in which to settle. But in the end he preferred to dispense with their services and to break his promise, and it was left to the king of Bithynia to put an end to the independent freebooting of the Gauls among the Hellespontine cities, by exterminating them.[1]

The military strength of Pergamum in the war with Antiochus the Great (191–188 B.C.) seems to have been very small. Eumenes had first to sustain a siege in his capital city, and he obtained help from his allies the Achaeans (1000 foot, 100 horse).[2] But at Magnesia the contingent of Pergamum in the Roman army seems to have been no more than two or three thousand strong. Eumenes was given the command of the Roman right wing, consisting of 3000 cavalry and 4000 infantry; but of these 2200 of the cavalry were Romans, and 3000 of the infantry were Achaean peltasts (*cetrati*), which leaves for Eumenes' own troops only 800 cavalry and 1000 light infantry (500 Cretan archers and 500 Trallians).[3] It is possible, however, that some of the Achaeans were mercenaries of Pergamum. The Achaean League was the ally of Eumenes, and probably the contingent of 1000 foot and 100 horse was the number stipulated in the treaty of alliance; but the same treaty may have contained a clause giving to the king of Pergamum rights of recruiting in the Achaean cities, which would account for the extra 2000 Achaeans at Magnesia (cf. the treaty of Rhodes and Hierapytna, p. 91).[4] The connec-

[1] Pol. v. 77. 2 sqq.; 78; 111. 2 sqq.   [2] Appian, *Syr.* 26.
[3] Livy 37. 39. 10; Appian, *Syr.* 31.
[4] Cf. *Insch. v. Perg.* i. 64, inscribed by "the Achaeans who crossed over in accordance with the alliance".

PERGAMUM AND PONTUS

tion of Attalus with Crete for military purposes is illustrated by a decree of Aptara in his favour, allowing him, among other privileges, that of recruiting mercenaries: and Cretans have appeared previously in Greece with Attalus, against Philip in 208 B.C.[1] Even so the mercenaries, and that is to say the army of Pergamum (for no citizens are to be found fighting at Magnesia), would seem to be less than 4000, a surprisingly low figure. It may be that another Pergamene force, of which we know nothing, was on duty elsewhere, perhaps in garrisons or guarding the line of communications with the Hellespont: in the following year a Roman expedition against the Galatians was accompanied by no more than 1000 infantry (apparently the same Cretans and Trallians) and 200 horse from Pergamum, though "the other troops" were under orders to follow later.[2] It is hard to believe that the war strength of the kings of Pergamum was restricted to an army of 4000 men; even as a peace strength that number would be exiguous. It must be concluded at the very least that Eumenes for some reason had not made any special recruiting effort for the war with Antiochus (though his position at one time was serious enough). And what has become of the Pergamene citizen troops it is difficult to imagine.

One may conclude this first part of the evidence by remarking that it would take a very bold man to postulate a "regular" army of military settlers for Pergamum in the period ending with the battle of Magnesia. The garrisons of Philetaireia and Attaleia (260 B.C.) cannot have been military settlers, or we should certainly have heard of it in the detailed contract that has survived. The garrison of Lilaea had no military settlers. And there can be no military settlers concealed within the absurdly small figures for the war with Antiochus the Great. Moreover, the collapse of Pergamum on land before Philip in 201 B.C. is an argument against a powerful "regular" army.[3] New cities the early Attalids did found (Philetaireia, Attaleia, Gergitha, Apollonis); but

---

[1] *O.G.I.S.* i. 270; Livy 28. 7.
[2] Livy 38. 12. 8; 21. 2. The operations of the Pergamene army in the winter before Magnesia do suggest a larger army, e.g. Livy 37. 18 shows Eumenes and his brother Attalus commanding separate forces, though each seems to have only cavalry and light infantry: this is before the arrival of the Achaean allies.
[3] Pol. xvi. 1.

there is no evidence for connecting them with the army in this period at least. The evidence in general is in favour of a small standing army, perhaps exclusively of mercenaries, for garrison purposes; in time of war citizens of Pergamum fought in the field army, and new mercenaries could be recruited as required. Magnesia remains a mystery.[1]

The evidence for the period after Magnesia is also very slight. The connection with Crete is maintained by a fragmentary treaty of Eumenes II with more than thirty Cretan cities. The most important part of the text is missing, but the part that remains contains plain references to reciprocal military assistance in case of need: this of course refers to contingents of allied troops from the cities, but it may well be that the treaty also provided for recruiting facilities, like the agreement of Attalus I with Aptara.[2] It is certain that this treaty was struck at the time of Eumenes' war with Pharnaces I of Pontus, a formidable enemy whose general could lead an invading army of 10,000 men into Cappadocia (183 B.C.). Eumenes "doubled his army and trained it energetically"—the one occasion on which we hear of a real recruiting campaign by a king of Pergamum: Polybius adds that he was anxious to impress the Romans and to show them that he was well able to defend himself.[3] In the third Macedonian War of Rome ten years later the army of Pergamum is much more conspicuous than in the war with Antiochus, for Eumenes was able to take a larger army much farther afield. He landed in Greece on his way to help the Romans at the head of 6000 infantry and 1000 horse:[4] and garrisons must have been left in the kingdom, which was now the largest territorial state of Asia Minor. Eumenes may again have added new recruits to his ordinary peace strength for this expedition to Greece; indeed we hear later of a further 1000

[1] *Insch. v. Perg.* i. 61 and 62 (*a*) show soldiers who went from Pergamum to Greece to fight against Nabis, 195 and 192 B.C. (cf. Livy 34. 29; 35. 25 sqq.). They are most likely Pergamene citizens; but if they are mercenaries they must be included in a standing army of Eumenes II, since they came back to Pergamum after 192 B.C.

In the same way there is nothing to show the standing of "Epigenes and the officers and men who fought against the Gauls and Antiochus" (= Hierax, 240 B.C.)—*Insch. v. Perg.* i. 29 and 30. Cf. also Pol. xxix. 6. 1 sqq.

[2] Ditt. *Syll.*³ ii. 627; cf. F. Halbherr, *Mon. ant.* 1890, p. 39, and G. De Sanctis, *ibid.* 1907, p. 310 n. 16.

[3] Pol. xxv. 4. 1 and 11.   [4] Livy 43. 55. 7 sqq.

Gallic cavalry in his service who can hardly have been part of his standing army.¹ The only other particulars are of a small body of possible mercenaries earlier in the war: they were employed as skirmishers and consisted of 100 Gallic horse and 150 light infantry, Mysians or Cretans.²

All this is of a piece with what we have noticed for the earlier period. It is not until we come to the very last days of Pergamum as a kingdom that we break fresh ground. The most important piece of evidence is the decree of citizenship in 133 B.C. (according to the testament of the last king of Pergamum, Attalus III) to various classes of the inhabitants of the kingdom. There are civilians among them (called πάροικοι), but most of the classes of beneficiaries by the decree are soldiers. The words must be quoted:

...καὶ τῶν στρατιωτῶν τοῖς κατοικοῦσι τὴμ πό
15. λιγ καὶ τὴγ χώραν, ὁμοίως δὲ καὶ Μακεδόσιν καὶ Μυσοῖς
καὶ τοῖς ἀναφερομένοις ἐν τῶι φρουρίωι καὶ τῆι πόλει τῆι
ἀρχαίαι κατοίκοις καὶ Μασδυηνοῖς καὶ......
καὶ παραφυλακίταις καὶ τοῖς ἄλλοις ἐ[μφρού]
ροις τοῖς κατοικοῦσιν ἢ ἐνεκτημένοις ἐν τῆι πόλει
20. ἢ τῆι χώραι, ὁμοίως δὲ καὶ γυναιξὶγ καὶ παισίν.³

Since the punctuation of this sentence must of necessity be perfectly arbitrary, it seems wasted labour to separate these soldiers into their different classes (some of the qualifications are probably redundant, and everything depends upon where one chooses to put a comma).⁴ The important fact is that here are κάτοικοι, like those of the Seleucids, and that some of them at least (ll. 16, 17) are active garrison troops, like the φρουροί of the Avroman parchment. One decision, however, must not be shirked. Does this inscription refer merely to the garrison of Pergamum, or to all the κάτοικοι of the kingdom? In other words, is the χώρα (l. 15) the land immediately round the city, or the kingdom in general? At first glance the former alternative seems preferable. But it saddles us with grave difficulties: first,

---
¹ Livy 44. 28. 9 sqq.   ² *Id.* 42. 57. 5 and 7.
³ *Insch. v. Perg.* i. 249 = *O.G.I.S.* i. 338. In ll. 18, 19 Dittenberger accepts the suggestion of Prote and Kolbe (*Comptes rendus de l'Acad. des Inscriptions*, xxvii. 1902, p. 109 n. 1), giving ἐ[πικού]ροις instead of Fränkel's ἐ[μφρού]ροις; but it is to be doubted whether this is an improvement (p. 182 n. 1).
⁴ Cf. Fränkel's commentary (*loc. cit.*); P. Foucart, *C.R. de l'Acad.* etc., 1903, p. 322; Cardinali, *op. cit.* p. 213 n. 2.

how did "Macedonians" come to be in Pergamum? That could be explained, but what is more difficult is the fundamental question of the χώρα, which, with this interpretation, must mean the land belonging to the city of Pergamum: in the first place it is at least doubtful if the city of Pergamum possessed any such land under the Attalids; and if it did, how did the king's soldiers come to be settled on the city's land? This seems impossible, and one must conclude that χώρα is the territory of the whole kingdom, and that these soldiers include all the military settlers who were settled on it.[1]

This conclusion is important, because it at once raises the question of the Seleucid κατοικίαι in Asia Minor, which after 188 B.C. were inside the frontiers of Greater Pergamum, and which, almost certainly, are indicated in a clause of the treaty of Apameia—μηδ' ὑποδεχέσθωσαν τοὺς ἐκ τῆς Εὐμένους τοῦ βασιλέως μήτε στρατιώτας μήτ' ἄλλον μηδένα.[2] Tscherikower pointed out, and with reason, that the Seleucid κάτοικοι could not possibly constitute an internal danger to the kingdom of Pergamum so long as the Seleucids themselves remained—as they did in fact remain —*ultra Taurum*.[3] And if there were no evidence at all one might easily have conjectured that these κάτοικοι, so far from being a danger to the Attalids, were positively useful, if they could still be employed as soldiers by the new government. The inscription quoted above is almost a proof that this is what actually happened. There must be a strong presumption that the Macedonians (l. 15) were the Seleucid military settlers: when they are found in conjunction with Mysians, whose presence has already been noticed in κατοικίαι and in the field army of Antiochus the Great, it becomes something more than a presumption.[4] It is unfortunate

[1] On χώρα, cf. M. Rostovtzeff, *C.A.H.* viii. pp. 597–8. I accept this view, for which this inscription is itself a support.
[2] Pol. xxi. 43. 7.   [3] *Op. cit.* pp. 180 sqq.
[4] Pp. 145, 167. The Mysians alone could perhaps be explained as Attalid κάτοικοι, since they occur once in an Attalid army before Magnesia (p. 172). To explain away the Macedonians in the same way would not be easy, unless one proposed that they were recruited as mercenaries from Macedonia after the fall of the monarchy (168 B.C.); and that is improbable. More improbable still is the idea that "Macedonians" here simply denotes a type of soldier, as in Egypt in the second century, for Pergamum differs from Egypt in that it has no previous tradition of "Macedonians" as an origin of the corruption. The Seleucid κάτοικοι, on the other hand, though they cannot have been anything like pure Macedonians at this date, have yet every right to the name because of their tradition of fighting in the phalanx.

that we cannot satisfy ourselves by actually seeing Macedonian κάτοικοι in action with the army; but Mysians do occur in 170 B.C.[1] And the Seleucid Macedonians can be seen in their κατοικίαι after they have passed into the kingdom of Pergamum.[2] The Masdyenes may be Seleucid κάτοικοι too; but they came probably from Masdye or Mastya in Paphlagonia, and Morzos, king of Paphlagonia, was in alliance with Eumenes II after 189 B.C.[3] Certainly the suggestion that they are to be equated with the *Mosteni Macedones* of Tacitus is to be scouted.[4] Perhaps the likeliest conclusion is that they were originally mercenaries from Paphlagonia who had been given land by Eumenes II or a successor according to the Seleucid system.

For it is not to be supposed that because Eumenes II had received Seleucid κατοικίαι among the spoils of war, he was therefore unable to form new κατοικίαι of his own, and there is evidence that he did so. First, all the garrison troops of Pergamum itself in 133 B.C. were κάτοικοι (above). Another (fragmentary) inscription of Pergamum (date uncertain) is undoubtedly concerned with the allotting of land to soldiers: the word μισθοφόρων occurs, but the context is much too doubtful to allow of anything but a bare mention of the fact.[5] But even this strengthens one's natural suspicion, that any new settlements formed by the last three kings of Pergamum would be formed mostly from their mercenaries. Eumeneia in Phrygia, a new city said to have been founded by Attalus II (Stephanus *s.v.*; Eutropius iv. 2: accepted by Tscherikower, pp. 33 and 180), produced coins (Imperial date) bearing the title ΕΥΜΕΝΕΩΝ ΑΧΑΙΩΝ, "showing

---

[1] Livy 42. 57. 5 and 7, "150 light infantry, Mysians or Cretans"—even if these particular 150 were in fact Cretans, the reference shows that there were Mysians in the army.
[2] E.g. at Nakrasa, *O.G.I.S.* i. 290.
οἱ περὶ Νάκρασαν Μακεδόνες
Μηνογένην Μηνοφάντου
συγγενῆ βασιλέως Εὐμένους
τὸν καὶ νομοφύλακα ἀρετῆς ἕνεκεν
καὶ ἀνδραγαθίας καὶ εὐνοίας
πρός τε τὸν βασιλέα καὶ ἑαυτούς.
At Doidye, *O.G.I.S.* i. 314. And cf. Schulten, *loc. cit.* p. 529; Schuchhardt, *Ath. Mitth.* xiii. (1888), pp. 3 sqq. and 13 sqq.
[3] Livy 38. 26.
[4] Tac. *Ann.* ii. 47, *quique Mosteni aut Macedones Hyrcani vocantur*; cf. Prote, *loc. cit.* p. 110, and Cardinali, *op. cit.* p. 214 n. 3.
[5] *Insch. v. Perg.* i. 158.

that a portion of the population claimed an Achaean ancestry".[1] The literary authorities quoted above say that Attalus II founded Eumeneia and called it after his elder brother Eumenes II, and it is dangerous to suspect this of being a mistake, because it is such an elaborate and unnecessary mistake for anyone to have made (the obvious mistake would be just the opposite, to have said it was founded by Eumenes II because it was called Eumeneia). All the same, the alliance and the cordial relations of Eumenes with the Achaean League are well established, and we have already found it probable that he had Achaean mercenaries at Magnesia (p. 174). It seems almost certain that Eumeneia contained Achaean settlers who had been mercenaries of either Eumenes II or Attalus II. Less certain is the conjecture of Ramsay that the name Smertorix which occurs on an Augustan coin of Eumeneia was introduced by Gallic mercenaries of the Attalids.[2] The same writer also suggested an Attalid κατοικία containing Trallians in the neighbourhood of Laodicea, from the Thracian names Molossus on an inscription and Sitalcas on an Imperial coin: this is possible but no more.[3] But one is right to look for mercenaries as the material from which the settlements were formed, and in this connection one remembers the recruiting of Eumenes II by which he "doubled his army": one effect is probably to be seen ten years afterwards in the comparatively large expeditionary force to Greece against Perseus (p. 176), and another effect may well have been new military settlers.

It is difficult to say how important were the Attalid κατοικίαι to the new cities founded in the kingdom after 188 B.C. Tscherikower discounts the military importance that has been attached to these cities by some earlier writers (e.g. Ramsay, Radet, Schulten, Schuchhardt, *locc. citt.*), and sees rather an economic and cultural importance: there was no question, he says, of founding rival κατοικίαι to those of the Seleucids (which could not possibly be dangerous again, and were probably useful), but rather of founding new cities in order to develop areas already partially hellenized by Seleucid colonization.[4] This is

[1] Head, *B.M. Catalogue—Phrygia* (London 1906), pp. lx–lxi; cf. Plate xxvii, No. 3.
[2] Ramsay, *Cities*, p. 371 n. 5.   [3] *Ibid.* pp. 34 and 77 n. 12.
[4] Tscherikower, pp. 180 sqq.

PERGAMUM AND PONTUS

probably sound in the main; but there may well have been a desire also to establish a military system for Greater Pergamum in imitation of the successful system of the Seleucids. The reason why such an imitation was never tried earlier (so far as we can tell) was that before 188 B.C. Pergamum was a relatively small kingdom, having neither the means nor the needs of the Seleucid empire. After 188 B.C. Pergamum practically supplanted the Seleucids in Asia Minor; and the Seleucid κατοικίαι which then fell into the hands of the Attalids provided them with a model if they wished to imitate. That they accomplished something the evidence above is sufficient to prove, but there is not enough of it to show how much they accomplished. For that we can rely only on conjecture based on general grounds.

The general impression that one draws from Pergamene history after 188 B.C. is that Pergamum was not even then a great military power: in fact, had the testament of Attalus III not survived (p. 177), to suppose a regular army including military settlers would have been extremely hazardous. Even as it is the indications are that the military strength did not increase proportionately with the size of the kingdom. The army needed to be doubled in size and specially trained in order to cope with Pharnaces. In the unsuccessful war against Prusias of Bithynia (155 B.C.), Attalus II was obliged to watch a hostile army advance to the very gates of his capital, unable to move in reply until he had received reinforcements from his allies the kings of Cappadocia and Pontus, and content to finish the war by appealing to Rome to make Prusias stop fighting.[1] The inference is that the "regular" army of Attalus II was either not very large or not very efficient (or both): nor do we hear of his recruiting mercenaries for the occasion. There is no evidence at all for mercenaries in the last thirty years of the kingdom.[2] There is no reason to consider as mercenaries any of the troops

---

[1] Pol. xxxii. 25; xxxiii. 10 sqq.
[2] Mention should perhaps be made of O.G.I.S. i. 330 (15th year of either Eumenes II or Attalus II = 183 or 145 B.C.), ... |νωι οἱ ἐκ Παραλείας| στρατιῶται οἱ διαβάν|τες ἐν τῶι ιε' ἔτει εἰς| τοὺς κατὰ Χερρόνη|σον καὶ Θράικην τό|πους εὐχήν. Paraleia is as much a mystery to me as it was to Dittenberger (n. 1 *ad loc.*); the reading seems certain, in spite of the earlier editions of the inscription (Sestinus, *Itin.* p. 136, Πακαλείας; *C.I.G.* 3568, (Ν)ακ(ο)λείας).

mentioned in the testament of Attalus III (above),[1] and it is possible that after the war with Perseus the kings discontinued the practice of hiring mercenaries, thinking their cleruch soldiers sufficient: certainly the occasion for a recruiting campaign arrived at the time of Prusias' invasion, and it seems to have been ignored. Great reliance may have been placed on the *pax Romana*, which had already begun to settle the quarrels of others with a word instead of a blow, and the kings of Pergamum were always (with one lapse on the part of Eumenes II) on the very closest terms of friendship with the Roman government, a fact which was in turn a guarantee of good alliances nearer home. This last period was one of almost unbroken peace, and even the κάτοικοι, though they continued to perform garrison duty at Pergamum and perhaps elsewhere, and were no doubt intended to become the field army in time of war, may well have degenerated through force of circumstances into little more than an elaborately organized militia.

2. Bithynia, Cappadocia and Pontus

Somewhat different from Pergamum, in resources and requirements, were the other three important kingdoms of Asia Minor. The civilization of Pergamum was that of a Greek state in close contact with barbarians. The civilization of Bithynia, Cappadocia and Pontus was that of barbarian kingdoms influenced more or less superficially by Greek neighbours or by an infiltration of Greek culture. Bithynia became a national kingdom independent of the Seleucids and of every other Greek power quite early in the third century, probably soon after the death of Lysimachus and the disruption of his Thracian empire (281 B.C.). Cappadocia and Pontus had never been truly conquered by Alexander or his successors. Cappadocia in particular, with few roads and no seaboard, was likely from the first to be impervious

[1] This remains true even if one reads ἐπικούροις instead of ἐμφρούροις (ll. 18, 19; cf. p. 177 and n. 3). Even in Hdt. and Thuc., where the word occurs most often, it is never safe to translate it by "mercenaries" unless it is supported by some word or phrase giving the idea of hiring. Plato's ἐπίκουροι, the military class of the Republic, are certainly something quite different. And I do not think ἐπίκουροι is used at all in the third century as a military word: certainly not in inscriptions. ἐμφρούροις is redundant, but inscriptions of this period are often that.

PERGAMUM AND PONTUS 183

to Greek penetration and development, and, in effect, though its Persian satrap Ariarathes was expelled soon after Alexander's death, the province was held permanently neither by Antigonus I nor by the Seleucids after him, and soon relapsed into the hands of an Iranian dynasty which counted this same Ariarathes as its eponymous founder. In the same way in Pontus it was probably the Persian satrap Mithridates, contemporary with Alexander, who is to be regarded as Mithridates the first king of the new kingdom:[1] Pontus was even more isolated than Cappadocia from Hellenistic Asia, and her main contact with Greek civilization was from the north, through the Greek cities of the Black Sea.

In these circumstances it would be surprising if we were to find that these kingdoms developed anything in the nature of an Hellenistic military system such as has been described in connection with the Ptolemaic and Seleucid empires, or even the kingdom of Pergamum: and no trace in fact of any such development exists. It is true that the evidence for the third and second centuries is very scanty, and yet contains references to mercenaries in the service of the kings. But there is nothing to make one think that they kept standing armies of mercenaries, much less were able to command a supply of Greeks from military settlements like those of the Seleucids, and in the absence of further evidence it seems more probable that their standing armies must have consisted of soldiers drawn from their own subjects, after the old Persian system.[2]

The evidence that exists is concerned principally with the Gauls of Asia. It was Nicomedes I of Bithynia who first invited the Gauls into Asia (278 B.C.): the terms of the agreement that he imposed upon them are preserved by Memnon, and included eternal friendship towards him and his friends, and enmity towards his enemies. He used them to win a civil war in his kingdom, probably against a rival to the throne.[3] The Gauls served his immediate purpose, but Nicomedes had imposed a

---
[1] On this question, see M. Rostovtzeff in *C.A.H.* ix. p. 218.
[2] I can see no justification for the two statements of Th. Reinach, *Mithridate Eupator*, pp. 264 and 265: "Les premiers rois de Pont avaient composé leur armée presque exclusivement de mercenaires étrangers: Galates d'abord, Grecs ensuite": and "Un des mérites de Mithridate" [i.e. Eupator] "fut de former le premier, à côté de cette armée mercenaire, une véritable armée nationale, recrutée parmi ses propres sujets".
[3] Livy 38. 16. 6 sqq.; Memnon 19 (*F.H.G.* iii. p. 535); Paus. x. 23. 14.

very bad neighbour on all the existing inhabitants of western Asia Minor, and not least on himself. Before his death he was obliged to fight for his kingdom with the Gauls against him, this time in the pay of his exiled son Ziaelas, who tried to return to Bithynia by force with their help.[1] It was not long before the kings of Pontus too made use of them. They occur in connection with Mithridates I and Ariobarzanes, but the circumstances are unknown.[2] As with Nicomedes, they seem to have fought as a nation rather than hired themselves out in small bands (they are said to have been only 10,000 fighting men in the first place).[3] When Ariobarzanes died they attacked Pontus, and were probably bribed to go away, as they certainly were later at Heraclea:[4] one can be sure that if they needed to be paid not to fight against a government they had certainly to be paid to fight for it, and in fact hired themselves as mercenaries for the duration of a campaign or a war, without prejudice for the future.

It is possible that nearly a hundred years later Pharnaces I used them regularly, for one of the clauses of the treaty that ended his war against Pergamum, Bithynia and Cappadocia (179 B.C.), said that "Pharnaces is on no account to set foot in Galatia, and his existing agreements with the Gauls are to be cancelled".[5] This may refer to an earlier agreement giving him a right of way through Galatia in order to attack Cappadocia and the Pergamene territory; but more likely it refers to an agreement allowing him to recruit soldiers from Galatia for his army[6] (other such agreements are frequent, pp. 257 sqq.). Pharnaces' agreement with the Gauls, if it was one of this kind, was most likely made soon after the Roman treaty with Antiochus III (188 B.C.), which may have placed Galatia in the area forbidden to Syrian recruiting officers. For the fifty years before Magnesia the Seleucids had been probably the leading employers of Gallic mercenaries, and when their competition was removed Pharnaces may have hastened to take their place.[7] His whole army was

[1] Memnon 22. [2] Apollonius 13 (*F.H.G.* ii. p. 312).
[3] Livy, 38. 16. 6 sqq. [4] Memnon 25.
[5] Pol. xxvi. 6. 2 sqq.
[6] Though Pharnaces was evidently hostile in this war to some at least of the Galatian chiefs, since he invaded Galatia and ravaged the land (Pol. xxv. 4. 1 sqq.).
[7] For the Rome-Antiochus treaty, and Gauls with the Seleucids generally, cf. pp. 146, 166 sqq.

10,000 strong.¹ Who took Pharnaces' place in turn after this treaty of 179 is not known; but there were Gauls again with Antiochus IV in 165 B.C. (p. 146), and it is possible that the mercenaries of Orophernes of Cappadocia (159-154 B.C.) were also Gauls, though we are not told so.² This Orophernes had usurped his brother's throne, and never held it securely, so that he probably kept a mercenary army of necessity: this may explain why he was obliged to tax his subjects heavily, but he had difficulty nevertheless in keeping his soldiers' pay up to date, and was obliged on one occasion to rob a temple in order to pay them.³ In the same way nothing is known of the mercenaries in Tios of Morzos, king of Paphlagonia, beyond the mere fact of their existence.⁴

Besides Gauls the kings of Bithynia may frequently have employed Thracian mercenaries, as one would expect considering the Thracian descent of the kings themselves, and their proximity to the Thracians of Europe. We hear of European Thracians in the service of Prusias I when he was at war with Byzantium (219-218 B.C.):⁵ and Prusias II sent for a bodyguard of 500 Thracians from a prince called Diegylis, his kinsman.⁶ But in both these cases the soldiers are recruited for a definite and immediate purpose, and are no argument for, but rather against, a standing army of Thracian mercenaries. All that can be said is that Prusias II was strong enough to overrun the territory of Attalus II of Pergamum and besiege him in his capital; but we have seen already that as a military power Pergamum was at this time extraordinarily weak (155 B.C.: pp. 181-2).⁷

[1] Pol. xxv. 4. 1.
[2] There is a notice in Polybius (xxxi. 2), Ὅτι τοῖς παρὰ τῶν ἐκ τῆς Ἀσίας Γαλατῶν πρεσβευταῖς συνεχώρησαν τὴν αὐτονομίαν μένουσιν ἐν ταῖς ἰδίαις κατοικίαις καὶ μὴ στρατευομένοις ἐκτὸς τῶν ἰδίων ὅρων. I think this must refer to a ban upon wars of aggression and not a ban upon mercenary service, since there were 5000 Gauls at the Daphne review very shortly after (ibid. 3. 5).
[3] Diod. xxxi. 43 and 45. For the general circumstances of his reign, cf. also Pol. iii. 5. 2; xxxii. 22. 8; Justin 35. 1. 2.
[4] Diod. xxix. 23. They may perhaps have been mercenaries of Eumenes II, since Morzos became his ally in 188 B.C. (Livy 38. 26).
[5] Pol. iv. 51. 8.   [6] Appian, Mith. 6.
[7] There is also a doubtful reference (Appian, Mith. 4 sqq.) to 2000 στρατιῶται sent by Prusias to Rome to kill (if necessary) his son Nicomedes there: in fact they were won over to Nicomedes and returned with him to Bithynia where he overthrew Prusias and became Nicomedes II. But I think, in the

So far nothing has been said of Greek mercenaries. There is no notice of Greeks with the kings of Bithynia or of Cappadocia, and the first notice of a Greek in the service of a king of Pontus is not until the reign of Pharnaces I (died *ca.* 170 B.C. or *ca.* 158 B.C., cf. *C.A.H.* ix. p. 221). A Greek called Metrodorus was φρούραρχος of the garrison of Amasia (the ancient capital of Pontus);[1] but it does not follow that the garrison consisted of mercenaries or that Metrodorus himself was a mercenary. The Greek city of Amisos had been in the power of Mithridates III as far back as 255 B.C.,[2] and Pharnaces himself is known to have won and held Sinope and other less important Greek cities on the coast.[3] Thus it may be that Greek soldiers in the service of the Mithridatids after these dates were in reality not mercenaries but citizens of these cities, to whom military service at the need of the king of Pontus was an obligation. What were the obligations of the cities in this respect is not known; but Hellenistic practice in general, and the practice of Mithridates Eupator at the time when most of the Greek cities of Asia were in his hands, both make it probable that the city Greeks were not obliged to serve as soldiers, or at least only in times of crisis.

Although Pharnaces I fought a great war in Asia Minor, not the smallest scraps of information about his army are known to us. The same would be true of the next warrior king of Pontus, Mithridates Euergetes (the father of the great Mithridates), had not Strabo (himself a native of Amasia) been happily inspired to air his knowledge of a celebrated Greek officer of Euergetes whose descendants were known to Strabo himself. "Dorylaus", says Strabo, "was a tactician (ἀνὴρ τακτικός), one of the Friends of Mithridates Euergetes. Because of his experience of military affairs he was appointed to recruit mercenaries (ξενολογεῖν) and became a great man in Greece and in Thrace, and also among the people who came from the neighbourhood of Crete, for the Romans had not at that time conquered the island, and it contained a great population of mercenaries and soldiers, from which the pirate ships too were manned."[4] One is not absolutely

circumstances (cf. esp. Appian, *Mith.* 4. 1 sqq.), that the 2000 are as likely to have been native troops as mercenaries.
[1] *Mith. Eup.* p. 456 (Appendix ii, *Les Inscriptions*, No. 1).
[2] Memnon 24.   [3] *Mith. Eup.* pp. 41 sq.   [4] Strabo x. 477.

PERGAMUM AND PONTUS 187

certain whether Dorylaus is an inhabitant of one of the Greek cities of Pontus, or a *condottiere* from Greece who has settled at the court of Euergetes (his nephew, also Dorylaus, is called Ἀμισηνός; but this is not conclusive).[1] But it is quite certain that Dorylaus, if he was not a mercenary officer in name, was at least a professional soldier of the approved style. And this passage is the first to establish that the kings of Pontus ever went west to the Aegean for mercenaries. The connection with Crete is of special interest, because it continues the Cretan tradition of mercenary service (combined with piracy), flourishing as we have seen throughout the third and well into the second century, now down to the year 120 B.C. at least: (and Strabo implies that it ceased only with the conquest of the island by the Romans in 67 B.C. In the year of Euergetes' death (121–120 B.C.) Dorylaus "chanced to be on a visit to Cnossus"; no doubt a recruiting campaign. But while he was there Cnossus became involved in a war with Gortyn, Dorylaus was made general, and quickly led the Cnossians to victory. Here he is the *condottiere* undisguised, and this engagement stood him in good stead, for just at this time he heard from Sinope that Euergetes had been murdered and the country was in the hands of the queen mother, and this decided him to renounce his interests in Pontus (which included a wife and three children), and to settle in Cnossus for good.[2]

Another interesting point about Dorylaus is that he is described as τῶν τοῦ Μιθριδάτου τοῦ Εὐεργέτου φίλων. There is no doubt that this is to be translated not as "a friend" but as "one of the Friends" of Euergetes.[3] Inscriptions dating from the reign of Mithridates Eupator show that the title τῶν πρώτων φίλων was a recognized title applied to the nearest counsellors or associates of the king, analogous to the ἑταῖροι of the Macedonian court.[4] All the Friends whose provenance is known are natives of cities within the kingdom of Pontus (all but one come from Amisos), and all are Greeks. It is probable that the Friends

---

[1] *Mith. Eup.* p. 459, App. ii, *Les Inscriptions*, No. 9 (*a*) (=*B.C.H.* vii. pp. 354 sqq.).
[2] Strabo, x. 477.   [3] *Ibid.*
[4] There are five such inscriptions, collected in *Mith. Eup.* App. ii, Nos. 9 (*a*) to (*e*): three refer to men who are τῶν πρώτων φίλων, the other two are called σύντροφος: the σύντροφοι may have comprised a kind of inner circle of the Friends.

were intended to supply the army with its highest officers, though *all* the Friends were not necessarily soldiers, and two were certainly civilians.[1] The title was in existence at least as early as the reign of Mithridates Euergetes (whose assassination was contrived by "the Friends" in Sinope).[2] The histories of the Roman wars of Mithridates Eupator contain many references to Greek officers in the Pontic army, and very likely many or most of these are really Friends, and not mercenary officers at all. Those who are called στρατηγοί are almost certainly Friends, and eleven such officers are known.[3]

The existence of these Friends must have been of the greatest importance to an ambitious king, for it gave him a supply of good officers for his army, whether native or mercenary. We have seen that Euergetes used Thracian, Greek, and Cretan mercenaries. About the early years of Eupator, before the beginning of his first war with Rome, practically nothing is known. They were certainly years of intense activity and almost constant fighting, by means of which he extended his kingdom as far as Colchis in the east, and became possessed of the Crimea. But the historians tell nothing of his methods or instruments, merely presenting us with the accomplished fact. The only one of his enterprises at this time of which anything at all is known is the conquest of the Crimea by his general Diophantus of Sinope, probably one of the Friends described above: this knowledge we owe to some remarks of Strabo and to an inscription of the Greek city of Chersonesus which by its position was intimately involved in the events described (*ca.* 107 B.C.).[4] The details of the two expeditions of Diophantus do not concern us, except that it appears that his army, though small, consisted of Greek

---

[1] *Mith. Eup.*, App. ii, Nos. 9 (*b*) and (*c*).   [2] Strabo, x. 477.
[3] Besides Diophantus (see below), and the well-known brothers Archelaus and Neoptolemus, there were the younger Dorylaus (Strabo, *ibid.*, etc.), Menophanes (Memnon 31; *F.H.G.* iii. 541); Taxiles (Appian, *Mith.* 70; Memnon 32 and 34; Plut. *Lucull.* 26. 3 sqq.); Hermocrates (Appian, *Mith.* 70); Eumachus (Appian, *Mith.* 75); Menander, Menemachus, and Myron (Plut. *Lucull.* 17. 1). I think these are all active officers with a military command, and not administrators of the στρατηγίαι of Cappadocia, on which see *Mith. Eup.* p. 256. Of the many other Greek officers the most interesting is Callimachus, the expert on siegecraft, Plut. *Lucull.* 19. 2.
[4] Strabo vii. 306; Ditt. *Syll.*³ ii. 709. He is described in the inscription as πιστευόμενος δὲ καὶ τιμώμενος οὐθενὸς ἧσσον ὑπὸ βασιλέως Μιθραδάτα Εὐπάτορος, = a Friend?

infantry and defeated a much larger army of barbarians: soldiers of Chersonesus fought with him, but the majority of his 6000 Greeks must have come with him from Pontus, and may have been mercenaries recruited from Greece like those of Euergetes.[1]

The results, however, of these campaigns are of the highest importance. Within a few years Mithridates[2] became the suzerain of the Scythian and Taurian kingdoms of the Crimea, of the Maeotians of the Cimmerian Bosporus, and perhaps even of some of the Roxolani and Sarmatians of South Russia. From such of these native kings as were his subjects he drew a valuable tribute (the revenue from the new province was 200 talents of silver and 18,000 medimni of grain—partly of course from the Greek cities); but even more valuable was his right of levying soldiers from their tribesmen. These levies, at least during the wars with Rome, formed the strongest part of his standing army, and may be regarded almost as foreign mercenaries. Other troops—such as his Thracians—were pure mercenaries, hired from nations on which he had no claim by conquest. In the present state of our knowledge it is impossible to differentiate accurately between so-called subjects and real mercenaries: nor is it of great importance to do so.[3] It is sufficient to realize that it was these immense reserves of man power that enabled him to

[1] Strabo, vii. 306, says: πρὸς μέντοι συντεταγμένην φάλαγγα καὶ ὡπλισμένην καλῶς τὸ βάρβαρον φῦλον ἀσθενὲς πᾶν ἐστι καὶ τὸ γυμνητικόν· ἐκεῖνοι γοῦν περὶ πέντε μυριάδας πρὸς ἑξακιλίους τοὺς Διοφάντῳ...συμπαραταξάμενους... οἱ πλεῖστοι διεφθάρησαν.

[2] In future "Mithridates" = Eupator.

[3] Appian's terminology is unreliable: e.g., *Mith.* 13, he mentions τοῦ τε ἰδίου στρατοῦ καὶ συμμάχων Θρᾳκῶν καὶ Σκυθῶν; the Thracians and Scythians, whatever either may have been, did not stand both in the same relationship to Mith.: *ibid.* 15, he says vaguely φίλοις δ' εἰς πᾶν τὸ κελευόμενον ἑτοίμοις χρῆται Σκύθαις τε καὶ Ταύροις καὶ Βαστέρναις καὶ Θρᾳξὶ καὶ Σαρμάταις καὶ πᾶσι τοῖς ἀμφὶ Τάναϊν τε καὶ Ἴστρον καὶ τὴν λίμνην ἔτι τὴν Μαιωτίδα; and *ibid.* 69 (third war), σύμμαχοί τε αὐτῷ προσεγίγνοντο, χωρὶς τῆς προτέρας δυνάμεως, Χάλυβες Ἀρμένιοι Σκύθαι Ταῦροι Ἀχαιοὶ Ἡνίοχοι Λευκόσυροι καὶ ὅσοι περὶ Θερμώδοντα ποταμὸν γῆν ἔχουσι τὴν Ἀμαζόνων λεγομένην....περασάντι δ' ἐς τὴν Εὐρώπην Σαυροματῶν οἵ τε βασίλειοι καὶ Ἰάζυγες καὶ Κόραλλοι καὶ Θρᾳκῶν ὅσα γένη παρὰ τὸν Ἴστρον ἢ Ῥοδόπην ἢ τὸν Αἷμον οἰκοῦσι, καὶ ἐπὶ τοῖσδε Βαστέρναι, τὸ ἀλκιμώτατον αὐτῶν γένος. For some of these nations mentioned by Pompey as conquered peoples, cf. Diod. xl. 4.

The evidence for the appearance of barbarian mercenaries actually on campaigns is: *Scythians*—Justin 38. 3. 7; Appian, *Mith.* 41 and 79; *Sarmatians*—Justin 38. 3. 6; Appian, *Mith.* 19; *Thracians*—Appian, *Mith.* 41; Dio Cassius 36. 11; *Bastarnae*—Justin 38. 3. 6; Appian, *Mith.* 71; Memnon 39; *Maeotians*—Plut. *Lucull.* 16. 1; *Gauls* (Danube?)—Appian, *Mith.* 111; cf. 109; Justin, *ibid.*—(Asiatic) Appian, *Mith.* 41 and 46; Justin, *ibid.* 4. 9.

be a danger to the Roman power in the East, a far more powerful adversary than any of his predecessors on the throne of Pontus. Another awkward point is in connection with the size of Mithridates' armies. Appian's figures are almost always fantastic.[1] Memnon has a very high figure for the army at the beginning of both the first and the third wars with Rome (150,000 in 88 B.C.; 150,000 infantry and 12,000 cavalry in 73 B.C.);[2] but it has been suggested that the figure 150,000 represents the nominal strength of the whole kingdom[3] (though it is misleading to speak in these terms of an army whose size depends so obviously not so much on the man power of a nation as upon the number of men that Mithridates wished, or could afford, to recruit). But Memnon does also produce some reasonable figures for the campaigning army—50,000 under Archelaus in Bithynia;[4] over 60,000 at Chaeronea;[5] over 30,000 and 48,000 against Lucullus.[6] If we accept these estimates as the nearest possible approach to the truth,[7] and bear in mind the number of troops who must have been kept employed in garrisons and communications, we must conclude that in the first war Mithridates must have had 80,000 men in arms at the very least. The proportion of these that were mercenaries is quite impossible to discover, for the reasons mentioned above. Nor is it known how he paid them, though it can be said that there is no sign of his having been short of money. In the first war he must have lived very largely on his conquests; but that he had also very large treasures in reserve is shown by Pompey's splendid haul at the end of the third war.[8] And when he finally retreated into Scythia he is said to have taken with him 6000 talents, out of which he paid a donative and

[1] E.g. 250,000 infantry, 50,000 cavalry in 88 B.C., Appian, *Mith.* 17; 120,000 in Greece (*ibid.* 41, cf. 45) + a reinforcement under Dorylaus of 80,000 (49): so Plut. *Sulla* 20. 2).
[2] Memnon 31 and 37.
[3] By M. Rostovtzeff, in *C.A.H.* ix. p. 240 n. 2.
[4] Memnon 31 (he represents this as only *part* of the whole army; but the rest of the army is the 150,000 of which mention has been made).
[5] *Id.* 32.
[6] *Id.* 40 and 43 (but he has previously made M. lose about 25,000 men, *id.* 40).
[7] In such a matter Memnon is more likely to be right than Appian, who used Roman sources and those not the best. Th. Reinach (*Mith. Eup.* p. 453) believes that Memnon used principally a chronicle or chronicles of Heraclea, which would at least be impartial.
[8] Appian, *Mith.* 116, cf. Pliny 37. 2. 16.

PERGAMUM AND PONTUS

a year's pay (whether arrears, or pay in advance) to the remnant of his army (certainly under 10,000 strong).[1]

Of this army, then, 80,000 strong or more, the northern auxiliaries or mercenaries were an important, perhaps the most important, part: and the king's Asiatic subjects will have played, numerically at least, scarcely less a rôle. What was the place of Greek soldiers in the army? Except for the inconclusive evidence about Diophantus and his Greeks in the Crimea (above) there is no evidence at all for Greek mercenaries in any of Mithridates' wars.[2] But we have seen that the army of Diophantus fought in phalanx (if Strabo is to be trusted on a point of military history): and in the same way a phalanx is to be found in the Pontic army during the Roman wars, starting from the first invasion of Bithynia and Cappadocia in 88 B.C., from which it is to be inferred that it was probably an integral part of Mithridates' regular army.[3] Here, one would think, if anywhere, Greeks should be the best soldiers for the place, for on the one hand the northern barbarians are likely to have been more useful fighting in their national formations and equipment than trained to a style to which they were unaccustomed, and on the other hand it is not likely that the Greeks of Sinope, Amisos and the other cities could be depended upon to supply contingents of regular soldiers for service on campaigns year in and year out.[4] The only piece of information we possess as to the composition of this phalanx is probably not to be taken at its face value. Plutarch says that at Chaeronea "in the forefront of Archelaus' army were 15,000 slaves, whom the king's generals had freed from the cities (? of Asia) and had enrolled among the hoplites".[5] The number 15,000 may be dismissed as impossible (Plutarch's figure for the whole army is 120,000, which must be

---

[1] Appian, *Mith.* 101.
[2] For Greek *allies* with Archelaus in Greece (Laconians and Achaeans), Appian, *Mith.* 29. The only other reference to Greeks is in the third war, where "some Greeks" (possibly only two) are captured by Lucullus: Plut. *Lucull.* 15. 3.
[3] Appian, *Mith.* 17: in 88 B.C. it was commanded by Dorylaus, the nephew of Dorylaus the Tactician. For the phalanx at the Amneius battle, *id.* 18; in Greece, Plut. *Sulla* 18. 4 sqq.; 19. 2.
[4] It is true that the Greeks of Tigranocerta fought against Lucullus (p. 193 n. 2), but to defend one's own city when it was besieged was quite a different thing from fighting abroad on annual campaigns.
[5] Plut. *Sulla* 18. 4.

at least double the real figure); but the fact itself may possibly be accepted as true, if we recollect how, even a hundred years after Alexander's death, the use of the phalanx had degenerated from being a matter of experience and skill to one of mere weight.[1] The phalanx of Mithridates may have been such that liberated slaves could be put to fight in it at the shortest notice, and this being so it is certain that Asiatics, or at least people other than Greek professional soldiers, could be trained to fight in it if required. Plutarch says that in the interval between the first and third wars with Rome Mithridates remodelled his army on the Roman style, arming and training his *barbarians* to fight with Roman weapons and methods, so that when he went to war in 73 B.C. he had "a Roman phalanx" (*sic*) of 120,000 men.[2] Here again though the numbers are impossible the fact is true, for Mithridates had entered into an alliance with Sertorius the Roman rebel in Spain, from whom he had received Roman officers for his army;[3] and he had collected in addition a considerable number of Roman deserters whom he formed into the most valuable fighting unit in his possession.[4]

There is nothing impossible, then, in the idea that Mithridates' phalanx consisted mostly of Asiatics, and in the absence of any references to Greeks it is probably sound to conclude that this idea is true. This is not to say that there may not have been a stiffening of Greek mercenaries also; they may be concealed in Plutarch's mention of "chalkaspids" with Archelaus in Greece, clearly part of the phalanx, and probably a "crack" corps of some kind.[5] In the same way Appian describes how Mithridates fleeing from his kingdom made his famous march round the east coast of the Black Sea to the Crimea "with the hypaspists only, and some mercenary horse and infantry whom he fell in with on his flight, about 3000".[6] These "hypaspists" are evidently such another "crack" corps as the "chalkaspids"; but not

[1] Cf. the remarks of W. W. Tarn, *Hellenistic Military and Naval Developments*, p. 28.
[2] Plut. *Lucull.* 7. 4.
[3] Appian, *Mith.* 68, cf. 70 and 90; Plut. *ibid.* 8. 5. In the same way Mithridates later set his officers to train the Armenian army of Tigranes to fight in the Roman style, at very short notice again (Appian, *Mith.* 87; Plut. *Lucull.* 26. 6).
[4] Dio Cassius 36. 45. 4; cf. Appian, *Mith.* 98.
[5] Plut. *Sulla* 16. 7 and 19. 2.   [6] Appian, *Mith.* 101.

the same corps, because it seems very likely that the "hypaspists" were no other than the corps of Roman deserters, who, as we learn by chance, "encamped nearest to Mithridates".[1]

In his last years in the Crimea, at all events, Mithridates cannot have had many Greek soldiers, for the whole history of the Greek settlements in that region betrays a population in the cities always too scanty in comparison with the prolific barbarian stocks of the interior. It was probably from these barbarians that Mithridates raised his last army, now certainly conscripting them as subjects and not recruiting them as mercenaries: he is said to have had 36,000 picked infantry trained in the Roman style as well as a horde of other arms, but the figures must certainly be too high.[2] Nevertheless there is no doubt that he did succeed in raising a fresh army, which inspired him with a hope of marching by land to the Adriatic and renewing the struggle with Rome, a second Hannibal, at her own doors. This last phase of his life reveals very clearly the chief source of his military strength, and confirms the unsatisfactory evidence for the Roman wars, which suggests, such as it is, that his military system, while it was to some extent dependent upon Greek tactics and formations, was never greatly dependent upon a Greek population for its man power, except indeed for its officers. And the silence of the first-century evidence in general on the subject of Greeks as mercenaries is quite in accordance with what we have already deduced elsewhere from the evidence for the second century, that Greece was no longer the land of soldiers *par excellence*.[3]

[1] Appian, *Mith.* 110.   [2] *Ibid.* 107–8.
[3] Appian, *Mith.* 86, has a reference to Greek mercenaries with Tigranes of Armenia against Lucullus (τοὺς Ἕλληνας οἱ ἐμισθοφόρουν); but it is clear from Plutarch's description of the siege of Tigranocerta (Plut. *Lucull.* 29. 2 sqq.) that these Greeks are not mercenaries but inhabitants of the city, transplanted thither by Tigranes in accordance with his regular policy (*ibid.* 26. 1 and 21. 4).

Other possible references to mercenaries in this period are at Athens (Appian, *Mith.* 28 and 39), mercenaries lent or given to the tyrant Aristion by Archelaus; at Delos (88 B.C.) (Posidonius, frag. 41) perhaps; at Olbia (*ca.* 60 B.C.) perhaps—nationality unknown (Ditt. *Syll.*[3] ii. 730).

CHAPTER VIII

THE WEST

1. SICILY[1]

IT seems that the history of mercenary service in Sicily was ruled throughout by conditions somewhat different from those prevailing on the mainland of Greece. In the first place, it is concentrated almost entirely within those periods when the greater part of the island was under the dominion of tyrants: the only occasions, of which we know, when the democracies employed mercenaries were in the times of great peril to Syracuse from the Athenian expedition and to Acragas and Syracuse from the Carthaginian devastations under Hannibal (410 B.C.).[2] It is generally agreed that the tyrannies in Sicily owed their existence at least in part to the need of a strong hand and central control against the Carthaginians, and it therefore follows that the mercenary armies of the tyrants were something more than mere bodyguards, more even than the mailed fist displayed in the view of possibly discontented citizens; that they were in fact intended from the very first to serve if necessary as field armies against a more dangerous enemy than the army of a rival Greek city. This fact probably accounts for the size of the mercenary forces which we meet. Gelon enfranchised more than 10,000 mercenaries in the course of his tyranny of only seven years, and we have no means of knowing how many others served in his army without receiving the franchise. The "bad" tyrants Thrasydaeus and Thrasybulus are said to have raised especially large armies in self-defence. And Dionysius I was certainly not behind his predecessors in this respect.

In the second place, it seems probable that the Greek inhabitants of Sicily were not sufficiently numerous to supply the demand for mercenaries when it was at its height. The Greeks occupied no more than a fringe of territory including about three

[1] For the relevant historical narrative before Agathocles, Parke, pp. 10 sqq. (Gelon, etc.), 63 sqq. (Dionysius I), 114 sqq. (Dion and Dionysius II), 170 sqq. (Timoleon).
[2] Diod. xii. 82; Thuc. vii. 48. 5; 58. 3. Diod. xiii. 63 and 75, 85; 88. 5.

THE WEST

parts of the coastline of the island, and taking in the occasional fertile plains or valleys near the sea. The interior was still in the hands of Elymians, Sicans and Sicels, and the western extremity belonged to Carthage. There is quite a strong probability that Sicels, as well as Greeks, served under the earlier tyrants;[1] but it is first to the tyranny of Dionysius I that we must look for a really wide range of recruiting. At different times he commanded mercenaries from Campania,[2] from the Peloponnese (including Messenians),[3] from the Celts and Iberians,[4] and probably from Locri and Medymna,[5] as well as the many whose provenance is not mentioned;[6] and we may guess that he left no recruiting ground untouched in Sicily and Southern Italy both Greek and barbarian. In addition to private recruiting, he recruited by means of alliances, and his officers were probably to be seen in all parts of Greece when the need for soldiers became great.[7] The story of the armourers who equipped the soldiers with their national arms testifies to the catholic character of his army, and the numbers of the arms manufactured can perhaps be used to deduce a possible figure for his mercenaries at the time. It becomes likely, from this passage, that Dionysius aimed at maintaining a force of about 10,000 mercenaries (infantry):[8] that he employed cavalry also is certain, but it is impossible to arrive at a total, since the numbers recorded probably

[1] The only evidence is Polyaen. v. 6; but it is suggested that the Sicel revival under Ducetius may have been partly due to the return of disbanded mercenaries of the tyrants. I owe this suggestion to Professor Adcock.
[2] Diod. xiv. 8–9, 61–2; [Aristot.] *Econ.* ii. 1349 sqq.
[3] Diod. *ibid.* 44. 2; 58. 1; 62. 1; 34. 3.   [4] *Id.* xv. 70. 1 sqq.
[5] *Id.* xiv. 78. 5.   [6] *Ibid.* 55. 6 sqq.—Sicans?
[7] *Ibid.* 44. 2. Cf. the very interesting suggestions of A. J. Evans—Suppl. III to E. A. Freeman, *Hist. of Sicily,* iv. p. 235—that Syracusan coin types found at Messene and Pheneus in the Peloponnese were due to Dionysius' mercenaries; also at Cnossus and Pherae (= Cretan archers, Thessalian peltasts or slingers?).
[8] Diodorus, xiv. 47. 7, gives 80,000 infantry, 3000 cavalry for the Syracusan army at the beginning of D.'s second war with Carthage (398 B.C.). These figures are certainly much too high, especially because it is unlikely that the army contained a large force of Syracusan citizens; D. had had serious trouble with them only four years before, and was to have trouble again the very next year. The only clue to the real figures is the passage about the arms (*ibid.* 41. 2 sqq.): 140,000 shields were made, 140,000 short swords, 140,000 helmets, and more than 14,000 breastplates of curious workmanship, which he intended for his cavalry, and the infantry officers, and the pick of the mercenaries. These multiples of 14 can hardly be fortuitous, and it seems probable that the mercenaries at this time were over 10,000 strong.

often include the citizen cavalry too.[1] But if 10,000 infantry may stand as a rough average figure, the total number of the soldiers who passed through his army is beyond computing, since we hear of at least ten recruiting campaigns in the course of his reign.[2]

It is very unfortunate that no figures or information should have survived concerning the payment of Dionysius' troops. If the stories about his heavy taxation and tricks with the currency contain any truth, then his army may have proved a serious drain upon his exchequer.[3] We are told of a trick by which he discharged some of his veterans.[4] And the colonies of soldiers at Leontini, Messana (?), and Tauromenium suggest that some arrangement may have been made whereby the soldiers should receive land after a certain term of service: possibly the gift of land may have been rather in the nature of compensation for arrears of pay than a real bonus or pension. But in addition to providing relief to the exchequer, the "colonies" almost certainly had another significance. All three towns occupied important strategic positions. Leontini commanded the most fertile plain in the east of the island, and may moreover have been in the tyrant's mind as a possible refuge should he ever be compelled to leave Syracuse: Messana commanded the straits, and was the obvious thorn with which to lacerate his enemy Rhegium: Tauromenium was a strong hill citadel commanding the coast road between Messana and Syracuse.

This strategic scheme is perhaps the most interesting feature of Dionysius' dealings with mercenaries. As a military inventor his name is always associated primarily with machines of war, and no new inventions in the sphere of tactics in the field have been ascribed to him. He may have been before his time (in relation to warfare in Greece) in his appreciation of a strong cavalry force, and he showed on one occasion at least that he knew something of the uses of light infantry; but it is not clear whether the peltast, as reformed by Iphicrates, ever served in

---

[1] Diod. xiii. 113. 1 sqq.
[2] *Ibid.* 96. 2; xiv. 8–9; 10. 4; 34. 3; 44. 2; 58. 1; 62. 1; 75. 8 sqq.; 78; xv. 14. 3.
[3] *Id.* xiv. 78. 5; Polyaen. v. 9. 5; [Aristot.] *Econ.* ii. 2. 6; 20. 2–5; cf. Freeman, *op. cit.* iv. pp. 230 sqq.
[4] Polyaen. v. 2. 2.

THE WEST

his army, though it is probable enough in view of his connection with Greek warfare through Sparta.[1]

Although there are serious gaps in our knowledge of Sicilian history after the death of Dionysius I there is no reason to think that they conceal any radical change in the methods of warfare. The information that we do possess, especially that which relates to Agathocles, all goes to suggest that mercenary service was in a particularly flourishing condition throughout the fourth century. Partly as a cause, and partly in effect, the condition of the island as a whole was deplorable. The most alarming result of the mercenary system, in its peculiar manifestation in Sicily, was the growth and influence of a barbarian element from abroad. The Carthaginians had always employed barbarian mercenaries.[2] Dionysius I had followed their example, and had probably settled them as military communities in cities which had previously been Greek. The younger Dionysius did likewise, and may have found in barbarian regiments the best means of terrorizing irreconcilable subjects: the two nights of terror which Syracuse endured at the hands of Nypsius' men form the worst page in the grisly chapter of Sicilian civil war. This means in effect that for fifty years there had been, from the part of the Carthaginians and that of the tyrants of Syracuse, a continual importation of foreign soldiers, many of whom must have remained in the island, and not to adorn it. The result may be judged from the fact that Plato, in a letter to the friends of Dion, can speak of the possibility of the Greek language being supplanted by that of Oscans and Phoenicians; and Plutarch, describing the state of Sicily immediately before the advent of Timoleon (*ca*. 345 B.C.), can say that the greater part of it is a desert, with most of the inhabited cities in the hands of barbarians of all races and discharged soldiers (perhaps a hendiadys).[3] Evidence exists of two such communities at Etna and Entella: the former must certainly have been the work of one of the Syracusan tyrants, and the barbarians were expelled by Timoleon.[4] But if Syracuse was the great prize to be fought and re-fought over, there were other smaller prizes too, and the

[1] Diod. xiii. 113. 1 sqq.; xiv. 42; 78. 1, etc.—his commander of mercenaries at one time was a Spartan, Aristoteles.
[2] Pp. 208 sqq. [3] Plato, *Ep*. VIII. 353 E; Plut. *Timol*. 1. 2.
[4] Diod. xvi. 67. 4 and 82. 4.

lesser tyrants whom Timoleon encountered (Hicetas, Mamercus, Leptines, Nicodemus and Apolloniades) no doubt used the same methods as the great tyrants of Syracuse, and so contributed to the difficulties and dangers of the Greek community.[1] Hand in hand with the increase of foreigners went the depopulation among the Greeks themselves, though the extreme instability of the governments meant that soldiers were always needed, and the great number of exiles arising out of the incessant party strife may have meant that there were always plenty of men in need of employment.[2] This was the situation in Sicily some thirty years before the tyranny at Syracuse was seized by Agathocles, the last of the great military despots in the West, and a worthy successor to the great Dionysius.

Agathocles served a stormy apprenticeship in the art of war. In the course of his early struggles he was twice exiled from Syracuse. On the first occasion he served for a time as captain of mercenaries to the government of Tarentum, and later captured Rhegium at the head of a band of exiles from the Italian cities.[3] His second exile he spent with a more immediate view to returning to Syracuse by force. Repairing to the Sicel town of Morgantia, he collected there another army of exiles reinforced with some of the Morgantines and inhabitants of other inland towns (that is to say presumably Sicel mercenaries); an army powerful enough to secure his return at its head, and for him to insist upon holding the office of "general". Once in Syracuse, he enlisted soldiers from the poorest classes and won the tyranny by a *coup d'État* (316 B.C.).[4] It appears that in the first place he had no bodyguard of mercenaries;[5] but the wars with his Greek neighbours in which he was at once involved, and especially the menace of interference by the Carthaginians, who had previously supported his political opponents in Syracuse and whose territory he had ravaged for the upkeep of his army at Morgantia, soon caused him to maintain a large field army which included foreign soldiers as well as Syracusans and allies.[6] In 311 B.C., when Carthage put a large army into the field against him, he may have had as many as 10,000 mercenary infantry and 3500

[1] Diod. xvi. 69, etc.; 72. 2 sqq.; 82. 4 sqq.
[2] Plato, *Ep.* VII. 337 C; Plut. *Timol.* 22. 3 sqq.   [3] Diod. xix. 3.
[4] *Ibid.* 5–6; 7–9; Justin 21. 2.
[5] Diod. xix. 9. 7.   [6] *Ibid.* 72. 2.

THE WEST

horse, but his whole army was considerably less than the 45,000 of the Carthaginians: the campaign ended in disaster for Agathocles, who suffered very severe losses especially in infantry, and in the winter 311–310 B.C. he was faced with the prospect of sustaining a siege in Syracuse.[1]

In the next year therefore Agathocles, with true strategic insight, resolved upon transferring the war to Africa. He left a sufficient garrison in Syracuse, almost certainly a mercenary garrison since his position was not such as to warrant his placing implicit confidence in his subjects; but the best of his troops sailed with him.[2] His army was a small one—3500 Syracusans, 2500 infantry who may have been Sicilian allies, 3000 Greek mercenaries, and 3000 barbarians from Central and North Italy ("Samnites, Etruscans, and Gauls"): probably many of the mercenaries were horsemen, though their mounts would have to be found when they arrived, and there was also a corps of 500 archers and slingers.[3] It would be tedious and irrelevant to describe the course of the four years' fighting. The Greeks were more than a match for the Carthaginian home levy,[4] so that one of Agathocles' objects was achieved when troops were recalled from Sicily.[5] Nevertheless, reinforced with the army of Ophellas the Greek governor of Cyrene, who by means of his influence at Athens had recruited from Greece a force of 11,000 mercenaries, and later with other reinforcements including at least 3000 more barbarians from Italy, Agathocles was in no danger of being annihilated.[6] His first difficulty may have been to preserve discipline in the ranks, since we hear of a mutiny of mercenaries, caused by lack of pay: indeed, a few of his soldiers deserted to Carthage.[7] The country in which they found themselves was rich in plunder, but Agathocles may well have experienced a shortage of actual money, since he took very little with him, and was probably afraid to make large demands on his African allies.[8] But the worst troubles arose when Agathocles himself was forced to pay a visit to Sicily. In his absence incompetent commanders lost nearly half the army in casualties, and when he returned he found the situation so changed that he could no longer hope to

[1] Diod. xix. 72. 2; 106–10; xx. 3.
[2] *Id.* xx. 4. 1 sqq.
[3] *Ibid.* 11. 1.
[4] *Ibid.* 11–12.
[5] *Ibid.* 15. 1.
[6] *Ibid.* 40–2; 61. 6; 64. 2.
[7] *Ibid.* 33–4.
[8] *Ibid.* 4. 5; Justin 22. 4. 4 sq.

meet the enemy in the field.[1] He promptly made his own escape by sea, leaving his sons to be put to death by the soldiers. The survivors of the expedition, about 9000 strong, came to terms with the Carthaginians: the few who waited in the hope of Agathocles' return were killed.[2]

The African expedition probably strained the credit of Agathocles as an employer, or indeed perhaps the available sources of man power, to the very utmost. In Sicily he was involved in a serious war against Deinocrates and his army of exiles and mercenaries. In 308 B.C. the Syracusan generals (in the absence of Agathocles himself with his expeditionary force) had been able to put into the field against Acragas an army of almost 10,000.[3] But shortly afterwards Pasiphilus, another of his generals, deserted to Deinocrates with his army,[4] and in 305 B.C. we hear of Agathocles himself starting a campaign with no more than 6000 men: financial troubles perhaps took their share in his difficulties. Nevertheless, he won his war, and when Deinocrates became one of his own generals his worst enemy in Sicily was removed.[5] Within a few years Agathocles had doubtless restored his credit and stability in the world of mercenaries, since he could afford (*ca*. 300 B.C.) to massacre 2000 Ligurian and Etruscan soldiers (possibly because he could not afford to pay them).[6] And we later find him campaigning in Italy against the Bruttians with an army more than 30,000 strong (*ca*. 295 B.C.).[7]

It is particularly unfortunate that no very accurate account of Agathocles' campaigns is preserved to us, because, judging by what we do possess, his battle tactics and formations are occasionally reminiscent of Alexander's. It appears that he had with him, in Africa at least, a battalion of especially good infantry, 1000 strong, which corresponds roughly to Alexander's foot-companions. In the first battle before Carthage he himself commanded them against the "Sacred Band", and we twice meet them later distinguished from the rest of the army:[8] they would almost certainly be picked mercenaries. In the same

---

[1] Diod. xx. 60 and 64.
[2] *Ibid*. 69.
[3] *Ibid*. 56. 2.
[4] *Ibid*. 77. 2.
[5] *Ibid*. 89; 90. 1.
[6] *Id*. xxi. 3.
[7] *Ibid*. 8.
[8] *Id*. xx. 11. 1, μετὰ τῆς θεραπείας αὐτὸς...χιλίοις ὁπλίταις πρὸς τὸν ἱερὸν λόχον. Cf. *ibid*. 17. 2, τὴν θεραπείαν ; *ibid*. 38. 6, 'Α. τοὺς ἀρίστους ἔχων ἀμφ' αὑτόν....

battle again Agathocles placed a company of his 500 archers and slingers on either flank, and they received and broke the charge of the Carthaginian war-chariots in much the same way as Alexander's archers and Agrianians disposed of the Persian chariots at Gaugamela:[1] the same slingers and archers are used with success against the Numidians, and again upon a siege-engine to shoot down upon a beleaguered city, in a manner rather out of the common run of Greek as opposed to Macedonian generalship.[2] Agathocles' misfortune was in the tools which he found to his hand. His needs were pressing, and it was, in any case, probably far too late in the day to try to build up a trustworthy Greek citizen army from the city rabbles and disaffected aristocrats who made up the Greek population under his rule. He was bound to rely mainly upon mercenaries, and mercenaries are dependable only so long as they are paid. There is ample evidence for believing that Agathocles, like Dionysius I, could not always pay his soldiers:[3] the remedy was to get rid of them and recruit new ones, so that when he saw the army of Africa dwindling and finally resolved to abandon it altogether, he probably did so without any great pangs of regret. It was the best army seen west of Greece since the elder Dionysius died.

The social and political question remained the same during the reign of Agathocles as it had been earlier, and is perhaps reflected in some information about the supply of mercenaries. Deinocrates, Hamilcar's Greek mercenary commander, is said to have raised an army of 28,000 mercenaries and exiles, of which the nucleus was 8000 Syracusans expelled on suspicion of disaffection during the siege (309 B.C.).[4] And out of 1000 Greek mercenaries in the pay of Carthage who were captured by Agathocles in Africa, more than half were Syracusans, and presumably therefore exiles from Syracuse. It is hard to say whether the demand for mercenaries at this time was greater than the supply: both were far too great to be healthy. The entry of Carthage too into the market for Greek soldiers may have upset the balance. The war in Africa withdrew for the time being at

[1] Diod. xx. 11–12. [2] Ibid. 38; 54. 4.
[3] Ibid. 33; xxi. 9 and 10; Justin 22. 4. 4 sqq. Also Diod. xx. 63. 5, κεραμεῦ καὶ καμινεῦ, πότε τοὺς μισθοὺς ἀποδώσεις τοῖς στρατιώταις ὅταν ταύτην ἐξέλω; he seems, too, often to have been obliged to make a war pay for itself (as in Africa).
[4] Diod. xx. 15; 31; 89.

least 15,000 Greeks, for none of the soldiers who sailed with Agathocles came back with him, though some no doubt returned later, after serving their time with Carthage: and this may explain the extraordinarily small numbers which we have noticed for Agathocles' army in Sicily shortly after the peace with Carthage. The shortage of men, if shortage there was, was probably no more than temporary, since the Carthaginians had no more fighting to do in Sicily, and it is unlikely that they would employ indefinitely the mercenaries left on their hands by Agathocles when he quitted Africa. In fact when Agathocles had established himself securely again in Sicily and appeared to have disposed of his enemies, it is probable that the military demands subsided to the normal. But even so he did not cease to employ barbarians, of whom some, a band of Campanians, made themselves famous by seizing and appropriating Messana, where they later became implicated in the events which led to the first war between Carthage and Rome.[1] This does not necessarily imply that there was a scarcity of Greeks, though this was perhaps so. But he may have preferred barbarians as less liable to interest themselves in Syracusan politics; or they may have been cheaper. Unfortunately our historians do not interest themselves in relative rates of pay, and there is not a single figure to quote on the subject.

Concerning the state of Sicily in the years between the death of Agathocles and the rise of Hieron the Second there is very little information.[2] They were years of trouble and distress occasioned by war among the Greeks themselves and against the old enemy Carthage, and it can accordingly be inferred that the mercenary system flourished under a variety of paymasters. Among its abuses, and not the least of them, may be reckoned the community of Campanian soldiers who had made the city of Messana their refuge and stronghold. The Mamertines, who

[1] Diod. xxi. 18; Pol. i. 7. 2 sqq.
[2] There are no details at all about the armies of the tyrants who ruled in the various cities after the death of Agathocles—e.g. Hicetas and Sosistratus in Syracuse, Phintias in Acragas, Tyndarion in Tauromenium, Heraclides in Leontini. Heraclides helped Pyrrhus with 4000 infantry, 500 cavalry, Sosistratus with 8000 infantry, 800 cavalry, "all picked men not inferior to the Epirotes". All the tyrants must have had mercenaries (Diod. xxii. 2; 8. 5; 10. 1).

THE WEST

won their name from their warlike temper and achievements, seem to have become pirates and brigands on a grand scale; they preyed ceaselessly upon their Greek neighbours, and from some of them even exacted a tribute, which was probably a species of "Danegeld" or doubtful guarantee of future immunity. They seem to have flourished and multiplied exceedingly, if we may believe Plutarch when he says that 10,000 of them harassed Pyrrhus on his retreat from Sicily: such a figure may be greatly in excess of the original number of mercenaries from Syracuse, but it is likely enough that the success that attended their evil ways should have attracted many ruffians from other parts of the island and from the neighbouring continent. Their hostility to Pyrrhus had won them the friendship of Rome, and it may perhaps be recorded as a triumph for insignificant rascality that this city of freebooters should have proved the means of embroiling the two great powers of the western Mediterranean. The story of the quarrel concerns us only in so far as the Syracusan Hieron was involved in it; but since perhaps he owed his elevation to the menace of the Mamertines, his story cannot fail to be of interest, besides being intrinsically relevant to our subject.[1]

The rise of Hieron is left far more obscure than that of his great predecessors Dionysius and Agathocles. We are told that "the Syracusan army was at variance with those in the city", that it elected in the field two magistrates (ἄρχοντες) on its own account, of whom Hieron was one, and that subsequently Hieron, with the help of a sympathetic party within the walls and a political alliance with the demagogue Leptines, procured his acceptance as general by the Syracusan people.[2] We may guess that this army was abroad in an endeavour to check the Mamertines; but when we come to examine its composition the situation is far from clear. In the first place there is no direct information whatever concerning the army before Hieron's elevation; but one of his first acts after becoming general of the

---

[1] The story of the Mamertines is to be found in Pol. i. 8 sqq.; Diod. xxi. 18; xxii. 7. 4; 13; Plut. *Pyrrhus* 23–4.
A similar community sprang up also in Rhegium, having its origin in a garrison of Campanian soldiers installed there by Rome: they massacred the citizens and became independent freebooters (Diod. xxii. 1).

[2] Pol. i. 8. 3 sqq.; 9. 1 sqq.

Syracusans was to lead against the Mamertines a force containing "the citizen cavalry and infantry" as well as "the old mercenaries", and it is added that he deliberately allowed the mercenaries to be cut to pieces because he saw that they were ill-conditioned and undisciplined.[1]

This brings us back to the question, what was "the Syracusan army" which had previously been "at variance with those in the city"? It is hard to see how it can have been a citizen army. For citizen soldiers in the field *are* "those in the city", except for the accident of their being absent on a campaign. And though factions of citizens in a democracy frequently become at variance, a Greek citizen army contained all able-bodied men who could provide themselves with arms, and therefore embraced presumably a variety of shades of political opinion: in short it is nearly incredible that the able-bodied men of Syracuse should have found themselves at variance with the other inhabitants of the city. The conclusion remains that the army in question consisted, or at least contained a preponderance, of mercenaries. The most obvious cause of variance between mercenaries and their employers is the question of pay. Probably the unpaid mercenaries chose two powerful citizens as their representatives in the hope of obtaining redress, and then the young Hieron used the position which they had given him in order to pull strings of his own inside the city. It is improbable that the mercenaries went so far as to impose their representative upon the people of Syracuse by forcing his election as general: at all events such a move would be without parallel in any other Greek city before or later. But if the theory set out here is correct, Hieron did owe his elevation in great measure to the action of the mercenaries, and they may not have allowed him to forget it, which would account for his sacrificing "the ill-conditioned and undisciplined" soldiers to the Mamertines.

"And so", as Polybius drily comments, "having accomplished his project with address and having rid himself of all the undisciplined and seditious element in the army, he recruited a sufficient number of mercenaries on his own account, and proceeded with his regimen in security."[2] He now marched against the Mamertines in earnest and defeated them severely, and on

---

[1] Pol. i. 9. 3 sqq.   [2] *Ibid.* 9. 6.

his return to Syracuse was recognized as king by the Syracusans and all their allies.[1] The fact of his being able to recruit new mercenaries immediately after his perfidious treatment of the old ones argues that the traffic in soldiers was in a healthy condition and that there was no shortage of mercenaries. The newly enlisted men owed their loyalty to Hieron himself and not to the city of Syracuse—so much can be read into the words of Polybius above—and there can be little doubt that Hieron throughout his long reign supported his position by hired troops just as the previous tyrants had done. After he had joined Rome against Carthage, he was expected to contribute reinforcements to the Roman armies in Sicily,[2] and it is unlikely that he would be willing to harass his Syracusan subjects with repeated campaigns throughout the long war. But apart from one reference in Polybius to Syracusan mercenaries at Acragas early in the war there is no explicit evidence.[3]

The second half of Hieron's reign was passed in profound peace—an unpromising condition for the present inquiry. That Hieron was a prosperous and a popular ruler is well known:[4] he had neither the wish nor the need for fresh conquests, and we may suppose that the military establishment of Syracuse was reduced to a minimum. That is not to say that Syracuse became a perfectly disarmed state, for the events of the two years after Hieron's death (215–213 B.C.) make it plain that there was at that time a mercenary army in the city, and the inference is that this was the army which Hieron himself had kept up while he was still alive: we hear of no recruiting when he died, though this alone is not conclusive. There is indeed one piece of evidence for this army before his death. In 218 B.C., after Trebia, the Romans sent to Hieron as their ally asking for a reinforcement: Hieron sent them 500 Cretans and 1000 πελτοφόροι.[5] (The "peltophoroi" were perhaps light-armed barbarians of some kind: the uncommon variant for "peltast" shows that Polybius

---

[1] Pol. i. 9. 7–8.
[2] *Ibid.* 17. 1—in the spring after Hieron's *volte face* the Romans sent to Sicily two legions only for that very reason.
[3] *Ibid.* 43. 2.
[4] E.g. Livy 24. 5. 3 sqq., for his free and open habit of life, without a bodyguard.
[5] Pol. iii. 75. 7.

206 HELLENISTIC MERCENARIES

probably did not consider them to be Greeks.[1]) The appearance of the Cretans is most interesting, because it is their first appearance in Sicily since the Athenian expedition 200 years before: that they should appear again now is quite in accordance with our evidence for the eastern Mediterranean in this period, a busy one for the Cretan pirates and mercenaries alike.

It is probably these same Cretans, and not a different contingent, who are to be found again at Syracuse in 213 B.C.[2] If this inference is right, the 500 had been caught in Hannibal's ambush at Trasymene along with the rest of Flaminius' army; but, more fortunate than the Roman legions, they had escaped with their lives by Hannibal's clemency, and returned to Syracuse in the interval. They were certainly not the whole of the mercenary strength in the city that played an important part in the tortuous politics of the two years after Hieron's death: here Greek politicians are seen at their worst and subtlest, and the tyrant's Greek soldiers were there to enforce their plans. The boy Hieronymus, Hieron's successor, was surrounded by foreigners who may or may not have been *condottieri*:[3] certainly he had an armed bodyguard in the style of Dionysius I, and the field army of Syracuse in 214 B.C. was at least 19,000 strong (partly of citizens, no doubt).[4] It was a soldier of the bodyguard that stooped to fiddle with his shoe and so gave the murderers of Hieronymus a moment's clear space while the boy was isolated from the guards

---

[1] Cf. Livy 22. 37. 7–8, for a reinforcement sent by Hieron to the Romans in this same year. Livy mentions no Cretans, but "1000 archers and slingers, a useful force against Balearians and Numidians and other people who fight with missiles".

[2] Livy 24. 30. 13 sqq., Prima forte signa sescentorum Cretensium erant, qui apud Hieronymum (*sic*) meruerant sub eis et Hannibalis beneficium habebant, capti ad Trasumennum inter Romanorum auxilia dimissique.

It seems that when Livy writes Hieronymum he must mean Hieronem, since Hieron's death was two full years after Trasymene, and the boy Hieronymus reigned for only one year in any case (215–214 B.C.). Livy gives 600 Cretans in 213, so that we are probably safe to suppose that Hieron in 217 sent to Rome only a part (500) of a larger total of Cretans in his army.

[3] Polybius vii. 2. 1 sqq.—Polyclitus of Cyrene and Philodemus of Argos sent as envoys to Hannibal 215 B.C. *Ibid*. 5. 2 sqq.—Aristomachus of Corinth, Damippus of Sparta, and Autonous a Thessalian, members of Hieronymus' συνέδριον.

[4] Livy, *ibid*. 5. 3 sqq.; 7. 1 sqq. Cf. 31. 11 for the two divisions of the army, mercenaries and citizens. Cf. also perhaps 28. 8—a council of war, where "duces ordinum praefectique auxiliorum simul consulere": duces ordinum = citizen officers, praefecti auxiliorum = mercenary officers?

who followed him.[1] In the hectic anarchy of Syracuse's last few months as a free city, the mercenaries were in their element: while the one party hoped to use them for its profit, the other dared not be rid of them for its safety.[2] A donative paid out of the tyrant's treasury attached them firmly to the pro-Carthaginian faction, and the alliance was powerful enough to impel Syracuse upon the course leading to a Roman siege, and the capture of the city hitherto uncaptured through all her adventurous history. During the siege the mercenaries must have borne the brunt of the stubborn defence. They were Spaniards and Africans, Cretans, and deserters from the Roman armies in Italy, a force well in keeping with the military tradition of the great Dionysius and his successors.[3] The deserters above all were desperate men, and it was they, along with the mercenaries, who kept the defence alive long after any real hope of safety was gone; they even turned their swords against the Syracusans when they spoke of peace. But in the end a Spanish captain betrayed his post by the fountain of Arethusa, and let the Romans in. The mercenaries escaped a general massacre while Marcellus restrained his men in his anxiety lest Hieron's treasure should fall into the wrong hands. They may have got clear away to Africa, but their fate is unknown.[4]

2. CARTHAGE

It is probable that in very early times the armies of Carthage were recruited from the Carthaginians themselves. About the middle of the sixth century a nobleman named Mago effected a military reform, described indeed in vague enough terms, but in which we are probably to recognize the occasion of a change of policy and method in warfare: henceforward Carthage relied more and more upon foreign soldiers commanded by Carthaginian officers.[5] The wars with the Greeks in Sicily were un-

[1] Livy 24. 7.
[2] Livy's account, *ibid.* 21 sqq.—esp. 21. 2; 23. 5 and 9; 24. 2 sqq.; 29. 1 sqq., 30 and 31.
[3] Africans and Spaniards, Livy, *ibid.* 24. 6. Roman deserters 2000 strong (= Italian allies, probably S. Italian Greeks, Bruttians, Lucanians, etc.?), *ibid.* 29. 2; 30. 6; 32. 7.
[4] For the siege, Livy 25. 25 sqq.
[5] Justin 19. 1; Diod. xiv. 75. 2.

doubtedly carried on principally with armies drawn from the subject Libyans and mercenaries from Europe. The advantages to Carthage of such a system are obvious enough, in view of the fact that she was essentially a commercial city: a nation of merchants has neither the time nor the inclination to subject its business to periodical interruptions for campaigning overseas. The situation of the Carthaginians has points in common with that of the English in the eighteenth century. Both peoples enjoyed a maritime supremacy that made them immune from all serious fear of invasion and encouraged them to forget that their fathers had known how to carry arms: and both peoples could easily afford to devote a part of the profits from their empire and their commerce to hiring barbarians to fight for them on the occasions when fighting became necessary.

It is difficult to reproduce even in outline the internal organization of the Carthaginian military system. It seems certain that a standing army of some kind must have been maintained in Africa; but the campaigns in Sicily, which provide the only field for our research, were undoubtedly undertaken with troops most of which were specially recruited for the occasion. It follows with equal certainty that there was never any lack of mercenaries when they were needed, and some idea of the principal recruiting grounds can easily be obtained from our material. We learn from Plutarch's *Timoleon* that Libya, Spain and Numidia were Carthage's great resource when she needed soldiers;[1] these were the regions where her influence was the greatest, and we may believe that it was in reality upon them that she relied for the bulk of her fighting material, though we shall see that her recruiting officers sometimes went much farther afield. At a very early date Balearic slingers seem to have been employed, and the story goes that since the laws of these people forbade them to use coined money, the soldiers were paid in women and wine and went home with empty pockets.[2] The army of Hamilcar was recruited from Italy and Liguria, from Gaul and from Spain (480 B.C.);[3] that of Hannibal (410 B.C.) from Spain as well as from the subject Libyans and Cartha-

[1] Plut. *Timol.* 28. 9. [2] Diod. v. 17. 1 sqq., esp. 5.
[3] *Id.* xi. 1. 5; Hdt. vii. 165. Cf. Polyaen. i. 28. 1, for Iberians with Carthaginians against Theron of Acragas.

ginians themselves.¹ When Hannibal was preparing to attack Acragas (407-406 B.C.) he sent recruiting officers with money to Spain and the Balearic Islands, and to Italy for more Campanians, who were highly prized.² Himilco, for his expedition of 397 B.C. against Dionysius, hired mercenaries from Spain who later distinguished themselves from the other troops of Carthage by their soldierly bearing in the disaster before Syracuse in the following year.³ Mago (393 B.C.) commanded "barbarians from Italy" as well as Libyans and Sardinians who were probably subject allies,⁴ and for the long war (*ca.* 383-373 B.C.) against Dionysius, the Carthaginians "spent great sums of money on hiring mercenary forces".⁵ In the war against Timoleon they used Iberians, Celts and Ligurians.⁶

We are expressly told by Plutarch that the first time Carthage used Greek mercenaries was when Gescon was sent to Sicily in 340 B.C., the year after the battle of the Crimisus.⁷ Plutarch appears to contradict here an earlier statement of his own about some Greek mercenaries with Mago and Hicetas of Leontini three or four years before. The Greek mercenaries with Timoleon and those of the opposite side had found a common interest in fishing, with the result that Mago deserted his ally in disgust; but it is always possible that the mercenaries who were fond of fishing were really in the service of Hicetas and not of the Carthaginians, and the action of Mago makes this the more likely.⁸ There are, however, other passages referring to Greeks in Carthaginian armies considerably earlier than the occasion noticed by Plutarch as the first of its kind. There were Greeks with Hannibal in 409 B.C., and with Himilco in 397. Himilco's Greeks can easily have come from the Carthaginian province in Sicily, which in 397 included Acragas, Selinus and Himera; but it is not easy to account for Hannibal's Greeks in 409 except by assuming them to be mercenaries, for the only inhabitants of Sicily mentioned as serving with Hannibal are some Elymians and Sicans.⁹ Polyaenus also has a story of Greek mercenaries with the Carthaginians in the time of Dionysius I.¹⁰ One imagines

¹ Diod. xiii. 44. 1 sqq.; 54. 1. ² *Ibid.* 80. 2 sqq. (cf. xii. 31).
³ *Id.* xiv. 55. 4. ⁴ *Ibid.* 95. 1. ⁵ *Id.* xv. 15. 2.
⁶ *Id.* xvi. 73. 3. ⁷ Plut. *Timol.* 30. 3. ⁸ *Ibid.* 20.
⁹ Diod. xiii. 58. 1; cf. 54. 6: and xiv. 53. 4; cf. xiii. 114. 1.
¹⁰ Polyaen. v. 2. 17.

that it would not be difficult for Plutarch to make a mistake on such a point as this, and if his statement is not absolutely accurate it nevertheless produces a true impression, namely, that it was at this time that the Carthaginians fully realized the excellence of the Greeks as soldiers. The fact had been brought to their notice at the battle of the Crimisus in the previous year, where a large army (it was said to number 70,000 men), recruited on the traditional principles and containing mercenaries from Spain, Gaul and Liguria with Libyans from Africa and a leavening of native Carthaginians, was utterly defeated by Timoleon and his 12,000 Greeks.[1] Crimisus proved conclusively that a horde of barbarians with a few picked troops from Carthage was no match for a much smaller army of trained and experienced Greek soldiers. In the very next year Carthage enlisted Greek mercenaries for the war against Timoleon, having found the Greeks, as Plutarch says, "the most irresistible soldiers of all mankind". This change of policy coincided with two minor successes in the field; but peace was made before it had received a fair trial.[2]

For nearly thirty years after Timoleon's peace the Carthaginians do not seem to have been involved in any serious warfare. It is known that they were active in the party struggles at Syracuse prior to Agathocles' seizing the tyranny; but no extraordinary army appears to have been called into being, nor is there evidence of Greek or other mercenaries having been retained in Sicily as a standing army of defence. In 311 B.C., however, a large force was collected against Agathocles, 40,000 infantry and 5000 horse. From Africa were sent 2000 Carthaginians and 10,000 Libyans, and recruiting officers brought in from the northern Mediterranean 1000 Etruscan mercenaries and 1000 slingers from the Balearic Islands: Hamilcar himself recruited mercenaries in Sicily (presumably Greeks) and received contingents from his Greek allies in the island.[3] Since the army was later divided before Syracuse into two camps, one of which contained Greeks only, it may be surmised that something like one half of the total strength was Greek.[4] A battle was

[1] Diod. xvi. 73. 3; Plut. *Timol.* 25. 1.
[2] Diod. *ibid.* 81. 4; Plut. *ibid.* 30. 3 sqq.   [3] Diod. xix. 106.
[4] *Id.* xx. 29. 6. They are called τῶν συμμαχούντων Ἑλλήνων; but cf. the text (above).

THE WEST

fought near Ecnomus in which the Carthaginian army, numerically the superior, defended a strong position against the assaults of Agathocles. Hannibal's Greeks stood firm, and his Balearic slingers caused great discomfiture to the enemy in their massed attack: unlike the Rhodian slingers, who shot missiles of lead, the Balearians used stones, which, though they are said to have weighed nearly a pound, were more likely to wound an enemy than to kill him.[1] The Greeks were probably responsible for the victory, but they were also to blame for its being wasted as soon as won. When Hamilcar sat down to besiege Syracuse he felt the need for segregating the Greek from the barbarian element of his army, and when he was himself taken prisoner the two elements were no longer able to combine. The Greeks elected a general of their own, a certain Deinocrates who had previously commanded the cavalry; the siege came to an end, and Deinocrates used his soldiers for his own purposes.[2]

Meanwhile Agathocles' landing in Africa was creating trouble for Carthage at her own doors. The feebleness of the Carthaginian resistance in the first few months argues against the presence of any foreign professional army (certainly no Greeks had as yet penetrated to Africa): in the first battle only an improvised army of citizens took part, and the only other immediate resources were the Libyan subject allies.[3] These were plainly not sufficient. Orders for reinforcements were sent to Hamilcar in Sicily, and it is almost certain that the 5000 soldiers that he sent were Greek mercenaries. At all events we hear later of Greek cavalry in Africa under Cleinon, who were severely handled by Agathocles, and of 1000 Greeks taken prisoners, of whom more than half were Syracusans.[4] Even after these losses, a little later the Carthaginian general Bomilcar made an attempt to overthrow the government with 4000 mercenaries, and since there had apparently been no recruiting campaigns in Spain or elsewhere these too were probably Greeks.[5] Finally, many of Agathocles' soldiers, when he returned to Sicily and abandoned them to their fate, became mercenaries of Carthage, and arrange-

---

[1] Diod. xix. 109. 1 sqq. For the Rhodians, cf. Xen. *Anab.* iii. 3. 17.
[2] Diod. xx. 29; 31.
[3] Ibid. 10. 5.　　　[4] Ibid. 15. 1 sqq.; 16. 9; 38. 6; 39. 4 sqq.
[5] Ibid. 44. 1: or 1000? Cf. MSS.

ments were made for others to be settled in the Carthaginian fortress of Solous in Sicily.[1]

There is another gap in the evidence between the invasion of Agathocles and the beginning of the first Punic War.[2] In the early stages of the war with Rome it seems likely that Carthage intended to rely for the defence of Sicily by land principally upon her ally Hieron of Syracuse. At all events, it is not until Hieron has changed sides that we hear of any extraordinary recruiting effort at Carthage with a view to reinforcing the permanent army of defence which presumably occupied the Carthaginian province. Hieron's defection was quickly followed by a recruiting campaign in the usual Carthaginian style, which brought to Sicily an army of Ligurian, Gallic and Spanish mercenaries: these may be "the mercenary forces" who are mentioned later as besieged in Acragas.[3] They included 3000 Gallic adventurers who gave nothing but trouble to the Carthaginians, as they did to their next employers the Romans, and later to the Epirotes (p. 253). To the relief of Acragas Carthage also sent from Africa an army of "the additional soldiers who had been collected", who may represent the Libyan levies; but they included Numidian horse, and it subsequently becomes clear that at least a great part of the reinforced army was mercenaries.[4] Thus it came about that a considerable force of mercenaries was concentrated in Sicily by the year 256 B.C. Meanwhile Carthage and Africa were denuded of troops. The unexpected landing of Regulus and his army threw the government into a state of justifiable panic. Five thousand soldiers were rushed from Sicily to the defence of the city, and probably

[1] Diod. xx. 69. 3 sqq. Two hundred of Agathocles' mercenaries had previously deserted to Carthage, *ibid.* 34. 7.
[2] But cf. Zonaras viii. 5. 377 *a*; *ibid.* 9. 383 *d*, for Italian mercenaries serving in Sicily against Pyrrhus, and again at the outbreak of the first Punic War. Gsell's suggestion that the former may have been recruited by permission of Rome (the ally of Carthage against Pyrrhus) is improbable, since Rome needed the Italians for her own levies; but he is right in judging that the two texts are of doubtful value (ii. p. 386 and nn. 3 and 5).
[3] Pol. i. 17. 4; 19. 3. Diodorus (xxiii. 8), on the authority of Philinus of Acragas, puts the Carthaginian army of 261 B.C. at 50,000 infantry, 6000 cavalry, which may be too high, as are all the figures of Orosius (*Adv. pag.* iv. 7 sqq.) and Eutropius (ii. 21. 3; 24): those of Polybius, when they occur at all, are reasonable.
[4] Pol. i. 18. 8; 19. 9. For the status of the Libyans, see below, p. 219.

THE WEST

constituted the bulk of the mercenary infantry who took part in the first engagement upon African soil: no other infantry is mentioned (the populace of Carthage, long unaccustomed to military service, must have been quite unfit to take the field at short notice); but the Carthaginian cavalry may have been recruited from the well-to-do citizens, and it was perhaps hoped that African elephants, used now for the first time, would cover a multitude of weaknesses.[1]

It was probably during their first alarm that the Carthaginian government had despatched recruiting officers to Greece. One of these officers now returned bringing with him a great number of soldiers and, better still, a competent Greek commander. His name was Xanthippus and he was a Lacedaemonian.[2] He saw at once that the strength of the Carthaginian army lay in its numerous cavalry and elephants, which should enable it to win battles in open country: he saw too that the generals of Carthage had failed to realize their strength, and he was not afraid to tell them so. His presence inspired the soldiers with a new confidence, and it is plain that in the decisive battle that ensued he virtually commanded the army.[3] He had at his disposal 12,000 infantry, 4000 cavalry and about 100 elephants: the infantry included a Carthaginian phalanx, but the majority must have been mercenaries.[4] The issue of the day completely justified Xanthippus' tactics. The mercenary infantry were roughly handled by the Romans—they lost 800 killed—but they fought well and gave Xanthippus time to win the battle with his cavalry and elephants.[5] Carthage owed everything to Xanthippus, and Polybius does not fail to give him his due: he considers him a striking vindication of Euripides' judgment that one good idea is worth more than the work of many hands.[6] His subsequent career is lost to us. He quitted Carthage in the very hour of his triumph, leaving the African campaign to be concluded by the Carthaginian generals, who, bunglers though they were for the most part, could now discover no loophole for error. Polybius commends the prudence of Xanthippus in departing before his own fortune could desert him or the jealousy of rivals work his

---

[1] Pol. i. 30. 2; 11 sqq.
[2] Ibid. 32. 1; Diod. xxiii. 14 sqq.
[3] Pol. i. 32. 3 sqq.; 33–4.
[4] Ibid. 32. 9; 33. 6.
[5] Ibid. 34. 8; 33–4.
[6] Ibid. 35. 4.

undoing: but he does not relinquish the subject without hinting that another story might be told concerning the mysterious departure, and indeed promises himself to tell it in a more suitable place, a promise which is unhappily never fulfilled. Why the Carthaginians let him go is in itself mystery enough.[1] Good ideas were not so common at Carthage in this period that they could afford to dispense with the services of a general who knew so well the lessons of Alexander and of the great Hellenistic commanders: they needed such a man in Sicily.

For this great victory, if the first prize goes to Xanthippus, the second must certainly go to the African elephants. Pyrrhus had introduced elephants into the warfare of the West, but this is the first time that Carthage is known to have used them, and in the first engagement with Regulus the Carthaginian commanders wasted their new weapon. Xanthippus knew better, for the correct use of elephants was a commonplace to the best Hellenistic generals. Xanthippus must have smiled grimly when he saw Regulus' order of battle, his infantry massed thick and deep in the pathetic hope of *stopping* the elephants:[2] and the Indian trainers on their backs probably regarded the battle as a party of pleasure, well worth the long journey from India. This long journey is itself of great interest, since it shows to what trouble and expense the great powers of that day were prepared to go in order to keep abreast with the very latest developments and inventions. The Indian trainers in Egypt were surprising enough, but their appearance at Carthage is almost astonishing, and we are perfectly in the dark as to the means by which they were procured. There must have been at least 100 of them, allowing

[1] Pol. i. 36. 1–4.
[2] *Ibid.* 30. 8; 33 sqq. It is interesting that Polybius himself seems to approve perfectly of Regulus' tactics (τῆς μὲν πρὸς τὰ θηρία μάχης δεόντως ἦσαν ἐστοχασμένοι), and relates almost with pride how, although the first ranks of the Romans went down "in heaps", the formation did not collapse until the rear ranks were obliged to turn to meet the attack by cavalry. He seems to have missed the point completely of Scipio's open order at Zama, and the explanation probably is that Polybius, practical soldier though he was, had had no experience of elephants, since Magnesia was the last great battle in the East at which they were in use. He may indeed have talked with Achaeans who had fought at Magnesia, but in any case the elephants of Antiochus never touched the Roman infantry, so that Magnesia was no guide.

For a fascinating account of elephants in the warfare of the period, cf. W. W. Tarn, *Hellenistic Military and Naval Developments*, pp. 92 sqq.

THE WEST

one Indian for each elephant. Their brilliant success against Regulus encouraged the Carthaginians to send them to Sicily, 140 strong, where they seem to have influenced the war for a short time almost to the extent that the war in Italy forty years later was to be influenced by Hannibal's cavalry and superior battle tactics: the Romans simply would not risk another battle with the elephants, and retired to broken ground to avoid them. When they did succeed in breaking the spell, and actually put the elephants to rout by a stratagem, they captured ten of them σὺν αὐτοῖς τοῖς Ἰνδοῖς (a triumph comparable with capturing a warship αὐτοῖς ἀνδράσι), and they succeeded later in rounding up all the others, which had stampeded and parted company with their Indians.[1] The resulting situation was ludicrous enough, for the Romans found themselves with over 100 elephants and only ten Indians, while the Carthaginians were left with over 100 Indians and no elephants. What the Romans can have done with their herd we do not know, for there is no further mention of elephants in the war in Sicily. But the Carthaginians for their part had not finished with elephants, and the Indian trainers must have spent some years in Africa, collecting and training the new recruits, for there were 100 again with Hanno in the Mercenaries' War, when they won another success at the storming of a fortified camp.[2] This evidently established both elephants and Indians as a permanent corps in the army of Carthage. Hannibal thought it worth his while to take them across the Rhone and through the Alps; but they did not thrive, for some of the men were drowned in the river and the animals nearly died of starvation in the mountains, and did die of cold in their first Italian winter, all except the one which survived to carry the sick Hannibal through Etruria in the spring.[3] Hasdrubal had better luck, for he produced ten elephants with their Indians at the Metaurus; but they were of little use in the battle.[4] Finally Hannibal had 70 at Zama, where again they were a failure; and this is the end of the picturesque specialists.[5]

To return to mere infantry, when the danger in Africa was past the Carthaginians sent back to Sicily the 5000 mercenaries

[1] Pol. i. 38. 2; 39. 11 sqq.; 40. 5 sqq.
[2] *Id.* i. 74.   [3] *Id.* iii. 46; 53. 8; 55. 8; 74. 11; 79. 12.
[4] *Id.* xi. 1. 12.   [5] *Id.* xv. 11. 1, etc.

who had sailed to defend the city. It is probable that the new mercenaries went with them, though some may have been kept in Africa as a restraint upon the Libyan subjects and the hostile Numidians.[1] We find a force of 10,000 mercenaries in Lilybaeum in addition to citizen troops, and later separate mercenary forces at Drepanum and at Eryx.[2] Since another reinforcement of 10,000 men was sent from Carthage to Lilybaeum, it becomes probable that the recruiting officers sent to Greece at the time of Regulus' landing in Africa continued to bring new soldiers after the urgent need for them was gone, for Xanthippus had fought Regulus with only 12,000 infantry, a number which is exceeded if the reinforcement mentioned here be added to the force of 5000 referred to above.[3] In fact the defensive warfare in Sicily waged by Carthage in the last ten years of the war would have been impossible without a permanent force of at least 20,000 mercenaries; it appears that they numbered Greeks among them, but how many it is impossible to say. The original force of 10,000 at Lilybaeum proved its loyalty to Carthage by refusing to mutiny and desert at the bidding of some of its officers: the conspiracy had been discovered by a Greek officer named Alexon, an Achaean, who had previously distinguished himself at the siege of Acragas, and whose great influence upon the soldiers in this crisis must mean that there was among them a good proportion of Greeks.[4] Again at Lilybaeum "some of the Greek mercenaries" rendered good service by burning the Roman siege-engines.[5] And in the last naval battle of the war at Drepanum, it was the Carthaginian plan to counter the Roman boarding tactics by using mercenaries as marines, "those of them who were suitable", which probably means the Greeks.[6] The plan miscarried, and the Carthaginians, compelled to fight without "the best of the infantry", were badly beaten.[7] In short, the evidence relating to the long weary struggle in Sicily, scanty as it is, does suggest that the mercenaries of Carthage, besides

---

[1] Pol. i. 38. 2, καὶ τὸν μὲν Ἀσδρούβαν ἐξαπέστελλον εἰς τὴν Σικελίαν δόντες αὐτῷ τούς τε προϋπάρχοντας καὶ τοὺς ἐκ τῆς Ἡρακλείας στρατιώτας. τοὺς προϋπάρχοντας probably refers to the soldiers who had remained in Sicily all the time.
[2] Ibid. 42. 11; 46. 1 sqq.; 53. 5; 60. 3.
[3] Ibid. 44. 1 sqq.   [4] Ibid. 43. 1 sqq.
[5] Ibid. 48. 3.   [6] Ibid. 60. 3.
[7] Ibid. 60. 8.

THE WEST

being numerous, were also both efficient and loyal. (Polybius says indeed that the Romans were much the better soldiers;[1] but they were better soldiers than most people.) It cannot be said that they lost the war for Carthage, and there is nothing to prepare us for the events of the peace which followed, more dangerous to Carthage than even the war and the Romans had ever been.

The so-called Mercenaries' or Truceless War arose out of a difficulty over the pay question, which was aggravated and magnified by the incredibly stupid behaviour of the Carthaginian government. The story of the quarrel throws valuable side-lights upon the ways and means by which mercenaries were paid, and will be discussed in detail in the section devoted to that subject.[2] It is enough to say here that Carthage had apparently not paid her soldiers by the month or at any other regular interval, but in the course of the war had run up a long account with the mercenaries in Sicily, who must now be evacuated from the island in accordance with the terms of the peace treaty with Rome.[3] Moreover, there was no choice but to transport them to Africa, there to receive their pay and collect their baggage and families (for it appears that all the mercenaries recruited during the war had at different times been concentrated at Carthage before proceeding to Sicily).[4] They numbered no fewer than 20,000 men,[5] so that the process of transport, payment and discharge was bound to be difficult and tedious, and in the event proved perilous in the extreme. It may be remarked that there seems to have been no idea of retaining the mercenaries in Africa on a permanent footing. Carthage had lost her possessions in Sicily and could accordingly with reason reduce her army to a figure lower even than the previous peace strength, an economy which became imperative in view of the financial drain of the war and the indemnity owing to Rome. The Carthaginians need not be censured for dismissing an army which had become an incumbrance, nor even for having laid themselves under the necessity of paying out a large lump sum at a time when they

[1] Pol. vi. 52. 2 sqq.   [2] pp. 288 sqq.
[3] Cf. Pol. i. 66. 3; 11; 67. 1, etc. For trouble earlier in Sicily, apparently due to the pay question, cf. Pol. ii. 7. 7 sqq.; Zonaras viii. 13. 392 a; 16. 396 d; 10. 386 b sqq.; Frontinus iii. 16. 3 (cf. ibid. 2); perhaps Diod. v. 11.
[4] Pol. i. 66. 7; 68. 1 sqq.   [5] Ibid. 67. 13.

could ill afford it. The payment of debts must always be an unpleasant duty, as the Carthaginians now felt; the serious charge against them is that they first contrived to place their creditors in a position to do them harm if they should be angered, and next proceeded to anger them.

Nevertheless the general, Gisgo by name, who was entrusted with the evacuation of the soldiers from Sicily brought reason and prudence to his task. He wisely sent them to Africa not all together but at intervals and in detachments, with the idea of giving the government time to pay and dismiss one batch before the next could arrive.[1] But his forethought was utterly wasted, for the authorities, "being short of money owing to their large outlay, and believing that they could beg off part of their debt to the mercenaries if they assembled and received them all into Carthage, were induced by this hope to keep the soldiers there as they arrived and hold them in the city".[2] The Carthaginians soon became disgusted with their rough ways, and next offered them a handsome gratuity if they would remove to a neighbouring city until their pay should be ready, a proposal which was gladly accepted. But the last and greatest blunder was over the mercenaries' belongings: the soldiers, perhaps preferring a bachelor's existence, wished to leave their wives and families in Carthage as before, but the government blindly insisted on their removal, thereby relinquishing its hostages for the mercenaries' good behaviour. So far the mercenaries had behaved as well as could be expected, but now, finding nothing for their idle hands to do, they began to employ their leisure in reckoning the amount of money due to them and formulating extravagantly high demands.[3] Even so the matter could probably have been settled by a prompt payment. The disorder did not become really serious until the general, Hanno, sent to parley with them, so far from conciliating, actually tried to persuade them to accept less than was admittedly due. Then all discipline was at an end. A great mixed army, which justly considered itself injured and abused, was at the mercy of its officers, upon whom it depended for interpreting the babel of foreign tongues which were in use in its ranks. Some of the officers unscrupulously fostered the sedition, and the army marched against Carthage in the ugliest

[1] Pol. i. 66. 1–3. [2] Ibid. 5. [3] Ibid. 6 sqq.

of humours.¹ The government was at last awake to the danger which it had courted, and did everything in its power to meet the soldiers' demands, exorbitant though they were. But it was too late. The men were thoroughly out of hand, and when they finally seized the envoy Gisgo and his suite it became clear that all hope of a compromise was at an end.²

Before proceeding to the story of the war, it will be as well to glance at the army itself which was causing all the trouble. We have seen that it was 20,000 strong: it appears that it contained cavalry as well as infantry and that a variety of nations was represented in it.³ There were Iberians, Gauls, Ligurians, Balearians, a good number of Greeks from many cities (described as "μιξέλληνες, of whom the majority were deserters and slaves"); but the greatest number were Libyans.⁴ These Libyans constitute something of a difficulty. It is true that it had always been the custom of Carthage in the past to include great numbers of Libyans in her armies, but it is equally true that the Libyans then served in the rôle of subject allies and not of mercenaries.⁵ Yet here Polybius always speaks of them as mercenaries, and there is nothing in his account which can be used to prove him wrong. There seem to be two possible explanations. First, and most obvious, that Polybius is in fact wrong, though he cannot be proved so. Second, that before or during the war with Rome, the Carthaginians had effected some reform whereby the custom of levying troops from their subjects was abolished or suspended. In support of this theory may be adduced the absence of Libyans from the Carthaginian army commanded by Xanthippus against Regulus (pp. 212 sqq.) in a crisis when Carthage needed every soldier she could obtain; though it may be said in opposition that the presence of Regulus then made it unsafe to employ the disaffected Libyans against him. Nevertheless, the Libyans had always been disaffected, and yet Carthage had long continued to use their levies overseas. It is thus possible that at the beginning of the war with Rome the government had decided that better soldiers than the Libyans could be found, and that the Libyans

---

¹ Pol. i. 67.   ² Ibid. 68. 8 sqq.; 69; 70. 3.
³ For cavalry, cf. Pol. i. 68. 8, etc.   ⁴ Ibid. 67. 7; Diod. xxv. 2.
⁵ Cf. O. Meltzer, *Gesch. d. Karth.* pp. 80–5, for the obligations of the Libyan subjects of Carthage.

themselves must find them: that the Libyan subjects should now contribute money in place of their usual quota of soldiers, as the allies of Sparta are said to have done in 383 B.C.[1] Some such arrangement may be concealed in Polybius' account of the excessive taxation endured by the Libyans during the war till "they needed no exhortation but merely the sign to revolt".[2] This explanation lacks proof to make it certain, but it may perhaps be considered plausible. If it is the true one, then the many Libyans found here among the mercenaries of Carthage are merely men who had volunteered for service in the same way as any other mercenary soldiers: and Carthage had thus eliminated from her army a possibly disaffected national element forced to serve against its will, while she employed such of her subjects as could be expected to remain loyal so long as they received the proper amount of pay.

Nevertheless it was a bad thing for Carthage in this new trouble that so many of the mutinous soldiers were Libyans. The ringleaders of the army were Spendius, a Campanian, a runaway slave and a deserter from the Romans whom he had perhaps served as a rower;[3] a Libyan named Mathos;[4] and a certain Autaritus the leader of the 2000 Gauls, a man who owed his influence to his excellent knowledge of the Phoenician tongue, which seems to have become the *lingua franca* of this polyglot army which had served Carthage for so many years.[5] But it was Mathos who incited the Libyans to sedition, and once the sedition broke out, it was the Libyans who persisted in carrying the affair to a decision of arms, for the obvious reason that, should a compromise be effected, the other mercenaries might depart in safety to their homes, but their own homes and persons would be at the mercy of Carthaginian vengeance.[6] They consequently strained every nerve to prevent a reconciliation, and when they had succeeded in this they had no difficulty in effecting a revolt of all the Libyan subject communities, who may have put as

[1] Xen. *Hell.* v. 2. 21.
[2] Pol. i. 72. 1 sqq., κατὰ γὰρ τὸν προγεγονότα πόλεμον εὐλόγους ἀφορμὰς ἔχειν ὑπολαμβάνοντες πικρῶς ἐπεστάτησαν τῶν κατὰ τὴν Λιβύην ἀνθρώπων, παραιρούμενοι μὲν τῶν ἄλλων πάντων τῶν καρπῶν τοὺς ἡμίσεις, διπλασίους δὲ ταῖς πόλεσι τοὺς φόρους ἣ πρὶν ἐπιτάττοντες, συγγνώμην δὲ τοῖς ἀπόροις ἢ συμπεριφορὰν οὐδ' ἡντινοῦν ἐπ' οὐδενὶ τῶν πραττομένων διδόντες....
[3] *Ibid.* 69. 5.
[4] *Ibid.* 6.
[5] *Ibid.* 77. 1 sqq.; 80. 5 sqq.
[6] *Ibid.* 69. 6 sqq.

THE WEST

many as 70,000 men into the field, though their fighting value was perhaps inconsiderable.[1] A much more valuable reinforcement was the money which the Libyans now gladly contributed to the cause of their freedom, and which more than made up the sum owed to the mercenaries by Carthage.[2] With such resources against her Carthage could not hope to win quickly, if at all, and so the event proved.

It would be tedious to describe the obscure campaigns of the three years' war which was necessary to stamp out the rebellion, a war chiefly memorable for the merciless cruelty with which it was waged by both parties.[3] No prisoners were taken, or at least none was preserved. And the numbers of slain in the battles which took place after the tide of victory had turned in favour of Carthage make it probable that few indeed of the mercenaries survived the end of the war. Carthage was victorious through the inflexible determination of Hamilcar Barca and the bad leadership of her enemies. The citizens of Carthage were compelled to practise the use of arms and fight for their city and their lives. But it is typical that when their existence was in danger at the hands of mercenaries, the Carthaginians even so did not abandon the mercenary system: the probability is that they had no choice. In the war they were greatly helped by a Numidian prince who fought for them with 2000 horse, and who was doubtless paid for his trouble.[4] And one of their first acts when they realized the seriousness of their danger was to collect new mercenaries, though in what numbers it is impossible to say.[5] Their need was pressing, and Sicily, the only quick recruiting ground, may have remained open to their recruiting officers through the magnanimity, or the policy, of Hieron of Syracuse.[6]

Carthage's victory over the Mercenaries was the inauguration of a new era in her history, coincident with the ascendancy of the Barcid family. Now for the first time the Carthaginian

---

[1] Pol. i. 70. 8 sqq.; 73. 3.   [2] Ibid. 72. 5.
[3] The account is in Pol. i. 73 sqq.; Diod. xxv. 3 sqq.
[4] Pol. i. 78. 1 sqq., 9, etc.
[5] Ibid. 73. 1. Early in the struggle the Carthaginian army was no stronger than 10,000, consisting of the citizen troops horse and foot, and of the mercenaries they had recruited, and deserters from the enemy.
[6] Cf. ibid. 83. 2 sqq.

government acquiesced in a policy of military imperialism, of which the fruits were an increase of subject territory in Africa, and conquests in Spain amounting practically to a great new province. The development of this policy is lost almost completely; we are left in possession of the accomplished fact, and its staggering effects. And for the present purpose the effect which is most relevant is the appearance in 218 B.C. of Hannibal's army, the second great army of antiquity. This army has been exhaustively discussed by modern scholars:[1] the task here and now is merely to try to find out how far (if at all) Hannibal had mercenary soldiers to thank for his victories, how far this appearance of a great army fighting for Carthage was due to a change of method.

When one speaks of a great army one is not thinking necessarily in terms of numbers (Alexander's army was less than 40,000 in the beginning). Hannibal's army is said to have been 102,000 men in Spain, but it was certainly no more than 26,000 when it reached Italy:[2] it stayed in Italy nearly sixteen years, and was of course strengthened by recruits and reinforcements in that time. Perhaps the best starting-point for our inquiry is a remark of Polybius referring to the year 202 B.C.: "having constantly fought the Romans for sixteen years, he never broke up his forces and dismissed them from the field, but holding them together under his own command, like a good ship's captain, he kept so large an army free from sedition against himself or within its own ranks, although the troops he used were not merely not all of the same nation, but not even of the same race (for he had Libyans, Spaniards, Ligurians, Celts or Gauls, Carthaginians, Italians, Greeks)".[3] This is really the text from which the whole

---

[1] Gsell ii. chap. 3 is devoted to the army of Carthage in general, and includes all the evidence for Hannibal's army: *id*. iii. chap. 4 contains the military history of the second Punic War.

[2] Pol. iii. 35 and 56. 4 (Hannibal's inscription). Most modern scholars believe that the former figure is much too high; e.g. B. L. Hallward, *C.A.H.* viii. p. 35, who supposes 40,000 as the maximum for the army after crossing the Pyrenees (Polybius gives 59,000 at that point). The difference is not really very material for our purpose, for there can be no question of statistics as far as Hannibal's mercenaries are concerned.

[3] Pol. xi. 19. 3 sqq. To this list Polybius might have added Indians. The African elephants still had Indian trainers, who are mentioned at Hannibal's crossing of the Rhone, and in Hasdrubal's army at the Metaurus (Pol. iii. 46. 7 sqq.; xi. 1. 12).

secret of Hannibal's success is to be expounded, though that is beyond the scope of this essay.

But in the first place those names of peoples have a familiar ring. One feels that the list could be transferred with perfect propriety from this particular army to any other army of Carthage in the two previous centuries; and in fact all those nations had provided soldiers for Carthage in the past. One must first try to see if the conditions of their service are the same. The Carthaginians may be eliminated at once, for obvious reasons; but the status of the Libyans (or Africans, as they are usually called in this connection) ought to be tested if possible, especially in view of the equivocal position of the Libyans in the Mercenaries' War (above). There Polybius classed them with the mercenaries, and it was hard to see whether he was merely making a mistake, or whether the Africans had really served as mercenaries in the first Punic War. It is no easier in the case of Hannibal's Africans, for Polybius merely calls them Libyans throughout and never qualifies them further; while Livy indulges in much loose talk about the Carthaginian armies in general, which makes it harder to be sure if he really knows what he is saying when he does say something to the purpose.

The state of our information, in brief, is as follows. The Africans were the foundation of the Carthaginian army in this war; they were perhaps the most numerous and certainly the best of the soldiers fighting in Italy, in Spain, and elsewhere (they were used mostly as infantry of the line, though we do hear of African light infantry, and of cavalry, as opposed to Numidian cavalry).[1] Of Hannibal's 20,000 infantry when he reached Italy, 12,000 were Africans:[2] he left 11,850 infantry and some cavalry in Spain with Hasdrubal:[3] and certainly most of the armies sent out by Carthage from Africa in the course of the war must have consisted mainly of native troops.[4] At Zama "the native Libyans and Carthaginians" formed Hannibal's second line of infantry, and here we have an important piece of evidence; for Polybius calls the first line "the mercenaries", and the third line "the

---

[1] The references are many, cf. Gsell ii. p. 360.
[2] Pol. iii. 56. 4.   [3] Ibid. 33. 15 sqq.
[4] Cf. Gsell ii. p. 340.

army of Italy", clearly regarding the Africans as a subject or national levy.[1]

The next step is to confront Polybius with Livy. Livy speaks of "hiring mercenaries throughout Africa" (210 B.C.);[2] and again (205 B.C.) appears to distinguish between the *levy* to be raised from Carthage itself and the country in its immediate vicinity (*dilectus in urbe agrisque*), and mercenaries to be recruited from the rest of the African province (*mittere ad conducenda Afrorum auxilia*).[3] There are two other passages in Livy where the Africans are called mercenaries (*mercede paratos milites*, and a similar phrase), but in each case the context shows a rhetorical tendency towards depreciating the resources of Carthage, and may be worth little.[4] References to pay for the army in general are of no value, since all soldiers took pay at this date whether they were mercenaries or not.[5] Finally, Livy in another passage of rhetorical tendency makes Scipio Africanus say that money is indispensable to Carthage, "because they keep mercenary armies" (the old argument of the Corinthians in connection with the Athenian rowers).[6] None of this is strong evidence, and one is merely led to suspect the value of the passages in which Livy uses such technical military words as *dilectus* and *conducere*, were it not that there is another general remark of the same kind from no less a person than Polybius, a remark of much greater worth perhaps from its context as well as from its author. Polybius is comparing the military arrangements of Rome and Carthage, and his (presumably) considered judgment is that the Carthaginians themselves are poor soldiers "because they use armies of foreigners and mercenaries" (and this certainly means "foreign mercenaries" in fact, as is clear from the next sentence); that Carthage "relies always for her freedom on the bravery of her mercenaries".[7] This seems plain enough. Polybius clearly applies his verdict to the army in general: the greatest part of the army was provided by the Africans and the Spaniards (who will be considered in a moment); there can be little doubt that he intends the verdict to apply to them—if it did not apply to

---

[1] Pol. xv. 11. 1 sqq.
[2] Livy 27. 5. 11.
[3] Id. 29. 4. 2.
[4] Id. 28. 44. 5; 29. 3. 13.
[5] They occur in Pol. iii. 13. 3 (ὀψώνια); and in Livy 22. 43. 3; 23. 12. 5; 28. 12. 5 (*pecunia in stipendium*, etc.).
[6] Thuc. i. 121. 3.
[7] Pol. vi. 52. 2 sqq.

THE WEST 225

them it would at once become false of the army in general, and patently so. If Polybius is to be believed, the armies of Carthage in Italy and Spain and Africa were almost entirely mercenary armies. Nevertheless, the probability is that Polybius is not to be taken quite at his face value, as will be shown presently.[1] But first let us consider the Spaniards also.[2]

There is just the same difficulty with the Spaniards as with the Africans. They appear constantly in the armies of Italy, Spain and Africa, and little reliance can be placed on the names applied to them by our authorities. The Spaniards with Hannibal himself are never qualified by Polybius. But we hear from Livy of Hannibal's *dilectus* in Spain before the beginning of the war, and after the capture of Saguntum he addresses the Spaniards as *socii*, whose *militia* might reasonably be expected to expire now that the Spanish province south of the Ebro was secure:[3] yet the same Livy speaks of *mercennarios milites, maxime Hispani generis* in Italy.[4] It is the same in Spain. One hears of the levy (*dilectus*, etc.) in 214, 208 and 206 B.C.;[5] of a huge recruiting campaign for 20,000 infantry and 4000 cavalry in 216 B.C. (Livy uses *conducere*, but these people cannot possibly be mercenaries);[6] of Spanish mercenaries in general (215 and 206 B.C.);[7] of Celtiberian mercenaries more than once.[8] The confusion is complete: it would be absurd to be dogmatic about these Spaniards, and it would probably be a mistake to regard them as an indivisible

---

[1] Apart from other considerations, it may be pointed out that this particular passage contains an elaborate series of antitheses. (1) The Romans are keen soldiers, the Carthaginians care nothing for it; (2) because C. use foreigners and mercenaries, R. use natives and citizens; (3) C. depend for freedom on the bravery of the mercenaries, R. on themselves and their allies. This is not the healthiest medium for conveying the exact truth. Nevertheless I do not suppose that Polybius was lying for art's sake: I am sure that he was speaking the truth to this extent, that the C. armies were *very like* mercenary armies in practice, even if they were not actually mercenaries (pp. 231 sqq.).
[2] For the mass of references to Spaniards in general, Gsell ii. pp. 368 sqq.
[3] Livy 21. 11. 13; *ibid.* 21. 3.   [4] *Id.* 22. 43. 3.
[5] Livy 24. 42. 6; Pol. x. 35. 6; Livy 28. 12. 13 sqq.; cf. *ibid.* 15. 1, *tironum Hispanorum*—i.e. the best of the Spanish levies had been killed long since or were fighting with Rome.
[6] Livy 23. 13. 8.
[7] *Ibid.* 29. 4, *in cornibus dextro Poenos locat laevo Afros mercennariorumque auxilia* (= Spaniards, who are not mentioned elsewhere by name): cf. *id.* 28. 30. 1 (4000).
[8] *Id.* 24. 49. 7 sqq.; perhaps 28. 1. 4 sqq.; Pol. xiv. 7. 5 (cf. Livy 30. 7. 10): Appian, *Ib.* 28; *Hann.* 52—contradicted by Livy 27. 48. 6 and 10.

whole, concluding either that they were all allies subject to the levy, or all recruited mercenaries. The only safe conclusion is that there certainly was a levy, and that it may account for the greater number of the Spanish troops. In this connection there is an interesting point relating to the Spaniards who went to Italy with Hannibal. Before he passed the Pyrenees he left Hanno with a garrison of 11,000 men to watch the country north of the Ebro. He also left with Hanno the baggage train (τὰς ἀποσκευάς) belonging to the army of Italy (as it was to become), and pushed on through the Pyrenees without baggage (στρατιὰν εὔζωνον). And before he started he detached a further 11,000 men from his army and sent them back to their own country, "wishing to leave behind these men themselves well disposed to him, and indicating to the rest a hope of the return home, not only to the soldiers of his own army, but also to the Spaniards who were remaining at home, in order that they might all start out eagerly, if he should have need of reinforcement from them".[1] Both these measures are the measures of a statesman nursing a levy of subjects or subject allies, and not of a general leading a mercenary army: mercenaries took their chance of returning home sooner or later or never, and one cannot imagine quite this consideration for their feelings. Nevertheless the importance of the levy does not necessarily exclude Spanish mercenaries altogether. In the first place, the powerful nations of the interior were never conquered by the Barcids, and may well have supplied mercenaries for hire: they include the Celtiberians, the most warlike of all the Spaniards.[2] And again in the later years of the war in Spain, when Scipio Africanus was confining the Carthaginian generals more and more closely in the south, the generals for their part had lost their power over many of the tribes, and the levy must have been greatly reduced. One hears of a levy in 206 B.C. before Ilipa (producing *tirones Hispanorum*); but in the same year after Ilipa Mago's lieutenant Hanno raises

---

[1] Pol. iii. 35. 3 sqq.
[2] Cf. Livy 24. 49. 7 sqq., where Celtiberians pass over from the C. to the R. army, to serve for the same pay as they had contracted for with C. Livy adds (wrongly) that these Celtiberians were the first mercenaries Rome ever employed. The two Scipios in 212 B.C. are said to have had 20,000 Celtiberians (an exaggeration ?): it was their desertion (bribed) that caused the defeat and death of Cnaeus (Livy 25. 32–3).

THE WEST

4000 men in the Baetis district *mercede Hispanos sollicitando*—which makes good sense.[1] Certainly the 4000 Celtiberians, who crossed over into Africa early in 203 B.C. and sold their lives dearly at the battle of the Great Plains, were pure mercenaries.[2] And about the same time Carthaginian recruiting officers were arrested at Saguntum.[3]

Of the other troops in the armies of Carthage by far the most important to Hannibal were the Numidians, the first light cavalry to make a great name for themselves in history. There are innumerable references to them on all fronts during the war, but nothing at all to our purpose.[4] It is known that the great princes of Numidia were allies of Carthage at one time or another, and presumably the Numidian cavalry were, in theory at least, allied troops; they are clearly so when they fight under their own princes, as Massinissa in Spain, Tychaeus in Africa. The experience of the Numidians who became veterans under the command of the Barcid generals, and especially those with Hannibal in Italy for sixteen years, must have produced a certain change, for one imagines that long before the end of that time they would have ceased to think of Syphax (or whoever their king might be), and recognized no higher authority than Hannibal himself. One remembers how Alexander's Greek allies were offered their discharge at Babylon, and how very many of them chose to stay with the army as mercenaries. The same idea must certainly have developed in Hannibal's army, though one never hears of a practical demonstration of it parallel to that at Babylon (there was no occasion for it).

The people whom Polybius calls "the mercenaries" in the front line at Zama were probably all fairly recent recruits; Ligurians, Celts (or Gauls), Balearians, Maurusii (Mauri).[5] There were some Mauri (cavalry) among the Numidians left behind in Spain by Hannibal in 218 B.C.: they appear again at the Ebro battle two years later, along with light infantry (*iaculatores*—the national weapon).[6] Hannibal had Mauri in Italy too, both light infantry and cavalry.[7] It is very possible that all these Mauri

---

[1] Livy 28. 12. 13; *ibid.* 15. 1; *ibid.* 30. 1.
[2] Pol. xiv. 7. 5, etc.; cf. Livy 30. 8. 6 sqq.   [3] Livy 30. 21. 3 sqq.
[4] For references, cf. Gsell ii. pp. 361 sqq.   [5] Pol. xv. 11. 1.
[6] *Id.* iii. 33. 15; Livy 23. 29. 14; *ibid.* 26. 11.
[7] Livy 22. 37. 8; 24. 15. 2; *ibid.* 20. 16.

were real mercenaries like those at Zama, for they inhabited the most westerly of the Numidian kingdoms (Morocco) and were certainly perfectly independent of Carthage: it is not known even that they had an alliance with Carthage at this date.[1] The Balearians were probably in the same position. Balearians had served as mercenaries of Carthage from an early date, and there is no indication that the islands became a Carthaginian province at the time of the Barcid conquest of Spain; certainly they no longer considered themselves allies of Carthage at least as early as 217 B.C., if they had ever done so.[2] The Balearians then were probably mercenaries, and were included in the standing army of Spain before Hannibal set out for Italy: he sent 870 of them to Africa in the winter of 219–218 B.C., left 500 with Hasdrubal in the spring, and took others in his own army to Italy.[3] It seems likely that the Carthaginian generals in Spain could still get mercenaries from the islands even after the supremacy on sea had passed completely into the hands of the Romans, for the Balearians are found both at Baecula and at Ilipa.[4] Finally Mago recruited 2000 from Minorca late in 206 B.C., and these were the troops who were included in the front line at Zama.[5]

It may be remarked in passing that this front line ("the mercenaries") cannot have been intended by Hannibal to act as very much more than a strong screen, though most modern writers have given the impression that the three lines at Zama had a more or less equal power of resistance, with the third line (the "old guard") perhaps rather the strongest. But among the mercenaries the Balearians and the Mauri were light infantry fighting with missiles (slingers and *jaculatores* = ἀκοντισταί, like Alexander's Agrianians for example); and the Gauls and Ligurians, though they were accustomed to fighting at close quarters, were not in the first class as infantry of the line. The same criticism applies to the Carthaginians and Africans of the second line, for

[1] Though they had one in the fourth century (Justin 21. 4. 7), and again about 150 B.C. (Pol. xxxviii. 7. 9; Appian, *Lib.* 111).
[2] Livy 22. 20. 9, *Baliaribus ex insulis legati pacem petentes ad Scipionem venerunt.* Livy appears to class them with the Spanish tribes north of the Ebro, who had never had anything to do with Carthage until Hannibal crossed the Ebro in 218.
[3] Livy 21. 21. 12 (cf. Pol. iii. 33. 11); Pol. *ibid.* 16; *ibid.* 72. 7; 83. 3; 113. 6, etc.
[4] Livy 27. 18. 7; 28. 15. 1 (cf. 27. 20. 7).   [5] *Id.* 28. 37. 9.

the Carthaginians themselves can have had little training or experience, and the African levy was the last levy of very many during the war, and may well have resembled the last Spanish levy at Ilipa—*tirones Hispanorum* (p. 226). The more one looks at it the more probable it seems that the third line was not the strongest merely but very much the strongest of the three, and the more certain it becomes that Hannibal's order of battle represents an elaborate plan of defence, by which the Romans were to break through—and were *expected* to break through—a succession of screens (first elephants, then missiles with a stiffening of heavy infantry, then more heavy infantry), before they reached the third line of infantry, the "old guard" strong and intact. The failure of the plan was due entirely to Hannibal's weakness on both wings, for Scipio by the rapid victory of his cavalry had time to pause in the centre and re-form before meeting the "old guard", which was soon encircled in addition by the victorious cavalry returning from pursuit. It is difficult to see how this could have been avoided, for if Hannibal had fought his defensive battle with the conventional single line, the probability is that everything except the "old guard" would have gone at once, and the result would have been the same, only quicker.[1]

One must return for a moment to Hannibal's army of Italy, more especially with a view to its reinforcements. Hannibal reached Italy with 26,000 men, and he stayed there nearly sixteen years, using his army all the time, so that the "army of Italy" which fought at Zama can have had little relation to the 26,000 who survived the Alps in 218 B.C.[2] His first reinforcements were from the north of Italy, Gauls and Ligurians.[3] One supposes that he made formal alliances with their chieftains very soon after his arrival, but probably the Gauls who appear in his army at that time were mostly volunteers and, for practical purposes,

[1] There is a good account of the battle by B. L. Hallward in *C.A.H.* viii. pp. 105 sqq., except that I think he overestimates the value as battle troops of the first line of infantry "the experienced mercenaries of Mago's army". The Balearians and Mauri were not infantry of the line at all, and the comparatively low value of Gauls against Roman legions can be seen from their performance at the Trebia, Trasymene and Cannae (especially in their casualties). I think the point is that Hannibal did not expect that any of his screens would stop the legions, but only delay them and impair their efficiency, and so give his third line a chance.

[2] His only reinforcements from Africa or Spain were 4000 Numidians in 215 B.C., Livy 23. 13. 7.   [3] Cf. e.g. Livy 21. 38.

mercenaries: that is the impression given by Livy, and it may be the right one.¹ Their numbers were certainly very great. Hannibal had had Ligurian mercenaries in Spain, and though they are not mentioned in the 26,000, nor in the three great battles (they are probably lumped together with the Gauls), he certainly had Ligurians in Italy, and must have recruited them before he moved south after Trasymene.² The numbers of the new reinforcements altogether can be judged only from the numbers given at the great battles: Polybius speaks of Gauls only, and the majority must in fact have been Gauls. At the Trebia the army was about 40,000 strong, which means about 14,000 new recruits, of whom over 4000 were cavalry:³ at Cannae his infantry alone exceeded 40,000, which means that over 20,000 of them were Gauls or Ligurians—and the Gauls had already suffered heavy losses (they were to lose 4000 men at Cannae).⁴ After Cannae his supply ceased, in the first place because he had found a better supply in the south, and later because he could not, if he would, regain touch with the Gauls of the north without sacrificing everything he had won elsewhere.⁵ But both Gauls and Ligurians did serve as mercenaries after this under Carthaginian generals, for Hasdrubal had them in his army at the Metaurus, and Mago recruited more in 205–203 B.C.⁶ Hasdrubal's Gauls came from the Rhone district as well as from Cisalpine Gaul.⁷ Mago's army is said to have numbered 30,000 in 203 B.C. (but a nucleus had sailed with him from Spain): some at least of his mercenaries accompanied him when he evacuated his army from Italy, and these are the Gauls and Ligurians of Zama⁸.

¹ Livy 23. 28. 5 sqq. But Pol. iii. 72. 9 speaks of τοῖς παρὰ τῶν Κελτῶν συμμάχοις; cf. vii. 9. 6 sqq. for these alliances with Gauls and Ligurians mentioned in Hannibal's treaty with Philip V (215 B.C.).
² Pol. iii. 33. 16; xi. 19. 4; Livy 22. 23. 4.
³ Pol. iii. 67. 1 sqq.; 72. 8 sqq.; 2000 Gallic infantry and nearly 200 cavalry had deserted from the Romans after the Ticinus engagement.
⁴ Ibid. 74. 10; 79. 8; 85. 5; 117. 6.
⁵ The only Gauls mentioned after Cannae are the 2000 picked Gauls at the capture of Tarentum (212 B.C.)—Pol. viii. 30. 1, etc.
⁶ Metaurus—Pol. xi. 1. 2; 3. 1 (no Ligurians mentioned); Livy 27. 48 and 49. 8. Mago—Livy 28. 36. 2, etc.
⁷ Livy 27. 36. 2; 39. 6; 44. 7 sqq.; 28. 10. 12; cf. Pol. ii. 22. 1 sqq. and 34. 1 sqq. for the Gaesatae, celebrated Gallic mercenaries of the Rhone (225 and 222 B.C.): and ibid. 41. 9, for Gauls serving as mercenaries at Massilia (218 B.C.). ⁸ Appian, Lib. 17 and 18.

THE WEST

Finally, Hannibal's Italian and Greek allies in the south of Italy occupied a peculiar position. Allies of Hannibal they certainly were, and not mercenaries, but their behaviour had left them with everything to fear from Rome in the event of her victory. In these circumstances many thousands of Italian soldiers, and some Greeks, attached themselves to Hannibal's army, and even preferred to leave Italy behind when he left it, sailing with him to Africa, where they formed perhaps the greater part of his "old guard" at Zama.[1] These men, whatever their motives and their name at the time when they became soldiers of Hannibal, clearly ended by remaining with him as pure professional soldiers.

This really brings us to the heart of the matter. Much of the evidence we have just considered involves us in a mere splitting of hairs. We have seen that in the case of the Africans and Spaniards the evidence is conflicting; they are called sometimes levies, sometimes mercenaries, and there may in fact have been some of each. Fortunately no one can possibly be interested in what they were called, except in so far as a name may help to show what they really were—and in most cases the names that we have noticed are of no such help. But when everything has been considered (and for the most part dismissed), one cannot easily dismiss the general statement of Polybius (pp. 224–5)—οἱ μὲν γὰρ (*sc.* Ῥωμαῖοι) τὴν ὅλην περὶ τοῦτο ποιοῦνται σπουδήν, Καρχηδόνιοι δὲ τῶν μὲν πεζικῶν εἰς τέλος ὀλιγωροῦσι, τῶν δ' ἱππικῶν βραχεῖάν τινα ποιοῦνται πρόνοιαν. αἴτιον δὲ τούτων ἐστὶν ὅτι ξενικαῖς καὶ μισθοφόροις χρῶνται δυνάμεσι, Ῥωμαῖοι δ' ἐγχωρίοις καὶ πολιτικαῖς. ᾗ καὶ περὶ τοῦτο τὸ μέρος ταύτην τὴν πολιτείαν ἀποδεκτέον ἐκείνης μᾶλλον · ἡ μὲν γὰρ ἐν ταῖς τῶν μισθοφόρων εὐψυχίαις ἔχει τὰς ἐλπίδας ἀεὶ τῆς ἐλευθερίας ἡ δὲ Ῥωμαίων ἐν ταῖς σφετέραις ἀρεταῖς καὶ ταῖς τῶν συμμάχων ἐπαρκείαις (vi. 52. 3 sqq.). Granted that this is an orgy of rhetorical antithesis, and that sentences can be found elsewhere in Polybius' history which seem to contradict what he says here, yet still one must believe (if one is to believe anything) that Polybius

---

[1] Many references for the war in Italy, cf. Gsell ii. p. 386 n. 6. The most important are Pol. vii. 9. 6 sqq. (their alliances with Hannibal); *id.* xi. 19. 3; Livy 30. 20. 6; 33. 6 (where he says the "old guard" were mostly Bruttians. Cf. E. Groag, *Hannibal als Politiker*, p. 100 n. 3, who computes that the "old guard" cannot have contained more than 8000 real veterans out of a possible 15,000).

would not have consented, in order to gratify a literary vice or to save himself the trouble of qualifying his words, to suggest a perfectly false idea to his reader. When he wrote this comparison of the two nations, it is impossible that he should not have had in mind principally the second Punic War, with its practical decision of their differences. One may say indeed that he is wrong in using the word "mercenaries" of the Carthaginian armies as a whole; and still no harm is done. For the important thing to realize is that, if the word is wrong, the idea none the less is right, for the idea of mercenary armies is exactly the idea that must occur to anyone who studies these armies of Carthage in general, and that of Hannibal in particular. Many nations and races were represented in it, and here there is a superficial parallel with the many mercenary armies of Carthage in the past. Other superficial resemblances can be found; a story of an incipient mutiny when pay was overdue, another story of some Numidian and Spanish cavalry who deserted to the Romans and served with them until the end of the war.[1] But these are trifles. The real distinguishing marks are the continuity of service under the same commanders and the same general; the complete severance from fatherland and civilian life, now superseded by the camp and the war;[2] the discipline and *esprit de corps* that must have become second nature to the men who were the instruments of Hannibal's elaborate tactical conceptions. To find an army its equal in these last qualities one must go back perhaps as far as Alexander's army, itself unique among armies requiring a citizen or national element as a core of strength.[3] And in other respects the closest counterpart to Hannibal's army may be the great mercenary armies of Antigonus I or Eumenes of Cardia. The truest description of it, as

---

[1] Livy 22. 43. 3; 23. 46. 6 sqq.
[2] Cf. Pol. iii. 33. 8 sqq. for the long service also of the troops shipped by Hannibal to Africa (winter 219–218 B.C.) to serve as an army of defence: they cannot possibly have returned to Spain before 215 B.C. (the year of the first big reinforcement to Spain), and even this is a very different thing from an annual levy for the summer months only.
[3] *Ibid.* 13. 3 (the election of Hannibal as general by the army in Spain, 221 B.C., cf. Livy 21. 3. 1—a more emphatic version) shows a remarkable parallel with the Macedonian procedure. But it is to be doubted if this information is sound, because its origin is probably the anti-Barcid tradition at Rome, which sought to depict the Barcids as almost independent rulers in Spain ranging for revenge against Rome.

of them, is to call it a professional army, and it was partly that already before Hannibal led it through the Pyrenees in 218 B.C.: the two elder Barcids had prepared a weapon very much as Philip prepared it for Alexander.[1] What is not always remembered is that Hannibal in Italy was obliged to save his weapon from perishing by attrition: no army can remain intact for sixteen years. It was an achievement to preserve it at all: to preserve it excellent was nearly a miracle, and the more so as it was not so much a question of merely hoarding the old as of replacing the old with new. But the tradition remained unbroken: the Bruttians or Campanians of Zama remained the same devoted professionals as the Spaniards or Africans of Trasymene. One must yield to Hannibal yet another notable quality: besides being a great statesman and a great strategist he must also have been a great contriver, one of those practical experts like Demetrius and Pyrrhus and Xanthippus the Spartan, who knew how to manage large mixed armies of disinterested soldiers, and induce them to fight and be killed like patriotic heroes.[2]

The peace of 202 B.C. meant the end of Carthage as an employer of mercenaries. According to one account, there was a clause in the treaty forbidding the recruiting in future of any mercenaries whatever (though this clause is not in Polybius' version).[3] If there was such a clause one may be sure that it was observed. Rome had her *agent provocateur* in North Africa, as eager to report (or fabricate) a breach of the treaty as to provoke it: and on this subject at least Massinissa was silent, so far as is known. This may of course be an argument against the "mercenaries" clause in the peace treaty, but, however that may be, they never appear again in the short remaining history of Carthage, not even in the last war with Rome. Then at length the citizens of Carthage were compelled to fight not for power or a province but for their lives, and with their own bodies, untrained and unwarlike as they were: and with a characteristic perversity they fought very well.

---

[1] Cf. Pol. iii. 89. 5.
[2] Cf. *id.* xi. 19. 3 sqq., the text from which I began, p. 222.
[3] Dio Cass. xvii, frag. 57. 82 (Boissevain); cf. Appian, *Lib.* 54 (cf. 32).

APPENDIX TO CHAPTER VIII

MERCENARIES WITH ROME

The evidence for mercenaries in the armies of the Roman republic is too slight to justify more than a mere notice. There are a few clear references to mercenaries, and more which are doubtful; but there is no sign of any system, and so far as mercenaries were used, they seem to have been recruited merely as the occasion called for them, and for an immediate purpose.[1] They thus appear to be without importance for the development of the Roman army in general, and are of interest chiefly as illustrating the use of the Hellenistic sources of supply by the Romans in their conquest of the East. It is nearly always difficult to distinguish the mercenaries from the other classes of *auxilia* in the Roman armies, and, especially in the last century of the republic, a study of the *auxilia* must certainly belong rather to the history of the client kingdoms than to that of the Hellenistic mercenary. It is possible that during the Civil Wars the armies of the East may have retained mercenaries on a more permanent footing, but here the sources do not help us. Even if this was so, the development came to an end with the army reforms of Augustus, and mercenaries play no part in the armies of the early Principate.

The references that I have noticed are the following:

Pol. ii. 7. 7 sqq.—(first Punic War, in Sicily), some Gauls who deserted from the Carthaginians and served with Rome until peace was made.

Livy 24. 49. 7 sqq.—(214 B.C., in Spain), Celtiberians.

Id. 25. 32 sqq.—(213 B.C., in Spain), 20,000 Celtiberians; the number probably much exaggerated.

Id. 33. 3. 10—(197 B.C., in Greece), Cretans with Flamininus.[2]

Id. 37. 39. 12—(188 B.C., at Magnesia), Macedonian and Thracian volunteers.

Id. 43. 7. 1 sqq.; cf. Plut. *Aemil.* 15. 3—(169 B.C., in Greece), Cretans with Aemilius Paullus.

Plut. *C. Gracch.* 16. 3—(121 B.C.), Cretans at Rome.

---

[1] I refer to real mercenaries and not to the *auxilia*, though there can sometimes have been little distinction between the two; cf. G. L. Cheesman, *The auxilia of the Roman imperial army*, pp. 8 sqq.

[2] The Cretans who fought against Hannibal at Trasymene were mercenaries of Hieron of Syracuse—Livy 24. 30. 13 sqq.; Pol. iii. 75. 7.

THE WEST

Appian, *Mith.* 20—(88 B.C., in Asia Minor), a mercenary garrison at Laodicea.[1]

Dio Cass. 36. 9. 3; cf. perhaps Plut. *Lucull.* 27 and Memnon, *F.H.G.* iii. p. 556—(68 B.C., in Asia), Thracians, originally mercenaries of Mithridates, who deserted to the Romans, and then reverted to Mithridates.

Caesar, *B.G.* ii. 7—(57 B.C., in Gaul), Cretans with Caesar.

[1] The position of the Galatians and other Asiatics serving with Rome in the Mithridatic wars is doubtful (Appian, *Mith.* 11, 17, and 19; Plut. *Lucull.* 27): the Greeks and Macedonians with Sulla at Chaeronea are not really mercenaries, though they had served with Archelaus previously (App. *Mith.* 41).

CHAPTER IX

THE PROVENANCE AND RECRUITING OF MERCENARIES

1. PROVENANCE

GREEK tradition named the Carians as the first mercenaries. The poet Archilochus was able to say "I shall be called a mercenary, like a Carian":[1] and the proverb ἐν τῷ Κᾶρι κινδυνεύειν has the same meaning as the Latin *facere experimentum in corpore vili*. The scholium to Plato's *Laches* explains its origin: "for the Carians seem to have been the first to serve as mercenaries",[2] and this explanation is supported by our evidence, for the earliest mercenaries of whom we know are those of the Saite kings of Egypt, beginning with Psammetichus I (*ca.* 650 B.C.). His mercenaries are described by Herodotus as "Ionians and Carians", later as "Greeks and Carians", and it is sufficiently clear that the Greeks were drawn first perhaps from Ionia proper, certainly later from the Dorian section of the seaboard of Asia Minor and the Dorian islands as well.[3] The mercenaries of the Lydian kings probably came from the same source, and also from Aeolia, though we hear of Croesus sending for mercenaries to the Peloponnese.[4] Though the Greek historians may have stressed the Greek side of the partnership, it is safe to say that the Carians and Asiatic Greeks between them monopolized the mercenary service under the Eastern and Egyptian dynasts in the seventh and sixth centuries B.C. Of the provenance of mercenaries who served under the tyrants practically nothing is known.[5] There is no evidence that Ionian mercenaries ever crossed over to Greece, and the very absence of all information on the subject suggests that there was no prevalent

[1] Archilochus, frag. 40 (Diehl, *Anth. Lyr.* iii. p. 221).
[2] Plato, *Laches* 187 B, and schol.
[3] Hdt. ii. 152, 154, 163; cf. Diod. i. 66. 12; Polyaen. vii. 3. 1 (Carians only). Hdt. iii. 11; *ibid.* 4; M. N. Tod, *Greek Historical Inscriptions*, 4.
[4] Diod. ix. 32, etc.: an anachronism suggested by later Persian practice?
[5] Hdt. i. 61; Aristot. *Ath. Pol.* 15. 2; 17. 4 show Pisistratus with Argive mercenaries for his second return from exile; he also married an Argive wife.

and well-known source, but that mercenaries were recruited at random and in the vicinity of their paymaster's own city. It would be tempting to suppose that they were actually citizens recruited from the poorer classes, to whom the tyrant usually stood as a champion against the rich, and that they were dubbed "mercenaries" by our authorities, who are unanimous in their anti-tyrannical bias. If this were true, it would explain the complete disappearance of the mercenaries as soon as the tyrants disappear. It would be strange if bands of foreign troops should have left no mark in the cities which they were employed to guard, and we should have expected that when the tyrannies were overthrown many mercenaries would have been left unemployed and might have made a considerable stir in their wanderings about the countryside in search of work or a home, as indeed trouble did arise out of the mercenaries of the expelled tyrants in Sicily, who plainly were foreigners.[1] But if we suppose the tyrants in Greece to have employed bodyguards of volunteer citizens, the absence, so far as we know, of such disorders would be well explained by the absorption of the soldiers into the ordinary citizen body.

In the fifth century the situation is rather clearer. It was then that the Arcadian hoplite began to come into his own, a process of which we can perhaps see the commencement in the Arcadian deserters who joined Xerxes.[2] We find Arcadians with Pissuthnes (427 B.C.), at Syracuse on both sides (415 B.C.) and on the expedition of Cyrus, where they were represented in far greater numbers than any other community (401 B.C.).[3] Lycomedes, the leader in the movement for Arcadian independence (*ca.* 370 B.C.), reminded his audience in a patriotic speech that theirs was at once the strongest and the bravest race of all Greece, and that "whenever anybody wanted mercenaries, they chose Arcadians second to none":[4] allowing for the enthusiasm of the speaker, there was probably much truth in what he said. The strength of the expedition of Cyrus lay in its hoplites, and the backbone of the hoplites was the Arcadians, as they were not slow to remind their comrades.[5] One of the clearest traces left by the tradition

[1] Diod. xi. 72. 3 sqq.; 76. 1 sqq.
[2] Hdt. viii. 26. 1.
[3] Thuc. iii. 34. 3; vii. 57 and 58, etc.; Xen. *Anab.* vi. 2. 10, etc.
[4] Xen. *Hell.* vii. 1. 23.
[5] *Id. Anab.* vi. 2. 10.

of mercenary service in Arcadia is the appearance, when the Arcadian federation came into being, of a standing army of 5000, the only non-mercenary army of its kind in Greece other than the Spartan.[1] This points to a population born and bred into the profession of arms, and indeed the Arcadian mercenary, like the Carian, became proverbial.[2]

The Peloponnese in the fifth century was a general recruiting ground of which Arcadia was the most particularly productive area. In the Peloponnesian War, in every case where a provenance of mercenary hoplites is mentioned, that provenance is the Peloponnese.[3] On the expedition of Cyrus the Peloponnesians were considerably more than half of the whole strength of the army, the Achaeans coming second to the Arcadians in numbers.[4] That is not to say that no hoplites came from elsewhere to serve as mercenaries in this period; but mercenaries from other quarters are usually light-armed specialists, such as Thracian peltasts, Rhodian slingers, Cretan and Scythian archers, Aetolian and Acarnanian javelin-men, peltasts again from Chalcidice and Thessaly: Thessalian hoplites also appear in the *Anabasis*.[5]

In the fourth century the situation is less simple. Mercenary service became so general that it is no longer possible to trace whence the soldiers came. Isocrates speaks of the great floating population in Greece, of homeless and unemployed wanderers, who were forced to become paid soldiers from sheer want. In the latter half of the century it was, he says, easier to collect a large and efficient army from the wanderers than from the dwellers in cities. This was especially true in Asia Minor, where the demands of the Persian governors may have attracted soldiers from the mainland of Greece, in addition to the existing supply.[6]

---

[1] Xen. *Hell*. vii. 4. 22; 33; 5. 3, etc.
[2] Ἀρκάδας μιμούμενος—Xenobius ii. 59 (E. L. Leutsch u. F. G. Schneidewin, *Paroem. Graeci*, i. p. 47); cf. Hermipp. 63 (Kock, i. p. 243), ἀπὸ δ' Ἀρκαδίας ἐπικούρους.
[3] Thuc. i. 60; iii. 109; iv. 76. 3; 80. 5; vii. 57. 9; 58. 3; viii. 28. 4. Xen. *Hell*. ii. 4. 29. [4] Xen. *Anab*. vi. 2. 10.
[5] *Thracians*—Aristoph. *Acharn*. 159 sqq.; Thuc. iv. 129; v. 6; vii. 27; Xen. *Anab*. i. 2. 9; *Hell*. i. 3. 10. *Rhodians*—Xen. *Anab*. iii. 3. 16, etc. *Cretans*—Thuc. vi. 43. 2; Paus. i. 27. 9; Xen. *Anab*. i. 2. 9, etc. *Scythians*—see P.-W. s.v. *Thessalians and Chalcidians*—Xen. *Anab*. i. 2. 6, etc. *Aetolians and Acarnanians*—Thuc. vii. 57. 9 sqq.
[6] Isoc. iv. 167 sqq.; v. 96; ix. 9.

PROVENANCE AND RECRUITING

It is true that the Peloponnese still held its own as a provider of mercenaries, as is shown by the fact that Dionysius I and the Phocians recruited from there.[1] But specialist "national" arms seem to have nearly disappeared, though we hear of more Cretan archers at the Isthmus with the Spartans (392 B.C.), of Elean slingers (not certainly mercenaries) at the same time and place, and of mercenary cavalry in common use in the armies of Greek cities and notably of Sparta.[2] But an officer could be sent to the Hellespont, or a message to Macedonia, apparently with the same certainty of result as if recruits were to be sought in the Peloponnese or in Boeotia. Athenian citizens could serve side by side with a Nisyrian, a Boeotian, a Cariandian, a Corinthian, a Rhodian, and a man from distant Cyrene.[3] Probably a chief cause, in addition to the economic one, of this disappearance of national divisions or monopolies, is that the mercenaries of the fourth century became standardized to a type, the type evolved by Iphicrates which may be called the "Iphicratean" peltast.[4] A natural consequence was that the Thracian peltast was driven from the field, or, more strictly speaking, from the market. There appears to be no trace of Thracian mercenaries in the seventy years before Alexander.

In Sicily the provenance of the mercenaries with the early tyrants is uncertain. Those of Dionysius I were recruited from the Peloponnese and possibly from other parts of Greece; and from the Campanians, Iberians and Celts, as well as from the Greeks and barbarians of Sicily itself. The Carthaginians obtained mercenaries from the same barbarian peoples as Dionysius, and also occasionally slingers from the Balearic Isles (see above, pp. 208 sqq.). Iapygian mercenaries fought with the Athenians at the siege of Syracuse.[5]

Alexander's army has been fully discussed. The original expeditionary force contained Balkan mercenaries as well as Greeks; but the mercenaries of the various reinforcements were far more numerous, and probably contained a preponderance of Greeks, though the information is slight (pp. 12 sqq.).

After Alexander the situation opens out considerably, partly

[1] Diod. xiv. 44. 2; 58. 1; 62. 1; xvi. 24.
[2] Xen. *Hell*. iv. 2. 5 sqq., etc.; *id. Hipp*. ix. 3.
[3] *Id. Hell*. iv. 8. 32 sqq.; v. 2. 38; *C.I.G.* 4702.
[4] Diod. xv. 44; Nep. *Iphic*. 2.   [5] Thuc. vii. 33. 3; 57. 11.

perhaps because we are better informed, but also partly because the field of recruiting did certainly become wider than ever before. Our best information comes from inscriptions containing lists of mercenaries with their provenance. They are four in number, and will give us a good start in our inquiry.

1. An inscription of Athens, near the end of the fourth century or a little later, certainly after 316 B.C.[1] There are 150 names, of which the first 46 may be barbarian, but no provenance is given: Köhler conjectured that they are the names of Thracians. A summary of the provenances is as follows:

Barbarians	51
North and Central Greece[2]	57
Peloponnese[3]	6
Islands and Asia Minor[4]	31
West[5]	4
Black Sea	1

2. An inscription of Athens, probably a little later than the one above. There are 21 names with provenance.[6] Summary:

North and Central Greece[7]	13
Peloponnese	5
Islands and Asia Minor	3

3. An inscription of Athens, about 230 B.C., containing the names of 23 mercenaries with provenance.[8] Summary:

North and Central Greece[9]	14
Peloponnese and Crete[10]	8
Asia Minor (Lycia)	1

4. An inscription of Lilaea, about 209 B.C., containing the names of mercenaries on garrison duty sent by Attalus I of

---

[1] *I.G.*² ii. 2. 1956.
[2] 5 Thessalians, 7 Aenianes, 6 Perinthians, 5 Cassandreians, 10 Locrians, 7 Euboeans.
[3] 4 Achaeans.   [4] 5 from Theangela, 6 from Lesbos.
[5] It is not perfectly certain whether the 3 Λευκανοί are from Lucania in Italy, or from Leuce in Ionia.
[6] *I.G.*² ii. 2. 1957.
[7] 5 Locrians.
[8] Ditt. *Syll.*³ i. 485 = *I.G.*² ii. 2. 1958.
[9] 3 Macedonians, 5 Phocians.   [10] 4 Cretans.

PROVENANCE AND RECRUITING 241

Pergamum (see above, pp. 171-2): the names are 73 or 74 in number.[1] Summary:

North and Central Greece[2]	43
Peloponnese and Crete[3]	9 or 10
Islands and Asia Minor[4]	12
West[5]	9

The figures speak for themselves. Their most striking feature is the marked decrease in the numbers of Peloponnesian mercenaries, and an increase in the numbers from northern and central Greece. Very interesting too is the presence of a strong barbarian (probably Thracian) element among the soldiers of the first inscription. This is not in the least surprising, as will be seen when the literary evidence is considered. But first it will be best to dispose of the only other statistical evidence available, that which comes from Egypt. Lesquier compiled a list of ethnical statistics collected from the papyri. He gives a warning that in the second century reliance can no longer be placed upon ethnical indications, because of the increasing specialization which gave ethnical names to different types of soldier (e.g. "Macedonian" = infantry of the phalanx; Cretan = archer or light infantry).[6] His collection of third-century provenances is likely to be more reliable, since in many cases both the race and the corps of the soldier are obtainable, and only such cases will be used here. All the soldiers mentioned are not mercenaries but cleruchs of the regular army: nevertheless, since the military settlements must in the first place have been filled to a great extent with mercenaries, the figures may be thought of some value. But since many new names have come

---

[1] An unpublished inscription used here by courtesy of the late M. Maurice Holleaux.
[2] 2 Macedonians, 17 Lysimacheians, 8 Thessalians.
[3] 3, or 4, Cretans.
[4] Including 2 Ἐλαῖται, from Elaea near Pergamum (?)—M. Holleaux' suggestion.
[5] The same doubt attaches to the 4 Λευκανοί here as to those of the Athenian inscription above.
[6] Lesquier, *op. cit.* pp. 106 sqq.; e.g. in P. Tebt. i. 32 (145 B.C. ?) a "Macedonian" becomes a "Cretan", and in P. Fay. 11 and 12 (115 B.C. and ? 103 B.C.) one and the same man occurs first as a "Persian", then as a "Mysian". Cf. too, Lesquier, pp. 142 sqq., on the πολιτεύματα, especially that of the Persians.

GHA 16

to light since Lesquier's book was published, the figures given here are based on the more recent work of F. Heichelheim: here too for the sake of safety only those provenances are used which certainly belong to the period before 200 B.C., except where they belong to high officers, who are not likely to have been subject to the same changes.[1]

1 a.

GREEKS	High officers	Military settlers	Soldiers not known to be settlers	[Ἐπιγονή]	Total
Macedonia	7	29	7	[12]	43 or 55
Central and North Greece	22	10	14	[4]	46 or 50[2]
Peloponnese and Crete	7	11	7		25[3]
Islands and Asia Minor	23	8	9		40[4]
The West (including Africa)	6	9	18	[22]	33 or 55[5]
GRAND TOTAL	65	67	55	[38]	187 or 225

Since the supply of high officers may have been governed by conditions different from those regulating the supply of ordinary soldiers, it may be convenient to see a table of statistics for soldiers and ἐπιγονή only.

1 b.

Macedonia	48
Central and North Greece	28
Peloponnese	18
Islands and Asia	17
West	49
TOTAL	160

[1] F. Heichelheim, *Die auswärtige Bevölkerung im Ptolemäerreich* (*Klio* Beiheft, xvii, Leipzig 1925), pp. 84 sqq. and *Archiv*, ix. pp. 47 sqq.: cf. Lesquier, pp. 110 sqq.

[2] Including 9 Aetolians, of whom 8 are high officers, mostly in the reign of Ptolemy IV and V, probably as a result of the ascendancy of Scopas (p. 121); 7 Athenians (2 τῆς ἐπιγονῆς); and 10 Thessalians (2 τῆς ἐπιγονῆς).

[3] 7 Achaeans; only 3 Cretans.

[4] Not more than four from any one city (four each from Magnesia, Miletus, and Samos). The proportion of high officers is very great, and is probably to be explained by the Ptolemaic domination over the islands and the coast of Asia Minor during most of the third century: the Egyptian service could perhaps take its pick of the best men.

[5] 46 from Cyrene (22 τῆς ἐπιγονῆς). The very high number of Cyrenaeans of the ἐπιγονή is suspicious, and it may be that the qualification denotes a class rather than an ethnic distinction, like the Πέρσαι τῆς ἐπιγονῆς in the second century (though Cyrenaeans are not found in anything like the same profusion).

PROVENANCE AND RECRUITING

	High officers	Military settlers	Soldiers not known to be settlers	['Επιγονή]	Total
2. BARBARIANS[1]					
Balkans	3	31	16	[6]	50 or 56[2]
Asia	3	13	2	[12]	18 or 30[3]
Italy	2	2			4
GRAND TOTAL	8	46	18	[18]	72 or 90

These lists are illuminating especially because they give us our only opportunity of judging to what extent the cleruch army in Egypt, organized after the Macedonian model, consisted of real Macedonians or their descendants. Of the Graeco-Macedonian common soldiers, less than one third are Macedonians (and if officers are included the proportion is lower). One must assume that in the third century these ethnic names were still genuine; but it is as well to remember that if they had already ceased to be genuinely ethnic, the "Macedonian" must be among the first to be suspected, so that the proportion may have been even lower than it appears.[4] This is only what one must have assumed, since there was no means of replenishing the original supply, which was certainly not large. Greek mercenaries must have formed the greater part of the Ptolemaic army especially in the first thirty years or so of the dynasty, before the settlements were well established: and the evidence for the years before Ipsus proves that this was so (pp. 109 sqq.). Among the barbarian soldiers in Egypt, the predominance of Thracians is not surprising, for the Ptolemies always had a foothold in Thrace throughout the third century. An interesting freak is the presence of a Roman military settler in Egypt as early as 252 B.C., but he has no fellow in later documents, and there is no evidence for supposing that it was a common thing for a Roman to enlist in a foreign army.[5]

[1] The distinction between Greeks and barbarians is useful for the present purpose, but it did not exist in Egypt itself for purposes of the administration: the distinction was purely between natives (Egyptians) and foreigners (including such races as Jews and Libyans as well as Greeks, Thracians, etc.). Cf. E. Bickermann, in *Archiv*, viii. pp. 229 sqq.
[2] 30 Thracians (6 τῆς ἐπιγονῆς).
[3] 23 Persians (12 τῆς ἐπιγονῆς): the name is to be suspected even in the third century.
[4] For the "racial" hipparchies in Egypt, whose ethnic names are almost certainly false, cf. p. 250, under "Tarentines".
[5] *Archiv*, vii. 19.

This completes the statistical evidence. It should perhaps be added that from two inscriptions containing names of mercenaries in the service of Egypt, P. M. Meyer drew numerous conclusions as to their provenance. Since in neither case does a single provenance appear in the inscriptions themselves, and the conclusions are drawn solely from the proper names, they are of little value.[1]

The literary evidence does not admit of so detailed an analysis, for in most of the cases in which Greek mercenaries are involved it is impossible to say more than that they were Greek, without being able to add from what part of the Greek world they may have sprung. Probably the most prolific period for Greek soldiers was that of the Successors' Wars (323–301 B.C.). We meet with them as far west as Cyrene and Carthage, and as far east as the Bosporan kingdom in the Black Sea.[2] It is established that all the successful generals of the time in Greece and Asia recruited mercenaries, and probably the majority of them was still Greek, though it is seldom that any indication is given. We have seen that the establishment in Syria and in Egypt of a "regular" cleruch army can hardly have been possible, except by the method of settling Greek mercenaries on the soil as a reinforcement to the scanty stock of real Macedonians. In the circumstances it would seem false to say that there was any great decline in the supply of Greeks, at any rate in the first half of the third century, the more especially as we still find them in the armies of Egypt and of Syria at Raphia (as mercenaries apart from the cleruch soldiers),[3] and earlier in the service of Carthage in the first Punic War.[4] Nevertheless by the end of the century a shortage may have begun to make itself felt. The Macedonian armies of Philip V and Perseus seem to have contained very few soldiers from Greece proper, though barbarian and Cretan mercenaries are often mentioned; and that of Antiochus the Great at Magnesia shows a falling-off from the numbers at Raphia, in spite of the fact that Antiochus had been in Greece

---

[1] P. M. Meyer, *op. cit.* pp. 18 sqq., 95 sqq. The inscriptions are *I.G.* xii. 3. 327 and *B.C.H.* 1896, pp. 177 sqq.; 1897, p. 166.
[2] *Cyrene*—Diod. xviii. 19–21; *Carthage*—*id.* xix. 106; xx. 29; *Bosporus*—*id.* xx. 22 sqq.
[3] Pol. v. 65. 3–4 and 6; 82. 8 sqq.
[4] *Id.* i. 32. 1 sqq., etc.

PROVENANCE AND RECRUITING

in the previous year.[1] After the great Roman wars against Macedonia and Syria, which reduced the number of armies likely to require Greeks, the situation may have been eased. At all events troops could still be raised in Greece for a king of Egypt or of Syria, and the "Cretan tyranny" at Antioch was conducted for the benefit of a mercenary army which may have been composed of Greeks of all kinds ("Crete and the isles").[2]

By far the most prominent Greek soldiers throughout the Hellenistic period were the Cretans. The population of Crete was hardy, warlike, and much given to piracy: the island was a ready-made nursery for mercenaries.[3] In consequence Cretans take a prominent place among the mercenaries of Egypt,[4] Syria,[5] Sparta,[6] the Achaean League,[7] Pergamum,[8] and Macedonia[9] (in the third Macedonian War they served in great numbers on both sides), and even of Syracuse[10]; in fact of all the principal employers of the time. A people of similar tendencies were the Aetolians. Although they appear not to have been in such universal demand as the Cretans (we never hear of them in strength in the service of a Greek state), yet we find Aetolian peltasts with Demetrius,[11] Aetolian pirates with Antigonus Gonatas and Philip V,[12] cavalry and infantry with Pyrrhus,[13] and at least 6500 Aetolians in the service of Egypt at one time.[14] Other northern Greeks with Pyrrhus were Acarnanians and Athamanians. Macedonians occurred as mercenaries in the Athenian and Lilaea inscriptions (see above), and Macedonian volunteers were in the Roman army at Magnesia.[15] Such was the

[1] Livy 37. 40.
[2] Pol. xxxiii. 8. 4 sqq.; Josephus, *Ant.* xiii. 129 sqq.; 1 Macc. 11. 38.
[3] Strabo x. 477; Pol. iv. 8. 11.
[4] Pol. v. 36; 65. 7; *O.G.I.S.* i. 153; *S.B. Ak. Wien*, 1915 (179), p. 60.
[5] Pol. v. 79. 10; 82. 8 sqq.; x. 29. 6; Livy 37. 40; Justin 35. 2: Josephus, *Ant.* xiii. 86, etc.
[6] Plut. *Pyrrhus* 32. 2; *Cleom.* 6. 3; 21. 3; Pol. iv. 80; xiii. 6. 8; Livy 32. 40. 4; 34. 27. 2; 35. 8; 35. 29. 1 sqq.
[7] Pol. xvi. 37. 3; xxxiii. 16. 5; Livy 35. 28 and 29; 39. 49. 2; Ditt. *Syll.*³ ii. 600.
[8] Livy 28. 7; 37. 39. 10; 38. 21. 2; *O.G.I.S.* i. 270.
[9] Pol. iv. 67. 6; *ibid.* 61. 1 sqq.; v. 66. 6; Livy 31. 35. 1 sqq.; 33. 18. 9 sqq.; *ibid.* 14. 3 sqq.; 42. 12. 7; 43. 7. 1; 44. 43. 8; Plut. *Aemil.* 16. 1; 23. 3 sqq.
[10] Pol. iii. 75. 7; Livy 24. 30. 13 sqq.: and later at Rome, cf. pp. 234-5.
[11] Polyaen. iv. 9. 2.
[12] *Id. ibid.* 6. 18; Pol. viii. 54. 7.
[13] Dion. Hal. 20. 1.
[14] Pol. xv. 25. 16; Livy 31. 43.
[15] Livy 37. 39. 12.

value, however, to the kings of Macedonia of their native troops, that it is to be supposed that the ordinary Macedonian was prohibited from leaving the country to fight as a mercenary (in the last cases cited above they were fighting for a friendly power), and that the odd Macedonians of the inscriptions were special cases—e.g. exiles or prisoners of war—who were able to fight for their living and not for their country. As for Peloponnesians, the four inscriptions and the statistics from Egypt would seem to indicate a much smaller proportion of them in mercenary service in the third century; nor do they fill the place in the literary evidence that they filled formerly—especially in Xenophon's *Anabasis*. Nevertheless Antigonus I was still in 315 B.C. able to get 8000 mercenaries from the Peloponnese.[1] Achaeans, probably mercenaries, fought with Philip V against the Aetolians,[2] and with Eumenes of Pergamum at Magnesia.[3] In Egypt, the army at Alexandria in 220 B.C. contained 3000 Peloponnesians, and one of the military clubs (κοινά) of Egyptian mercenaries in Cyprus was that of "the Achaeans and the other Greeks", which implies that Achaeans predominated.[4] In view of the perpetual anti-Macedonian interference of Egypt in Peloponnesian politics of the third century, the presence of Peloponnesians in her armies is not surprising. The only remaining known κοινόν of Greek soldiers in Cyprus is that of the Ionians,[5] and Ionia and the islands was another region much influenced by Egyptian policy. Finally, there were considerable numbers of Rhodians in the service of Egypt at the time of the siege of Rhodes by Demetrius.[6]

A word must be said about the soldiers known as "Tarentines". They make their first appearance in 316 B.C., and they occur later frequently enough to make it certain that the name cannot mean simply men from Tarentum in Italy. They have been described as "originally mercenaries from Tarentum", but it is not certain if even this qualification is enough: it is safest to begin by saying that certainly no band of "Tarentines" that we meet can possibly have come from Tarentum, and that it is not always clear that they are mercenaries. In these circum-

[1] Diod. xix. 57. 1; 60. 1.
[2] Pol. iv. 61. 2.
[3] Livy 37. 39. 10; Appian, *Syr*. 31; cf. p. 174.
[4] Pol. v. 36. 1 sqq.; *O.G.I.S.* i. 151.
[5] *Ibid.* 145.
[6] Diod. xx. 82.

PROVENANCE AND RECRUITING 247

stances it becomes probable that the name refers to a *style* of fighting, though the connection of that style with Tarentum is lost completely: was the "Dokimos Tarantinos", who became infamous in the army of Philip of Macedon for using warm water for washing, a genuine citizen of Tarentum serving as a mercenary, or the first exponent of this new style on record?[1] It is impossible to say; but one can say definitely that the 2200 "Tarentines" with Antigonus at Gabiene (316 B.C.) did not come from Italy, but were probably recruited near the seaboard of Asia Minor, whether as mercenaries or as a levy.[2] They were probably light cavalry (ἐπιλέκτους ἐν ἐνέδραις), and, whatever their origin, they made a permanent place for themselves in the army of Antigonus, since they are mentioned later with Demetrius at Gaza and at Athens.[3] After that "Tarentines" disappear for eighty years (which is not surprising, where the sources for that period are so scanty), only to come up again in quick succession in the armies of Sparta, the Achaean League, Elis, and Antiochus the Great. The "Tarentines" fighting on both sides at the battle of Mantinea (207 B.C.) were certainly mercenaries; whereas there is a slight probability that those of Elis in 218 B.C. were really the Elean citizen cavalry:[4] those of Antiochus may have been anything, except that they are distinct from the cataphract cavalry and the "Companion" cavalry, and may thus be light horse, as we suspected originally.[5] But this crop of

---

[1] Polyaen. iv. 2. 1, Φίλιππος ἐπὶ στρατοπέδου Δόκιμον Ταραντῖνον λούτρῳ θερμῷ χρησάμενον τὴν ἡγεμονίαν ἀφείλετο, φήσας· ἀγνοεῖν μοι δοκεῖς τὰ τῶν Μακεδόνων, παρ' οἷς οὐδὲ γυνὴ τεκοῦσα θερμῷ λούεται.

Does this mean that Dokimos was himself a Macedonian, and ought to have known "the customs of the Macedonians"? Or does it mean that he was *not* a Macedonian, because if he had been one Philip would not have needed to remind him of the circumstances of maternity in Macedonia? If the former, then he may be the excellent officer who fought with Alexander, Eumenes, and Antigonus (Berve, *s.v.*). But more probably he was ἡγεμών of mercenaries: ἡγεμών = an *infantry* officer, and hence he really came from Tarentum—and may still be Berve's Dokimos.

[2] Diod. xix. 29. 2, ἑξῆς δὲ τοὺς ἀπὸ θαλάττης συναναβεβηκότας Ταραντίνους δισχιλίους καὶ διακοσίους, ἐπιλέκτους ἐν ἐνέδραις καὶ καλῶς διακειμένους ταῖς εὐνοίαις πρὸς αὑτόν. [3] *Ibid.* 82. 2; Polyaen. iii. 7. 1.

[4] Mantinea—Pol. xi. 12. 6 (cf. 11. 4 sqq. and 13. 1); Elis—*id.* iv. 77. 7, ὃς παραγενόμενος εἰς τὴν Ἠλείαν, καὶ παραλαβὼν τοὺς μισθοφόρους τῶν Ἠλείων, ὄντας εἰς πεντακοσίους, καὶ πολιτικοὺς χιλίους, ἅμα δὲ τούτοις τοὺς Ταραντίνους, ἧκε βοηθῶν εἰς τὴν Τριφυλίαν....

[5] Pol. xvi. 18. 7. The other references tell us nothing (Plut. *Cleom.* 6. 3; *Phil.* 10. 2).

references indicates that the "Tarentine" style, whatever it may have been, was in general use in Greece and in Asia at the end of the third century. And inscriptions from Athens, Boeotia and Thessaly prove that in the second century the style was still in use in the cities of Greece, where its exponents were certainly not mercenaries but the citizen cavalry.[1] It is even possible that *all* the Athenian ἱππεῖς at this date were "Tarentines",[2] and the Polybian reference to Elis (above) might be interpreted as using the word "Tarentines" to denote simply "the cavalry", or "the citizen cavalry".

So much for the spread of the Tarentine style: what of the style itself? It is described in the late works on tactics, but first one must notice one earlier piece of evidence, more authoritative because its source must date from a time when "Tarentines" were still to be seen in Greece. Livy, in a section almost certainly transcribed from the Greek of Polybius, describes the Tarentines of Philopoemen operating against Nabis: *dein Cretenses auxiliares et, quos Tarentinos vocabant, equites, binos secum trahentes equos, ad prima signa misit*.[3] One's instinctive reaction to this piece of information is most probably one of pure scepticism: What was the use of having two horses? Suidas tells us the use: ἱππική· τοῦ δὲ ἱππικοῦ τὸ μὲν ἁπλῶς οὕτω καλεῖται ἱππεῖς καὶ ἱππικόν, τὸ δὲ ἄφιπποι· καὶ ἄφιπποι μὲν οἱ ἐπὶ δυοῖν ἀστρώτοιν συνδεδεμένοιν ὀχούμενοι· οἱ καὶ μεταπηδῶσιν ἀπ' ἄλλου ἐπ' ἄλλον ὅταν ἡ χρεία καλῇ.

The tactics described by Suidas are those, one imagines, of barbarians from the steppes of South Russia or the Iranian plateau, where horses were plentiful and horsemanship a matter of second nature: the idea that this style ever became common in Greece is absurd. Its only real advantage was the presence of the second horse if one horse was disabled: its disadvantages were, that Greece produced very few horses, that two horses per man would have been too expensive, and that if one can imagine a situation whereby any Greek general had horses to

---

[1] At Athens, *I.G.*² ii. 1. 958, ll. 56 sqq.; 960. 33; 961. 34; and *I.G.* ii. 3. 1218. In Boeotia, *I.G.* vii. 1. 2466. In Thessaly, *I.G.* ix. 2. 509.

[2] A. Martin, *Les cavaliers athéniens* (Paris 1886), pp. 422 sqq., mentions this possibility, but rejects it. This book contains a short section on "Tarentines" (pp. 418–23), which collects most of the evidence.

[3] Livy 35. 28. 5.

spare, one may be sure that he would not have wasted them by letting them be led, but would certainly have put men on their backs. What then did Livy mean by saying what he did say? Either one is to accept what he says in spite of its improbability, or one must suspect that he has made a mistake: and perhaps it is a mistake in translation. His *binos secum trahentes equos* is probably a translation of the Greek ἀμφίππους (of which Suidas' ἄφιπποι must surely be a corrupt form): the question is, did Polybius write ἀμφίππους? Or is there another word that he could have written, a word which Livy could have confused with ἀμφίππους? One thinks immediately of the ἄμιπποι of Thucydides and Xenophon—people who could keep up with horses. These people were light infantry trained to operate with cavalry, and may have been a Boeotian specialty.[1] Is it possible that somebody—perhaps at Tarentum—went one step further, and put these light troops on horseback, and that the new light cavalry came to be called "Tarentines"? Perhaps; but there is still the difficulty of the new light cavalry being qualified in Polybius by the same adjective—ἄμιπποι—formerly used of the old light infantry, an adjective which is slightly absurd, moreover, when applied to cavalry, or even to what is called "mounted infantry".

The theory is, then, that the "Tarentines" were a type of light cavalry or mounted infantry, perhaps a development of the old ἄμιπποι. The ἀμφίπποι heresy may be discarded as an absurdity; and if further persuasion is needed, one may mention that in Antigonus' order of battle at Gabiene "Tarentines" and

[1] Thuc. v. 57. 2, Βοιωτοί μὲν πεντακισχίλιοι ὁπλῖται καὶ τοσοῦτοι ψιλοὶ καὶ ἱππῆς πεντακόσιοι καὶ ἄμιπποι ἴσοι....
Xen. *Hell.* vii. 5. 23, καὶ μὴν τοὺς ἱππέας οἱ μὲν πολέμιοι ἀντιπαρετάξαντο ὥσπερ ὁπλιτῶν φάλαγγα βάθος ἐφεξῆς καὶ ἔρημον πεζῶν ἀμίππων.
Id. *Hipp.* 5. 13, Ἱππαρχικὸν δὲ καὶ τὸ διδάσκειν τὴν πόλιν ὡς ἀσθενὲς τὸ πεζῶν ἔρημον ἱππικὸν πρὸς τὸ ἀμίππους πεζοὺς ἔχον.

In both these last two passages πεζοὶ ἄμιπποι is clearly a technical name for a type of light infantry, and not merely infantry in general: if Xenophon had meant merely infantry, he would have said merely πεζοί.

This style, like that of the ἀμφίπποι, probably came from the barbarian nomads. Cf. Hdt. i. 215 and Aristarchus, *ad loc.*, in P. Amh. ii. 12, correcting the strange ἄνιπποι to ἄμιπποι; Hdt. is speaking of the Massagetae. Cf. Caesar, *B.G.* i. 48. 5 sqq. for the Germans of Ariovistus, who had a light infantry trained to keep up with the cavalry and escape by jumping up behind the horseman if necessary. Cf. also Livy 44. 26 (the Bastarnae).

ἀμφιπποι are mentioned as two perfectly separate contingents.¹ Moreover, the late tacticians would have gloried in the description of the "two-horse" style, picturesque and of little practical use: whereas in fact Arrian's description of the Tarentine "style" is circumstantial enough, and shows clearly that the people he describes were ordinary light cavalry, ἱππακοντισταί, akin to the mounted archers, though sometimes they were armed with swords for close fighting in addition to their missiles.² That is plausible, and must content us, since we know less about them than Arrian knew. The origin of the name must remain a mystery, and in the circumstances we can never be certain (unless by deduction) whether any particular "Tarentines" are Greeks or Asiatics, citizen cavalry or mercenaries. It may be suggested that in the early days, while the style was still a novelty, it may have called for the professional soldier as its exponent; but we have seen that certainly in the second century, and perhaps by 218 B.C. in Elis, it had been adopted by Greek cities for their own cavalry. But the "Tarentines" are chiefly interesting as the first manifestation of a tendency in Hellenistic military affairs, which is itself important for this question of provenance: the tendency to use an ethnic name to describe a type of soldier. The most obvious example is the use of the word "Macedonian", but there are closer parallels to the "Tarentines" in the so-called "racial" hipparchies of the Ptolemaic regular cavalry—the hipparchies of the Mysians, the Persians, the Thessalians, and the Thracians. In the first place it must have been very difficult for the Ptolemies to procure real Thessalians and real Persians, to say nothing of real Mysians; and again all the names known to us of soldiers who belonged to these corps are Greek names, and all of the third century (though admittedly barbarians with Greek names are common in later Egyptian documents): and finally in the one and only case where the provenance of such a soldier is known, the "Thracian" is a Pergamene.³ These hipparchies are clearly named after a type, not after a race. The question next arises as to how far this principle may have been applied to other

---

[1] Diod. xix. 29. 2, τοὺς ἀμφίππους ὀνομαζομένους.
[2] Arr. *Tact.* 4. 5 sqq.
[3] P. Petr. iii. 112 (f), ll. 13–14. Cf. Lesquier, p. 296 (tables).

PROVENANCE AND RECRUITING 251

mercenaries. K. Grote suggests that the names "Cretan" and "Thracian" in general are to be viewed with suspicion.[1] It is a very difficult question to decide; but there is no intrinsic reason (as there is in the case of Tarentum) why Crete and Thrace should not in fact have produced all the mercenaries credited to them by our authorities, so that it seems best to take the names at their face value, except in this branch of the Egyptian army, and in the case of all provenances attached to soldiers in Egypt in the second century.[2]

Greek mercenaries were only a part of the mercenary population of the Hellenistic world. There is abundant evidence to show that each of the great powers, while it used Greek mercenaries to a smaller or greater degree (perhaps to the largest degree possible), yet drew also for its supplies of soldiers upon the barbarian fighting stocks which lay nearest or most convenient to its hand. Thus Carthage, accustomed by long tradition to the use of barbarian mercenaries, continued to use them in this period too: to employ Greeks was, in fact, to Carthage an innovation of the period, and the majority of her foreign soldiers must still have been barbarian, recruited as of old from the best fighters of Spain, Gaul, Italy, the Balearic Islands and northern Africa.[3] In the same way the Seleucid army at Raphia, and more especially at Magnesia, reveals a predominance of Asiatic over Greek mercenaries. It is difficult, in the case of Asiatic contingents serving with the Seleucids, to define the exact status of each. Such people as the Arabs, Mysians, Scythians and Jews are certainly mercenaries (perhaps the Cilicians too, and others from the nations of Asia Minor), as well as the Gauls and Thracians of whom more will be said.[4] Pergamum employed Mysians and Masydenians, but perhaps the greater part of her mercenaries were Greeks.[5] Clubs (κοινά) of Lycians and Cilicians are among those discovered in inscriptions dating from the Egyptian occupation of Cyprus, and Lycian and Pamphylian

---
[1] K. Grote, p. 97.
[2] Lesquier, pp. 124 sqq. The κοινά in Cyprus are of the second century, but since, so far as is known, they are quite unofficial in their character, their names may really represent the nationality of their members.
[3] Pp. 208 sqq.
[4] Pol. v. 79; xxx. 25. 3 sqq.; Livy 37. 40; Josephus, *Ant.* xiii. 129 sqq. (Jews).
[5] *O.G.I.S.* i. 338.

mercenaries occur at Aspendus along with Cretans and Greeks.[1] Macedonia drew a supply from the barbarian nations surrounding her, Illyrians, Thracians and Gauls. To the Illyrians the same doubt attaches as to the Asiatic contingents of the Seleucids. They appear several times with Macedonian armies, but also with the army of the Achaean League at Mantinea, and in this last case they must certainly be mercenaries.[2]

But by far the most generally employed of barbarian mercenaries were the Gauls and Thracians. First the Gauls. Their striking successes against the first Greek armies which they encountered marked them out as a most valuable tool in the hands of the man who could turn them to his own profit. That man was Antigonus Gonatas, one of whose earliest acts after becoming the first general to defeat Gauls in an open field, was to take some of them into his own service.[3] Pyrrhus followed his example[4], and the custom spread rapidly elsewhere. We have seen how Gauls were invited into Asia by the king of Bithynia, and were there employed by him, by the kings of Pontus, and finally by the Seleucids themselves.[5] It is uncertain whether Pergamum ever employed the original Gallic nations which crossed to Asia (the Galatians); but Attalus I brought others from Europe on his own account, and his successor had Gauls among the troops with which he helped Rome against Perseus.[6] As early as 274 B.C., or less than five years after the first Gallic irruption into Greece, Gauls had made their way into the Egyptian army. These or later recruits must have been settled in cleruchies in Egypt, whence they were called out to fight at Raphia.[7] In Macedonian armies they are to be found at Sellasia with Antigonus Doson, and later with Philip V and Perseus.[8] Finally some Gauls (probably from Italy) appear as the garrison of the independent Epirote city of Phoenice. Their history is so

---

[1] O.G.I.S. i. 146, 147, and 162; ibid. 148 and 157; S.B. Ak. Wien, 1915 (179), p. 60.
[2] With Macedonia, Pol. ii. 65. 1; Livy 33. 14. 3 sqq.; ibid. 4. 4 sqq.; 44. 11. 7. With Achaeans, Pol. xi. 11. 4 sqq.
[3] Polyaen. iv. 6. 7; Plut. *Pyrrhus* 26. 3. Apollodorus of Cassandreia had Gauls, perhaps before Antigonus, Diod. xxii. 5. 2.
[4] Plut. *Pyrrhus, ibid.*   [5] Pp. 183 sqq.
[6] Pol. v. 77. 2 sqq.; 78; 111. 2 sqq.; Livy 42. 57; 44. 28. 9 sqq.
[7] Paus. i. 7. 2; Pol. v. 65. 10, cf. O.G.I.S. ii. 757.
[8] Pol. ii. 65. 2; v. 2 sqq.; Livy 42. 12. 7; 44. 2. 6 sqq. (the Bastarnae).

PROVENANCE AND RECRUITING 253

varied, and perhaps so typical, that it is worth telling. In the beginning they had been expelled from their own land by their compatriots. Having entered the service of Carthage they were sent to Sicily, where they quarrelled with their general about pay, and attempted to sack the city of Acragas which they were supposed to be guarding (at this time they were about 3000 strong). In the same way at Eryx they first tried to betray the city and its garrison to the Romans, and, foiled in this, they deserted to the Romans themselves. Next they sacked a temple and made themselves so unpopular with their new masters that, when the war was over, they were at once disarmed, put on board ship, and forbidden to set foot in Italy. It was then that they sailed to Epirus, where they were entrusted with the garrison of Phoenice. By now they were reduced to 800. The last that we hear of them is that they betrayed Phoenice to the Illyrian raiders of Queen Teuta.[1]

Hardly less striking than the influx of the Gauls is the renaissance of the Thracians as a power in Greek armies. In the fourth century, before Alexander, they disappeared completely, driven out perhaps by the improved Greek peltast, until they were restored probably by the rise of Macedonia with her ascendancy over the neighbouring nations of Thrace. We saw that Thracians helped Alexander to conquer the East, and from that time they continued to play an important rôle as auxiliaries in the principal Hellenistic armies. Some of Alexander's Thracian settlers reappear at Paraitacene, where other Thracians fought on the opposite side with Antigonus.[2] Thracians fought on both sides again at Raphia a century later: those of the Egyptian army were military settlers, which implies that there was an established tradition of recruiting from Thrace, which is probable enough in view of the Egyptian possessions there.[3] In the Seleucid army Thracians are present several times during the reigns of Antiochus III and IV;[4] and in that of the Attalids as early as 260 B.C., and later at Magnesia.[5] But it is to the armies of Macedonia that we should naturally look for their

[1] Pol. ii. 5. 4; 7. 6 sqq.
[2] Diod. xix. 27 and 29.   [3] Pol. v. 65. 10 and 79. 6.
[4] Id. xxx. 25. 3 sqq.; Livy 37. 40; Polyaen. iv. 16; Appian, *Syr.* 6. 1 sqq. With Rome at Magnesia, Livy 37. 39. 12.
[5] *O.G.I.S.* i. 266; Livy 37. 39. 10; 38. 21. 2.

most constant attendance, and there they are indeed to be found with unfailing regularity under Philip and Perseus, who may have valued them sufficiently highly to make military settlers of them in Macedonia proper, and so ensure a constant supply.[1]

At the end of the third century and the beginning of the second, barbarian mercenaries probably outnumbered Greek in the great armies. The Greek states themselves seem not to have taken kindly to Gauls, Thracians and the like; apart from Philopoemen's Illyrians at Mantinea, and some Thracians with the Achaean League army of 197 B.C., we know only of the barbarian bodyguards of Aristotimus at Elis and Apollodorus at Cassandreia:[2] and if there was any movement to enlist barbarians on the scale of Dionysius I and his successors at Syracuse, it has escaped us completely. But even allowing that the Greek states were conservative and employed Greek mercenaries, the use of barbarians by the kings of Macedonia and Syria was sufficient to turn the numerical scale in their favour. At that time the situation may have approached that of the Italian cities in the late Middle Ages—the exponents of civilization striving to destroy one another with the help of the uncivilized. Whether Greek soldiers later in the second century recovered the position of pre-eminence which had formerly been theirs in the world of mercenaries, our information does not allow us either to prove or to disprove. The indications are that they did not, that Greece had ceased to be the foremost nursery of soldiers before she became a battlefield for the Romans, and after fifty years of Roman wars she was something not unlike a desert.[3]

2. Recruiting

One of the favourite methods of obtaining soldiers was that of recruiting through diplomatic channels and by means of political influence and interest. A state or a ruler that needed mercenaries would procure them from a friendly power that controlled a source of supply. This arrangement was simple and

---

[1] Pol. iv. 66. 6; v. 2 sqq.; xviii. 22. 2; 26. 8; xxii. 13. 6; Livy 31. 35. 1 sqq.; 33. 4. 4 sqq.; 18. 1 sqq.; 42. 51. 5 sqq.; 44. 42. 2; Plut. *Aemil*. 18. 1 sqq.
[2] Livy 33. 15. 1 sqq.; Plut. *Moral*. 251 sqq.; Diod. xxii. 5. 2.
[3] Pol. xxxvi. 17. 4 sqq.

PROVENANCE AND RECRUITING 255

effective, and requires no explanation: it can be seen in use from the very earliest times. Psammetichus I of Egypt very probably got his Greek and Carian mercenaries from Gyges of Lydia:[1] Pisistratus had an Argive wife, and obtained 1000 mercenaries from Argos.[2] In the Peloponnesian War Sparta controlled the main source of supply of heavy infantry; consequently the allies of Sparta profited by being able to engage Peloponnesian mercenaries when necessary, while we hear of only one occasion, while the war was in progress, when Peloponnesians served on the opposite side.[3] The classic example in the fourth century is that of the Persian and Egyptian employers. Both the Great King himself and his governors, and his disaffected subjects, used the Greek cities unscrupulously as suppliers of mercenary armies and generals, so that the best Greek commanders of their day are to be seen fighting for one barbarian power against another, sometimes with soldiers sent officially by their mother-cities.[4] Dionysius I and the Phocian Philomelus also obtained soldiers from the Peloponnese by virtue of their friendly relations with Sparta.[5] Diplomacy reached its highest mark in this direction when the Great King thought fit to try to compose the inter-city wars of the Greeks in order that soldiers might be released to serve as mercenaries in his own army.[6]

When recruiting was not reinforced by diplomacy, the ordinary method was to send recruiting officers to the locality whence mercenaries were to be raised: this seems to have been done in a perfectly haphazard way as the occasion might arise. Thus Brasidas and Lysander doubtless had no difficulty in raising an army in their native Peloponnese, where they were the most distinguished generals of their time.[7] Cyrus recruited the greater number of his Greeks by sending to Greece a few trusted friends of his own who were also officers of repute. He also set his garrison commanders to work in Asia Minor, but of their methods, as of the methods of the satrap Pissuthnes who had

---

[1] Cf. G. Smith, *History of Assurbanipal*, pp. 64 sqq.
[2] Aristot. *Ath. Pol.* 15. 2; 17. 4.
[3] Thuc. i. 60; iii. 109; iv. 76. 3; vii. 58. 3.
[4] Diod. xiv. 39. 1 sqq., etc.; xv. 29; xvi. 22. 1 sqq.; 34. 1 sqq.; 44. 1 sqq.; Xen. *Ages.* ii. 26 and 28 sqq.
[5] Diod. xiv. 44. 2, etc.; xvi. 24. [6] *Id.* xv. 38.
[7] Thuc. iv. 80. 5; Xen. *Hell.* ii. 4. 29.

recruited Peloponnesians before that date for his army in Asia, nothing can be learnt.[1] No particular system indeed is apparent anywhere. But an interesting remark of Isocrates sheds a little light upon the subject: "In those times [i.e. about 400 B.C.] there was no mercenary service at all (*sic*), so that whoever found it necessary to recruit mercenaries from the cities spent more upon the gifts which were given to the recruiting officers, than upon the wages of the soldiers".[2] Allowing for the pamphleteer's exaggeration, it is still easy to believe that in those times the task of recruiting was not a sinecure, and perhaps required officers of proved tact and ability. But Isocrates was writing of what had happened more than fifty years ago, and in the same passage he points out the difference which those years had brought about: it was now, he says, easier to collect a large and efficient army from the wanderers than from the city-dwellers. So that in the fourth century recruiting may have presented few difficulties, and the casual method have still been effective. There is evidence, however, that at Athens, where the use of mercenaries was almost unbroken, the office of recruiting became in the fourth century a recognized "liturgy" (possibly something between military service and a trierarchy in importance), and that the "commissioners of the mercenaries" also mark a systemization of what had become an important branch of the public business.[3] It is possible too that such conveniently situated cities as Athens and Corinth became permanent rallying points for soldiers who wanted occupation and recruiting officers or *condottieri* who wanted soldiers, though the evidence on this point is not sufficient to justify a very positive assumption.[4] The recruiting arrangements of the Sicilian tyrants and of the Carthaginians in the West have been described in chapter VIII, and to that there is nothing to add.

Mention should perhaps be made of a suggestion about recruiting put forward by Aeneas in his manual of "Siegecraft": "The richest men in the city should be bidden to provide mercenaries each according to his means, some three, some two, others one". He says that this method of recruiting through

---

[1] Xen. *Anab.* i. 1. 6 sqq.; Thuc. i. 115. 4; iii. 34. 2.   [2] Isoc. v. 96.
[3] Demosth. xl. 36; Aeschines i. 113; cf. Demosth. l. 10.
[4] Xen. *Hell.* vi. 5. 11; vii. 3. 4.

numerous individuals, followed by a similar method of paying and maintaining the mercenaries, would be "the quickest and safest and cheapest way".[1] The superiority, in general, of private enterprise over management by the State has been demonstrated in many walks of life; but it does seem that in this particular case too much is expected of the individual, and that, in any but the very smallest community, there would be almost unlimited openings for the bungler or the evader to do his worst. Aeneas is of course suiting his thesis to a special situation, that of the besieged town, and there is no evidence of his plan having ever been put into practice. The nearest approach to it that suggests itself is the plan of Agesilaus in Asia, whereby he recruited mercenary cavalry by the expedient of conscripting the richest citizens in the allied cities, and allowing each, if he so wished, to provide a horse and an armed man to fight in his stead (the notorious method of Scutage).[2]

In the Hellenistic age no striking new ways of recruiting come to light; it is merely that there are more and better examples of the old ways. The diplomatic method has perhaps become more common, and we possess the text of a treaty between two states which grant to each other "most favoured nation" rights of recruiting in their respective spheres of influence (Rhodes and Hierapytna). Such rights meant that a Rhodian ξενολόγος in Crete received a safe-conduct, in so far as that was possible, from the Hierapytnians, who further lent him all possible assistance in his task (and *vice versa*); no enemy ξενολόγοι were allowed in the neighbourhood of Hierapytna, and Hierapytnian citizens were prohibited from taking service against Rhodes.

This last clause is instructive, because there are penalties for its being broken, but exempt from these penalties are "those of the Hierapytnians who are already serving abroad before this treaty". This is not surprising, since the Cretans were at the height of their fame as mercenaries at about this time; but what is more significant is that the same clause is binding on the Rhodians also, who were never famous mercenaries. It may have been merely a legal precaution, but even legal precautions bear, originally at least, some relation to an existing set of facts,

---

[1] Aeneas Tacticus 13. 1 sqq.; cf. 10. 7.
[2] Xen. *Hell.* iii. 4. 5; *Ages.* i. 24; Plut. *Ages.* 9. 4.

and this clause must be at least a survival from a time when it was applicable to almost any Greek city.[1] It may have been these rights that the city of Aptara, also in Crete, gave to Attalus I of Pergamum, when the council and assembly passed a decree granting him, among other privileges, that of "recruiting" (without further qualification).[2] On the other hand, this may merely be a permission to recruit, unreciprocated, and unaccompanied by such promises of assistance as occur in the treaty mentioned above; and this permission may have been always necessary before recruiting officers could enter a free Greek city. Every government was, or ought to have been, bound to prevent too great a drain upon the man-power of its citizens, as in fact the Aetolian government was once obliged to limit the number of its citizens who could be permitted to take service with Egypt.[3] If this permission was in fact a necessary preliminary to recruiting, it is the easier to sympathize with the cold reception by the Roman senate of ambassadors from Cretan cities, on the ground that as many Cretans were mercenaries of Perseus as of Rome.[4] The probability is that it *was* a necessity: the great Antigonus obtained the permission of Sparta before recruiting mercenaries from the Peloponnese.[5] Similar to these diplomatic advances to Greek states were the agreements between a prospective employer and a nation or tribe of barbarians represented by their king or chief, as in the cases of the Thracians of Cotys and the Bastarnae of Clondicus (dealing in each case with Perseus).[6] It was an invitation of this kind by Nicomedes of Bithynia that first brought the Gauls into Asia, and Attalus I of Pergamum later introduced another of their nations in the same way.[7] Carthage got Numidians from friendly princes,[8] and the

---

[1] Ditt. *Syll.*³ ii. 581, ll. 45 sqq., 77 sqq. There are traces of similar undertakings in the (incomplete) treaty of Antigonus Doson with Hierapytna (*B.C.H.* xiii. 1889, pp. 51 sqq.).
[2] *O.G.I.S.* i. 270, ll. 10 sqq., ἧμεν δὲ αὐτῶι| καὶ προεδρίαν καὶ ἀσυλίαν καὶ ἀτελείαν καὶ ἀσφαλείαν καὶ πο|λέμω καὶ εἰρήνας καὶ ἐν πόλι καὶ ἐν τοῖς λιμένοις, καὶ ξενολογῆσθαι καὶ ὁρμίζεσθαι....
[3] Livy 31. 43.
[4] *Id.* 43. 7. 1 sqq.
[5] Diod. xix. 60. 1.
[6] Livy 42. 67. 5; 44. 26 sqq. (cf. Appian, *Mac.* 18. 4; Diod. xxx. 4; Plut. *Aemil.* 12. 1 sqq.).
[7] Livy 38. 16. 6 sqq.; Pol. v. 77. 2 sqq.
[8] Pol. i. 78, etc.

PROVENANCE AND RECRUITING 259

Seleucids obtained Jewish mercenaries through the good offices of the High Priests at Jerusalem.[1] Armies could still be raised, however, without any diplomatic preliminaries, and it may have been that there were certain places which became known as fixed rallying-points for soldiers in want of employment. One such place was certainly Taenarum, for some years in the fourth century. It has been supposed that Taenarum first became important in this connection during the last two years of Alexander's life, when the flight of Harpalus, the exiles' decree, and the demobilization of the satraps' armies, brought thousands of mercenaries back from Asia to the Aegean. Actually one ought perhaps to carry the search to an earlier date. In 332 B.C., when the Spartan king was preparing for war, he sent the money and ships that he had collected from Asia to Taenarum where his brother Agesilaus was waiting:[2] it looks as if Taenarum was already a Spartan naval base, if it was nothing more. The advantages of the place are obvious. From the land it could be approached only through Spartan territory, and even supposing that a hostile army reached the neck of the promontory, an assault was still almost out of the question; the two possible routes are difficult even to-day, and could have been made impassable by a small defending force. The defenders could be reduced only by starvation, and this demanded a great naval superiority, which Macedonia never possessed in Alexander's lifetime. When Harpalus fleeing from Asia reached Greece, after he had failed to win over Athens, he went with his army to Taenarum and stayed there until he heard of a job in Crete for himself and his men.[3] In the same way Leosthenes concentrated his mercenaries at Taenarum, where they stayed for some time until the outbreak of the Lamian War:[4] it was the one place in Greece where one could be perfectly safe from the Macedonians. (It must have been with similar motives that Phalaecus at the end of the Phocian War had taken his army to the adjacent promontory of Malea.[5]) This motive of self-preser-

[1] 1 Macc. 10. 36 sqq.; 15. 26.
[2] Arrian ii. 13. 6; cf. [Plut.] *Moral.* 848 E (*Vit.* x *Orat.*). If the name Chares here is right, which is doubtful (p. 35), Taenarum was already occupied by mercenaries some months earlier: so Parke, p. 201, and Berve, p. 404.   [3] Diod. xvii. 108. 7 sqq.
[4] *Ibid.* 111, etc.; cf. p. 35.   [5] Diod. xvi. 62. 3.

17-2

vation may have made Taenarum a rallying-point for mercenaries even before Leosthenes, for Harpalus had arrived there with 6000 men and departed with 7000. Certainly after Leosthenes it must have become a sort of rest-camp and recruiting market, for Thibron could get 2500 men from Taenarum to reinforce his army at Cyrene (p. 43),[1] and as late as 303 B.C. Cleonymus of Sparta recruited 5000 mercenaries there.[2] Besides being almost impregnable to a land attack, the place was ideally situated for piracy, and this may account for its popularity with soldiers for more than twenty years. Promontories in general were notoriously dangerous in antiquity to the civilian traveller, and to-day the Greeks of Kalamata will tell you (though probably quite groundlessly) that the people over there (pointing to Taenarum) are "not good people". This function of Taenarum disappears in the third century, nor is it possible to cite any other town or locality as a parallel case in that period. The city of Aspendus has indeed been mentioned repeatedly in this connection, but this seems to be an example of what one may call "scholars' myth", having its origin in an over-free statement made by one scholar about forty years ago:[3] in reality there is no ground whatever for believing that Aspendus was an Asiatic parallel to Taenarum, though its position as a seaport and its proximity to fighting populations may have made it a market for mercenaries in common with other cities on the coast of Asia Minor.

It is not known how a recruiting campaign such as that of Carthage in the first Punic War was carried out: all that can be said is that recruiting officers went to Greece, and returned with plenty of mercenaries and a brilliant commander (Xanthippus).[4] It is unlikely that Carthage can have had previous agreements with any Greek cities, and the inference is that the recruiting officers must have known where to go in order to find what they

---

[1] Diod. xviii. 19. 1 sqq.; 21. 1 sqq.; Arrian, τὰ μετὰ Ἀλεξ. 16 sqq.
[2] Diod. xx. 104; cf. xix. 57. 5; 60. 1—Aristodemus, Antigonus' general, recruits 8000 mercenaries in the Peloponnese by permission of Sparta: this looks like Taenarum again (so P.-W. s.v.).
[3] Graf Lanckorowski, *Städte Pamphyliens u. Pisidiens* (1890), pp. 85 sqq.; using Xen. *Anab.* i. 2. 12; Nepos, *Datames* 8; Appian, *Syr.* 32; Pol. v. 64, all references to soldiers from the neighbourhood of Aspendus.
[4] Pol. i. 32. 1 sqq.

PROVENANCE AND RECRUITING 261

required. The same is true of the recruiting of Heraclides the minister or officer of Alexander Balas (152 B.C.), who, armed with the approval of Rome, was able to summon the notable mercenary captains of Greece to his aid (τῶν ἐπιφανῶν ἀνδρῶν). But when he reached Asia he probably used Ephesus as a recruiting base, and Ephesus may have been a recognized market for mercenaries, in view of its situation convenient for both Attalid and Seleucid purposes.[1] The coast cities of Asia Minor in general were likely places for recruiting. Eumenes of Cardia sent his officers from Cappadocia into Pisidia, Lycia and Cilicia, others to Coele-Syria and Phoenicia and as far as Cyprus, and the news of his requirements spread rapidly and brought him 12,000 men.[2] As to the more intimate details of the recruiting process we are utterly in ignorance. The Miles Gloriosus conducts his affairs in the market place of Ephesus. His business was merely to recruit the soldiers and give them an advance of pay, not, apparently, to become their commander;[3] nor is there anything to suggest that ξενολόγοι were habitually ἡγεμόνες as well. There must have been some form of contract upon enlisting. If soldiers were needed for a short expedition only, they perhaps required to know what was its nature and object.[4] If they were engaged for a long period, probably the period was specified, and the contract was after the style of the agreement between Eumenes I and his mercenaries (pp. 282 sqq.). The rate of pay and ration allowances was the most important thing to be settled, after which there were probably minor details such as the length of the service year, accommodation for families, possibilities of bonuses or grants of land. In fact the contract of mercenaries and their employers may have been the model for the procedure adopted by the great Roman generals after Marius.

Finally, there were what may be called casual methods of obtaining mercenaries. The most obvious of them was that of winning over mercenaries in the service of the enemy. Desertion and surrender on the part of the mercenaries are symptoms most common in the generation of the Successors, when the rapid rise

---

[1] Pol. xxxiii. 16. 12 sqq.; cf. v. 35. And Ephesus is the scene of the *Miles Gloriosus*.
[2] Diod. xviii. 61. 4 sqq.   [3] *M.G.* 72 sqq., 948 sqq.
[4] Plut. *Arat.* 6. 2; 7. 1; cf. Xen. *Anab.* i. 1. 6 and 9; 2. 1; 3. 2 sqq. and 21.

and fall of the great employers was perhaps a hindrance to personal loyalty among soldiers, and an excuse for their keeping an eye to the main chance. The general who could place his opponent's army at an obvious disadvantage to his own could reasonably hope to command both armies in the near future. Relevant examples are very numerous: in addition to epidemics of gradual desertion (such as the desertion of the troops of Perdiccas to Ptolemy, of Antigonus to Ptolemy, of Lysimachus to Antigonus),[1] there are also cases of wholesale surrender by mercenaries during or after a losing battle; the more important instances concern the armies of Craterus at the Dardanelles, Eumenes at Gabiene, Demetrius at Gaza, Ptolemy in Cyprus, and Antigonus at Ipsus.[2] Later examples can be collected also, but they do not involve important issues, and in this respect the soldiers of the Successors left a blemish upon Greek mercenary service, which could otherwise show a tolerably fair face.

There remains to be mentioned a form of recruiting which has something of the casual in it, and something too of the diplomatic method mentioned earlier. This was, to employ for one's own ends a section of the community of pirates that abounded in the Greek seas. The profession of piracy, particularly towards the end of the fourth century, had much in common with the mercenary calling, and probably embraced much the same types of unemployed Greeks.[3] Perhaps the mercenary's was the steadier, the pirate's the riskier but more rapid way of seeking a fortune, and men who were in need of a fortune tried their hands at both—the classic example is Charidemus. Pirates could be, and were, used as mercenaries through the connivance of their leaders. Thus Demetrius employed them at the siege of Rhodes and as guardians of Ephesus.[4] Antigonus Gonatas captured Cassandreia with the help of Ameinias the "pirate king" (ἀρχιπειράτης), who became one of his generals.[5] Some of his pirates were Aetolians; and an Aetolian pirate leader Dicaearchus was employed by Philip V at a later date.[6] More

---

[1] Diod. xviii. 33 sqq.; xx. 75 sqq.; 113. 3.
[2] *Id.* xviii. 32. 3 sqq.; xix. 40 sqq.; 85. 3; xx. 53. 1; Plut. *Dem.* 29. 2 sqq.
[3] H. A. Ormerod, *Piracy in the Ancient World*, pp. 119–20; cf. Isoc. iv. 115; v. 96; Aeschines i. 191.
[4] Diod. xx. 85. 3; Polyaen. v. 19.
[5] Polyaen. iv. 6. 18; Plut. *Pyrrhus* 29. 6.   [6] Pol. xviii. 54. 7.

PROVENANCE AND RECRUITING 263

Aetolian pirates are found serving the Eleans in 218 B.C.[1] Aratus surprised Sicyon with "soldiers" (στρατιώτας) obtained through Xenophilus, a brigand chief.[2] It was to this type that the service of Nabis particularly appealed. He was hand in glove with the pirates of Crete, but employed brigands of the Peloponnese as well, and indeed ruffians from all over the world (if Polybius' pious horror has not seduced him into an overstatement).[3] Another of the *archipiratae* is discovered in the service of Antiochus the Great in 190 B.C.;[4] but Ormerod professes to trace a decline in the influence of the mercenary pirates and *archipiratae* after the Gallic invasions, a decline perhaps due, as he suggests, to the greater numbers of barbarians who entered into the armies of the kings.[5] Nevertheless the pirates of Aetolia and of Crete continued to flourish, a fact which in itself sufficiently illustrates that piracy and mercenary service were mutually sympathetic trades.[6]

[1] Pol. iv. 68. 1.   [2] Plut. *Arat.* 6. 2.
[3] Pol. xiii. 6. 3 sqq.; 8. 2. For the importance of Cretan support to Nabis, cf. Livy 34. 35. 8, "Ne quam societatem cum ullo Cretensium, aut quoquam alio institueret" (proposed terms of peace dictated by Flamininus).
[4] Livy 37. 11; Appian, *Syr.* 24.   [5] *Op. cit.* p. 126.
[6] Pol. iv. 6; Strabo x. 477.

CHAPTER X

THE PAY AND MAINTENANCE OF MERCENARIES[1]

1. σῖτος (ETC.) AND μισθός: THE PROCESS OF PAYMENT IN THE CLASSICAL PERIOD

THE question of how mercenaries were paid is probably more awkward of approach than any that has been considered already. In effect, it is not too much to say that in this connection there is nothing that can be taken for granted: even the word μισθός, indicating the basis of every transaction between a soldier and his employer, is to be regarded as a preliminary hazard, to be mastered indeed if possible, but at all events to be approached with care.

First, then, the receiving of μισθός was not peculiar to the soldiers whom the Greeks agreed to call μισθοφόροι—mercenary soldiers. The history of the subject is as obscure as it well can be, but one supposes that in the earliest times Greek citizen armies of hoplites undertook their short campaigns at their own expense. Perhaps the first relief came in the form of rations provided by the State (σῖτος).[2] Certainly at some time in the fifth century Athens took the next step, and paid her citizen soldiers a sum of money in addition: and probably from the first (though this is not certain) this payment in money, like the payments for the other public services at Athens in the high

[1] I have thought it best to begin at the beginning of this subject, partly because the early evidence is not to be found collected in one place in Parke's book, and partly because it is the easiest form of introduction to the somewhat complicated procedure of the Hellenistic period, which would be confusing without an introduction of some kind. Valuable information on the subject is to be found in P.-W. *s.v.* μισθός and σιτηρέσιον (Schulthess). It was not until this book was in the press that I was able to obtain the work of B. A. Van Groningen, *Aristote: le second livre de l'Économique* (Leyden, 1933): I was glad to find that, in the interpretation of several texts from the *Economics* (see below, pp. 268 sqq.), he had previously reached the same conclusions.

[2] σῖτος τριῶν ἡμερῶν—Aristoph. *Acharn.* 197; *Vesp.* 243; *Pax* 311, cf. Thuc. i. 48. 1—was perhaps the usual issue to a citizen force on a short expedition; but these references are much too late to be of any use towards showing when such issues were first begun.

democratic period, was called μισθός.¹ The first task is to put μισθός and σῖτος in their respective places. The evidence, such as it is, is against the idea that μισθός was ever a mere substitute for σῖτος, merely a payment in money which the soldier was to use for buying his rations for himself: σῖτος and μισθός existed together in the same army and at the same time, so much seems clear.² The situation will become less clear when the process known as *adaeratio* makes itself known (as it presently will): the "rations" cease to be food and become an equivalent payment in money, with the result that a soldier receives *two* payments in money, and it is sometimes difficult to tell, when a payment is made, which of the two it may be. But there is of course a difference between the two, and a fundamental difference at that. Reduced to the simplest possible terms, it is this: Rations, or money for rations, are something without which a soldier cannot begin to fight, and they must consequently be paid *in advance*; pay (μισθός) is something which a soldier receives in return for having done some work, and consequently, like any other wages or salary, it is paid at the *end*. This is a point which has never been made sufficiently clear, perhaps because it is too obvious. Nevertheless it will be of great help in the troubles that are approaching, for the distinction governs all armies actually on campaign in time of war, though it will be less reliable when applied to the standing armies of the Hellenistic period.

The *Expedition of Cyrus* provides us with our only intimate picture of a mercenary army in action, and includes a little information about pay, though not very much (the rate of pay will be discussed later, pp. 295 sqq.). The only actual payment Cyrus ever made to the Ten Thousand was in Cilicia, when he gave them four months' μισθός, of which "more than three months'" was already overdue.³ This suggests at once that μισθός was

---

¹ Aristoph. *Eq.* 1367 uses μισθός of a rower's pay (and *Acharn*. 159, μισθός as a mercenary's pay); and Aristot. *Ath. Pol.* 27 has ὁ δῆμος...συνεθισθεὶς ἐν ταῖς στρατείαις μισθοφορεῖν, in the same category as καὶ μισθοφόρα τὰ δικαστήρια (*ibid.*). But cf. also p. 267, on Thuc. v. 47. 6.

² Cf. n. 1 and p. 264 n. 2, all of which references deal with the period of the Peloponnesian War: also for σῖτος Thuc. v. 47. 6; Diod. xiii. 95. 3 (Syracuse, 405 B.C.).

³ Xen. *Anab.* i. 2. 11 sqq.

reckoned by the month, and ought to have been paid at the end of each month: and the suggestion is made certain by later references to occasions when Cyrus raised the rate of μισθός *per month*, and when the army, returned from its travels, was offered a certain rate of pay "reckoning from the 1st of the month" (ὑπισχνοῦμαι... ἀπὸ νουμηνίας μισθοφορὰν παρέξειν κυζικηνὸν ἑκάστῳ τοῦ μηνός).[1] This information accounts perfectly for the μισθός of the army. But how would it subsist in the meantime, at the best until the end of the first month (if the μισθός had been paid regularly), and as it actually happened during more than three months before the first (and last) instalment of μισθός was paid? Either it must have received real food (σῖτος), or else payments in money for its purchase. It is almost certain in fact that it received real food—σῖτος and οἶνος requisitioned by Cyrus from the countryside through which he passed on the march, including a surplus which he carried with him in a provision-train in case he should find himself in difficulties.[2] This train was captured by the Persians at Cunaxa, and subsequently the "Cyreians" were marching through a hostile country, taking what they could get without paying for it, so that the question of rations did not arise till they reached civilization again. Then Trapezus provided an ἀγορά, in which the soldiers paid for what they took;[3] but Sinope and Heraclea were advised to pay the army some money (it is not clear whether it was actually paid in fact) in order to get rid of it—τῇ στρατιᾷ μισθὸν ὥστε ἔχειν τὰ ἐπιτηδεῖα ἐκπλέοντας. This phrase looks awkward at first, with μισθός appearing to mean "money for rations"; but the context shows quite clearly that it is not used here in the technical (military) sense, and what it really means in the circumstances is "a bribe".[4] When the remnant of the army took service in Thrace under Seuthes the contract was the same as that of Cyrus, a μισθός in money and rations in kind—(1) ὑπισχνοῦμαι ὑμῖν δώσειν τοῖς στρατιώταις κυζικηνόν, etc.; (2) ἔξω δὲ τούτων τὸν ἄξιον τιμήσω; (3) σῖτα δὲ καὶ

[1] Xen. *Anab.* i. 3. 21; v. 6. 23.
[2] *Ibid.* i. 4. 19; 5. 9 sqq.; 10. 18. The last passage suggests that the surplus was to be distributed free (διαδιδοίη), and not to be bought by the soldiers in ἀγορά, as was the practice where ration-money was given instead of rations. Other arguments against ration-money in this case are that (1) we never hear of it, (2) Cyrus was short of money, at least when he began the march (i. 2. 11).
[3] *Ibid.* v. 5. 14.   [4] *Ibid.* vi. 6. 19.

PAY AND MAINTENANCE 267

ποτά ὥσπερ καὶ νῦν ἐκ τῆς χώρας ἕξετε.[1] This contract includes everything that a mercenary soldier at this period could hope to get—(1) pay (μισθός); (2) a possible bonus;[2] (3) rations (or their equivalent in money): one reminds oneself that he would receive these three things in a different order from that in which Seuthes is said to have mentioned them (3: 1: 2).

It may be said that this "money for rations", mentioned already more than once, has never yet appeared in fact. It is impossible to say when it first began to be used. The phrase σῖτος τριάκοντα ἡμερῶν, in the Athens-Argos treaty of 419 B.C., rouses one's suspicions. Could a hoplite, or even a hoplite's servant, be expected to carry with him "rations for thirty days" (armies in Greece had no elaborate provision-trains as a rule)?[3] One would suspect that σῖτος might have come to mean "ration-money", except indeed that σῖτος is so essentially a basic word that it has no business to mean anything but what it does really mean—"corn": if people begin to say "corn" when they mean "money" one is almost helpless. Nevertheless Thucydides (v. 47. 6) does once use σῖτος for a payment in money. In this same Athens-Argos treaty he says, τοῖς δὲ βοηθοῦσιν ἡ πόλις ἡ πέμπουσα παρεχέτω μέχρι μὲν τριάκοντα ἡμερῶν σῖτον,... ἢν δὲ πλέονα βούληται χρόνον τῇ στρατιᾷ χρῆσθαι ἡ πόλις ἡ μεταπεμψαμένη, διδότω σῖτον, τῷ μὲν ὁπλίτῃ καὶ ψιλῷ καὶ τοξότῃ τρεῖς ὀβολοὺς Αἰγιναίους τῆς ἡμέρας ἑκάστης..., etc. There is no circumventing this plain statement of fact: all that one can say is that this use of the word is unique, and one may explain it by suggesting that it belongs to the period when *adaeratio* was in its infancy, and a new word describing it was not yet coined.[4] For it is not so long after this date that the word we are needing —"corn-money"—duly presents itself. Lycon the Achaean, one of the "Cyreians", addresses his comrades, "I am surprised

---

[1] Xen. *Anab.* vii. 3. 10.
[2] *Ibid.* i. 7. 7. Cyrus had promised στέφανον ἑκάστῳ χρυσοῦν.
[3] Thuc. v. 47. 6; cf. Diod. xiii. 95. 3 (Syracuse, 405 B.C.). It may be mentioned that the Peloponnesians invading Attica in 431 B.C. brought their provisions with them (Thuc. ii. 23. 3); presumably they did the same for their subsequent invasions (cf. iii. 1. 3), and that of 430 B.C. (the longest in duration) lasted 40 days (*ibid.* 57. 2).
[4] I know of no other case in which σῖτος must mean a payment in money, and very many where it clearly means "food", for which ἐπιτήδεια is also used sometimes (below).

268 HELLENISTIC MERCENARIES

that our generals make no attempt to furnish us with a σιτηρέσιον: for the free food" (ξένια, from Heraclea) "cannot possibly be more than three days' corn (σιτία) for the army: and the means for provisioning ourselves for our march do not exist".[1] 'The means for provisioning oneself", then, is σιτηρέσιον (or kindred words, σιταρχία, -κία; σιτώνια, etc.). It is σιτηρέσιον that we are to expect to find being paid *in advance* (for without it how is a soldier to fight—or march?); and it ought to be perfectly distinct from μισθός paid at the *end* of a period.

This distinction is well exposed in a set of texts from the *Economics*, dealing with examples of military economy mostly in the fourth century.[2] (1) The distinction between rations in kind and pay in money. "Datames the Persian in command of an army was able to provide the daily necessaries from the enemy's country, but since he had no money, he used the following device"; the device itself is of no consequence, but its result was that Datames was enabled to make use of his army for a considerable time while paying out rations only (τὰ ἐπιτήδεια μόνον διδούς).[3] A story of Timotheus at Samos tells of a device for raising money in order to pay μισθός to the soldiers, who receive their rations in kind (ἐπιτήδεια): here the commodities are bought from the Samians by the officers (ταξίαρχοί τε καὶ λοχαγοὶ ἀγοράζοντες), and are then distributed to the soldiers (διεδίδοσαν), who appear to pay nothing for them.[4] (2) Between ration-money (σιταρχία) and pay-money (μισθός). By far the clearest example is the device of Memnon of Rhodes, τῶν τε στρατευομένων παρ' αὐτῷ παρῃτεῖτο τὰς σιταρχίας καὶ τοὺς μισθοὺς ἐξ ἡμερῶν τὸν ἐνιαυτόν, φάσκων ταύταις ταῖς ἡμέραις οὔτε φυλακὴν αὐτοὺς οὐδεμίαν οὔτε πορείαν οὔτε δαπάνην ποιεῖσθαι, τὰς ἐξαιρεσίμους λέγων. This proves that the two words were not merely synonymous, but did denote two

---

[1] Xen. *Anab.* vi. 2. 4; cf. (e.g.) *I.G.* ix. 1. 694, ll. 33 sqq. for the same distinction between the σιτηρέσιον and μισθός of workmen (third or second century).

[2] The anecdotes contained in the second book of the *Economics* vary in value, but those that I propose to use, relating to the fourth century (those of them that can be dated), make such excellent sense that I feel sure, for my own part, that they are trustworthy: the use of the technical terms (σιταρχία and μισθός) is almost always consistent, and this set of texts taken as a whole is illuminating in a way that can hardly be accidental. Cf. Van Groningen, *op. cit.* pp. 37 sqq., 53 sqq., and Commentary (cited below).

[3] [Aristot.] *Econ.* ii. 24. 1350 *b*.

[4] *Ibid.* 23. 3. 1350 *b*; cf. Isoc. xv. 111; Polyaen. iii. 10. 9.

entirely different things. But next comes the really valuable piece of information about σιταρχία, confirming what one was bound to assume whether confirmation could be found or not: τόν τε πρὸ τοῦ χρόνον διδοὺς τοῖς στρατιώταις τῇ δευτέρᾳ τῆς νουμηνίας τὴν σιταρχίαν, τῷ μὲν πρώτῳ μηνὶ παρέβη τρεῖς ἡμέρας, τῷ δ' ἐχομένῳ πέντε· τοῦτον δὲ τὸν τρόπον προῆγεν, ἕως εἰς τὴν τριακάδα ἦλθεν.[1] This proves that σιταρχία was paid by the month, and normally at the beginning of the month: and one is not entitled to object that this may not have been true of employers other than Memnon, because the whole point of the "device" lay in delaying the payment later and later each month, till finally it had worked round to the beginning of the month again, that is to say to the normal date. In order to make this point doubly sure one may mention a device of Cleomenes very similar to that of Memnon, except that his object was to save a month's μισθός (instead of a month's σιταρχία, as in Memnon's device), by delaying the payment of σιταρχία until it overlapped the date when payment of μισθός was due.[2]

The object of paying a σιταρχία was of course to enable the soldiers to buy their food for themselves. No doubt the first care of a general in a foreign land was to ensure that the local traders provided an ἀγορά for the army, as Trapezus had done for the "Cyreians" (above). If a general had no money for σιταρχίαι he was obliged to allow his army to support itself by plunder, unless he could contrive to make a shift by the use of his wits: most Athenian generals in the fourth century found themselves in this difficult position, and Timotheus had the reputation of being a unique contriver.[3] One shrewd and sound piece of finance was to mint an emergency coinage of copper for the use of the army in its ἀγοραί: the soldiers disliked it until they found that the tradespeople honoured it just as if it were Athenian silver; and Timotheus had in fact told the traders to get rid of as

[1] [Aristot.] Econ. ii. 29. 1351 b; cf. Van Groningen, op. cit. pp. 175 sqq.
[2] Ibid. 39. 1353 b. I confess that I cannot see quite how the device worked: Κλεομένης προσπορευομένης τε τῆς νουμηνίας καὶ δέον τοῖς στρατιώταις σιταρχίαν δοῦναι κατέπλευσεν ἐξεπίτηδες, προσπορευομένου δὲ τοῦ μηνὸς ἀναπλεύσας διέδωκε τὴν σιταρχίαν, εἶτα τοῦ εἰσιόντος μηνὸς διέλιπεν ἕως τῆς νουμηνίας. οἱ μὲν οὖν στρατιῶται διὰ τὸ νεωστὶ εἰληφέναι τὴν σιταρχίαν ἡσυχίαν εἶχον, ἐκεῖνος δὲ παραλλάξας ἕνα μῆνα παρὰ τὸν ἐνιαυτὸν ἀφῄρει μισθὸν ἀεὶ μηνός. Van Groningen holds the last four words suspect.
[3] Isoc. xv. 120 (cf. 108 sqq., 111, 113)—panegyrical, but not worthless.

much of it as they could in payment for the commodities that they bought from the countryside, and the remainder he guaranteed to redeem with good silver.[1] There is a case on record (date uncertain, but probably fourth century) of a government itself providing ἀγορά for its own soldiers, and the curiosity here is the motive (it would have been much simpler merely to distribute the commodities as rations). The government of Heraclea Pontica was short of money (οὐκ εὐπορούμενοι χρημάτων), and decided to buy up the commodities from the traders, with a guarantee to pay at a future date: then on the campaign ἀγορά was provided in which the soldiers paid for their food with money: and finally when μισθός became due to the soldiers it was paid to them in the same money that they had themselves paid for their rations! It follows that σιταρχία must have been paid to them previously—how else could they have paid for the rations?—a fact that is not mentioned in the anecdote as it stands, one phrase of which is undoubtedly corrupt.[2]

On a campaign, then, σιταρχία must be paid at the beginning, and μισθός must follow if possible. A general who had the confidence of his men could tide over a lean period by paying σιταρχία regularly and crediting μισθός to their account. Timotheus at Corcyra paid three months' σιταρχία but had no money for μισθός, and when the soldiers became difficult to control he restored his credit by telling them that they could regard what they had already received as a donative; that is to say that they would receive it again when his funds arrived, in addition to the μισθός overdue.[3] The same sort of thing must have happened at Chalcedon and at Clazomenae (the date in each case is uncertain),

[1] [Aristot.] *Econ.* ii. 23. 1. 1350 *a*; cf. Isoc. xv. 113; Polyaen. iii. 10. 4.
[2] *Ibid.* 8. 1347 *b*. The whole anecdote is too long to be quoted in full. I now find that Van Groningen (*op. cit.* p. 85), accepting the emendation of Kirchhoff (*Hremes*, xiii. pp. 139 sqq.), reads the suspected passage as follows: 'Ἐκεῖνοί τε (*sc.* Ἡρακλεῶται—after buying up all the commodities to provide ἀγορά) διαδόντες διμήνου μισθὸν παρῆγον [ἀλλὰ] τὴν ἀγορὰν ἐν ὁλκάσιν... I still think that this will not do, because people who are short of money do not pay two months' μισθός (perhaps in advance), and because, in this event, the soldiers would have been using this μισθός instead of their σιταρχία. Clearly the sense requires σιταρχία, and I would read: διαδόντες σιταρχίαν, οὐ μισθὸν παρῆγον ἀλλὰ τὴν ἀγορὰν ἐν ὁλκάσιν... This is certainly less happy palaeographically—but it does make sense of ἀλλά (by the "device" ἀγορά was to supply the deficiency in μισθός): and *a priori* σιταρχίαν is necessary.
[3] *Ibid.* 23. 2. 1350 *a*; cf. Isoc. xv. 109.

PAY AND MAINTENANCE 271

where we hear of governments that had run up a long debt of μισθός to their mercenaries: Clazomenae at first temporized by paying an annual interest on the principal of the debt (the rate was 20 %!), but both governments resorted in the end to extraordinary measures in order to pay the mercenaries off. The important point in these transactions is that in the meantime the soldiers cannot possibly have consented to live on air, or even, in the case of those at Clazomenae, on their 20 % interest—that would have been pure philanthropy: during all the time that μισθός was overdue, σιταρχία (or σῖτος) must have been paid, and paid regularly.[1]

Finally there is the crucial passage in Demosthenes' *First Philippic*, much used (and misused) as evidence for the rate of pay in the fourth century, in which connection it must be mentioned later. But the form, as well as the amount, of payment is of great interest. Demosthenes proposes that a small standing army be kept in the field, of which one quarter shall be Athenians, the rest mercenaries, and he outlines a scheme for keeping them in pay and maintenance with the smallest possible sacrifice to the city: ἔστι μὲν ἡ τροφή, σιτηρέσιον μόνον, τῇ δυνάμει ταύτῃ τάλαντ' ἐνενήκοντα καὶ μικρόν τι πρός (40 talents for the fleet; 40 talents for the infantry), ἵνα δέκα τοῦ μηνὸς ὁ στρατιώτης δραχμὰς σιτηρέσιον λαμβάνῃ (and 12 talents for the cavalry). εἰ δέ τις οἴεται μικρὰν ἀφορμὴν εἶναι, σιτηρέσιον τοῖς στρατευομένοις ὑπάρχειν, οὐκ ὀρθῶς ἔγνωκεν· ἐγὼ γὰρ οἶδα σαφῶς ὅτι, τοῦτ' ἂν γένηται, προσποριεῖ τὰ λοιπὰ αὐτὸ τὸ στράτευμ' ἀπὸ τοῦ πολέμου, οὐδένα τῶν Ἑλλήνων ἀδικοῦν οὐδὲ τῶν συμμάχων, ὥστ' ἔχειν μισθὸν ἐντελῆ. Now this could be construed so as to put a rather different complexion upon the two payments σιτηρέσιον and μισθός: one could suppose from this passage that μισθὸς ἐντελής is σιτηρέσιον + something (a payment at the end), that σιτηρέσιον is in fact a part of the μισθός paid in advance. If it were a mere question of words it would be absurd to waste time and labour on the matter; but it may be important later, when we consider the *amount* of money paid to soldiers, to be absolutely certain what these words exactly mean. The foregoing pages have been based

[1] [Aristot.] *Econ.* ii. 10. 1347 b; 16. 2. 1348 b; so also Van Groningen, *op. cit.* p. 153.

on evidence showing σιταρχία (= σιτηρέσιον) and μισθός as two perfectly distinct payments to soldiers on campaign: is the issue to be obscured now by these words of Demosthenes? To speak impartially, there is at least no need for the obscurity, if it is to exist. The passage can equally well be translated "the army will make the rest for itself from the war...so as to have full pay" (i.e. it will make not merely part of its μισθός but all of it, assuming μισθός to be perfectly distinct from σιτηρέσιον). And fortunately one can quote a parallel use of this very phrase by Aristophanes (*Eq.* 1367):

πρῶτον μὲν ὁπόσοι ναῦς ἐλαύνουσιν μακράς,
καταγομένοις τὸν μισθὸν ἀποδώσω 'ντελῆ.

Here surely the poet cannot have in mind a previously paid σιτηρέσιον as part of the μισθός: he merely means "to the sailors, when they come ashore, I will pay their full pay"—i.e. without deductions or delays. It seems almost certain that Demosthenes must mean the same thing.[1]

To examine this passage as we have just examined it is to see the Athenian military finance of the period in a cruel light. Now Demosthenes was not a practical soldier: he did not possess a fraction of Timotheus' knowledge of the realities of warfare. With this in mind one is shocked to realize that this proposal of his, produced with such an air of the practical man, was in reality an improvement on the existing state of affairs—of this there can be no doubt. Yet the proposal itself was far from being

[1] Demosth. iv. 28 (and 21); cf. Arrian, *Anab.* ii. 13. 6, for the same phrase, with no special meaning apparently; also Isoc. xv. 120. Parke, pp. 232 and 233 n. 6, uses the quoted passage as authority for saying that Demosthenes' mercenaries were to serve for 2 obols a day only, and for denying that there was in the fourth century "the distinction commonly found in the third century between ὀψώνιον = σιτηρέσιον (*sic*), and μισθός....The μισθός had probably been introduced then" (i.e. third century) "to compensate soldiers who were being employed as a standing army in peace time without hope of other supplements to their wages. Demosthenes' reference shows that during campaigns in the fourth century this was unnecessary. Cf. the use of the word ἐπισίτιος which was applied to those who served for their keep only: Plato, *Rep.* iv. 420 *a* of ἐπίκουροι μισθωτοί..." (and other references).

I cannot follow this line of thought, for it appears to ignore the μισθὸν ἐντελῆ of the Demosthenes passage: and the reference to Plato, *Rep.* iv. 420 *a* is extremely misleading. There Adeimantus has objected that Socrates' φρουροί would be mere ἐπίκουροι μισθωταί, and Socrates agrees: Ναί, ἦν δ' ἐγώ, καὶ ταῦτά γε ἐπισίτιοι καὶ οὐδὲ μισθὸν πρὸς τοῖς σιτίοις λαμβάνοντες ὥσπερ οἱ ἄλλοι. This needs no comment.

a sound piece of business, for it left much—too much—to speculative hopes of the future and the fortunes of war: it was a display of patriotic optimism. And the policy of Athens was directed by a democracy no less optimistic indeed than Demosthenes, but less patriotic where patriotism led to expenditure. In such an age the situation of a general is to be deplored, and that of his soldiers to be pitied. But this situation must have arisen very often, for if smaller cities may have been more willing than Athens to spend their money on their armies, yet they had far less money to spend. In these circumstances a speech of the Spartan general Teleutias may well be typical of the way in which a good commander was obliged to behave (its opening words contain a touch of the ludicrous): "Soldiers, as for money, I come to you with empty hands; but if God wills it and you assist with your endeavour, I will try to find you your rations (ἐπιτήδεια), as copious as I can". And the tenor of his speech is that it is a sweet and comely thing to live on the enemy's country. Demosthenes proposed to find μισθός from the proceeds of a successful campaign; but the poor Spartan was obliged to begin his campaign with an inglorious hunt for ἐπιτήδεια.[1]

This was how mercenaries of the Greek cities must have lived in the fourth century, from hand to mouth. There were exceptions of course; the enthusiastic hopes and prospects of the "Cyreians" setting out on their anabasis, the bonuses of Jason of Pherae, the ten glorious years for the mercenaries of the Phocians among the treasuries at Delphi. But even these high moments of prosperity convey a sense of something feverish, as if the hour and the money must be seized before they are gone: even Jason is said to have had recourse to playing theatrical tricks in order to wheedle money out of his poor old mother—an absurdity whether true or fictitious.[2] To the modern mind the proposal of Demosthenes and the appeal of Teleutias are scarcely less bizarre, and when we turn from them to the evidence of the next century it is like turning from fantasy to the sober facts of life.

[1] Xen. *Hell.* v. 1. 14 sqq.
[2] Polyaen. vi. 1. 2 and 3.

2. σιτώνιον (ETC.) AND ὀψώνιον: THE PROCESS OF PAYMENT IN THE HELLENISTIC PERIOD

The best documents in our possession throw light upon the military finance of Egypt, Pergamum and Carthage in the third century, in a period when each of these powers was dependent, to a greater or less degree, upon corps of mercenaries in its standing army. But, before we examine the documents, there is still one more point of terminology to be fixed. In the third century one meets with a new word, ὀψώνιον, which is common in papyri, occurs in inscriptions, and in literary sources seems to be almost peculiar to Polybius. Its meaning appears to be "salary" or "wages", covering a wide range from an allowance to a child or a slave or a student to the wages of a soldier or the fee of a magician! (Finally, death is ὀψώνια ἁμαρτίας.)[1] Its importance lies in the fact that, for military purposes at least, it has probably taken the place of μισθός, and means what μισθός has been shown to have meant in earlier texts: and the fact that it occurs earliest in official documents, with a time-lag of more than a century before it becomes known to us in a literary source, may mean that it was primarily a specialists' word, and its history is not without interest for its own sake. The derivation is of course ὄψον-ὠνοῦμαι, parallel to σιτ-αρχία (σιτ-ώνιον occurs in Egypt, below). The question is, what was the relation of ὄψον to σῖτος where two payments of money were involved? And the answer is not very difficult. To an Homeric hero bread and wine and ὄψον constituted a really good meal—σῖτον καὶ οἶνον ἔθηκεν| ὄψα τε....[2] To a Greek mercenary in the pay of Cyrus σῖτος (and οἶνος) were the necessaries of life (p. 266), and it was to purchase these that he received his σιταρχία. But necessaries are the better for a relish, and the relish was ὄψον in real life, and in proverbs some unsatisfying abstract to take the place of ὄψον—"hunger is the best sauce".[3] So ὀψώνιον was the means

---

[1] Cf. L. and S. *s.v.* ὀψώνιον.
[2] *Od.* 3. 480.
[3] Cf. Xen. *Cyr.* 1. 5. 12, λιμῷ ὥσπερ ὄψῳ διαχρῆσθε; *id. Mem.* 1. 3. 5, ἡ ἐπιθυμία τοῦ σίτου ὄψον—not the best reply to a mercenary demanding his ὀψώνιον. There is a curious use of ὀψώνιον = ὄψον in *U.P.Z.* i. 91. 13 (a private account of a month's expenditure, kept by the ἐπίγονος Apollonius at Memphis—τῶν ἀνηλωμάτων πάντων σίτου καὶ ὀψόνιον [*sic*] τοῦ Φαρμοῦθι).

PAY AND MAINTENANCE 275

of purchasing one's relish or dish, as opposed to one's bare necessaries, for which one had already received an allowance. There is thus a strong presumption that ὀψώνιον will mean wages, and that it will resemble μισθός in remaining perfectly distinct from σιταρχία, etc.: and in fact there are many cases, both in military and in other contexts, where the distinction is explicit.[1] The warning should be added, however, that in dealing with payments made to soldiers of a standing army one is not on perfectly safe ground, for here the payments both of ὀψώνιον and of rations or allowance for rations would be made regularly each month and on approximately the same days, so that it would not be surprising if the issue were to be confused. We shall in fact find that in Egypt, which gives us more detailed information than any other source, the distinction is usually between ὀψώνιον (wages) and σιτώνιον (an allowance in cash) or σιτομετρία (rations in kind): the word σιταρχία on the other hand is used rarely in the papyri, and more loosely, and (what is worse) perhaps not always with just the same meaning.[2] This confusion appears also (as it seems) in two treaties made by Greek cities in the third century; the one treaty has ὀψώνιον and the other

---

[1] Some clear cases of the distinction are P. Cairo Zen. iii. 59507. 5, τό τε ὀψώνιον καὶ σιτομετρίαν καὶ τὸ ἔλαιον; U.P.Z. i. 14. 26, μετρήματα καὶ ὀψώνιον; Wilcken, Ostraka, ii. 714 and 1538; O.G.I.S. i. 229, l. 106; Pol. i. 67. 1, etc. (pp. 288 sqq.); and the following pages of my text.

Parke, however, p. 233 n. 6, holds that the distinction is "between ὀψώνιον = σιτηρέσιον and μισθός"; but I know of no use of μισθός for military pay in Hellenistic documents.

[2] The relevant texts are (1) Dikaiomata, 1. iv. 157 sqq., ὅσοι ἂν...ἐγκαλῶσι περὶ σιταρχιῶν καὶ σιτομετριῶν καὶ παραγραφῶν τῶν σιταρχίας ἢ σιτομετρίας γινομένων, where the editor rightly points out that σιτομετρία always means an allowance in kind, and concludes that σιταρχία here means "allowance in cash" (cf. P. Amh. 29. 11 and 22, where ἀγοραί and σιταρχίαι are clearly in contrast). If this is right, σιταρχία is used here in its original sense.

(2) U.P.Z. i. 16. 12 sqq., καὶ τὰς σιταρχίας οὐκ ἀποδίδωσι, a complaint that a contract is not being fulfilled: we possess the details of the contract in U.P.Z. i. 14. 24 sqq., 47 sqq., and 64 sqq., which show that the payments in question ought to have consisted of wages in cash (ὀψώνιον) + allowances (μετρήματα) + an additional allowance (σιτώνιον). Here then σιταρχία appears to embrace all these things, though this is not perfectly certain.

(3) Archiv, viii. pp. 202 sqq., no. 8, ll. 12 sqq. (B.G.U. iii. 1748), προοῦ τὸ καθῆκον ἐκλόγισμα εἰς Μεσορή (= composite pay), ἑκάστῳ χαλκοῦ δραχμὰς γ (= certainly ὀψώνιον, cf. ibid. no. 9, l. 6), πυροῦ ἀνηλωτικῷ ἀρτάβας β (= σιτομετρία)...καὶ ἀπὸ τοῦ ιθ ἔτους (the following year) τιθέσθωσαν αὐτοῖς εἰς δεκάμηνον αἱ σιταρχίαι. Here too σιταρχία seems to mean composite pay (ὀψώνιον + σιτομετρία).

σιταρχία, but the two words seem to mean exactly the same thing, namely composite pay (*everything* that a soldier was to receive). Nevertheless, Polybius in his account of the great mutiny of the Carthaginian mercenaries preserves the old distinction between ὀψώνιον and σιταρχία throughout his narrative, except for one sentence in which he writes σιταρχία when it looks as if he means ὀψώνιον (i. 66. 6). It may be thought strange that there should be no single word which regularly means composite pay (ὀ. +σ.), but it will seem much less strange if the original and fundamental difference between the two things is kept in mind (pp. 264 sqq.). But the lack of such a word probably explains the occasional use of ὀψώνιον (once) and σιταρχία (several times) to denote composite pay: the correct word for the *part* was occasionally used loosely and incorrectly to supply the missing word for the *whole*. These difficulties will be discussed in their place, but in general one may assume that ὀψώνιον nearly always means (and *ought* to mean) a soldier's wages as opposed to his rations or ration-allowance: it may have originated as a piece of workmen's or soldiers' slang, but in the third century it had established itself in military parlance in the sense for which μισθός was used formerly.[1]

We are now in a position to receive the evidence relating to the pay and maintenance of soldiers in the great standing armies of the third century.

[1] I have noticed that in non-military contexts in the papyri ὀψώνιον often means "salary", i.e. payment made regularly by the month (P. Cairo Zen. ii. 59176. 51, 72, 76, 93, etc.; iii. 59326. 132; *P.S.I.* iv. 332. 33; ix. 1011. 5; P. Mich. Zen. 49. 10 sqq.; P. Tebt. iii. i. 701. 151, etc.). μισθός is, however, still in use (e.g. in same texts as ὀψώνιον, P. Cair. Zen. iii. 59326. 126 and iv. 59782 (*b*). 2–3); but μισθός in some cases is paid for piecework (P. Cair. Zen. iii. 59494; P. Mich. Zen. 62. 12), and in other cases for work done under contract (P. Cair. Zen. iv. 59621. 7; 59642; P. Hamb. 27. 15 sqq.; *B.G.U.* iv. 1122. 9; vi. 1258. 5, etc.; *B.G.U.* iv. 1107–9 are three contracts for wet-nurses, who are to get μισθὸν κατὰ μῆνα for a fixed number of months). My notes do not pretend to be exhaustive, and there are certainly many examples of both ὀψώνιον and μισθός used in a very general sense; but if ὀψώνιον *could* mean "monthly salary" and μισθός could *not*, this would account for the complete disappearance of μισθός in military contexts in the post-classical period, because ὀψώνιον would in that case be clearly the right word for the regular payments made to soldiers of a standing army.

PAY AND MAINTENANCE 277

i. *Egypt.*

There is a valuable series of papyri illustrating an elaborate organization for paying and keeping a standing army in time of peace—whereas almost all the texts noticed hitherto are devoted to expedients in war. We begin with three documents of the third century which represent the official correspondence necessary to produce a month's wages for a garrison of soldiers, the whole business a matter of mere routine, which must have been repeated, with slight variations, in every month of every year.[1] (The soldiers are called simply τοῖς ἐν τῶι Τεχθὼ φρουρίῳ στρατιώταις, and may be mercenaries.) The procedure is as follows. On the 22nd of the month the military secretary (Dion) of the soldiers at Techtho addresses a demand for the month's wages to the civilian official of finance for the district (ἐπιμελήτης—Protarchus by name): the demand mentions the number of the soldiers and the amount of money required. On the 29th of the month a subordinate of Protarchus (Agathocles) in reply to the demand sends an order to the cashier of the royal bank (τραπεζίτης—Hermias) to pay to the military secretary, Dion, a certain sum of money for the soldiers' wages, slightly smaller indeed than the sum demanded, for Dion seems to have made a mistake in his calculation; and this involves a second letter to Hermias from another subordinate of Protarchus, confirming the figures of Agathocles' letter, and enclosed with it under the same seal.[2] Hermias receives the two letters on the 30th of the month,[3] and one hopes that the soldiers got their wages in time. The wages are called ὀψώνιον; they are paid monthly, and at the end of the month.

With this transaction in mind one can hardly fail to ask two pertinent questions: (1) Where is the σιτηρέσιον (or whatever it

[1] P. Strassb. ii. 103, 104 and 108. The editor, F. Preisigke, adds to the same category *ibid.* 105, 106 and 107; but in this matter, and in some details of interpretation, I am guided by the masterly comments of U. Wilcken, *Archiv*, vii. pp. 89 sqq., who shows that only 103, 104 and 108 are military, and that even in them all the officials except one are civilian (see text).

[2] The deduction of Wilcken, *loc. cit.* The conflicting calculations of the military secretary and the civilian office of finance are probably due to a mistake of the former with regard to the number of men for whom pay is to be calculated (103, l. 16); there is also a divergence in the two calculations of ἀλλαγή, a specialists' topic which fortunately does not concern us.

[3] Here again Preisigke's interpretation (*loc. cit.*) seems impossible, and Wilcken's correct.

may be called in Egypt)? (2) Supposing that there is a σιτηρέσιον, and that both σιτηρέσιον and ὀψώνιον are paid monthly, why do not the officials take the obvious course of paying them both together, since the ὀψώνιον of the past month and the σιτηρέσιον of the coming month will fall due within two days of each other? One hopes to be able to answer these questions from the next evidence.

Three documents of the royal bank at Thebes about 130 B.C. record a transaction precisely similar to that which we have just noticed—arrangements for the month's pay of a troop of mercenary cavalry (μισθοφόροι ἱππεῖς).[1] The process is the same, the matter passes through the same offices; from military secretary (γραμματεύς) to a civilian official, from him to an official of the bank, from the bank back to the military secretary (who presumably does receive the money, though we are not told so). One humane touch comes to light—the soldiers are evidently allowed to anticipate their pay: for the bank is instructed to pay money εἰς πρόδομά τι if required, and it is not the first time that this has been done.[2] But the important thing is that in these documents the pay is divided again into the two old categories, wages (ὀψώνια) and ration-allowances (σιτώνια) + a small allowance for the horses (ἱπποτροφικόν). The arrangement is confirmed by other documents of the same period,[3] and there is an additional point of interest in connection with the σιτώνια. This word in its derivation is the exact parallel to ὀψώνια, and ought therefore to mean "money for corn".[4] But in this bank document of Thebes it includes rations in kind as well as an allowance in money, in fact in reckoning the σιτώνιον the unit is not a coin of the realm but a measure of corn, the *artabe*: the garrison receives as its σιτώνιον 56 *artabai*, of which 13 are paid in kind, the remaining 43 commuted into cash (*adaeratio*) at stipulated rates.[5] In the same way, we learn, the pay of an ἐπίγονος at Memphis (158 B.C.) was divided into

---

[1] Wilcken, *Aktenstücke*, v–vii, and commentary, pp. 49 sqq.
[2] *Ibid.* vii. ll. 8, 9, 18.
[3] Cf. especially P. Tebt. iii. i. 723, l. 4, ὀψώ[νια καὶ σιτώνια?]; l. 11, καὶ εἴ τι προδέδοτ[αι....
[4] Cf. Ditt. *Syll.*³ i. 304, l. 13 (*ca.* 330–325 B.C.) for σιτωνία = a buying of corn; xxx : δραχμὰς εἰς σιτωνίαν.
[5] *Aktenstücke*, vi. 8 sqq.

PAY AND MAINTENANCE 279

ὀψώνιον and μετρήματα, and the μετρήματα were paid partly in kind (1 *artabe* per month) and partly in cash (2 *artabai* commuted into drachmae). At Memphis every ἐπίγονος received μετρήματα, but another allowance too seems to have been paid only to some of them, and this is called σιτώνιον, and is paid in cash (the nominal value of 1 *artabe*) as it ought to be:[1] why the general allowance is called μετρήματα and the special allowance σιτώνιον is a mystery, but μετρήματα is perhaps the more accurate name for an allowance partly in cash and partly in kind, and used for the purchase of other commodities besides corn.[2]

Finally, it is possible to get an even closer insight into the process of payment from documents of a somewhat later date. In two papyri of the first century B.C.[3] there has survived the record, first, of the total sum required by a military official for a month's pay for his soldiers, partly in cash and partly in kind;[4] second, the request for payment of the allowance in kind, addressed to the σιτολόγος, the official of a royal granary;[5] third, the request for payment of the pay in cash, addressed to the τραπεζίτης, the official of a royal bank.[6] It seems that this must certainly have been the rule at all times,[7] for it would be surprising enough to find that a banker was responsible for the payment of corn as well as of money.[8] Now this information answers our questions on the previous page concerning the first document that was considered—where is the σιτηρέσιον (*sic*) if any, and why is it not paid at the same time as the ὀψώνιον? The answer is that it probably *was* paid at the same time: it was not a σιτηρέσιον (or σιτώνιον as it is called in Egypt) but a σιτομετρία, a payment of rations in kind (Wilcken deduced this

---

[1] *U.P.Z.* i. 14 = P. Lond. i. 23. Cf. P. Grenf. 1. 42 for σιτώνιον again, but with no further information.
[2] E.g. Revillout, *Mélanges*, p. 333 (*adaeratio* of allowance for wine).
[3] W. Kunkel, "Verwaltungsakten aus spätptolemäischer Zeit", in *Archiv*, viii. pp. 201 sqq., nos. 8 and 9 (=*B.G.U.* viii. 1749-50); cf. above, p. 275 n. 2, for a discussion of the meaning of ὀψώνιον and σιταρχία in these texts.
[4] *Ibid.* no. 8, ll. 10 sqq.   [5] *Ibid.* no. 8, ll. 3 sqq.
[6] *Ibid.* no. 9; cf. no. 8, ll. 15 sqq.
[7] Cf. Kunkel, *ibid.* pp. 178 sqq. and 202 sqq. (=*B.G.U.* viii. 1747-8).
[8] A. S. Hunt, in his note on P. Tebt. iii. i. 722, points out that in the three documents relating to the royal bank at Thebes quoted above (*Aktenstücke*, v-vii), although there is mention of the wheat-payments, nevertheless in the order to the banker the 13 *artabai* of wheat which are *not* subject to *adaeratio* are omitted (*ibid.* vi. 17).

truth some years ago, for a different purpose),[1] and therefore the order for payment would be addressed not to an official of finance but to a σιτολόγος (or his ἀντιγραφεύς). The reverse of this situation can now be seen in a recently published papyrus (second century B.C.), which is an order to the ἀντιγραφεύς of a σιτολόγος to produce a payment in wheat to soldiers stationed in his district, and naturally this order contains no mention of any payment in cash, which was doubtless obtained through a bank.[2]

Confirmation of several points mentioned above is to be found in other Ptolemaic documents. One hears for example of ἀγοραί, which ought to mean "markets", perhaps provided by the State, in which the soldiers could buy food and wine with their σιτώνια. In some contexts it certainly does mean this:[3] in others there seems no reason why this should not be the meaning:[4] and there is one text which says that some cavalrymen were to get wine from καπηλοί, which seems to indicate ἀγορά in this sense, though the word ἀγορά does not actually occur.[5] In other texts, however, ἀγορά seems to mean not so much "market" as "payment in kind", so that Wilcken describes ἀγοραί in general as "*Naturalverpflegung*":[6] with this sense the word is synonymous with σιτομετρία, except that it can include other commodities besides corn. The truth seems to be that the word had more than one meaning.

The advances of pay (προδόματα) were used by the Aetolian Scopas as a bait to catch recruits on his recruiting campaign in Greece, though this example is hardly in line with our previous one, where long-service mercenaries were allowed to overdraw, as it were, from the royal bank, in anticipation of their pay which was to come.[7] The allowance for upkeep of horses to mercenary cavalry is also established,[8] and there can be little doubt that the horses were in the first place given to the soldiers by the

[1] *Archiv*, vii. p. 90; cf. Schmoller's *Jahrbuch*, 45. 2, p. 83.
[2] P. Tebt. iii. i. 722.
[3] *B.G.U.* vi. 1271. 6; 1281. 8.
[4] E.g. P. Grenf. i. 42; P. Lille 4. 5 sqq.; P. Tebt. i. 48. 1 sqq.
[5] P. Tebt. iii. i. 724. 5 sqq.
[6] E.g. *P.S.I.* iv. 354. 4; 436. 5; v. 504. Wilcken in *Archiv*, v. p. 224.
[7] Pol. xv. 25. 6.
[8] P. Grenf. i. 46; P. Petr. iii. 62 (*b*); P. Tebt. iii. i. 723. 23; and perhaps 724. 2.

PAY AND MAINTENANCE 281

State.[1] The arsenals of Philadelphus and Philopator make it probable that arms too were provided by the State: non-mercenary cleruchs certainly regarded their arms as private property, and could dispose of them by testament.[2] One would have thought that with all this elaborate machinery devoted entirely to the needs of the army, a fixed standard of pay would have been realized, but such does not seem to have been the case. We possess a petition addressed by certain cavalry mercenaries to their *strategos*, complaining that they received less pay than other soldiers. The petition is unfortunately not perfectly preserved, but it certainly covers the σιτώνιον and the allowance for horses (εἰς τὴν κράστιν τῶν ἵππων), and draws unfavourable conclusions by comparing the pay of mercenary horsemen in other garrisons.[3] It is of course possible, even supposing that there was in existence some sort of sliding scale of wages corresponding to merits and length of service, that certain special cases might find themselves with a grievance. But to return to the petition, it is most interesting as illustrating the contrast between a great standing army like that of Egypt, a machine running smoothly, in which a slight imperfection might easily be brought to notice and adjusted, and the rough-and-ready gangs of soldiers who made up an army of mercenaries in the fourth century, or indeed in the Hellenistic age in the case of the small employer. There, if a difference of opinion arose about pay, it was settled by a word and a blow, and the blow often came first. In Egypt we never hear of strikes or mutinies, or even of soldiers' pay in arrears, the condition most common to Greek military finance. The army was so necessary to the rulers of Egypt that it must always have been treated with consideration and probably with liberality. There is perhaps some truth behind the flattery of the court poet when he makes his country boy say to a friend:

[1] P. Freib. 6. 7. P. Petr. ii. 35 (*a*) is a document dealing with cavalry horses, in which occurs the phrase ἐδόθη εἰς τοὺς μισθοφόρους. Mahaffy (note *ad loc.*) suggests that the numerical predominance of mares over horses mentioned in the document may indicate that the cleruchs were intended to breed horses as well as to keep them. For inspectors of horses (ἱπποσκοποί), cf. P. Petr. iii. 54; P. Hib. i. 162; and, in general, M. Rostovtzeff, in *J.E.A.* vi. p. 174.
[2] The arsenals—Appian, *Prooem.* 10 (Athen. v. 206); Pol. v. 64; testaments—P. Petr. iii. 12. 1; iii. 6 (*a*), etc.
[3] P. Grenf. i. 42.

"If you really want to be a soldier, Ptolemy is the best paymaster for a free man".[1] In time liberality may have degenerated into licence, producing the pampered mercenaries of the Alexandrian court who became a by-word for their arrogant and intemperate behaviour.[2]

ii. *Pergamum.*

Here we can use only one document, but that one of more than ordinary interest. We are shown the army of Pergamum, or the better part of it, in a state of mutiny, demanding and obtaining concessions from its employer. But the agreement between man and master is so intimately concerned with straightening out the small tangles which had probably arisen in previous years of the connection (the precise occasion of the mutiny is unknown), that it presents a reasonably good reproduction of what may have been the regular form of contract in standing armies. It consists of seven points or clauses, which had better be examined separately.[3]

(1) σίτου τιμὴν ἀποτίνειν τοῦ μεδίμνου δραχμὰς τέσσαρας, οἴνου τοῦ μετρήτου δραχμὰς τέσσαρας.

Quite literally, the translation must be: "As the price of corn to *pay* 4 dr. the m. etc." (the infinitive ἀποτίνειν is governed by the preceding words of the inscription Εὐμένης ὁ Φιλεταίρου ⟨ἐπεχώρησεν⟩...). Reinach interpreted it, "Eumenes the son of Philetairus agreed to *sell* corn at 4 dr. the m. etc.", which does violence to the Greek. The literal translation above not merely does justice to the Greek, but plainly gives the right sense. The question is not one of selling corn to the soldiers, but of converting their ration-allowance from a corn basis to a money basis, as we have just seen it converted in Egypt. And here the soldiers fix the rate of conversion. Reinach appended some pricelists for corn, and admitted that "for a valley so fertile as that of the Caicus, this price" (meaning the price at which the soldiers, as he supposed, were to *buy* the corn) "will not seem very low". The reason for its not being very low is explained, if we suppose the money to have been money *received* by soldiers in lieu of

---

[1] Theoc. xiv. 52 sqq.   [2] Caesar, *Bell. Civ.* iii. 110.
[3] *Insch. v. Perg.* i. 13 = *O.G.I.S.* i. 266. Cf. A. J. Reinach, in *Rev. Arch.* 1908, pp. 196 sqq.

corn, and not money paid by soldiers for corn: no doubt they would have fixed the rate of conversion higher had they dared, but people who wish to exchange goods in kind for cash can never expect the top prices.

(2) Ὑπὲρ τοῦ ἐνιαυτοῦ· ὅπως ἂν ἄγηται δεκάμηνος, ἐμβόλιμον δὲ οὐκ ἄξει.

The campaigning year is to be limited to ten months. In the wars of the Greek city states the season for war had been a short one of no more than the seven or eight months when the weather was good. Naturally the professional army was expected to endure a longer season; but this clause shows that even the professional army jibbed at campaigning in the heart of winter. How did the close season affect the pay of the soldiers? The only evidence is in an inscription of Cos (probably 204–201 B.C.).[1] Coan citizens subscribe money for their mercenaries' ration-allowances (σιτηρέσιον). A "year's" ration-allowance is 151 drachmae, but 6 months' allowance is 99 drachmae, 4 obols: the obvious inference is that the "year" at Cos was a 9-month year, the monthly allowance being about 16 drachmae. It is clear, therefore, that the σιτηρέσιον was not paid during the three months of idleness, and the probability is that the soldiers were expected to support themselves. (If no σιτηρέσιον was paid, it is still less likely that an ὀψώνιον, or pay proper, was given.) It is a little hard to see how the 10- or 9-month year was workable with garrison troops, since the essence of a garrison lies in its being always there. Perhaps in the four winter months at Pergamum (and the six at Cos) one half of the army was always on duty while the other half was free (e.g. one half might take its two months off in November–December, the other half in January–February). The part of the clause referring to an intercalary month is not perfectly clear (ἐμβόλιμον δὲ οὐκ ἄξει). Alexander is supposed to have intercalated a second Artemisios because he did not want to start a campaign in the unlucky month of Daisios.[2] The question in Pergamum may have arisen out of the difference between the Ionian and the Macedonian calendar, which may have given an opening to employers who tried to make their men do two months' fighting for one month's

---

[1] Paton and Hicks, *Inscr. of Cos*, 10.   [2] Plut. *Alex.* 16. 2.

pay.[1] Or the soldiers may merely have objected to a campaign which lasted a month longer, even if they were paid for it.

(3) Ὑπὲρ τῶν τὸν ἀριθμὸν ἀποδόντων τὸν κύριον καὶ γενομένων ἀπέργων· ὅπως τὸ ὀψώνιον λαμβάνωσι τοῦ προειργασμένου χρόνου. Reinach translates: "Pour ceux qui ont fait leur temps de service et qui sont devenus invalides, qu'ils reçoivent la même indemnité de nourriture qu'au temps de leur activité". This may be correct, but it is a little hard to believe it. One has heard of veterans receiving land in their old age, and of cleruchs receiving pay when they were not actually fighting,[2] but one has never heard elsewhere of their continuing to be paid for being old and useless at the same rate as when they were active servants of their employer. That is not to say that it never happened, but it does justify a second glance at the words which have given rise to such an assumption. One notices that Reinach has translated the Greek ἀπέργων by "invalides", perhaps to suit a preconception that the clause must refer to soldiers who are about to quit the service and become pensioners. But ἀπέργων means simply "idle", and has no implication of sickness or unfitness for military service, for which the ordinary Greek word is ἀπόμαχος.[3] Let us translate ἀπέργων by "idle" (literally): "For those who have fulfilled the regular number and have become idle: let them receive the pay of the time they have worked". "The regular number" of what? Why not of *months*, the number of which to a year's service has just been stipulated in the previous sentence? When the soldiers have served their 10-month year, and are entering upon their 2-month period of idleness, they are to receive the 10 months' pay which is due to them. In other words, this clause has nothing to do with pensions, but merely demands a prompt payment of the ὀψώνιον at the end of the military year (the σιτηρέσιον doubtless having been paid from month to month): the demand is all the more comprehensible if the men received nothing at all during the two idle months, and the two months of idleness may explain

---

[1] So Reinach, *loc. cit.* p. 204; see above, pp. 268–9, for other such devices.
[2] Josephus xiii. 129 sqq.; p. 162.
[3] E.g. in Xen. *Anab.* and Arrian, *Anab.* often. L. and S. *s.v.* ἄπεργος, has missed this reference. For ἀπόμισθος, used in a similar sense, cf. Demosth. xxiii. 154; Aen. Tact. 5. 2 and 11. 4; Diod. xvii. 111. 1.

PAY AND MAINTENANCE 285

why they received their ὀψώνιον at the end of the year, and not monthly as in Egypt and elsewhere.

(4) <u>Ὑπὲρ ὀρφανικῶν· ὅπως ἂν οἱ ἄγχιστα γένους λαμβάνωσι ἢ ᾧ ἂν ἀπολίπῃ.</u>

Here is revealed a previous agreement by which the employer has undertaken to pay an allowance to a soldier's family in the event of his decease. This clause seems merely to confirm the existing agreement, and ensures that the allowance be paid to the proper persons, the guardians of the orphaned children.

(5) <u>Ὑπὲρ τελῶν· ὅπως ἂν ᾖ ἡ ἀτελεία ἡ ἐν τῷ τετάρτῳ καὶ τεσσαρακόστῳ ἔτει.</u> Ἐάν τις ἄπεργος γένηται ἢ παραιτήσηται, ἀφιέσθω καὶ ἀτέλης ἔστω ἐξάγων τὰ αὑτοῦ ὑπάρχοντα.[1]

This too refers to an existing privilege of the army, an immunity from fiscal obligations. Reinach shows that τέλος is used properly of indirect taxation,[2] so that the soldiers may have obtained imported goods free of duty (as the personnel of the British Navy obtains tobacco). The clause also provides that soldiers whose term is finished or who obtain leave (see below) may be released and leave the country without paying a duty on the property which they take with them.[3]

(6) <u>Ὑπὲρ τοῦ ὀψωνίου, οὗ ὡμολόγησεν τῆς τετραμήνου· ἵνα δόθῃ τὸ ὁμόλογον καὶ μὴ ὑπολογιζέσθω εἰς τὸ ὀψώνιον.</u>

The pay in question is obviously something special, and Reinach conjectures with probability that the "4 months" is the period of the mutiny, and that Eumenes, as a preliminary to opening negotiations, had been obliged to promise to give the army its pay for that period. There is no mention of σιτηρέσιον, perhaps for the reason that the army had fed itself during the mutiny by plundering the countryside, in which case it would be too unreasonable to demand that Eumenes should give them the ration-money which they would have had, had they not mutinied.

[1] The "44th year" may refer to the Seleucid era, which makes it 269–268 B.C. (Dittenberger). Or it may reckon from the death of Alexander? = 279–278 B.C. Or from the death of Alexander's son = 268–267 B.C. These two suggestions are made by Reinach, *loc. cit.* pp. 210–11.
[2] *Loc. cit.* p. 212.
[3] For a similar ἀτελεία, cf. *Insch. v. Perg.* i. 158.

(7) Ὑπὲρ τῶν λευκίνων· ὅπως καὶ τὸν σῖτον λάβωσιν τοῦ χρόνου, οὗ καὶ τὸν στέφανον.

There must have been a system of bonuses awarded to soldiers who had distinguished themselves, and perhaps, as Reinach suggests, it took the form of σίτησις ἐν πρυτανείῳ, an institution which existed in the city of Pergamum.[1] This would account for the evident anxiety of the army lest the bonus be set off by a cessation of rations.[2]

Let us review the position of a mercenary serving in the army of Eumenes I of Pergamum. He was expected to remain on active service for 10 months out of every 12. At the end of his 10 months he received his pay. He received an allowance of money in lieu of rations during the 10 months, the allowance probably paid monthly.[3] He could hope to win a recognized bonus for distinguished conduct. His family was safeguarded against destitution if he should himself be killed. He enjoyed fiscal privileges while he remained in Eumenes' service, and when he quitted it (if he did so in a regular manner) he was at liberty to remove himself and his whole property elsewhere.

Two difficulties remain, and one an important one, namely our ignorance as to the term of service for which a new recruit contracted upon joining the army. Did he at once "sign on" for a fixed term of years, or was the contract renewed from year to year? The only possible indication lies in the phrase referred to above—ἀπεργος γένεσθαι. It occurs twice, in clause 3 and again in clause 5. If, as has been proposed above, clause 3 must be taken in close conjunction with clause 2, then the phrase in question must refer to soldiers finishing their military year of service. But in clause 5 the same phrase admittedly seems to denote soldiers who have fulfilled their contract. It would be presumptuous to assert dogmatically that the interpretation of

[1] *Insch. v. Perg.* i. 252.
[2] It will be noticed that this is the only mention of rations (apart from "the price of corn" above) in the inscription. Does the word σῖτος mean that they were given in goods and not in money? We have seen that in Egypt they were given partly in money, partly in corn, and there is nothing to prevent the same arrangement having been adopted in Pergamum: in which case clause 1 refers to the *adaeratio* of a part of the rations due, clause 7 to the rations paid in kind.
[3] Or perhaps, in lieu of *part* of his rations. See above.

PAY AND MAINTENANCE 287

clause 3 above *must* be the only correct one, and that therefore soldiers finishing their year of service are to be equated with soldiers who had fulfilled their contract—i.e. that the contract was a yearly one: nevertheless, that is the conclusion which, on the evidence of this particular document, seems the more probable.

The second difficulty arises out of two words occurring in Eumenes' oath to the soldiers: he refers to some of them as ἔμμισθοι and to others as ἄμισθοι. His oath begins: "I will be reconciled to Paramonus and the officers and the others τοῖς ἐμμίσθοις who are in Paramonus' command at Philetaireia under Ida, and to Arces and the soldiers in garrisons under him, and to Philonides and τοῖς ἀμίσθοις who have conspired, to these and all who belong to them: also to Polylaus and the officers and all the other soldiers in his command at Attaleia, foot, horse, and Trallians, as long as they are in my service". At first glance it appears as if there were two classes of soldiers in the army, those who were in receipt of pay (ἔμμισθοι), and those who were not. If this were really so, it would saddle us with a grave difficulty, the difficulty of accounting for the presence of unpaid soldiers in such an army as that of Eumenes would seem to have been. Fortunately that difficulty does not arise. Compare with the oath of Eumenes just quoted, the oath of the soldiers to Eumenes: "The oath which was taken by Paramonus and the officers and men in his command at Philetaireia under Ida, and Polylaus and the officers and men in his command at Attaleia, and Attinas the cavalry commander and his men and Oloichus and his Trallians". (The oath follows.) It will be noticed that all the persons mentioned in the soldiers' oath are accounted for in Eumenes' oath (the commanders of the cavalry and of the Trallians are not mentioned by name in Eumenes' oath, but they are no doubt included with their men, who are mentioned). But the oath of Eumenes includes also two other sets of people, namely Arces and his men (φρουροί) who are plainly soldiers; and Philonides and his ἄμισθοι. These latter can be quite well accounted for if we suppose that Philonides at the head of some irregular corps had associated himself with Paramonus and the mutineers at Philetaireia. The irregular corps could have consisted of native inhabitants (i.e. Mysians), or disbanded veterans, or even of disaffected friends of the king.[1] They were not regular soldiers, and so were not included in the soldiers' oath. Eumenes, however, did include them in his oath, and called them ἄμισθοι to distinguish them from the men of the Philetaireia command, the ἔμμισθοι of the regular army.

iii. *Carthage.*

Our third standing army is that of Carthage in the first Punic War. Polybius has a good account of the events leading up from the peace with Rome to the outbreak of the mercenaries' mutiny, which turned in the first place on the question of pay. The mercenaries of Carthage in Sicily had not been paid regularly each month, or even, perhaps, each year, so that when they assembled in Africa at the end of the war there were due to them considerable arrears of pay, always referred to as τὰ προσοφειλόμενα τῶν ὀψωνίων or an equivalent.[2] As to their ration-allowances we are not fully informed. Clearly, during the years of continuous warfare, they must have received regular rations in some form or other. For the time which they spent in Africa waiting for their pay to be prepared, they received each a gold stater—εἰς τὰ κατεπείγοντα χρυσοῦν—which must have been their σιτηρέσιον:[3] the Carthaginians then provided ἀγοραί, and in their eagerness to conciliate them, allowed them to fix their own prices for the commodities they required.[4] But there was some trouble, too, about ration-money (σιταρχίαι, etc.). As the mercenaries became more and more irritated by the dilatory pusillanimity of the Carthaginians (who actually tried to beg off a part of the money which they admittedly owed as pay),[5] they began to make extravagant demands, and among them "that in respect of the ration-money due to them over a considerable period of time they ought to receive the highest value which had been

---

[1] The last words of the soldiers' oath quoted above imply that the mutiny had been abetted in high quarters.
[2] Pol. i. 66. 1 sqq.; 67. 1; 72. 6; ὀψωνιασμός—69. 7; 72. 5. For the antecedents of the mutiny, cf. pp. 217 sqq.
[3] *Ibid.* 66. 7.
[4] *Ibid.* 68. 4 sqq., σπουδάζοντες ἐξιλάσασθαι τὴν ὀργὴν αὐτῶν τάς τε τῶν ἐπιτηδείων ἀγορὰς ἐκπέμποντες δαψιλεῖς ἐπώλουν, καθὼς ἐκεῖνοι βούλοιντο καὶ τάττοιεν τὰς τιμάς....
[5] *Ibid.* 66. 5; 67. 1.

PAY AND MAINTENANCE 289

reached in the course of the war ".[1] The question is obscured by a very legitimate doubt on our part as to whether there *was* in reality any ration-money due to the mercenaries at all. Obviously they must have received it as they needed it, and Polybius makes it clear that this was among the more exorbitant of their demands. The truth may be that they had received their ration-money at regular intervals, but that it varied from time to time according to the fluctuations in commodity prices, due perhaps to the state of war as well as to the ordinary causes. The mercenaries now, in their grasping mood, preferred that all their past ration-allowances for the whole period of service should have been reckoned at the highest prices touched during the war (i.e. supposing that an infantryman's allowance over 6 months varied as follows: 12 drachmae, 15d., 17d., 18d., 20d., 17d., amounting in all to 99d.; if, as the mercenaries demanded, the whole 6 months were reckoned at the highest rate of 20d., giving a total of 120d., the sum of 21 drachmae was still owing). This was of course a monstrous imposition, and if it was actually attempted it was very properly refused. It is interesting chiefly as proving that the *adaeratio* of ration-allowances was the rule in the West, as it was in Egypt and in Pergamum. The only other fact of interest which emerges from the quarrel has to do with allowances for horses. The mercenaries demanded the value of such of their horses as had been killed in the war. This too was one of their preposterous demands, and was likewise refused; which suggests that Carthage had supplied her mercenaries with horses as we have seen it done in Egypt. A word in conclusion should perhaps be said of Polybius' use here of the word σιταρχία, which should mean ration-allowance. He uses it twice, and in the second case it carries the right meaning, referring to the προσοφειλομένη σιτομετρία which the mercenaries tried to extort.[2] In the first case, however, it seems to be equivalent to ὀψώνιον which occurs several times immediately before and after it.[3] This is perhaps another indication that σιταρχία was used in a more general sense than the other words

---

[1] Pol. i. 68. 8, τῆς προσοφειλομένης σιτομετρίας ἐκ πλείονος χρόνου τὴν μεγίστην γεγονυῖαν ἐν τῷ πολέμῳ τιμὴν ἔφασκον αὐτοὺς δεῖν κομίζεσθαι.
[2] *Ibid.* 70. 3.
[3] *Ibid.* 66. 6; cf. *id.* v. 50. 1 sqq., for another doubtful use of σιταρχία, where either translation will make sense of the passage.

290   HELLENISTIC MERCENARIES

denoting payments of rations or ration-money (σιτομετρία, σιτώνιον, σιτηρέσιον, etc.; cf. p. 275).[1] It remains to add that the evidence for the pay of Athenian soldiers in the garrisons of Attica is scanty, but presents few difficulties, so far as it goes. One inscription (210 B.C.) shows that at that date the soldiers received an ὀψώνιον certainly, and probably a σιτώνιον or σιτηρέσιον also (σῖτόν τε παρατιθέμενος ἐξ ἑτοίμου ὅπως ἔχωσιν ὡς λυσιτελέστατον): and one particular commander gave προδόματα so that the men could clothe themselves adequately (προδιδοὺς ἀργύριον εἰς ἐσθῆτα).[2] But from earlier inscriptions it appears that σῖτος was paid in kind: one hears of granaries built for the garrison at Sunium,[3] and of coupons (ἐκκλησιαστικά) issued to soldiers at Eleusis, which were evidently to be presented when a soldier received his allowance.[4] The same inscription relating to the garrison at Sunium shows that arms were provided by the State. From Erythrae comes evidence that Ptolemaic mercenaries there received probably σιτηρέσιον and ὀψώνιον.[5] At Palaimagnesia near

[1] The pay of the Roman army is summarized by Polybius, and makes an interesting comparison: Pol. vi. 39. 12 sqq., Ὀψώνιον δ' οἱ μὲν πεζοὶ λαμβάνουσι τῆς ἡμέρας δύο ὀβολούς, οἱ δὲ ταξίαρχοι διπλοῦν, οἱ δ' ἱππεῖς δραχμήν. σιτομετροῦνται δ' οἱ μὲν πεζοὶ πυρῶν 'Αττικοῦ μεδίμνου δύο μέρη μάλιστά πως, οἱ δ' ἱππεῖς κριθῶν μὲν ἑπτὰ μεδίμνους εἰς τὸν μῆνα, πυρῶν δὲ δύο, τῶν δὲ συμμάχων οἱ μὲν πεζοὶ τὸ ἴσον, οἱ δ' ἱππεῖς πυρῶν μὲν μέδιμνον ἕνα καὶ τρίτον μέρος, κριθῶν δὲ πέντε. δίδοται δὲ τοῖς μὲν συμμάχοις τοῦτ' ἐν δωρεᾷ. τοῖς δὲ Ῥωμαίοις τοῦ τε σίτου καὶ τῆς ἐσθῆτος, κἂν τινος ὅπλου προσδεηθῶσι, πάντων τούτων ὁ ταμίας τὴν τεταγμένην τιμὴν ἐκ τῶν ὀψωνίων ὑπολογίζεται.
This may be supposed to refer to the Roman army at least as late as 150 B.C., which means that the Romans were still very backward in the amenities of the camp. (One wonders if their defeated competitors spoke of "sweated labour"!) The outstanding characteristics are: 1. ὀψώνιον: a very low rate indeed (cf. pp. 302 sqq.). 2. σῖτος: still paid in kind. (a) The allies, who received it in addition to ὀψώνιον, were in the position of, say, Athenian soldiers in the Peloponnesian War. (b) The Romans themselves, who had the value of their rations deducted from their ὀψώνιον, were in a very poor position: one never hears of any Greek soldiers, receiving pay at all, who surrendered part of it to pay for the rations they had received.
[2] *I.G.*[2] ii. 1304. 31 sqq.   [3] *Ibid.* 1281. 3 sqq. (*ca.* 266 B.C.).
[4] *Ibid.* 1272. 9 sqq. (280 B.C.; cf. W.W. Tarn, in *J.H.S.* 54 (1934), pp. 30 sqq.), ...πολλὴν σπουδὴν πεποίηται περὶ τὴν τοῦ σίτου δόσιν καὶ τῶν ἐκκλησιαστικῶν τῶν διδομένων ἐπὶ τὸν σῖτον. 1264. 5 sqq. (300 B.C.) appears also to refer to σῖτος in kind.
[5] Ditt. *Syll.*[3] i. 410. 16 sqq.; the restoration of these lines is probably right, but I cannot see exactly what they mean—Φροντίσαντες δὲ τῶν τοῖς παρ' Ἑρμοκράτει ταττομένοις διαγραφέντων χρημάτων ὑπ' Ἀθη[ναίου, καὶ τῶν τοῖς Πτολε]μαϊκοῖς προσοφειλομένων ε[ἰς σιτηρέσιον, τοῖς δὲ μισθο]φόροις τῶν ὀψωνίων ἐκ πλείονος λειπόντων, ...

PAY AND MAINTENANCE 291

Smyrna a Seleucid garrison got ὀψώνιον and probably rations in kind.[1]

So much light can be thrown upon the methods of paying a standing army. Other evidence which is forthcoming from scattered sources illustrates the procedure in actual warfare, and confirms in the main what has already been noticed. The first necessity was to feed the army while it was fighting in the field: rations or their equivalent in money must be distributed in advance. In Achaea Philopoemen ensured that when the citizen army was mobilized it should take the field with provisions for ten days, half in food, half in money.[2] In the Macedonian army under Philip V the rations may have been paid monthly—we twice hear of "rations for thirty days".[3] In the field it must have been very common for the allowances to be paid not in cash but in kind. In Aetolia Philip V used the produce of the conquered countryside,[4] but in a friendly country food was to be paid for. Whether the payment was made by the commander to contracting authorities, or by the individual soldiers to private vendors, it is usually quite impossible to say, though we hear of Philip V's paying for Magnesian figs with a town which he handed over to the city of Magnesia.[5] But in the majority of cases where ἀγοραί are mentioned, there is every likelihood that the soldiers paid for their goods with ration-money given out by their employers.[6] Even in a hostile country, it was obviously a bad policy to allow an army to loot privately.[7] Eumenes of Cardia in Cappadocia,[8] and Philip in Aetolia, plundered systematically in order to supply their men with what was no more than their due, and although in special cases, such as the capture of an enemy's camp or of a rebel city, soldiers may have received

---

[1] *O.G.I.S.* i. 229. 106 sqq., τά τε μετρήματα καὶ τὰ ὀψώνια τἆλλα....
[2] Pol. xvi. 36. 1 sqq., ἔχοντας τὰ ὅπλα καὶ πενθ' ἡμερῶν ἐφόδια καὶ πεντ' ἀργύριον. Cf. *id.* frag. 218, apud Suidas, *s.v.* σῖτα. Ὅτι Φιλοποίμην μετὰ δευτέραν ἡμέραν ἀπὸ τῆς πρὸς πόλεμον ἐξόδου παρήγγειλε τὰ δύο σῖτα τρία ποιεῖν, ὅτε βούλοιτο μίαν ἡμέραν προσλαβεῖν, ποτὲ δὲ τὰ δύο τέτταρα.
[3] *Id.* iv. 63. 10; *id.* frag. 75, apud Suidas, *s.v.* σιτομετρεῖν.
[4] *Ibid.* Cf. Diod. xxviii. 5, where he is said, in his need of supplies, to have ravaged the territory of Pergamum up to the very gates of the capital city.
[5] Pol. xvi. 24. 9.
[6] E.g. *id.* xi. 34. 10 and 12; xxviii. 10. 4.
[7] Hamilcar Barca did not allow his soldiers to plunder in Sicily (Diod. xxiv. 9). [8] Plut. *Eum.* 8. 5.

opportunities for private gain (as the Jewish mercenaries of Demetrius II are said to have enriched themselves at the sack of Antioch),[1] it is likely that a system of bonuses or στέφανοι would be preferred by a wise commander. The most obvious occasion for a bonus was as a reward for something well done, and as such it figured in the promises of Cyrus the Younger and the Thracian king Seuthes, and in the performance of Jason of Pherae and Alexander.[2] But it was used, apparently, in another sense too, namely as an incentive to doing something well. Thus there are several cases known of commanders distributing what was probably extra pay, or if not that then certainly pay in advance, on the eve of some critical engagement.[3] Another form which it took was that of a consideration in advance paid to soldiers upon their first entering a new service (πρόδομα, here = *aurum tironarium*?). Scopas the Aetolian, when he sailed from Egypt to Greece in order to recruit mercenaries, took with him large sums of money for the preliminary payments, and the picture of the same procedure in the *Miles Gloriosus* makes it probable that it was a custom already well established early in the third century.[4] But it is found at its subtlest in an agreement between the captured town of Theangela and its captor (late fourth century).[5] Theangela was by its position almost impregnable, and it was probably through famine, and the consequent pressure brought to bear upon its citizens by the mercenary garrison, that its gates were thrown open to the besieger Eupolemus. (The occasion may even have been an act of treachery by some of the mercenaries.) At all events the mercenaries inside had clearly deserved well of Eupolemus, who undertook to pay the wages due to them from their old employers

[1] Josephus, *Ant.* xiii. 129 sqq.; 1 Macc. 11. 38 and 44 sqq.
[2] Pp. 267, 273, 299.
[3] E.g. Eumenes of Cardia—6 months' pay, Diod. xix. 15. 5; Antigonus—3 months' pay, *id.* xx. 108. 2; Sosibius—2 months' pay, Pol. xv. 25. 11; Antiochus IV—1 year's pay, 1 Macc. 3. 27—perhaps exaggerated?
[4] Pol. xv. 25. 16; *M.G.* 72 sqq.

       M.G.—Videtur tempus esse ut eamus in forum
            Ut in tabellis quos consignari hic heri
            Latrones, ibus dinumerem stipendium.

The Greek play Ἀλάζων, the prototype of *M.G.*, was written probably about 287 B.C. Perseus, too, paid a small sum in advance to the Bastarnae: Livy 44. 26 sqq.; Appian, *Mac.* 18. 4 sqq.

[5] M. Rostovtzeff, in *R.E.A.* 1931, pp. 5 sqq.

PAY AND MAINTENANCE 293

in Theangela. But one mercenary captain seems to have deserved especially well, so that he and some of his men were taken into Eupolemus' service, and received, in addition to their overdue wages, a donative (δόμα) of 2 months' pay on Eupolemus' own account, the bonus here serving the double purpose of reward for past and incentive to future services.

Apart from such cases, however, the pay proper (ὀψώνιον) was not paid in advance; in practice it may not even have been paid by the month, but more probably at the end of the year's campaigning. The Pergamene inscription discussed above lent grounds for believing that the contract of the *regular* mercenary (i.e. in a standing army) may have been a yearly one; it also defined the campaigning season, and, most probably, insisted upon a prompt distribution of pay when the season was over (p. 284). But troops could also be hired for short periods to meet an emergency, and here the procedure certainly seems to have been to engage them for a campaign upon definite terms of pay, which was not forthcoming until the campaign had been completed. (All casualties were thus a clear financial gain to the employer.) Antigonus Gonatas hired some Gauls for an unknown period at the rate of 1 Macedonian stater (= rather more than 20 Attic drachmae) per man. The Gauls did their fighting, and when pay day came the sum due to them was 30 talents. Were it a question of Greek soldiers one would say without hesitation that the pay day must have come after only one month's fighting (this supposing a very plausible rate of pay for Greeks).[1] But it is quite likely that the Gauls, new to the game, were induced to fight at a very cheap rate, and that 1 stater represents each man's pay not for one month but for a campaign of several months. Perseus certainly hired his Bastarnae for a campaign, and was prepared to pay no more than a small percentage of their pay in advance (perhaps the σιτηρέσιον).[2] In the same way he paid Cotys' Thracians at the end of their campaign.[3] Indeed this was plainly the employer's most convenient time for paying soldiers, since it freed him from the encumbrance of large sums of money in his baggage. For the soldiers themselves it may have been less convenient, since it provided greater opportunities for delay or

[1] Polyaen. iv. 6. 17; cf. pp. 302 sqq.
[2] Livy 44. 26 sqq. [3] *Id.* 42. 67. 5.

default. The most notable example is that of Carthage at the end of the first Punic War; but even a Seleucid king could find himself embarrassed by the demands of his army for pay overdue (Antiochus III in 221 B.C.).[1] Among the small employers the dilemma was probably common: when Theangela surrendered to Eupolemus the mercenaries were owed some of them 7 months', others 4 months', pay.[2]

3. Rates of Pay

It remains to consider the *amount* of pay, and here the tradition treats us badly, for whereas there is some little information about the pay of citizen troops, that of mercenaries remains largely a matter of conjecture. The topic is one that must be approached through the chronological method, and with an eye to the definitions of technical terms attempted above (on the one hand σιτηρέσιον, etc., on the other μισθός and ὀψώνιον).

In the Peloponnesian War Athenian hoplites at Potidea are said to have received a drachma a day each, with another drachma in addition for their servants.[3] By the terms of the Athens-Argos treaty, hoplites and other infantry were to receive 3 Aeginetan (= 4 Athenian) obols a day σῖτος, and cavalry double that amount.[4] Confining ourselves to hoplites only, we are likely to guess at once that the reason for the larger sum at Potidea is that it includes μισθός as well as σιτηρέσιον (or σῖτος as Thucydides might have called it). If we assume that hoplites at Potidea took the same σιτηρέσιον as that proposed in the Athens-Argos treaty (4 Athenian obols), and that their servants took a σιτηρέσιον of 2 or 3 obols (and no μισθός), there remains a sum of 5 obols or 1 drachma as a hoplite's daily μισθός. The purpose of this calculation is to try to obtain some basis for comparison with our evidence for a mercenary's wage at about the same period.

[1] Pol. v. 50. 1 sqq.
[2] Cf. also Pol. iv. 60. 2; v. 30. 5 sqq. (Achaean League).
[3] Thuc. iii. 17. 4: a suspected passage; but I hope to show that this is not an impossibly high rate.
[4] *Id.* v. 47. 6. Schulthess (P.-W. *s.v.* σιτηρέσιον, p. 384) sees in this σῖτος, "offenbar Verpflegungsgeld und Sold zugleich bezeichnet". I cannot follow him so far, for this seems to put too great a strain upon the capacity of the word σῖτος, which is sufficiently strained by being used for ration-money only: and the word μισθός was in use long before this date, cf. p. 265.

PAY AND MAINTENANCE 295

First, we hear of some Thracian peltasts hired by Athens in 414 B.C. They came too late to sail to Syracuse with Demosthenes, and were considered too expensive a luxury to be kept for the war in Attica: "for they received a drachma a day each".[1] There is no indication as to what the drachma a day includes. If it includes μισθός only (in which case they received their σῖτος in kind), then their composite pay (μ. + σ.) was equivalent to that of the Athenian hoplites at Potidea, and they were an expensive luxury indeed. If, as is perhaps the more likely, a drachma a day represents their μισθός and σιτηρέσιον together, they were receiving two-thirds of what the hoplites at Potidea received, and that was probably more than Thracian peltasts were worth.[2] Fortunately we are able to see exactly what a Greek hoplite was worth to Cyrus fourteen years later. The μισθός of the "Cyreians" was originally 1 daric a month (about 25 Attic drachmae = 5 obols a day): and the σῖτος was given in kind in addition.[3] And since this was the rate offered to them by their subsequent employers, including the Spartan commander Thibron, it becomes probable that it was the recognized rate for Greek mercenary hoplites about 400 B.C.: the *lochagoi* received double (διμοιρία), and the *strategoi* quadruple pay (τετραμοιρία).[4]

[1] Thuc. vii. 27. 2.
[2] Aristoph. *Acharn.* 159 sqq. may be ignored as serious evidence either for the pay or for the military value of Thracian mercenaries.

ΘΕΟ. τούτοις ἐάν τις δύο δραχμὰς μισθὸν διδῷ,
καταπελτάσονται τὴν Βοιωτίαν ὅλην.
ΔΙ. τοισδὶ δύο δραχμὰς τοῖς ἀπεψωλημένοις;

The "2 drachmae" is a joke directed perhaps partly against the rapacity of Thracians and partly against the lavish expenditure of Athenians on military pay. The last line of the quotation may indicate a genuine conviction that, for fighting, an Athenian soldier was likely to be more useful than a Thracian.

[3] Xen. *Anab.* i. 3. 21; Cyrus raised the rate to 1½ darics a month to persuade the soldiers to follow him to the East (*ibid.*).
Schulthess (*loc. cit.* p. 386) takes this rate of pay of the "Cyreians" to include σιτηρέσιον throughout, as well as μισθός. The arguments against this view are set out above (p. 266); in brief, if μισθός included σιτηρέσιον, how did the soldiers live, since μισθός was not paid regularly (and in the contract of Seuthes μισθός and σῖτα are mentioned separately)? But not the weakest argument is that after all Xenophon was in a better position for knowing the truth of the matter than either Schulthess or myself; he was a practical soldier and one of the "Cyreians", and I for my part am willing to believe that when he wrote μισθός he meant μισθός, and neither more nor less.

[4] *Ibid.* v. 6. 23; vii. 3. 10; 6. 1.

For the fourth century before Alexander the information is not so good, being limited to two pieces of evidence both of which are to be used with care. In 383 B.C. Sparta made it possible for cities of the Peloponnesian League to contribute money instead of soldiers, at the rate of 3 Aeginetan (4 Attic) obols per man (and four times that amount for a cavalryman).[1] That the intention of the Spartans was to recruit mercenaries to take the place of their allies is perfectly plain. But it is impossible to be certain whether the 4 Attic obols per man to be paid by the allies was equivalent to the contemporary rate of pay for mercenaries, or to the contemporary rate for citizen soldiers of the League—if indeed the two rates were different. It is important to notice that Xenophon calls the 4 obols μισθός, and here too it is to be assumed that he meant exactly what he said, and that σῖτος was still paid in kind, as it was to the League army in the Peloponnesian War. It follows then that the rate of composite pay (μ.+σ.) in 383 was perhaps an Attic drachma or 7 obols a day, a little less than the pay of the "Cyreians"; this was the rate for citizen hoplites or for mercenaries, or perhaps for both, for there is no intrinsic reason why the two rates should not have been the same. Indeed our second piece of evidence suggests that they can have been the same, though this too cannot be proved conclusively. Demosthenes, in the passage quoted previously, proposed to pay a σιτηρέσιον of 10 drachmae a month (2 obols a day) to a force which was to consist of Athenian citizens and mercenaries together: the war itself was to provide the μισθός ἐντελής.[2] Mercenaries and Athenians were to receive the same σιτηρέσιον, but it does not necessarily follow that they were to receive the same μισθός, though it is perhaps likely. Nor does it follow that because the σιτηρέσιον was so low, the μισθός was to be correspondingly low, for it is clear from the context that the σιτηρέσιον of 2 obols was an extraordinary act of economy, and it may be that the whole point of the proposal was to economize on the σιτηρέσιον, which had to be paid out of cash in hand, and to make up the deficiency by means of a

---

[1] Xen. Hell. v. 2. 21, ἀργύριόν τε ἀντ' ἀνδρῶν ἐξεῖναι διδόναι τῇ βουλομένῃ τῶν πόλεων τριώβολον Αἰγιναῖον κατὰ ἄνδρα· ἱππέας τε εἴ τις παρέχοι, ἀντὶ τεττάρων ὁπλιτῶν τὸν μισθὸν τῷ ἱππεῖ δίδοσθαι.

[2] Demosth. iv. 21 and 28; cf. pp. 271-2.

PAY AND MAINTENANCE 297

higher μισθός, which was to be paid out of future profits. One can safely say that mercenaries of Athens about 350 B.C. received at least 4 obols a day composite pay (μ.+σ.); but a composite pay of a drachma a day may be nearer the truth, though this must be regarded as a maximum figure. This means that between 400 and 350 B.C. the rate has fallen, perhaps as much as from 8 to 4, and certainly as much as from 7 to 5 or 6 obols; a development which is to be remembered when we approach the question of pay in the army of Alexander, because there is no direct evidence for the pay of mercenaries, and one is reduced to making some rather insecure deductions from the known rate for Macedonian soldiers.

A start is to be made from the fragmentary Attic inscription recording the rate of pay of Alexander's hypaspists: ὑπασπιστῆι δραχμὴν καὶ τοῖς... | ἑκάστης τῆς ἡμέρας· is almost the only intelligible fragment that has been saved from the wreck.[1] That seems clear as far as it goes; a hypaspist is to receive a drachma a day. But what does this drachma a day represent: σιτηρέσιον, or μισθός, or both together? It would be absurd to be dogmatic on the strength of isolated words and phrases in this inscription; but it may be pointed out that the words ἔ]χειν σῖτο[ν (l. 4), and ...σιν οἴκοθεν μὲν ἔχειν σ[ῖτον (l. 7), and [δέ]κα ἡμερῶν δόντας σῖτον ἀποπέμπ... (l. 12), must have some bearing on the ὑπασπιστῆι δραχμὴν, etc. (l. 9). If we assume that the *whole* of this fragment is devoted to the question of σῖτος and nothing else, it will follow that the hypaspist's drachma a day is his ration-allowance; but there is the alternative, that the σῖτος here is rations in kind, in which case the drachma a day will be the hypaspist's μισθός, and this is the more probable (below).[2] Finally it is possible that the drachma a day includes both his μισθός and σῖτος (in money) together; this seems the

---

[1] *I.G.*[2] ii. 1. 329, ll. 9–10.
[2] For three possible reasons: (1) I think it unlikely that at this date σῖτος could mean ration-money, because by this time the words σιτηρέσιον and σιταρχία were well established (cf. pp. 267 sqq.). (2) A ration-allowance of a drachma a day would be very high indeed. (3) Alexander must have counted on making the war in Asia pay for itself, and in that event σῖτος in kind was perhaps the more convenient form, since the country could supply it easily. Certainly later, in the Far East, anything except σῖτος in kind seems almost out of the question (see below).

least likely of the three possibilities, though it is not out of the question.[1]

This is our only guide towards finding the rate at which Alexander's mercenaries were paid: if his citizen soldiers (including perhaps the troops of the League as well as his own Macedonians) received a drachma a day μισθός and their rations in kind, what, are we to think, did his mercenaries receive? The evidence of Demosthenes makes it almost certain that the rate for mercenaries had fallen by 350 B.C. There is no reason to assume that by 335 B.C. it had fallen still further, but perhaps it may be assumed that at least it had not risen. In the case of Demosthenes' mercenaries, one deduced, given a σιτηρέσιον of 2 obols a day, that they must have got at least 4 obols and at most 1 drachma (μ. + σ.). The μισθός alone therefore was probably between 2 and 4 obols a day. Is a μισθός of, say, 3 obols a day for Alexander's mercenaries impossible, given a μισθός for citizen soldiers of a drachma a day? Probably not, for the general statements of Isocrates and Demosthenes relating to the economic conditions of the period, which were reflected in the great increase in the numbers of mercenary soldiers, make it likely enough that mercenaries were now to be found who were willing to serve at a lower rate than that of citizen soldiers. How much lower, it is impossible to say without more information; but if one were compelled to estimate a mercenary's pay with Alexander, it might be safest to say that it consisted of 3 or 4 obols a day μισθός, and σῖτος probably in kind.

Hazardous though these calculations may be, they are less dangerous than others which have been made, based on two passages in the literary sources for Alexander's campaigns,

[1] Reasons (1) and (3) of the previous note are valid here too. And also I think it more likely (though I may be wrong) that, if μισθός and σῖτος are both being discussed in this fragment, they would be kept separate throughout: they would be paid at different times, and once their respective amounts had been defined separately, there could be no good purpose served by performing in stone a very simple sum of addition which anyone could do in his head within five seconds. When Thucydides speaks of "a drachma a day" he may very well mean μ. + σ.; but when an official document mentions a rate of payment it is far more likely to mean either one or the other. I do not know of any official document that confuses the two by adding them together, though there are two third-century inscriptions which appear to use one word for the two things (pp. 302 sqq.); on the other hand, numerous official documents distinguish the two things very clearly (p. 275 etc.).

PAY AND MAINTENANCE 299

neither of which can tell us anything more about the pay of mercenaries, though one of them does establish that the mercenaries of the original expeditionary force were not forgotten when Alexander reached Babylon and was able to distribute bonuses to the army (their bonus amounted to two months' pay —διμήνου μισθοφοραῖς).[1] This ought to mean two months' μισθός, and if one was right in assuming that Alexander paid σῖτος in kind (above), then this is what it must mean. The assumption cannot be verified, for we are told nothing of Alexander's arrangements for commissariat, except for one notice of an ἀγορά provided to the army on its return march from India.[2] So far as can be seen, ἀγορά usually implies payment of money in return for commodities, but in this case there is no indication as to who paid the money for the food, though the food certainly changed hands. It is possible that it was bought by officers and then distributed to the army as σῖτος (rations in kind), since there is an earlier example of this procedure (Timotheus at Samos).[3] One hears nowhere of the payment of σιτηρέσιον, and certainly it seems that the most convenient way of feeding the army would have been by requisitioning supplies from the country, supplies which might be paid for, or not, according to the circumstances.

[1] Diod. xvii. 64. 6 (cf. Curt. v. 1. 45) mentions these bonuses distributed by Alexander at Babylon: to the "Companion" cavalry 6 minae each, to the allied cavalry 5, to the Macedonian infantry 2, and to the mercenaries two months' μισθός. Arrian vii. 23. 3 shows that in the Macedonian infantry there were three grades of pay: (1) common pay, (2) 10 staters (δεκαστάτηρος), (3) double pay (διμοιρίτης). (Cf. however, K. Grote, p. 82, for a different view, though I think he mistranslates the passage.) The Diodorus passage proves nothing, except that the sum of 6 minae was *not* two months' μισθός for the "Companions", and similarly the other bonuses were not two months' μισθός for anybody, except that of the mercenaries, which *was* two months' μισθός, as Diodorus' source has taken the trouble to explain, obviously because in this respect it differed from all the other bonuses. I think this is the only reasonable interpretation. Nevertheless in Kromayer u. Veith (*op. cit.* p. 111 n. 3) the writer assumes that all the bonuses represent two months' pay; he thus arrives at amazingly high rates for everybody, and incidentally falls foul of the Arrian passage which I have cited above. In reality Arrian merely confirms what we suspect already from our inscription, *I.G.*[2] ii. 1. 329 (which is ignored by Kromayer u. Veith). Arrian says there were three grades of pay, and tells us the amount of the middle grade— 10 staters = 40 drachmae a month (the staters here must certainly be silver): the inscription says that a hypaspist is to get a drachma a day = 30 drachmae a month. If we assume this last to be common pay, we conclude that the three grades were 30, 40 and 60 drachmae respectively.

[2] Arrian vi. 23. 6. [3] [Aristot.] *Econ.* ii. 24. 1350 *b*; cf. p. 268.

It is difficult to think that Alexander carried vast sums of money about with him during his Indian campaign, and in fact it is certain that he did not pay μισθός regularly by the month, for when he returned from India and discharged 10,000 Macedonian veterans, he had arrears of pay to make up;[1] and the same considerations may have made it impossible for him to feed the army except with rations in kind. Nevertheless, the mercenaries of the field army probably made as good a livelihood as mercenaries could hope to make, for if μισθός came irregularly it came in full in the end, and there were handsome bonuses by way of interest.[2] But perhaps the quickest road to wealth was by plunder. Plutarch says that the treasure of Damascus made the whole army rich: the Thessalian cavalry were sent in advance to occupy the city and so got first pick as a reward for their splendid fighting at Ipsus.[3] Probably all towns were plundered that were taken after a siege, and there were sieges enough. It is said that the plunder of Ecbatana alone, exclusive of what Alexander reserved for himself and for the army's pay, exceeded 20,000 talents.[4] Finally, Alexander is said to have paid out a further 20,000 talents in freeing the whole army of its debts.[5]

It is well known that Alexander's conquests were responsible for an economic upheaval in the western Mediterranean. With the release of gold long hoarded in the Persian treasuries, money became cheap, prices rose, and, for a time at least, wages rose also.[6] The famous Epidaurus inscription recording the Greek League re-formed by Demetrius (303–302 B.C.) contains a clause which stipulates the fines to be paid by a city failing to produce its levy of soldiers to the League army: the fines are calculated on a basis of money per soldier, and it has been shown, with probability, that they represent ten times the pay of the soldier in question.[7] If this is right, the pay of a citizen hoplite in

---

[1] Arrian vii. 12. 1 sqq.—τὴν μισθοφορὰν...τοῦ ἑξήκοντος ἤδη χρόνου. Also at Ecbatana (330 B.C.), when he discharged some of the Greek allies (*id.* iii. 9. 6—τὸν μισθὸν...ἐντελῆ τὸν ξυντεταγμένον; Plut. *Alex.* 12; Diod. xvii. 74. 3).
[2] Arrian iii. 19. 6; v. 26. 8; vii. 12. 1 sqq. (cf. Diod. xvii. 64. 6; 74. 3).
[3] Plut. *Alex.* 24.   [4] Diod. xvii. 74. 5.
[5] Arrian vii. 5. 1 sqq.; Diod. xvii. 109. 2 (nearly 10,000 talents); Plut. *Alex.* 70 (9870 talents).
[6] Cf. G. Glotz, *Journal des Savants*, 1913, pp. 207 sqq.
[7] G. A. Wilhelm, *S.B. Ak. Wien*, 1911 (165), 6, pp. 34 sqq. (*Attische Urkunden*, i); cf. Xen. *Hell.* v. 2. 21 sqq.

PAY AND MAINTENANCE 301

303 B.C. was 2 drachmae a day (of a cavalryman 5 drachmae, and of a ψιλός 1 drachma).[1] Unfortunately there is again absolutely nothing to show whether this is composite pay (μ. + σ.), or μισθός only.[2] To try to determine a plausible rate of composite pay here, by calculating what would be a plausible increase since 335 B.C., would be extremely risky even if the composite pay in 335 were certain—and it is not certain.[3] Here at least, calculation becomes a sheer waste of time, and it is best to leave a choice of alternatives to the preference of the individual.[4] Whatever may have been the rate for citizen soldiers, the rate for mercenaries can hardly have been higher, but there may have been a *rapprochement* of the two rates, because the wars of the Successors created an unparalleled demand for mercenaries, and, especially, it must have been part of the policy of Antigonus and Ptolemy to attract Greek soldiers to Asia and Egypt. In the circumstances it is difficult to take seriously the "4 obols a day", a phrase which occurs twice in plays of Menander, and which has been supposed to refer to the pay of mercenaries.[5] And similarly the τετρωβόλου βίος of Eustathius, though he certainly intends it as a reference to the pay of mercenaries at *some* period,

---

[1] *I.G.*[2] iv. 1. 68, ll. 95-9; and Wilhelm, *loc. cit.*

[2] The argument used above (p. 298 n. 1), that official documents probably never confused the two component parts by adding them together, does not apply here, because this official document is not itself concerned with establishing a rate of pay—it is merely a piece of good fortune for us if we can deduce the rates of pay from it.

[3] P. 298, where the rate suggested is merely that which seems the most probable from the evidence available.

[4] The choice is, roughly, this: If the Alexander inscription does *not* include σῖτος in its rate of pay, the actual value of the composite pay may have been, say, 1½ drachmae a day (= 3 obols σῖτος). If it does include σῖτος, then the composite pay is a drachma a day. In the same way, if the Demetrius inscription does not include σῖτος, the composite pay may have been 3 drachmae a day (= 1d. σῖτος). If it does include σῖτος, the composite pay is 2 drachmae a day. Thus the increase may be (1) from 1½d. a day to 2d. a day or (2) from 1d. to 2d. or (3) from 1½d. to 3d. or (4) from 1d. to 3d. My own preference is for (1).

[5] By Parke, p. 233, using Men. *Olynthia* frag. 357 (Kock) apud Suidas, *s.v.* φέρειν, and *Circumtonsa* 189 sqq. The first of these texts refers to the year 314 B.C.

μετ' Ἀριστοτέλους γὰρ τέτταρας τῆς ἡμέρας
ὀβόλους φέρων.

But it is clear from Diod. xix. 68. 3 sqq. that Aristoteles is an Athenian ναύαρχος, and the man who is supposed to be "drawing 4 obols with

302 HELLENISTIC MERCENARIES

seems more appropriate to almost any other period than to this.[1] In the third century, just where one would hope and expect to find evidence establishing the pay of mercenaries for certain, the evidence in fact breaks down almost completely. All that can be done is to mention the information relating to citizen troops, which itself presents serious difficulties. Three inscriptions record rates of payment to citizen soldiers about the years 270, 228 and 200 B.C. The first is a treaty between the Aetolians and the Acarnanians providing for reciprocal military assistance in case of need. The reinforcements are to be maintained for the first 30 days by "the senders" (σιταρχούντω δὲ τοὺς ἀποστελλομένους στρατιώτας ἑκάτεροι τοὺς αὑτῶν ἀμερᾶν τριάκοντα): after the first 30 days by "the receivers" (οἱ μεταπεμψάμενοι...διδόντω τὰς σιταρχίας...), at the following rates: for a cavalryman, 1 Corinthian stater a day (= about 16 Attic obols); for a hoplite 12 Corinthian (= 8 Attic) obols; for a peltast (?) 9 C. (= 6 A.) obols; for a light-armed soldier 7 C. (= 4⅔ A.) obols.[2] A." is very likely an Athenian too, and not a mercenary: he may even be a rower.

The second text runs:

ΣΩΣΙΑΣ. πότερα νομίζετ᾿ οὐκ ἔχειν ἡμᾶς χολὴν
οὐδ᾿ ἄνδρας εἶναι;
ΔΑΟΣ. ναὶ μὰ Δία, τετρωβόλους.
ὅταν δὲ τετραδράχμοις τοιοῦτος συλλάβῃ,
ἢ ῥᾳδίως μαχούμεθ᾿ ὑμῖν.

If these figures are to be used as serious evidence, they must surely mean that the *cheapest* soldier got 4 obols a day (i.e. perhaps a ψιλός), and that the most expensive (an officer of some kind, or perhaps διμοιρίτης—cf. Men. *Adulat.* 28) got 4 drachmae. I do not see why the cheapest rate is to be attached to the ordinary mercenary.

[1] Eustathius, *ll.* 951; *Od.* 1405; cf. Schulthess in P.-W. *s.v.* σιτηρέσιον, who seems to apply the proverb to the late fourth century.
[2] Ditt. *Syll.*³ i. 421, ll. 35 sqq.; cf. G. A. Wilhelm, Ἀρχ. ἐφ. 1910, p. 147, and *loc. cit.* The three classes of infantry are τῷ τὰμ πανοπλίαν ἔχο[ντι; τῶι τὸ ἡμιθωράκιον ἔχοντι; and ψιλῶι (ll. 40 sqq.).

It will be noticed that the ratio of the rates of pay for cavalry, hoplites and light-armed, is very much the same here as in the inscription of 303 B.C.

The ratio of cavalry to hoplites varied in the course of time as follows: 421 B.C., 2:1 (Thuc. v. 47. 6); 383 B.C., 4:1 (Xen. *Hell.* v. 2. 21 sqq.); 351 B.C., 3:1 (Demosth. iv. 28, figures for σιτηρέσιον only); 303 B.C., 5:2; *ca.* 270 B.C., 2:1; 169 B.C., 2:1 (Livy 44. 26, Bastarnae). It is just possible that the very high ratio in 383 B.C. may reflect an increase in the value of cavalry (particularly scarce in the Peloponnese), as the best weapon against the new peltasts, who began to make their name about 10 years earlier; e.g. Xenophon's account of the famous engagement in which the Spartan *mora* was destroyed by peltasts, makes it clear that a good cavalry charge would have saved the situation (Xen. *Hell.* iv. 5. 16).

PAY AND MAINTENANCE 303

It is important to notice that the only payment mentioned is called σιταρχία. The second inscription represents a treaty between Antigonus Doson and the Cretan city of Hierapytna, in which Antigonus proposes to give 1 Alexander drachma (= 1 Attic drachma) to citizen soldiers of Hierapytna: the surviving fragment does not indicate whether this represents σιταρχία or ὀψώνιον or both together.[1] The third inscription again concerns Hierapytna, this time entering into an obligation to supply soldiers to Rhodes (about 200 B.C.).[2] The treaty tells us three important things: (1) The amount of money to be paid to the soldiers is 9 Rhodian (= about 8 Attic) obols, and 2 Rhodian drachmae for a ἡγεμών (ll. 25 sqq.). (2) This amount is almost certainly ὀψώνιον.[3] (3) The Hierapytnian contingent is allowed to consist half of mercenaries and half of citizens (ll. 19 sqq.). This last piece of information is really important, because it means that some mercenaries at this date could command an equal rate of pay with Cretan citizen soldiers, and it may perhaps be inferred that this was true of Greek mercenaries in general at the end of the third century. The slump in the market value of a Greek mercenary in the fourth century was thus not permanent. One inferred that it may have ceased with Alexander's conquests and the wars of the Successors; and now one may be reasonably confident that by 200 B.C. the recovery was complete. If the supply of Greeks was really beginning to run short by that date, this fact would go far to explain how the mercenary had regained the position that he had held two centuries earlier, before mercenary service had become a form of relief for economic necessity.

This part of the Rhodes-Hierapytna treaty may perhaps be thought satisfactory enough; but what is less satisfactory in it is the description of the money to be paid, especially if it is considered in relation to the Aetolia-Acarnania treaty described above. In a word, the Aetolia treaty of 272 B.C. provides for

---

[1] *B.C.H.* xiii. (1889); cf. Wilhelm, *loc. cit.*   [2] Ditt. *Syll.*³ ii. 581.
[3] ll. 25 sqq., which give the amount, do not indicate what the amount represents; but ll. 30 sqq. provide for a contingency in which the Hierapytnian soldiers are to be paid during the first 30 days not by Rhodes but by Hierapytna, and here the word used is ὀψώνια—παρεχόντων Ἱεραπύτνιοι τοῖς ἀποσταλεῖσι συμ|μάχοις τὰ ὀψώνια ἀμέρας τριάκοντα, τοῦ δὲ ὑπολοίπου χρόνου| διδόντων Ῥόδιοι καθὰ γέγραπται (= in ll. 25 sqq.).

citizen hoplites to be given 8 Attic obols a day σιταρχία: the Hierapytna treaty about seventy years later provides for citizen soldiers and mercenaries to be given about the same amount daily—but it is called ὀψώνιον. The two documents represent a very real difficulty, and it would be absurd (though not impossible) to try to explain them away by sophistry. It would be absurd to say that the rates of pay mentioned represent, in each case, only part (perhaps only *half*) of the full amount which was actually paid, for the rates as they stand are high enough, and the people who drafted the treaties were not perfect fools.[1] One could say, with some show of reason, that the Aetolians and Acarnanians may have called their composite pay σιταρχία from a desire to present a false show of patriotism by eliminating ὀψώνιον in name if not in effect; but this does not explain why the Rhodians and Hierapytnians should have gone out of their way to call their composite pay ὀψώνιον and eliminate σιταρχία! The fact is that there seems to be no good reason for believing that in these two treaties σιταρχία and ὀψώνιον do not mean precisely the same thing—composite pay.[2] Moreover this interpretation is supported by the inscription of Cos mentioned previously (p. 283), of almost the same date as this inscription of Hierapytna. At Cos the σιτηρέσιον of mercenaries was 16 drachmae a month (about 3 obols a day): if one is to assume any approximation of the rates of pay at Cos and at Hierapytna (a reasonable enough assumption in itself), then it is the 3 obol σιτηρέσιον of Cos which must be only half the full sum that a soldier received, and his composite pay must have represented at least 6 obols a day, presumably of Rhodian standard.[3]

It seems, then, impossible to explain away these two awkward pieces of evidence in these terms: here at least ὀψώνιον and σιταρχία both mean composite pay. Are we then to renounce the idea that there was ever any difference between the two? It is a matter of choice. If one is content to ignore the fundamental

---

[1] The treaty of Antigonus Doson and Hierapytna says simply, "Antigonus shall give to each man for each day 1 Alexander drachma", which must be composite pay—and is of lower value than the pay in the two treaties under consideration.
[2] E.g. especially the payments for the first 30 days—σιταρχούντω in the one, παρεχόντων τὰ ὀψώνια in the other.
[3] Paton and Hicks, 10.

PAY AND MAINTENANCE

difference in origin of σῖτος and μισθός (pp. 263 sqq.), and the examples of its practical working during the fourth century, and in the great majority of the Hellenistic documents, then the idea must be renounced by all means. But to do this would be to take one's stand upon what appear to be exceptions in order to deny that there was ever a rule. It will probably be thought safer to accept what appears to have been the rule, and to admit frankly that the exceptions *are* exceptions, and that the word σιταρχία may have been subject to a more elastic usage than other words with which one would expect it to be synonymous (σιτηρέσιον, etc.; cf. pp. 275–6, and p. 289).

The conclusion therefore is, that throughout the last seventy years of the third century the composite pay of a citizen soldier (perhaps in most cases a hoplite?), serving for a campaign abroad under the command of an allied government, may have varied between 6 and 8 Attic obols a day; and that by the end of the century at the latest the pay of a Greek mercenary had risen to the level of that of a citizen serving in those conditions.

There are also two literary texts which give rise to speculations as to the rate of pay of mercenaries serving the last two kings of Macedonia. In 218 B.C., when the army of Philip V in the Peloponnese consisted of 6000 Macedonians and 1200 mercenaries, his allies the Achaeans agreed to provide wages (μισθοδοτῆσαι) for part of the year, at the rate of 17 talents a month: it is certain that this sum did not include σιτηρέσιον also, because σῖτος was provided separately.[1] Now 17 talents divided equally among 7200 men would give each man a μισθός of about 14 drachmae and 1 obol a month (about 3 obols a day—of whatever standard), so that the *average* composite pay of this army (μ. + σ.) cannot have been worth more than a drachma a day.[2] This calculation may be right, in spite of the higher rate given in the third-century inscriptions; because Macedonians in the royal army may well have been paid a little less than allied citizen soldiers serving abroad, and because these mercenaries of Philip were probably barbarians, in which case they too probably received less than Greek citizens or mercenaries. This text may therefore

[1] Pol. v. 1. 11 sqq.; 2. 11.
[2] An average pay of 1 drachma might mean that the pay of an infantryman was worth about 5 obols (officers and cavalry got higher pay).

be taken as a useful confirmation of the inscriptions. The second text is much less satisfactory. In 171 B.C. Perseus hired from the Thracian king Cotys 1000 infantry and 1000 cavalry; but after 6 months they went back home again, and Cotys received from Perseus 200 talents, representing "6 months' pay for the cavalry".[1] This gives a rate of 200 drachmae a month for each horseman, a monstrously high rate for Thracian horse: indeed it becomes difficult to accept this text as it stands.[2]

Finally, the documents from Egypt, though they throw little further light on the amount of pay for mercenaries in general, are useful because they show the relative value of σιτώνιον and ὀψώνιον; but it is important to realize that they are evidence only for the procedure in one army and at one period. At Thebes about 130 B.C. a troop of mercenary horse received 56 *artabai* of wheat as a month's σιτώνιον, and 2785 copper drachmae ὀψώνιον; which makes the value of the σιτώνιον about three-and-a-quarter times that of the ὀψώνιον.[3] Similarly the ἐπίγονοι at Memphis in the second century took μετρήματα of nearly six times the value of their ὀψώνιον, and some of them got a σιτώνιον in addition which increased the ratio to exactly 6 : 1.[4] It is impossible to explain with certainty why this ratio

---

[1] Livy 42. 67. 5.

[2] 200 talents as 6 months' pay for the whole force would be a little more reasonable. In the Aetolia-Acarnania treaty a horseman got 16 Attic obols a day, a peltast 6, and the same proportion in this case would give a horseman 145 drachmae a month, a peltast about 55d.; even this would be very high, if the drachmae were Attic. Altogether, I do not think this text is to be accepted as good evidence.

Livy's information (44. 26) about the proposed pay of Perseus' Bastarnae (169 B.C.) cannot help us much, because we are not told the term of service. Perseus is supposed to have promised 10 gold staters to each horseman, and 5 to each infantryman, = 24 silver drachmae a month for the infantry, if the campaign were one of 10 months: this is a plausible rate for barbarians, but it is pure conjecture.

[3] Wilcken, *Aktenstücke*, vi and commentary. The market price of wheat about 130 B.C. was 400 c. d. per *artabe*; but the price here, for the purpose of *adaeratio*, was 100 c. d. for 29 *artabai*, 66⅔ c. d. for 14 *artabai* (the remaining 13 *artabai* were paid in kind). Thus the value of the σιτώνιον is: 13 *artabai* in kind at 400 c. d. = 5200 c. d. 29 *artabai adaeratae* at 100 c. d. = 2900 c. d. 14 *artabai adaeratae* at 66⅔ c. d. = 933⅓ c.d. Total—9033⅓ c.d.

For corn-prices, cf. Heichelheim, *Wirtschaftliche Schwankungen*, pp. 120 sqq. (tables).

[4] *U.P.Z.* i. 14; cf. p. 279. μετρήματα—1 *artabe* of wheat in kind = about 600 c. d.; 2 *artabai* of wheat *adaeratae* = 200 c.d.; ὀψώνιον, 150 c. d. (The extra σιτώνιον was 100 drachmae.)

PAY AND MAINTENANCE 307

was so high, especially when it is remembered that in Demosthenes' proposal quoted earlier (p. 296) σιτηρέσιον is perhaps the smaller part of the total payment, and that in payments to civilians at Delos throughout the third century, σῖτος and ὀψώνιον are normally about equal.[1] But a possible explanation is that these payments to mercenaries in Egypt are payments made to soldiers of a standing army in time of peace, and that on a campaign the ὀψώνιον may have been paid at a higher rate, though there is no evidence in support of this suggestion either from Egypt or elsewhere.[2] One other interesting point is the current rate of *adaeratio*, probably always 100 copper drachmae for 1 *artabe* of wheat. In 159 B.C. the ἐπίγονος at Memphis got 100 drachmae in place of his *artabe* of wheat; but the market price of wheat at the time was about 600 drachmae: and about 130 B.C., when the rate of *adaeratio* for the mercenary horse was still 100, the market price of wheat was probably about 400.[3] The Ptolemaic government, when it decided to commute payments in *artabai* into payments in cash, no doubt intended from the first to throw the risk upon the recipient, and when the rate of *adaeratio* remained constant in defiance of the increase in market prices, the risk must have been a very serious matter. Incidentally, it has been suggested that at the time when payments in cash were first introduced they must have borne some reasonably close relation to market prices, and this was only possible before the inflation of the copper currency in 170 B.C.:[4] judging from the extant corn-prices, the most likely period for the change seems to be not later than about 230 B.C., before prices began to rise.

[1] Cf. G. Glotz, *loc. cit.* p. 212.
[2] E.g. one cannot compare this ὀψώνιον in Egypt in time of peace with contemporary ὀψώνιον elsewhere in time of war, because none is known; and even if one were known, comparison would still be difficult, in view of the peculiar state of the Egyptian currency in the second century, and the lower cost of living in Egypt compared with the Aegean. I do not see how the purchasing power of the Egyptian copper currency can be brought into any satisfactory relation to that of the silver standards outside Egypt. For the Egyptian currency and the cost of living, cf. Heichelheim, *op. cit.* pp. 16 sqq. and 97 sqq.
[3] *U.P.Z.* i. p. 409; P. Paris 8, l. 6; cf. Heichelheim, *op. cit.* pp. 120 sqq.
[4] Heichelheim, *op. cit.* p. 64.

4. THE STANDARD OF LIFE

All the foregoing figures remain merely figures unless they can be related to the real life and times to which they are relevant. To know that a man earned a drachma a day is to know nothing; one must know also how much his drachma would buy, and how his own power of purchase compared with that of his contemporaries following different trades or professions. Fortunately much valuable work has been done on the subject of wages and the cost of living in general, so that comparisons may be brief and easy.[1] The basis of all comparisons must be an established "existence-minimum", by which is meant the smallest wage or salary upon which a man could reasonably be expected to keep himself alive. For the period before Chaeronea we have a good indication—the 2 obols a day of paupers at Athens subsisting on support from the State. In the same period the Athenian dicasts were paid 3 obols a day, and they were recruited from the poorer citizens. But when we turn to mercenary soldiers we find the "Cyreians" receiving 5 obols a day in money and (almost certainly) σῖτος in kind as well (p. 295): a composite pay of 7 obols at least. And Thracians at Athens got a drachma a day (414 B.C.). In the fourth century, as the numbers of the mercenary profession rose, the rate of pay fell, so that about 350 B.C. mercenaries with Athens got 1 drachma at the most and perhaps as little as 4 obols a day (composite pay: pp. 295–6). It is most probably to this period that the τετρωβόλου βίος is to be traced; but even so the mercenary is comfortably removed from the Athenian pauper. Then came the economic revolution resulting from the conquest of the East. Money poured into the Aegean, prices rose, and wages rose too. One cannot be certain how soon the change began to take effect, but at Eleusis in 329 B.C. the wages are definitely high, ranging from 1 drachma a day for young boys to 2½ drachmae for skilled stonemasons and carpenters: at Delos early in the third century skilled workmen get at least

---

[1] Cf. especially Glotz, *loc. cit.*; Heichelheim, *loc. cit.*, especially pp. 99 sqq. and 123 sqq. (tables of salaries and wages in Egypt, and at Delos); W. W. Tarn, in *The Hellenistic Age* (Cambridge 1925), pp. 108 sqq.; and in *Economica*, 1930, pp. 315 sqq. (review of Heichelheim). The general conclusions of these scholars are so well established that I shall use them without constantly referring to chapter and verse.

PAY AND MAINTENANCE

1½ drachmae a day, and labourers in 279 B.C. 5 obols. It was in these conditions that Demetrius undertook to pay 2 drachmae a day (at least) to citizen hoplites of the Greek League: there is no evidence for mercenaries, unless the "4 obols" in Menander be applied to them, which seems in the circumstances unreasonable (p. 301, and n. 5).

These figures have almost a prosperous ring. But in the meantime one must expect a corresponding rise in the "existence-minimum", for no doubt the man who could reasonably be expected to live on 2 obols a day in 340 B.C. would require more money in 300 B.C. to produce an equal standard of life. But the fact is that in the period after Alexander's conquests, the poor of Greece and the Aegean were obliged to reduce their budget, and we must accordingly reduce our ideas of what constituted a reasonable minimum for existence. Although there was more money in the world, the very poor received no more of it than they had received previously, but rather less, and since the purchasing power of money had decreased, the poor were now living (one supposes) at a standard well below that which was considered the minimum a hundred years before. Glotz has calculated that a reasonable minimum at Delos in the third century was about 120 drachmae a year—the same sum in currency as the 2 obols a day of the earlier period, but perhaps not much more than half that sum in purchasing power: and one is shocked to find that in the lowest grades of employment it is by no means the rule for people to receive as much as 120 drachmae. Of the permanent employees of the Delian Apollo, a clerk gets usually about 80d.; a κρηνοφύλαξ about 90d.; a temple inspector between 60 and 200d.; a flute-girl usually 120 or 130d. (occasionally more, once as much as 195d.); a ὑπηρέτης about 160d.[1] Compared with these pittances, the 1⅓ Attic drachmae a day of the Aetolian and Acarnanian citizen hoplites in 272 B.C. seems almost princely, and even if we suppose

---
[1] Cf. the table in Heichelheim, *op. cit.* pp. 125 sqq.: one cannot be perfectly certain, however, that these people had no other employment besides.

The daily wage of unskilled workers seems to have averaged about 2½ obols a day (Heichelheim, *loc. cit.* p. 125, with Tarn, *Economica*, p. 317 n. 2), = about 150 drachmae a year if the worker were regularly employed. But Tarn has shown that regular employment cannot be assumed, for skilled workmen at least (see below).

that mercenaries at that date received less, we can still be sure that they were easily above the level of starvation. Certainly mercenaries in a reinforcement sent by Hierapytna to Rhodes about 200 B.C. would have been quite well off with their composite pay of 8 Attic obols a day; and even the mercenaries in the Macedonian army in 218 B.C had no reason to complain, if their composite pay was worth a drachma a day or more (pp. 303 sqq.).

One conclusion, then, is self-evident. The campaigning mercenary was entitled to be confident that he would at least escape death by starvation: he could easily buy the necessities of life, and ought to have had money to spare, not indeed for luxuries, but for pleasures, and so far Mars was a kinder master than the Delian Apollo. But it may be said that the daily wage of the skilled workman (at Eleusis certainly, and even at Delos later) was higher than the highest wage known to have been paid to a mercenary soldier. That is true as far as it goes, but it goes only this far: if a skilled mason were at work every day in the year, he could live better than the mercenary serving under a year's contract. And in actual fact our daily wages for skilled workmen were paid indeed for work done under contract; but in no case of which we have knowledge did a single contract last a year or anything near to a year, and it has been calculated that the best workmen at Delos could not make more than about 240 drachmae a year, representing an *average* daily earning of 4 obols.[1] This is pitiful enough when one remembers that a man required probably a drachma a day to keep a wife and two children. Now the difficulty is to compare the mercenary's prospects of employment with those of the skilled workman, and the only method is to choose two imaginary cases, first of the mercenary casually employed, and then of the mercenary serving in a standing army. Let us imagine a young man of (say) Megalopolis leaving home to better his prospects. In the first place, he will be a little unlucky if there is not a war either in progress or at least imminent somewhere within 200 miles of his home. One spring morning he will arrive at one of the headquarters of the war (if he has not been picked up by a recruiting officer already), and will probably be able to enlist for the year's campaigning season. Suppose that the war ends after six months and that the recruit has not

[1] Tarn, *Hellenistic Age*, pp. 121 sqq.

PAY AND MAINTENANCE 311

been killed—he will be discharged with perhaps 180 drachmae for pay, of which he will not have spent more than the half on his food. Now 180 drachmae represent quite a good year's earnings for a skilled workman at Delos working whenever he could find a job: whereas our imaginary mercenary can now afford to take his ease for six months, or to travel overseas in search of new employment, and the probability is that he has only to reach Alexandria or Ephesus to be certain of becoming a permanent soldier if he wishes. But even if he is content to travel about enlisting for short periods as the opportunity appears, the odds are that he will be able to live either comfortably all the time or riotously in short bursts, though he may have to forgo the pleasures of a legal wife and legitimate children. Such a life would be risky and unsettled, but it would not be a dog's life like the life of an unmarried clerk or a mason with a large family at Delos.

It is more difficult to estimate the standard of life of a mercenary in a standing army, because there is no evidence at all for the prevalent rates of pay, though one imagines that the small permanent garrisons so frequently employed in the Hellenistic period may have been paid at a lower rate than the mercenaries in a field army in time of war. Even in Egypt there is no safe basis for calculating how much soldiers of the standing army were paid in peace time, though it may perhaps be inferred from the wages of φυλακῖται in the third century, that the mercenaries must have got a very comfortable living wage.[1] In that period the cost of living in Egypt was low, and everyone seems to have had enough money.[2] By about 150 B.C. conditions had

[1] P. Petr. iii. 128 (214 B.C.) An ἐπιστάτης τῶν φυλακιτῶν gets 300d. a month (by far the highest salary known, cf. Heichelheim, *loc. cit.* pp. 123 sqq.), the φυλακῖται themselves get respectively 80, 50, 40 and 30d. a month, in proportion to the importance of their nome. The existence-minimum at this time was probably about 120d. a year (Heichelheim, *loc. cit.* p. 100). On the other hand the ὀψώνιον of an ἔφοδος attendant on the ἐπιστάτης is 1d. a month—which is quite inexplicable.

[2] Tarn (*Economica, loc. cit.*) criticizes this conclusion of Heichelheim (*loc. cit.* pp. 101 sqq.) on the ground that it does not take into account (*a*) that the Egyptian *artabe* is a doubtful quantity (varying from 24 to 40 *choinikes*), (*b*) that, in the present state of our knowledge, daily wages in Egypt must be subject to the same caveat as those at Delos before they can be used as the basis for reckoning *yearly* wages (i.e. did the man who received 1 drachma a day receive it *all the year round*?). Granted the soundness of this criticism, and

changed greatly for the worse, and many cases are known of people working at rates below the probable "existence-minimum". Yet the ἐπίγονος at Memphis in 158 B.C. gets just about the minimum, and he is not an active soldier, and may be a mere boy.[1] One must assume therefore that the standing army, such as it was, was still paid a living wage, and indeed the assumption is necessary on external grounds also, for in the second century the Ptolemaic *régime* became extremely insecure, and a loyal army must have been a necessary weapon against the native population, among which rebellions were frequent. For Asia and the Aegean there is even less information than for Egypt; but the contract of the mercenaries of Eumenes I suggests a certain stability in the life of regular mercenaries, if that contract was never broken, and if it is to be taken as typical (pp. 282 sqq.). The soldiers of Eumenes received a σιτηρέσιον perhaps monthly, representing σῖτος and οἶνος commuted into money by *adaeratio* at a rather low rate; and in addition they received ὀψώνιον probably at the end of each campaigning season. They enjoyed ἀτέλεια while they lived and remained in the service, and if they died provision was made for their families (ὀρφανικά). Against these benefits must be set a period of two months' unemployment in the winter (at Cos a few years later the period was three months), during which probably neither ὀψώνιον nor σιτηρέσιον was paid (p. 283); and this period of idleness was probably common to all standing armies.[2] Nevertheless the soldiers at Pergamum were not dissatisfied with it, but rather were anxious to keep it in its entirety: they could contemplate two months' unemployment with equanimity, and perhaps even looked forward to spending the time comfortably with their wives and families. All this tempts one to believe that they must have been at least reasonably near the drachma-a-day mark, the level at which a man is supposed to have been able to support a

that Heichelheim's proposed "existence-minimum" is probably too low, our φυλακῖται (p. 311 n. 1) would still be safe from real hardship even if the cost of living were twice as high as Heichelheim supposed, and I think one may assume that Heichelheim's theory of a "golden age" in the third century remains true for the Ptolemaic army, though not perhaps for the Egyptian poor.
    [1] Heichelheim, *loc. cit.* pp. 103 sqq.
    [2] Cf., in Egypt, *B.G.U.* viii. 1749 (p. 275 n. 2 (3)); and perhaps in Macedonia, 169 B.C., p. 306 n. 2.

PAY AND MAINTENANCE 313

wife and two children. Admittedly this state of affairs at Pergamum had been brought about only by means of a successful mutiny, and it is legitimate to argue that the general standard was lower; but even with this qualification it seems unlikely that a mercenary serving under a long contract can ever have experienced the desperate hardship which we have seen at Delos.

A soldier's wage in general was certainly in the category of "working-class" wages, and certainly must have been small compared with the profits of a successful merchant or the salary of a successful professional man;[1] but still, as "working-class" wages went, the soldier's was not a bad one.

Even the garrison duty in time of peace may thus have been comfortable enough, if tedious. The outbreak of war transformed the mercenary from something like a steady-going family man into something like an adventurer. On the one hand war might bring death, or worse—pay heavily in arrears, poor facilities for marketing, perhaps even the danger of starvation in a devastated country where good money was no better than none. Or it might bring bonuses and plunder after victory.[2]

But one has still to mention the greatest reward of all, the highest good pursued, one imagines, by most soldiers of fortune —land. Just as shortage of land had always been at the root of all the economic troubles in the mainland of Greece, and γῆς ἀναδασμός was foremost in the programme of every radical reformer, so it follows that, to many of the Greeks who emigrated into Asia and Egypt after 330 B.C., a piece of land was at the summit of their ambition, and if they gained it the world's great age began anew for them. And perhaps the most interesting thing about the mercenary profession at that time is that it did enable some of these emigrant Greeks to get what they

[1] E.g. an architect at Delos, who could earn anything up to five times as much as a skilled workman; Glotz, pp. 243 sqq.; Heichelheim, pp. 125–6.

[2] There is an interesting point in the Aristeas Letter (22), suggesting the profits that could be made out of prisoners; the soldiers in Egypt appear to have been allowed, as a rule, to sell any prisoners they had taken (or in some cases perhaps to receive a ransom for them): τοῦ βασιλέως προστάξαντος, ὅσοι τῶν συνεστρατευμένων τῷ πατρὶ ἡμῶν εἰς τοὺς κατὰ Συρίαν καὶ Φοινίκην τόπους ἐπελθόντες τὴν τῶν Ἰουδαίων χώραν ἐγκρατεῖς ἐγένοντο σωμάτων Ἰουδαϊκῶν καὶ ταῦτα διακεκομίκασιν εἴς τε τὴν πόλιν καὶ τὴν χώραν ἢ καὶ πεπράκασιν ἑτέροις, ὁμοίως δὲ καὶ εἴ τινες προῆσαν ἢ καὶ μετὰ ταῦτά εἰσιν εἰσηγμένοι τῶν τοιούτων, ἀπολύειν παραχρῆμα τοὺς ἔχοντας, κομιζομένους αὐτίκα ἑκάστου σώματος δραχμὰς εἴκοσι, τοὺς μὲν στρατιώτας τῇ τῶν ὀψωνίων δόσει, τοὺς δὲ λοιποὺς ἀπὸ τῆς βασιλικῆς τραπέζης. Cf. ibid. 20.

wanted. Although there is little positive evidence, it must be perfectly certain that the majority of the military settlers in Egypt and in the Asiatic empire of Antigonus and the Seleucids were originally mercenaries:[1] they may not have become settlers until they were veterans, but their descendants in time became the material from which the regular (i.e. non-mercenary) armies of the Ptolemies and the Seleucids were drawn. In Pergamum too in the second century it seems that all the new military settlers of the Attalids (as opposed to the old Seleucid settlers) must originally have served in the Pergamene army as mercenaries. The barbarian settlers established in Macedonia by Philip V and Perseus *may* have been mercenaries, though this is not certain.[2] Are we then to assume that it became part of the contract between soldier and employer, that if a man served a reasonable term of years he might expect a *kleros* as his right? Unfortunately there is no single piece of evidence in support of this theory. The elaborate contract at Pergamum in 218 B.C. certainly did *not* contain any such clause; but it does not follow from this that a Seleucid or a Ptolemaic contract might not have contained it, because at that date military settlements were not yet part of the Attalid policy (p. 175). There are in fact only two cases on record of the assignment of land to mercenaries. At Cassandreia in 279 B.C., when Eurydice had abdicated and left the city free, the demagogue Apollodorus established a festival in her honour, and procured for her mercenaries, who now evacuated the citadel, lots of land in Pallene, "so that they might remain as guardians of liberty".[3] Does this mean that they were to continue to form a standing army? If so it is extremely interesting, for it represents the only certain attempt on the part of a Greek city to imitate the military systems of the two great monarchies. But the incident must not be considered apart from its context: the story goes on to say that very soon afterwards Apollodorus made himself tyrant of Cassandreia, so that the allotments of land to the mercenaries may have been merely a tactical move, his method of identifying their interests with his

---

[1] Cf. p. 242, for a few statistics from Egypt.
[2] Cf. pp. 149 sqq.; 179 sqq.; 77 sqq.; for the evidence for Syria, Pergamum, and Macedonia.
[3] Polyaen. vi. 7. 2.

PAY AND MAINTENANCE 315

own. In any case we do not know how the scheme worked out, or whether it was continued. There is, however, a rather similar incident recorded at Theangela (pp. 292 sqq.). When the city had capitulated to Eupolemus (perhaps the tyrant of Mylasa), some of the former mercenaries of Theangela took service with Eupolemus and were rewarded not only with a donative but with some land: unfortunately it is not certain whether they were being allowed to keep land which had been given to them already (by Theangela) or whether they were now receiving grants of land from Eupolemus, though the second alternative is perhaps the more likely.[1] But this must almost certainly be an imitation, whether by the tyrant or by the Greek city, of the contemporary methods of Antigonus.

These two examples are not enough to establish a rule, especially when there is a very strong argument against the rule's existence: very few employers outside Egypt and Asia had land to spare. In Greece especially, if many of the inhabitants emigrated because there was not enough land, it would be curious in the extreme if we were to find that cities made a practice of giving grants of land to veteran mercenaries. The thing is plainly out of the question, unless in exceptional circumstances. Dionysius I of Syracuse and Nabis of Sparta, both in possession of despotic power, were in a position to give land to their soldiers, the one using conquered territory for the purpose, the other distributing the confiscated property of his political enemies.[2] The ordinary Greek city could not afford to be so generous; but there were occasions when a city gave its mercenaries all that it could give, namely its citizenship. This happened at Aspendus (probably 310–306 B.C.), at Ephesus (*ca.* 297 B.C.), at Smyrna (*ca.* 244 B.C.), at Dyme in Achaea (217 B.C.), and perhaps at Pharsalus (third century).[3] What may have been the value of such a gift it is hard to say. For a man who had married and founded a family (or wished to do so) in a city where he had

[1] So Rostovtzeff, *loc. cit.* p. 19, who interprets the passage very fully. The disputed phrase is τοῖς τε στρατιώταις τοῖς ἐκ Θεαγγέλων, ἐάν τινες στρατεύωνται παρ' Εὐπολέμῳ ὑπάρχειν αὐτοῖς τὰ Πεντάχωρα.
[2] For Dionysius, p. 196; for Nabis, Pol. xiii. 6. 3 sqq.; Diod. xxvii. 1.
[3] G. A. Wilhelm, "*Neue Beiträge*", in *S.B. Ak. Wien*, 1915 (179), p. 60 = *Mon. Ant.* xxiii. pp. 116 sqq. (Aspendus—a Ptolemaic garrison); Ditt. *Syll.*[3] i. 363 (a garrison, probably of Demetrius, at Ephesus); *O.G.I.S.* i. 229 (Smyrna —a Seleucid garrison); Ditt. *Syll.*[3] i. 529 (Dyme); *I.G.* ix. 2. 234 (Pharsalus).

served as a soldier, the citizenship must have been useful and convenient, but it can hardly have been an economic advantage to him; in fact if it meant that he ceased to be a mercenary soldier, it took away his livelihood and exposed him again to the fierce economic competition of civilian life, in which his chances of survival cannot be estimated without knowing more of the circumstances. But a phrase in the Aspendus decree seems to make it certain that the soldiers on whom the citizenship was bestowed were not necessarily expected to settle down in the city; in this particular case some of the mercenaries are known to have been barbarians (Pamphylians, Lycians and Pisidians), and to them a Greek citizenship may have been of some advantage.[1] And the soldiers of the Seleucid garrison of Palaimagnesia near Smyrna must certainly have served their contracts before they could be allowed to settle down in Smyrna as civilians.[2] In any case the gift of citizenship may not have been very common except as an honorific measure, and a mercenary in the service of a small Greek city probably had no guarantee of anything beyond his yearly contract of service. If he really wanted to settle down to a new life with new hopes, his best plan was to go to one of the great kings abroad.

[1] ll. 15 sqq., ἐὰν δέ| τις αὐτῶν βούληται [κατ]αχωρ[ισθῆ]]ναι εἰς φυλήν, [ἐξέστω, ἀρ]γύριον| [δότω] ἡ πόλις βου[λομένῳ. The restoration of the last line is by no means certain. It is rejected by Wilhelm (*S.B. Ak. Wien, loc. cit.*), who rightly says that such a transaction would be improbable in the extreme.
[2] Pp. 154–5.

CONCLUSION

THE purely military importance of the Hellenistic mercenary is easily summarized. In the fifth century Greek mercenaries had conformed for the most part with the Peloponnesian hoplite type, and in the fourth century a lighter type of infantry came into vogue, partly as the result of the reforms of Iphicrates.[1] But Alexander had demonstrated what could be achieved by the use of different styles of fighting in perfect combination—the irresistible charge of Macedonian heavy cavalry, the immovable stand of the phalanx, and the mobile tactics of light-armed troops (among which most of his earliest mercenaries were to be found). What influence had this demonstration upon mercenaries after his time? It may be said at once that the heavy-cavalry style seems never to have attracted mercenaries: for one thing, the equipment was probably too expensive. The Companions of Alexander were the outcome of years of training and the national spirit of generations; the Successors tried to maintain their troops of Macedonian "Companion" cavalry, but by the end of the third century the use of such cavalry as shock troops had almost disappeared, perhaps because the material could not be found outside Macedonia itself.

The experience of the phalanx, however, was rather different. In the light of what had gone before, it was considered a necessity to make the phalanx the backbone or the kernel of an army, and the expense of hiring and training mercenaries to fight in phalanx was not out of the question. Accordingly, we find in the armies of the Successors mercenaries fighting in the phalanx, doubtless because there were not enough Macedonians to go round. Mercenary phalangites appear early, in the armies both of Eumenes (6000) and of Antigonus (9000).[2] The phalanx of Demetrius at Gaza consisted of mercenaries almost entirely (8000 out of 11,000),[3] and the same must have been true of the phalanxes of both Ptolemy I and Seleucus I, since neither had a

[1] Cf. Parke, pp. 50 sqq. [2] Diod. xix. 27. 6 and 29. 3.
[3] Ibid. 82. 4.

sufficient supply of real Macedonians. The armies of the Ptolemies and Seleucids during the greater part of the third century are an unknown quantity; but we know that both governments built up a "regular" phalanx out of their military settlers, and this same shortage of real Macedonians must have meant that the settlements were originally populated to a great extent with mercenary phalangites. In Europe too the phalanx had come to stay: a remark of Polybius gives the impression that in the second century the Macedonian sarissa was the weapon of all Greek soldiers in general[1], and it is known that the citizen infantry of Sparta was converted to the Macedonian style of fighting by Cleomenes, and that of the Achaean League by Philopoemen.[2] But the tendency here seems to have been to rely upon a citizen or a national phalanx, and to use recruited mercenaries for other purposes. This was of course quite in the original Macedonian tradition, which still held good in the Macedonian armies of Philip V and Perseus, and also at the end of the third century and later in the Egyptian and Seleucid armies, which had been deliberately constructed after the Macedonian model. Mercenaries had reverted for the most part to the status of auxiliaries, in which capacity they must be examined further.

The clearest way of arriving at an idea of the functions of mercenaries is to look at their performance in the great battles, where they are to be found fighting with or against the regular forces of the principal armies. At Raphia various contingents of mercenaries fought in the two armies. Of them all, only the 8000 Greeks of Ptolemy fought as heavy infantry (they had been drilled with the regular phalanx, and were stationed in the battle next to the new phalanx of native Egyptians); the rest seem to have been light-armed infantry or cavalry, including even the corresponding contingent of Greek infantry in the Seleucid army.[3] At Magnesia again the mercenaries of Antiochus are all light-armed, and mostly barbarians.[4] In Europe, Antigonus

---

[1] Pol. xviii. 18. 1 sqq., οἱ μὲν γὰρ Ἕλληνες μόλις αὐτῶν κρατοῦσι τῶν σαρισῶν ἐν ταῖς πορείαις....
[2] Plut. Cleom. 11. 2; 23. 1 sqq.; Phil. 9. 1 sqq.; Paus. viii. 50. 1; Polyaen. vi. 4. 3.
[3] Pol. v. 65 and 82.
[4] Livy 37. 40: Appian, Syr. 32; cf. Pol. xxxi. 3. 3 sqq. (Daphne review).

CONCLUSION 319

Doson and Cleomenes each had mercenaries at Sellasia, but they were used as light skirmishing infantry in front of the phalanxes, which were composed of the national levies of Macedonians and Lacedaemonians respectively:[1] the mercenaries in the army of Perseus were likewise mainly light troops and barbarians.[2] At Mantinea the two phalanxes consisted of Achaean and Lacedaemonian citizen infantry, and although the mercenary infantry fought under the two commanders-in-chief, they were partly if not wholly light infantry (εὔζωνοι).[3] At a later date some garrison troops of the Achaean League (and therefore probably mercenaries) are described as peltasts.[4] It may be, therefore, that εὔζωνοι are to be taken as the equivalent of peltasts. On the other hand some εὔζωνοι of Philip V were plainly lighter troops than his peltasts; were the Macedonian "peltasts" really *hypaspistae*?[5]

Perhaps the clue to the three kinds of Greek infantry is to be found in the treaty between Aetolia and Acarnania, in which different amounts of pay are prescribed for the different classes of reinforcement which might be sent. The classes are: (1) τῶι τὰμ πανοπλίαν ἔχοντι; (2) τῶι τὸ ἡμιθωράκιον (ἔχοντι); (3) ψιλῶι.[6] (1) is the heavy infantryman;[7] (2) is probably the peltast; (3) is the lightest type of infantryman, who fought with missiles (archer, slinger, or javelin-thrower) and without defensive armour. It is probably to the second of these classes that most of the non-phalangite Greek mercenaries of the period are to be assigned. The most prominent exponents of the third style of warfare were the Cretans, whose national weapon was the bow. They may have had some very light protective armour,[8] but they were valuable chiefly for their mobility, and Polybius says that they were useless as phalanx troops.[9] The special

---
[1] Pol. ii. 66. 5-8; cf. 69. 3, where Doson's mercenaries are called "5000 mercenaries and εὔζωνοι".
[2] Livy 42. 51; cf. 33. 4. 4 (Cynoscephalae).
[3] Pol. xi. 11. 5 sqq. [4] *Id*. xxiv. 12. 10.
[5] *Id*. v. 23. 1 sqq. The peltasts are included among the βαρέων ὅπλων. Cf. Livy 33. 4. 4.
[6] Ditt. *Syll*.³ i. 421, ll. 39 sqq.
[7] It is impossible to say whether at that date (about 275 B.C.) and in a backward part of Greece the heavy infantryman means the phalangite or the hoplite.
[8] Livy 42. 55. 10, *Creticus armatus*; Pol. x. 29. 6, ἀσπιδιῶται: and cf. p. 144 and n. 2 for "Neocretans". [9] Pol. iv. 8. 11.

barbarian contingents (Gauls, Thracians, Illyrians, etc.) fought each in their own style and never appear in phalanx formation. The use of such troops is exemplified under the command of Eumenes II at Magnesia, where he broke up the charge of Antiochus' war chariots with his Cretan archers and slingers and mounted javelin-men (probably Trallians), precisely as Alexander had broken the charge of Darius' war chariots with his Agrianians.[1] But the limitations of the Greek ψιλοί were exposed when they came into contact with the Roman *velites*, who were as mobile as they and better able to bear punishment.[2]

The heyday of mercenaries seems to have been the last thirty years of the fourth century and perhaps the first thirty years of the third: for although our principal literary source happens to end with the battle of Ipsus, it would be surprising if this historical symptom should have ended equally abruptly. In this unique period military history appears almost as the whole of history, and here alone in antiquity the mercenaries were for a short time perhaps the most important soldiers in the service of the great army commanders; important not merely as members of armies then in existence, but also because they might become the means of producing the armies of the next generation. After Ipsus the Hellenistic world slowly settled down not indeed to peace but to warfare under a new and a more settled system. In particular the two great new powers in Egypt and Asia had time to develop a military machinery, and naturally it was designed after the Macedonian model. When one first has the opportunity of seeing it at work (by bad luck it is not until nearly a century later, at Raphia), one sees an organization not so very different from that which Alexander himself had used—and this means that the mercenaries have relapsed into their subordinate place, while the most important functions are perfomed by soldiers whom we have called "regulars"; who are, however, in many cases the ἐπίγονοι of earlier mercenary settlers. There are hints indeed that at Raphia the Egyptian machinery is unsound: it has broken down once and has been refitted for an occasion, and one suspects that it broke down again later, and then the mercenaries may have come into their own again, but worse and few compared with those of the earlier period. The second century in general

---

[1] Livy 37. 41. 9 sqq.   [2] *Id.* 41. 35. 1 sqq.

was for this profession a period of decline, naturally enough, when the great employers one by one collapsed and retired from the market. The arrival of Rome in the East very soon meant the end of war as a profitable trade.

The decline of the Greek mercenary (as opposed to mercenaries collectively) seems to have set in even earlier, and for a different reason. It may be presumptuous to say that one knows the reason, when really it is only the event that is made known to us; but at least there is a reason which is not absurd in itself and which, if accepted, explains everything. It is simply that the population available for mercenary service may no longer have existed. The generation of Alexander and the Successors was a time of dispersal for the Greeks. It was not only that thousands of Greeks fought as mercenaries in the conquest of the East and its partition, nor only that many of them remained in the East as military settlers. The movement of emigration must have far transcended mere movements of troops. For every one of the new cities for which a military origin is known or even suspected, there are two or three which have nothing to connect them with soldiers. There can be no doubt that the opening of Asia and Egypt to the Greeks was something not unlike the discovery of a new world. The new capitals Alexandria, Antioch and Pergamum rapidly outgrew all but the very greatest of the old Greek cities. Naturally these new populations contained many non-Greek ingredients; but the fact remained that in them any Greek man or woman was welcome merely for being Greek. The effect on the race as a whole can have been hardly less than that of the early age of colonization—and the details of the process have disappeared even more completely: we know merely the names of about 100 new cities. Statistics are out of the question, but it is known that the pressure of governments was occasionally introduced to reinforce private enterprise.[1] And one authority mentions 300,000 as the number of "Greeks" deported by Tigranes from Mesopotamia into Armenia at the beginning of the first century B.C.[2] For the other side of the picture turn to Polybius' description of the Peloponnese about 150 B.C: it is a picture of depopulation

[1] Magnesia and Antiochus II (*O.G.I.S.* i. 233).
[2] Plut. *Lucull.* 21. 4 and 26. 1 sqq.

and race-exhaustion.[1] This abrupt contrast is perhaps historically false in some of its implications, but it is true in so far as it illustrates the general truth that by the time of Polybius the strength had gone out of Greece and was scattered over a wide area in foreign lands. The decline in Greek mercenary service early in the second century is another illustration of the same truth. It marks the end of a long and slow process, and one that implies more than a mere record of marches and sieges, victories and defeats; for the mercenaries were certainly among the chief assistants in the process which we call vaguely hellenization, embracing the carrying abroad among foreigners of the Greek language and institutions, and all the arts for which Greece was the school and Greeks the teachers, including the art of war.

It requires imagination to see what these mercenaries did, and still more to see what they themselves were like, for the reason that they were nonentities almost to a man.[2] Although there are a few men who, because they rose to the top of the profession, have left some mark on the history of their time, there is none that one knows instinctively to have been a great man, and perhaps the only one of them all in whom one feels a keen interest for his own sake is the Spartan Xanthippus, who saved Carthage from the Romans, and then disappeared. Of able officers there must have been hundreds, and the ablest of them became famous, like Leosthenes the Athenian, the "mystery man" of Hellenistic history, or the Aetolians Theodotus and Scopas,[3] who rose in the Egyptian service to be the one a governor of a province, the other commander-in-chief of the Ptolemaic army, drawing a salary of 10 minae a day and living dangerously among the intrigues of the Alexandrian court. Another such adventurer was the Cretan Lasthenes who helped the boy Demetrius II to win the throne

---

[1] Pol. xxxvii. 4. 4 sqq.
[2] There exists a certain body of archaeological evidence throwing some light upon the arms and accoutrements of Hellenistic soldiers, but it is both difficult to collect (much of it is unpublished), and of a highly specialized interest which makes it impossible for me to deal with it summarily. It awaits (I hope) a more able pen than my own.
[3] Theodotus—Pol. v. 40; 79. 4; he surrendered his province and his services to Antiochus the Great, became one of his leading generals, and fought against Egypt at Raphia (cf. an Epigenes, first an officer of Attalus I, later of Antiochus the Great—*Insch. v. Perg.* i. 29; Pol. v. 41. 2; 49 sqq.). Scopas—Pol. xiii. 1 sqq.; xv. 25. 6; xvi. 18; xviii. 53 sqq.

CONCLUSION 323

of Syria, and as his minister was responsible for a remarkable period of misrule.[1] But perhaps the most attractive in this gallery of rogues was the man who rose from the ranks of the Syrian mercenaries by the simple expedient of declaring himself to be the son of Perseus, king of Macedonia; he was sent to Rome for his pains, but escaped and embarked on a triumphant and luxurious tour of the Near East, and even a former mistress of Perseus was deceived (or professed to be) by the face and figure of the Pseudophilippus.[2] These men lived by their wits, and hardly one of them died in his bed. They are the stars of their profession—falling stars with a brief and vivid career, before they vanish suddenly and for ever. And as soon as one begins to descend towards the rank and file, one's vision is obscured, or, what is worse, deluded. What are we to make of the *miles gloriosus* of the New Comedy, a fantastic desperado who may have appeared on earth and lived in human shape once, or perhaps even twice, but surely not more often than that? It would be as absurd to swallow the *miles* as a typical Hellenistic mercenary or subordinate officer as it would be to swallow the clergyman of a Victorian farce as a typical clergyman of that or any other date. The origin of the two caricatures is obvious. Both the mercenary and the clergyman belonged to a class set apart from almost all its contemporaries by a unique experience, and it is more than possible that their experience may have been reflected in their general bearing and demeanour. When the *miles* boasts of the many and distant lands that he has visited and the appalling dangers and difficulties that he has overcome, he is ridiculous indeed (as he is meant to be), but the fact remains that the people who are laughing at him have perhaps never been abroad at all, or have seldom exposed their bodies to a greater risk than that of snakebite on a country excursion. The mercenary's manner of life must have been unsympathetic to the quiet and orderly citizen, and this is the most probable reason, as Parke has pointed out, for the series of unsympathetic portraits which has survived from the New Comedy. The soldier led a strenuous life and yet remained poor, and there is always something laughable in the idea of a man's taking very great

---

[1] Justin 35. 2; Joseph. xiii. 86, etc.; 1 Macc. 10. 67, etc.
[2] Diod. xxxi. 40; xxxii. 15—Andriscus.

pains to win almost nothing: or if he made some money he made it discreditably—and the man who "lives by his wits" is generally unpopular with the majority that lives by rule.[1]

What one would most wish to discover is a diary kept by a common soldier, or even a letter written by such a soldier to his parents or his wife. But nothing of the kind has survived (it would be surprising if it had been otherwise). There is indeed a document which *may* be the letter of a Ptolemaic soldier campaigning in Syria; but this "letter" (if it is a letter at all) is concerned with describing the events of the campaign in a very impersonal style, and tells us nothing of the life and habits of the man who wrote it.[2] One is thrown back upon the bare records of historical events, which have formed the basis of this inquiry, and the imagination is left free to pursue at will the themes suggested by them; the confused mass of motives and impulses and memories which were once the lives of individual men, the life of wandering with poverty never far behind, the moments of intense excitement in action, the years of intense tedium in a garrison of Asia or Egypt, the settling, perhaps, in a new country with a piece of King's Land on which to found a family —all these things are forgotten for ever, unless they have chanced to be implied in the casualty list of an ancient historian, or some letters chipped in a slab of stone, or a memorandum written on Egyptian papyrus.

[1] Cf. Parke, pp. 234 sqq., where the evidence is collected: add Plautus, *M.G. passim*; *Curculio* 437 sqq.; *Truculentus* 482 sqq.; Terence, *Eunuch.* 397 sqq. The *miles* usually serves, or has served, in Asia, as one would expect in the generation of the Successors; cf. also Terence, *Heaut. Tim.* 110 sqq.

[2] P. Petr. ii. 45; the occasion is supposed to be the Syrian War of Ptolemy III (247-6 B.C.).

INDEX OF TECHNICAL TERMS

ἄγημα (Ptolemaic), 118, 119 n. 1, 127 sqq.
ἀγορά, 266, 269 sq.; definition of, 280; 288, 299
adaeratio, 265, 267; in Egypt, 278, 279 n. 8, 306 n. 3, 307; at Pergamum, 282 sq.; at Carthage, 289
ἄμιπποι, 249
ἀμφιπποι ("amphippoi"), 49, 248 sqq.
ἀποσκευή, importance in period of Successors of, 40; 226
ἀποστολεῖς, 83
ἀποτελεῖος, 106
auxilia, 74, 75, 234
ἄφιπποι, see ἄμφιπποι

δεκαστάτηρος, 299 n. 1
διμοιρία, 295
διμοιρίτης, 299 n. 1
δόμα, 293

ἐκκλησιαστικά, 290
ἐπιγονῆς, οἱ τῆς, 115 n. 1
ἐπίγονοι, 115, 118, 126, 137, 163, 306 sq., 312
ἐπίλεκτοι (Achaean League), 101 sq., 106; (Ptolemaic), 127
ἐπιτηδεία, 266, 268, 273
"eponymous commanders" (Ptolemaic), 131 n. 1, 135 n. 3
εὔζωνοι, 71 n. 2, 104, 106 n. 5, 319

ἡγεμών, 84 n. 3, 91, 154 sq., 172, 261, 303

θωρακίτης, 104

κατοικίαι (Seleucid), 148 sqq., 162 sqq., 314; (Attalid), 179 sqq., 314
κάτοικοι (Ptolemaic), 118, 124 n. 1; (Seleucid), 151, 153 sqq.; (Attalid), 177 sqq.
κλῆρος (Ptolemaic), 114, 159 n. 2, 314, 324; (Seleucid), 155, 157 sqq., 162, 314, 324
κληροῦχοι (cleruchs) — (Ptolemaic), 114 sqq., 122 sqq., 129, 135 n. 3, 148, 162 sqq.; provenance of, 241 sqq., 314

κληροῦχοι μισθοφόροι, 78 n. 2, 116, 135 sqq.
κοινόν, in Cyprus, 134, 246, 251
μάχιμοι, Egyptian, 112 sq., 118, 127
μετρήματα, 155, 275 n. 1, 279, 291 n. 1, 306
μισθός, definition of, 264 sqq., 294, 295 n. 3, 296; ἐντελής, 271 sq.; supplanted by ὀψώνιον in military contexts, 275 sq.; rates of, 294 sqq., 305
μισθοφόροι, synonymous with ξένοι, etc.? 16, 29 sq.
μισθοφόροι κληροῦχοι, see κληροῦχοι μισθοφόροι

ξεναγός, 84 n. 3, 91, 172
ξένοι, synonymous with μισθοφόροι? 16, 29 sq.; ἀρχαῖοι of Alexander, 17, 28 sq.; distinct from παντοδαποί? 49
ξενολόγος, 84, 257, 261

ὄψον, used wrongly for ὀψώνιον, 264 n. 3
ὀψώνιον, 155, 272 n. 1; definition of, 274 sqq., 294, 304 sq.; in Egypt, 277 sqq. passim; at Cos, 283; at Pergamum, 284 sq.; at Carthage, 288 sq.; at Athens, 290; in Roman army, 290 n.1; of a Seleucid garrison, 291; not paid in advance, 293, 312; once only wrongly used for composite pay? 303 sqq.; ratio to σιτώνιον (etc.) of, 306 sq.

παντοδαποί, perhaps Asiatics, distinct from ξένοι? 42, 48 sq.; from Asiatic levies, 49; armed in Macedonian style, 49
περίπολοι, 86 sqq.
πρόδομα, 85, 278, 280

σιταρχία (-κία), definition of, 268 sqq., 304 sq.; used loosely? 275 sq.; at Carthage, 288 sqq.; used wrongly to denote composite pay? 303 sqq.
σιτηρέσιον, definition of, 268 sqq.,

294, 305, 312; at Cos, 283; at Pergamum? 284 sq.; at Athens? 290; of a Ptolemaic garrison, 290; of Bastarnae? 293; rates of, 294 sqq.; ratio to μισθός of, 307
σιτομετρία, definition of, 275 nn. 1 and 2; 279, 289 sq.
σῖτος, 85 n. 2; definition of, 264 sqq., 312; used wrongly for σιτηρέσιον? 267, 294; at Pergamum, 282 sq., 286 n. 2; at Athens, 290; in Roman army, 290 n. 1; in 4th century, 296 sqq. *passim*; in 3rd century, 305; ratio to ὀψώνιον, at Delos, of, 307

σιτώνιον, 274 sqq., 278 sqq., 290; ratio to ὀψώνιον of, 306 sq.
στέφανος, 267 n. 2, 286, 292
στρατηγὸς ἐπὶ τῶν ξένων, at Athens, 84, 91
στρατιώτης, not necessarily "mercenary" at Athens, 84 sq.; and in Egypt, 126, 132 sqq.
στρατιωτικῷ, οἱ ἐν τῷ σ. φερόμενοι, 113, 125 sq.
συνταγματάρχης ἐπὶ τῶν ξένων, at Rhodes, 91
σωματοφύλαξ, 160 n. 4

τετρωβόλου βίος, 301, 308

GENERAL INDEX

NOTE.—The names of mercenary officers are printed in italics.

Acarnania, 4
Acarnanians, mercenaries with Pyrrhus, 61 sq., 245; in 5th century, 238; rate of pay to citizen soldiers of, 302 sqq.; its value, 309 sq.
Achaean League, an employer, 80, 90 sqq.; 94 sq., 97 sq.; resources of, 99 sqq., 107; 121, 180; maintenance of soldiers of, 291; 318; peltast? mercenaries of, 319
Achaeans, κοινόν of, 134, 246; allies and? mercenaries of Eumenes I, 174, 179 sq., 246; mercenaries in 5th century, 238; 305
Achaeus, an employer? 143; 173
Achillas, 130
Acragas, 194, 200, 205, 209, 212, 216, 253
Adriatic, sea, 193
Aegae, 63
Aegosagae (Gauls), mercenaries of Attalus I, 173 sq.
Aegosthena, 59
Aemilius Paullus, L., 234
Aenianes, mercenaries at Athens, 240 n. 2
Aeolis, early mercenaries from? 236
Aetolia, 58; man-power of, 81; a recruiting ground, 81, 121, 258; 94; Ptolemaic connection with, 242 n. 2; plundered by Philip V, 291
Aetolians, in Lamian War, 36; with Polyperchon, 46; mercenaries with Pyrrhus, 61 sq.; with the Antigonids, 67, 74, 77; as employers, 80 sqq.; 101; Ptolemaic mercenaries, 121, 133, 242 n. 2; with Antiochus III? 165; allies of Attalus I, 171; mercenaries in 5th century, 238; summary, 245; as pirates, 262 sq.; rate of pay to citizen soldiers of, 302 sqq.; its value, 309 sq.
Africa, Agathocles in, 199 sqq.; Carthage and, 208 sqq. *passim*
Africans, *see* Libyans
Agathocles, minister of Ptolemy IV and V, 128 sqq., 135, 137 sq.

Agathocles, of Syracuse, an employer, 197 sqq.; *condottiere*, 198; influence of Alexander on? 200 sq.; 210 sqq.
Agathocles, Ptolemaic official, 277
Agesilaus, king of Sparta, his recruiting through individuals, 257
Agesilaus, brother of Agis III, 259
Agis III, of Sparta, 33
Agis IV, 94
Agrianians, mercenaries? of Alexander, 12 sqq., 20, 201, 228, 320; with the Antigonids 70, 72, 74, 75 n. 1, 78; with Antiochus III, 144
Alcetas, an employer, 44
Alexander, son of Polyperchon, 46
Alexander the Great, an employer, 12 sqq., 27; his reinforcements, 17 sqq.; his cities and garrisons, 22 sqq., 48, 149, 152; his military policy for the Empire, 23, 33, 37; value of mercenaries to, 23 sqq.; his "second line" of mercenaries, 30 sqq.; his field army and *Occupationsarmee*, 32; his "exiles' decree", 34; "the luck of", 38; the subsequent importance of his military system, 39, 317; the number of his mercenaries? 39; 200 sq., 214, 222, 227 sq., 232 sq., 239, 259, 283; bonuses, etc. of, 292, 297 sq.; rate of his pay to mercenaries, 297 sqq.; to citizen soldiers, 297 sqq.; economic results of his conquests, 308 sq.; 320
Alexander Balas, 167 sq., 261
Alexandria, Royal Guard at, 124 sqq., 135, 137 sq., 140; 163, 169, 311, 321
Alexandrians, 130
Alexon, Achaean, 216
Alps, 215, 229
Amasia, 186
Ambraciots, levy of Pyrrhus, 62
Ameinias, Phocian, 67, 262
Amisos, 186 sq., 191
Amphipolis, 10; garrisoned by Perseus, 75

INDEX

Ancyra, battle of, 166
Andromachus, officer of Ptolemy IV, 122
Andron, ἀρχιπειράτης, 59
Antigoneia (Macedonia), 75
Antigoneia (near Cyzicus), 150
Antigoneia (Orontes), a military settlement? 149 sq.
Antigonus I, Macedonian soldiers of, 39, 44, 49 sqq.; 44, 47 sqq.; the greatest employer of his day, 44, 46, 51 sqq.; 110 sq., 114; military settlements of, 149 sq., 152 sq., 301, 314 sq.; 232; recruits through Sparta, 258; receives deserters from Lysimachus, 262; his mercenaries desert, 262; 317
Antigonus Doson, an employer, 65, 69; 95, 102; rate of his pay to citizen soldiers, 303; 318 sq.
Antigonus Gonatas, 58 sq., 63; an employer, 65 sqq.; 78 sq., 262, 293
Antimenidas, 1
Antioch, 150, 169, 293, 321
Antiocheia, a dynastic name, 152
Antiochus I, military settlements of, 152, 155
Antiochus II, 166
Antiochus III (the Great), 121, 123; an employer, 143 sqq., 161, 165 sq., 174 sqq., 294, 318
Antiochus IV, 121, 124, 128, 142; military settlements of, 152 sq., 156 sq., 166
Antiochus VIII (Grypus), 162
Antiochus Hierax, an employer, 166
Antipater, 36; Macedonian soldiers of, 39, 41; his garrisons in Greece, 46
Apameia, a dynastic name, 152
Apameia (Orontes), treaty of, 146, 165, 178; 150
Apameia (Rhagai), a military settlement? 150
Apollo, Delian, 309 sq.
Apollodorus, of Cassandreia, an employer, 67, 254; gives land to mercenaries, 314
Apolloniades, an employer? 198
Apollonis, 175
Apollonopolis, 133
Aptara, allows Attalus I to recruit, 175 sq., 258
Arabs, mercenaries? of Antiochus III, 144 sq., 167, 251

Arachosia, 22, 51
Aratus, of Sicyon, 94, 99 sqq.; 106, 263
Arcadians, 82; mercenaries in 5th and 4th centuries, 237 sq.
Arces, officer of Eumenes I, 173, 287
Archelaus, 190 sq.
Archilochus, 236
Arethusa, 207
Areus, king of Sparta, 93 sq.
Argos, 10, 64 sq., 67, 69; tyranny at, 89; 94; garrisoned by Nabis, 98; 99 sq.; Pisistratus recruits through, 255; treaty with Athens of (419 B.C.), 267, 294
Ariarathes I, of Cappadocia, an employer, 43; 183
Ariobarzanes, of Pontus, an employer, 166, 184
Aristippus, of Argos, an employer, 89
Aristodemus, officer of Antigonus I, 52
Aristomachus, of Argos, an employer, 89; 100
Aristomachus, Corinthian, 206 n. 2
Aristonax, mortgages κλῆρος at Doura, 156 sq.
Aristonicus, 121
Aristophanes, Athenian, 85
Aristotimus, of Elis, an employer, 68, 88 sq.; 254
Armenia, Greeks in, 191 n. 4, 193 n. 3; 321
Arrhidaeus, Macedonian general, mercenaries of, 44
Arsaces, 165
Arsinoe (Peloponnese), 133 n. 4, 134
Arsinoe II, of Egypt, 63
Artaxerxes Ochus, an employer, 7; his edict to his satraps, 33
Artemisios, Macedonian month, 283
Asclepiodorus, officer of Perseus, 74
Asculum, battle of, 61 sq.
Asia Minor, Greek mercenaries in (4th century), 238; a recruiting ground, 240 sq.; coast of, Ptolemaic domination over, 242 n. 4
Asiatics, trained to fight in phalanx, 26, 41, 48, 51; in the armies of the Successors, 42, 48; among the mercenaries of the Successors? 43
Aspendians, Ptolemaic mercenaries, 133, 134 n. 1

INDEX

Aspendus, 131; a recruiting base? 260; mercenaries receive citizenship at, 315 sq.
Astyphilus, Athenian, 6
Athamanians, mercenaries of Pyrrhus, 61 sq., 245
Athenagoras, Macedonian, 72
Athenians, mercenaries in Asia Minor, 43 n. 2; with Demetrius at Ipsus, 52, 55; in Egypt (4th century), 239; in Ptolemaic army, 242 n. 2
Athenodorus, led rising of military settlers in Bactria, 34, 36
Athens, military service relaxed at, 2; Harpalus at, 33, 259; her relations with mercenaries at Taenarum, 35 sq.; permits Demetrius to recruit? 52; garrisoned by Demetrius, 58; by Antigonus Gonatas, 66, 68; an employer, 80, 82 sqq., 240; "Tarentines" at, 86, 248; helps Ophellas to recruit, 199; treaty with Argos of (419 B.C.), 267, 294; military finance of (4th century), 269 sqq.; pay of mercenaries at, 290, 295 sqq.; of citizen soldiers at, 294, 296; hires Thracian peltasts (5th century), 295; allowance of paupers and dicasts at, 308
Attaleia, 173, 175, 287
Attalids, the, employers, 171 sqq.
Attalus, Macedonian general, 16
Attalus I, of Pergamum, mercenaries of, 171 sqq., 240 sq.; 258
Attalus II, military policy of, 179 sqq.; 185; 258
Attalus III, testament of, 177 sqq., 181
Attinas, officer of Eumenes I, 173, 287
Augustus, 234
Autariatae (Thracians), mercenaries of Lysimachus, 54
Autaritus, Campanian, 220
Autonous, Thessalian, 206 n. 3
Avroman parchments, the, 160, 177

Babylon, 21, 22, 49, 53 sq., 227, 299
Bactra, 20
Bactria, Alexander's army of occupation in, 23, 33; risings of military settlers in, 27, 34, 36 sq.
Baecula, battle of, 228
Baetis, river, 227

Balearians, slingers, mercenaries of Carthage, 208 sqq., 219, 227 sqq.
Balearic Islands, a recruiting ground, 209 sq., 251
Balkan mercenaries, with Alexander, 239; in Egypt, 243; (*and see* Thracians, Illyrians, etc.)
Barbarians, mercenaries of Macedonia, 68 sqq., 78 sqq.; of Aristotimus of Elis, 68; in Sicily, 197, 239; at Athens, 240 sq.; in Egypt, 243; in general, 254; rates of pay to? 293, 305; their styles of fighting, 320
Barcids, family of, 221, 226 sq., 232 n. 3, 233
Bastarnae, relations with Perseus of, 75 sq., 258; mercenaries of Mithridates VI, 189 n. 3; ἄμιπποι, 249 n. 1; σιτηρέσιον of? 293; pay of? 306 n. 2
Berenice, Seleucid queen, 166
Beroia, 151
Bithynia, 166; kings of, 174; their mercenaries, 182 sqq.; 190 sq.
Biton, led rising of military settlers in Bactria, 34, 36
Black Sea, 192; mercenary from, 240
Blaundos, κατοικία and πόλις? 154
Boeotia, 239; "Tarentines" in, 248
Boeotians, mercenaries? of Perseus, 74, 77; a mercenary (4th century), 239; ἄμιπποι, 249
Bomilcar, 211
Bonus, to mercenaries, 267, 286, 292 sq., 297 sq.
Botrichus, Arcadian, 98
Brasidas, 255
Bruttians, 200; in Hannibal's army, 231 n. 1, 233
Byzantium, 185

Cadusians, 144
Caesar, C. Julius, 130 sq., 235
Caicus, river, 282
Calas, 13
Calymnus, 91
Campania, a recruiting ground, 195
Campanians, mercenaries of Agathocles, 202; the Mamertines, 202 sq.; mercenaries of Carthage, 209, 233, 239
Cannae, battle of, 229 n. 1, 230

INDEX

Cappadocia, 43, 47, 176; mercenaries with kings of, 182 sqq.; 191, 261; plundered by Eumenes of Cardia, 291
Cappadocians, cavalry of Eumenes of Cardia, 42; in army of Antiochus III, 145
Cardaces, 144
Caria, 109; Ptolemaic garrisons in? 127
Cariandian, a mercenary (4th century), 239
Carians, an officer of Demetrius, 58; mercenaries? of Philip V, 72; subject to Ptolemy II, 132; in army of Antiochus III, 145; the earliest mercenaries? 236, 255
Carmania, 21
Carmanians, 143 sq.
Carthage, 92, 133, 198 sqq.; an employer, 207 sqq.; her dependence upon mercenaries, 224 sq., 231 sqq.; summary of their provenance, 251; methods of recruiting of, 258, 260; payment of mercenaries at, 288 sqq., 294
Carthaginians, 194, 197 sqq.; mercenaries of, 207 sqq.; 234, 239
Carystian, a Ptolemaic soldier, 134 n. 1
Carystus, 91
Caspian, sea, 144
Cassander, Macedonian soldiers of, 39, 46; 45 sqq.; his garrisons in Greece, 46; 52 sqq.; 77
Cassandreia, garrisoned by Perseus, 75; inscription of, 77; mercenaries receive land at, 314
Cassandreians, mercenaries at Athens, 240 n. 2
Cavalry, rates of pay to, 302; heavy cavalry style unsuitable for mercenaries? 317
Celtiberians, mercenaries of Carthage, 225 sqq.; of Rome, 234
Celts, mercenaries of Dionysius I, 195, 239; of Carthage, 209, 222, 227; *and see* Gauls, of Gaul and Italy
Chaeronea, battle of, 5, 11 sq.; second battle of, 190 sq.
Chalcedon, financial device of, 271
Chalcidice, peltasts of, 10, 238
Chaonians, 62
Chares, Athenian general, 10, 35

Charidemus, his career, 6; 262
Charimortus, Aetolian, 132 n. 7
Chersonese (Thracian), 11, 57
Chersonesus (Crimea), 188 sq.
Chios, 20
Chremonidean War, 93
Cilicia, a recruiting ground, 47, 261; pirates, etc. of, 130; 265
Cilicians, 132; κοινόν of, 134, 251; mercenaries? with the Seleucids, 143 sqq., 167, 251
Cimmerian Bosporus, 189
Cineas, officer of Pyrrhus, 61
Cissians, 144
Citium, 126 n. 2, 133 n. 5
Clazomenae, financial device of, 271
Cleander, Macedonian, 28
Clearchus, Macedonian, 28
Cleinon, Greek officer of Carthage, 211
Cleitus, Macedonian, 36
Cleomenes, king of Sparta, 94 sq.; 100 sqq.; in Egypt, 127 sq.; 318 sq.
Cleomenes, minister of Alexander in Egypt, 109; financial device of, 269
Cleonae, battle of, 89
Clondicus (or Cloelius), 76, 258
Cnossians, as mercenaries, 81
Cnossus, treaty with Aetolian League of, 81; employs Dorylaus, 187; coin types of, perhaps due to mercenaries, 195 n. 7
Coele-Syria, recruiting in, 47, 261
Coenus, Macedonian, 26
Coeratadas, Theban, *condottiere*, 6
Colchis, 188
Conon, κλῆρος at Doura of, 157
Contract, of mercenaries, 99, 172 sq., 261, 266, 282 sqq., 293, 314
Coprates, river, 49
Corcyra, 270
Corinth, garrisoned by Polyperchon, 45; by Cassander, 46 n. 1; by Antigonus Gonatas, 66 sqq.; by Philip V, 71, 105; tyranny at, 89; 100, 110
Corinthian, mercenary (4th century), 239
Corn, *see* σῖτος, etc.
Cos, an employer, 90; payment of mercenaries at, 283, 304, 312
Cotys, 74 sq., 258, 293, 306
Craterus, Macedonian general, 36, 41 sq.; his mercenaries surrender, 262
Cratesipolis, an employer, 47, 89

INDEX

Cretans, mercenaries of Alexander, 13 sqq.; of Demetrius, 53; with the Antigonids, 69 sqq., 74 sqq., 92; of Rhodes, 69; of Rome, 92, 234 sq.; of Sparta, 94 sqq.; of the Achaean League, 105 sqq.; of the Ptolemies, 118 sqq., 127 sq., 133 sq., 242 n. 3, 252; κοινόν of, 134; mercenaries of the Seleucids, 143 sqq., 165, 169 sq.; of Pergamum, 174 sq., 177, 241 n. 3; of Mithridates V, 186 sqq.; at Syracuse, 195 n. 7, 205 sqq.; in 5th century, 238; a *type* of soldier? 241, 251; at Athens, 240 n. 10; summary, 245; as pirates, 263; rate of pay to citizen soldiers of, 303 sqq.; to mercenaries of, 303; their style of fighting, 319 sq.

Crete, Harpalus in, 33; Thibron in, 43; a recruiting ground, 69, 81, 91 sqq., 105, 121, 161, 165, 176, 186, 240 sqq., 257 sq.; mercenaries employed in, 92; Areus in, 93; relations with Nabis of, 98, 263; Philopoemen in, 103 sqq.; Ptolemaic garrisons in, 133 sq.; treaty of Eumenes II with cities of, 176

Crimea, 188 sqq.

Crimisus, battle of the, 209 sq.

Critolaus, Achaean, 105

Croesus, 236

Cunaxa, 266

Cyclades, 132

Cynoscephalae, battle of, 72

Cyprus, 47, 53; Ptolemaic troops in, 109 sqq.; 126 n. 2, 133 sq., 246, 251; 261 sq.

"Cyreians", the, how paid, 266 sqq., 273; how much paid, 295; value of their pay, 308

Cyrenaeans, in Ptolemaic army, 134, 242 n. 5; a mercenary (4th century), 239

Cyrene, Thibron at, 43, 260; 109 sq., 120; Ptolemaic garrisons at, 131; Ophellas at, 199

Cyrtaeans, 145

Cyrus, the Younger, 99, 237; recruits in Greece, 255; how he paid his mercenaries, 265 sq.; bonuses of, 292; rate of his pay, 295

Cyzicus, 150

Dahae (Scythians), mercenaries? of the Seleucids, 143 sqq., 167, 251

Daisios, Macedonian month, 283

Damascus, sack of, 300

Damippus, Spartan, 206 n. 1

"Danegeld", 203

Daphne, review of Antiochus IV at, 142, 146 sqq., 153, 161, 165 sqq.

Dardanelles, 262

Darius III, 20, 320

Datames, financial device of, 268

Deinocrates, officer of Philip V, 72

Deinocrates, Greek officer of Carthage and of Agathocles, 200 sq., 211

Delos, wages and standard of life at, 307 sqq.

Delphi, 273

Demetrias, garrisoned by Antigonus Gonatas, 66; by Perseus, 75

Demetrius (Poliorketes), 52 sqq.; an employer after Ipsus, 57 sqq.; temperamentally a *condottiere*? 57; army strength of, 58 sq.; garrisons of, 58 sq.; his last mercenaries in Asia, 59; 86, 110 sq., 116, 133, 233; his mercenaries desert, 262; rate of his pay to citizen soldiers, 300 sq.; to mercenaries? 301; its value, 309; 317

Demetrius I (Seleucid), 168

Demetrius II, 161, 164, 168 sq., 292, 322

Demosthenes, Athenian general, 295

Demosthenes, Attic orator, his tendencious account of the Macedonian army, 11

Desertion, of mercenaries, 261 sq.; *and see* Macedonians

Dicaearchus, Aetolian, 262

Didas, Paeonian, 74

Diegylis, 185

Diodorus, officer of Demetrius, 59

Dion, in Sicily, 197

Dion, Ptolemaic military secretary, 277

Dionysius I, an employer, 194 sqq.; 201, 203, 206, 209, 239, 254 sq.; gives land to mercenaries, 196, 315

Dionysius II, an employer, 197

Dionysodorus, military theorist, 5

Diophantus, of Sinope, 188, 191

Diospolis, Magna, 132; Parva, *ibid.*

Dioxippus, at Athens, 86

Docimus, of Tarentum? officer of Philip V, 247

Dorian islands, etc., early mercenaries from? 237

332 INDEX

Dorylaus, officer of Mithridates V, 186 sq.
Dorylaus, of Amisos, nephew of above, officer of Mithridates VI, 187
Drepanum, 216
Dymaeans, employers, 101
Dyme, mercenaries receive citizenship at, 315

Ebro, river, 225 sqq.
Ecbatana, 33, 150; plunder of, 300
Ecnomus, 211
Edessa, 151
Egypt, earliest mercenaries in, 3, 236; Alexander's army of occupation in, 18, 22, 25, 30; 51; under the Ptolemies, 108 sqq.; statistical evidence from, 241 sqq.; process of payment, etc. in, 277 sqq.; rate of pay in? 306 sq.; its value, 311 sq.
Elaites, mercenaries of Pergamum, 211 n. 4
Elephants, African, of Carthage, 213 sqq., 222 n. 3
Eleusis, Athenian garrisons at, 84 sq.; civilian wages at, 308, 310
Eleuthernae, treaty with Antigonus Doson of, 69
Elis, under Aristotimus, 68, 88; an employer, 82; 101; "Tarentines" at, 247 sqq.
Elymians (Asia), 145
Elymians (Sicily), 195, 209
Entella, 197
Ephesus, 57; garrisoned by Demetrius, 59; by Ptolemy II, 133; scene of *Miles Gloriosus*, 165; Heraclides recruits at, 168; a recruiting base? 261; 311
Epidaurus, inscription of, 300
Epirotes, of Phoenice, 212, 252 sq.
Epistratus, Acarnanian, 106 n. 5
Erythrae, 133
Eryx, 216, 253
Ethiopians, 132
Etna, 197
Etruria, 215
Etruscans, mercenaries of Agathocles, 199 sq.; of Carthage, 210
Eumeneia (Phrygia), a military settlement? 179
Eumenes, of Cardia, Macedonian soldiers of, 39, 41; Cappadocian cavalry of, 42 sq.; his war with Antigonus, 44, 47 sqq.; his relations with Polyperchon, 47; his recruiting, 47, 261; 150, 232; his soldiers desert, 262; systematic plundering of, 291; 317
Eumenes I, of Pergamum, famous inscription of, 172 sq., 261, 282 sqq.; 312, 320
Eumenes II, 73; mercenaries of, 176 sqq.; military settlements of? 179 sqq.
Euphrates, 23, 156
Eupolemus, an employer, 292 sqq.; gives land to mercenaries? 315
Euripidas, Aetolian, 82
Euripides, 213
Europos, 150 sq., 159
Eurydice, queen of Macedonia, 8
Eurydice, an employer, at Cassandreia, 314

Flamininus, T. Quinctius, 98, 103, 234
Flaminius, C., 206
"Friends", of Mithridates V and VI, 187 sq.

Gabiene, battle of, 53, 109 sqq., 116, 139, 262, 319
Gaesatae, Gallic mercenaries, 230 n. 7
Galatians, 146, 166 sq., 175, 252; *and see* Gauls
Garsyeris, 143 n. 1
Gaugamela, mercenary infantry at, 17, 28, 30; mercenary cavalry at, 29; second line of mercenaries at, 31 sq.; 201
Gaul, a recruiting ground, 208, 210, 251; Cretan mercenaries in, 235
Gauls, mercenaries with Pyrrhus, 63 sq.; with Antigonus Gonatas, 66 sqq.; with Apollodorus of Cassandreia, 67; with Antigonus Doson, 70; with Philip V, 71; with Perseus, 74 sq.; military settlers? in Macedonia, 78; 79; of Asia Minor, 90; in Ptolemaic army, 118 sqq., 137, 142; in Seleucid army, 143 sqq., 166 sq.; in Pergamene army, 173 sqq., 177, 180, 258; with kings of Bithynia, 183 sq., 258; with kings of Pontus, 184 sq., 189 n. 3; with Orophernes of Cappadocia? 185; of Gaul and Italy, with Agathocles, 199; with Car-

INDEX

thage, 210, 212, 219, 222, 227 sqq.; with Massilia, 230 n. 7; with Rome, 234; summary, 252 sq.; pay of? 293
Gaza, battle of, 53, 109 sqq., 116, 139, 262, 319
Gedrosia, 23
Gelon, tyrant of Syracuse, mercenaries of, 194
Genthius, 75 sqq.
Gergitha, 175
Germans, ἄμιπποι, 249 n. 1
Gescon, 209
Gisgo, 218 sq.
Gordium, 20
Gortynia, 105, 187
Granicus, mercenary infantry at, 31
Great Plains, battle of, 227
Greece, North and Central, a recruiting ground, 240 sqq.
Greek mercenaries (*see also under* provenance), before Alexander, 2 sqq.; with Alexander, 13 sqq., 239; with the Successors, 42 sqq.; with Pyrrhus, 61 sq.; with the Antigonids, 68 sqq., 74 sqq., 78 sqq., 244; with Greek leagues and cities, 81 sq., 87 sq., 91 sqq., 104 sqq.; with the Ptolemies, 117 sqq., 127 sq., 132 sqq., 136 sqq., 241 sqq., 320; with the Seleucids, 143 sqq., 149, 161, 165 sqq., 244; with Pergamum, 171 sq., 174 sqq., 179 sqq., 240 sq.; with kings of Pontus, 183, 186, 188 sqq.; in Sicily, 194 sqq., 239; with Carthage, 209 sqq., 216, 219, 222, 231; in the earliest times, 236 sqq., 255; as military settlers in Egypt, 242 sq.; with Bosporan kings, 244; at Cyrene, *ibid.*; heyday of, 244, 320; decline of, 244, 251 sqq., 320 sqq.; κοινόν of, 246; pay, etc. of, chap. x *passim*; armament of, 319 sq.
Gyges, 3, 255
Gythium, garrisoned by Nabis, 98

Halicarnassus, Alexander's garrison at, 22
Hamilcar (309 B.C.), 201, 211
Hamilcar Barca, 221
Hannibal, 206, 215; his army, 222 sqq.; his genius, 233
Hannibal (410 B.C.), 208 sq.
Hanno, the Great, 215, 218

Hanno (218 B.C.), 226
Hanno (206 B.C.), 226
Harpalus, Macedonian, flees from Alexander with mercenaries, 33; at Taenarum, 259
Hasdrubal Barca, 215, 223, 230
Helenus, 64
Hellenization, mercenaries instrumental in, 321 sq.
Hellespont, 175, 239
Heraclea, battle of, 62
Heraclea (Pontica), 266, 268; financial device of, 270
Heraclea (Rhagai), a military settlement? 150
Heracleon, 162
Heracles, bastard of Alexander, 46
Heraclides, Macedonian governor at Athens, 58 n. 3
Heraclides, officer of Demetrius II (Seleucid), 168; his recruiting campaign, 261
Hermias, Ptolemaic bank-cashier, 277
Hermoupolis Magna, 132
Hicetas, an employer? 198, 209
Hierapytna, treaty with Antigonus Doson of, 69, 303; with Rhodes, 69, 91 sq., 174, 257, 303 sqq., 310
Hieron II, an employer, 202 sqq.; 212, 221
Hieronymus, successor of Hieron II, an employer, 206 sq.
Himera, 209
Himilco, 209
Hindu Kush, 33
Hipparchus, officer of Antigonus I, 52 n. 2
Hoplites, citizen, rate of pay of, 294, 296 sqq. *passim*; mercenaries, rate of pay of, 295 sqq. *passim*
Hyperides, his conspiracy with Leosthenes (or with Chares?), 35

Iapygians, mercenaries (5th century), 239
Iberians, mercenaries of Dionysius I, 195, 239; at capture of Syracuse (Spaniards), 207; mercenaries of Carthage, 209 sq., (Spaniards) 212, 219, (Spaniards) 222; position in Hannibal's army of, 225 sqq., 231 sq.
Ilipa, battle of, 226, 228

334 INDEX

Illyria, possible recruiting ground for Philip II, 10
Illyrians, "masters" of Macedonia, 359 B.C., 8; mercenaries (5th century), 9; of Alexander, 13 sqq.; of the Antigonids, 68, 70 sqq., 75 n. 1, 252; military settlers? in Macedonia, 78, 314; mercenaries of Achaean League, 104, 252
India, Alexander's mercenary reinforcements in, 21; his cities and garrisons in, 23; mutiny in the garrisons in, 26; *mahouts* from, 214; Alexander's method of paying his troops in, 300
Indian trainers, of African elephants, 214 sq., 222 n. 3
Ionia, early mercenaries from? 236; Ptolemaic influence in, 246
Ionians, κοινόν of, 134, 246
Iphicrates, his reformed peltast, 5, 17, 196, 317; 83, 239
Ipsus, battle of, 52, 53 sqq.; 149, 243, 262, 320
Islands, the, a recruiting ground, 240 sqq.
Isocrates, 2, 4, 7
Issus, mercenaries of Alexander at, 27, 29; "second line" of mercenaries at, 31
Italian city-states, 2; *condottieri* of, 5
Italians, in Hannibal's army, 222, 231
Italy, a recruiting ground, 199, 209, 243, 251; Hannibal in, 222

Jason of Pherae, standing army of, 5; its efficiency, 6; bonuses of, 273, 292
Jerusalem, 258
Jews, mercenaries? of later Seleucids, 167 sqq., 251, 258, 292
Jonathan, High Priest, 167
Judea, 167 sq.

Kalamata, 260
Keteus, 48
Kyinda, 57

Lachares, Macedonian? 67
Lamia, 36
Lamian War, 35 sq., 38 sq., 43
Laodicea (Asia Minor), an Attalid military settlement near? 180; mercenary garrison of Rome at, 235

Laodicea (Rhagai), a military settlement? 150
Larissa (Syria), a military settlement? 151 sq.
Larissa (Thessaly), 152
Larissa Cremaste, 75
Lasthenes, Cretan, officer and minister of Demetrius II (Seleucid), 169, 322
Leonidas, Spartan, 74
Leonidas, king of Sparta, 94
Leonnatus, Macedonian general, 36
Leontini, 196, 209
Leosthenes, Athenian, organizer of Alexander's disbanded mercenaries, 34 sqq.; at Taenarum, 35, 259 sq.; general in Lamian War, 36; his collusion with military settlers in Bactria? 37; 322
Leptines, an employer? 198
Leptines, demagogue, 203
Lesbians, mercenaries at Athens, 240 n. 5
"Leukanoi", mercenaries at Athens, 240 n. 5; of Pergamum, 241 n. 5
Leukios, officer of Aristotimus of Elis, 68 n. 5
Libya, 132
Libyans, in Ptolemaic army, 118 sq.; mercenaries at Syracuse (Africans), 207; subject levies of Carthage, 208 sqq., 216; perhaps mercenaries in first Punic War, 219 sqq.; position in Hannibal's army of (and Africans), 222 sqq., 231
Liguria, a recruiting ground, 208, 210
Ligurians, mercenaries of Agathocles, 200; of Carthage, 209 sq., 212, 219, 222, 227 sqq.
Lilaea, inscriptions of, 171 sq., 240
Lilybaeum, 216
Locri, 195
Locrians, mercenaries at Athens, 240 nn. 2 and 7
Longarus, 14
Lucullus, L. Licinius, 190
Lycia, a recruiting ground, 261
Lycians, mercenaries with Lysimachus, 54; subject to Ptolemy II, 132; in army of Antiochus III, 145; mercenaries at Athens, 240; at Aspendus (Ptolemaic), 251, 316
Lycomedes, Arcadian, 237
Lycon, Achaean, 267
Lycurgus, king of Sparta, 70, 95

INDEX 335

Lycus, Achaean, 74
Lycus, river, 173
Lydiades, of Megalopolis, 94
Lydians, in army of Antiochus III, 144 sq.
Lysander, 255
Lysimacheia, 66 sq., 172
Lysimacheians, mercenaries of Pergamum, 172, 241 n. 5
Lysimachus, an employer, 53 sq., 59; 57, 60, 66, 142, 182; his mercenaries desert, 262

Macedonia, a backward country before Philip II, 8; man-power of, 9, 18, 40, 54, 69, 72, 74 sq.; mercenaries in the armies of, chap. III; their provenance, 252 sqq.; military settlements in? 77 sq.; 239
Macedonians, of Philip and Alexander, chap. I *passim*; their displeasure at Alexander's pro-Persian policy, 26, 38; under the Successors, 39 sqq., 44, 48 sqq., 317 sq.; their equivocal position, 39 sq.; their numbers, 40 sq.; desert Cassander for Demetrius, 53; desert Demetrius for Lysimachus and Pyrrhus, 60; with Pyrrhus, 61 sq., 64; desert Antigonus Gonatas for Pyrrhus, 63, 67; under the Antigonids, 65 sqq.; peltasts? 71, 75 n. 1, 119; in the Ptolemaic army, 109 sqq., 139, 243; in the Seleucid army, 149, 162; mercenaries with Rome, 234; at Athens, 240 n. 9; of Pergamum, 241 n. 2; summary, 245 sq.; rate of their pay, 297 sqq., 305
"Macedonians", infantry of the phalanx, not necessarily of Macedonian birth, perhaps already in period of the Successors, 41; with the Ptolemies, 109 sqq., 129, 131, 136, 139 sqq., 241 sqq.; with the Seleucids, 143, 146, 147 sqq., 161 sqq., 168 sq.; with Pergamum, 177 sqq.; in general, 250
Machanidas, tyrant of Sparta, 95 sq., 104
Maeotians, 189
Magas, 120 sq.
Magnesia (Maeander), battle of, 142, 143 sqq., 153, 161, 165 sqq., 174 sqq., 180, 251 sqq., 291, 318, 320

Magnesia (Sipylus), Seleucid κάτοικοι at, 154 sqq.
Magnesians, mercenaries in Egypt, 242 n. 4
Mago (6th century), army reforms of, 207
Mago (393 B.C.), 209
Mago (344 B.C.), 209
Mago Barca, 226, 228, 230
Malea, Cape, 259
Mamercus, an employer? 198
Mamertines, 202 sq.
Mantias, 9
Mantinea, battle of, 95, 104, 252 sqq., 319; garrisoned by Achaean League, 102, 105; inscription of, 106
Maracanda, 22
Marcellus, M. Claudius, 207
Marius, C., 261
Maroneia, 72
Mars, 310
Masdye, 179
Masdyenians, in Pergamene army, 177, 179, 251
Massagetae, ἄμιπποι, 249 n. 1
Massilia, an employer, 230 n. 7
Massinissa, 227, 233
Mathos, Libyan, officer of Carthage, 220
Mauri, mercenaries? of Carthage, 227 sqq.
Maurusii, mercenaries? of Carthage, 227
Medes, in army of Antiochus III, 144
Media, Alexander's mercenary reinforcements in, 20; 51; provides levies for Seleucus I? 54; 143; Seleucid military settlements in, 160
Medius, Thessalian, 44
Medymna, 195
Megalopolis, 94, 100, 106, 310
Megara, 10; inscription of, 59
Memnon, Rhodian, financial device of, 268 sq.
Memphis, 20, 25; payment of ἐπίγονοι at, 278 sq., 306 sq., 312
Menander, his "Recruiting Officer", 6; his "4 obols", 301, 308
Menander, Macedonian, commanding mercenaries of Alexander, 25 n. 4, 28
Menelaus, Macedonian, 109 sq.
Mercenaries' War, 215, 217 sqq.

336 INDEX

Mesopotamia, 49, 142, 321
Messana, 196, 202
Messene, 10; coin types of, perhaps due to mercenaries, 195 n. 7
Messenians, mercenaries of Dionysius I, 195
Metaurus, battle of the, 215, 230
Methana, 133 n. 4
Metrodorus, 186
Miles Gloriosus, 165, 261
Milesians, mercenaries in Egypt, 242 n. 4
Miletus, 18, 20, 27, 29
Military settlements, *see* κατοικίαι, κάτοικοι, κληροῦχοι
Minorca, 228
Mithridates I, of Pontus, an employer, 166, 183
Mithridates III, an employer, 186
Mithridates V (Euergetes), an employer, 186 sqq.
Mithridates VI (Eupator), an employer, 186 sqq., 235
Mnesimachus, mortgages κλῆρος, 157 n. 3
Moiragenes, 128 sq.
Molon, an employer, 143, 165
Molossus, Thracian name, 180
Morgantia, 198
Morgantines, 198
Morocco, 228
Morzos, king of Paphlagonia, 179; an employer, 185
Mosteni Macedones, 179
Mylasa, 315
Myrmidon, Athenian, 109
Mysia, 172
Mysians, mercenaries? with Seleucids, 143 n. 1, 145 sqq., 167, 251; with Pergamum, 171 sq., 177, 251; a *type* of soldier in Egypt? 241 n. 6, 250
Mytilene, 22, 27

Nabis, tyrant of Sparta, an employer, 96 sqq., 263; 105 sq.; gives land to mercenaries, 315
Nakrasa, κατοικία and πόλις, 151 nn. 2 and 4, 179 n. 2
"Neocretans", 146
New Comedy, its portraits of soldiers, 323 sq.
Nicaea, an employer, 89
Nicanor, founder of Doura, 156
Nicanor, of Stagirus, 34

Nicocles, of Sicyon, an employer, 89, 99
Nicodemus, an employer? 198
Nicomedes I, of Bithynia, an employer, 106, 183 sq., 258
Nile, 109, 111
Nisaeans, 146
Nisyrean, mercenary (4th century), 239
Nora, 47
Numidia, a recruiting ground, 208
Numidians, 201, 216; mercenaries? of Carthage, 212, 221, 223, 258; position in Hannibal's army of, 227; 229 n. 2, 232
Nypsius, Campanian, 197

Odrysians, mercenaries? with Alexander, 13 sqq.
Oloichus, Thracian? 173, 287
Olympia, 34, 82
Omanes, 155
Ophellas, an employer, 199
Orchomenus (Peloponnese), 53
Oscans, language of, prevalent in Sicily, 197

Paeonia, 73
Paeonians, mercenaries? with Alexander, 13
Palaimagnesia, Seleucid κάτοικοι at, 154 sqq.; pay of garrison at, 290; 316
Palestine, 110 sq., 132
Palmyra, 156
Pamphylians, mercenaries with Lysimachus, 54; subject to Ptolemy II, 132; in army of Antiochus III, 145; at Aspendus (Ptolemaic), 251, 316
Pangaeus, Mount, 10
Paphlagonia, 179, 185
Paraitacene, battle of, 39, 42, 48 sqq.; 253
Paramonus, officer of Eumenes I, 173, 287
Parmenion, 11
Parthia, kings of, 156; their policy towards Greeks, 160 sq.
Pasiphilus, officer of Agathocles, 200
Pausanias, Macedonian pretender, 8
Pay, etc., *see* μισθός, ὀψώνιον, σιτηρέσιον, etc.
Peithon, Macedonian general, suppresses rising of military settlers in Bactria, 37; supports Antigonus

INDEX

against Eumenes, 48 sqq.; recruits mercenaries in the East, 51
Pella, review of Perseus at, 74
Pella (Apameia), a military settlement? 150 sq.
Peloponnese, garrisons of Cassander in, 46, 53; mercenaries of Antigonus I in, 46, 52; a recruiting ground, 52, 195, 236, 239 sqq., 246, 255, 258
Peloponnesian League, rate of pay to soldiers of, 296
Peloponnesian War, influence of, on mercenary profession, 4; 255; rate of pay during, 294 sq.
Peloponnesians, Ptolemaic mercenaries, 127 sq., 246
Peltasts, reformed by Iphicrates, 5, 17; in Sicily? 196 sq.; weight of armour of? 17, 319; Macedonians? 71, 75 n. 1, 119, 319; εὔζωνοι? 319
Pelusium, Alexander's garrison at, 25; 109; Ptolemaic garrison at, 131
Peraea, Rhodian, 72
Perdiccas, king of Macedonia, 8
Perdiccas (Regent), Macedonian soldiers of, 41 sq.; co-operates with Eumenes, 43; 109, 114; his soldiers desert, 262
Pergamum, 142, 147; inscription of, 151, 282 sqq.; an employer, 171 sqq.; provenance of mercenaries of, 251; contract and payment of mercenaries at, 282 sqq., 312 sq.
"Periclean strategy", 4
Perinthians, mercenaries at Athens, 240 n. 2
Perseus, an employer, 73 sqq.; military settlements of? 73, 77 sq., 314; military policy of, 73 sqq., 258; garrisons of, 75, 92, 181; rate of his pay to barbarian mercenaries? 306; 318 sq., 321
Persians, in Alexander's army, 24, 26; cavalry with Eumenes of Cardia, 48; with Seleucus I? 54; with Antiochus III, 144; with Seleucus II, 155; a *type* of soldier in Egypt? 241 n. 6, 243 n. 3, 250
Peucestas, Macedonian general, 48
Phaedrus, Athenian, 84
Phalaecus, Phocian general, 259

Phalanx, of Philip II, 9; of Alexander at Issus and Gaugamela, 31 sq., containing Persians? 36, 42, containing mercenaries? 42, 317; of Demetrius at Gaza containing mercenaries, 53, 317; of Pyrrhus, 61; of Sparta, 95; of the Ptolemies, 114, 117 sq., 121 sqq., 317 sq.; of Seleucus I, 317
Phalinus, of Zacynthus, 6
Pharaeans (Achaea), employers, 101
Pharcedon, 10
Pharnaces I, of Pontus, 176, 181, 184 sqq.
Pharsalus, mercenaries receive citizenship at? 315
Pheneus, coin types of, perhaps due to mercenaries, 195 n. 7
Pherae, Jason of, 5, 273, 292; coin types of, perhaps due to mercenaries, 195 n. 7
Philetaireia, 173, 175, 287 sq.
Philetairus, 282
Philip II, of Macedonia, an employer, 8 sqq.; 233, 247
Philip V, 65, 68; an employer, 70 sqq.; garrisons of, 70 sqq.; 86, 91 sq., 124, 175; his methods of maintaining soldiers in the field, 291; rate of his pay? 305; its value, 310; 314, 318
Philippides, comic poet, ransoms Athenian mercenaries 301 B.C., 52 n. 2
Philodemus, Argive, officer of Hieronymus of Syracuse, 206 n. 2
Philomelus, Phocian general, 255
Philonides, officer? of Eumenes I, 287
Philopoemen, 92, 96, 98 sq., 102 sqq.; his methods of payment to soldiers, 291; introduces Macedonian style for citizen soldiers, 318
Phocians, mercenaries of (4th century), 239, 273; mercenaries at Athens, 240 n. 9
Phocion, 36
Phocis, 10
Phoenice (Epirus), an employer, 252 sq.
Phoenicia, recruiting of Eumenes of Cardia in, 47, 261; 132 sq.
Phoenicians, language of, prevalent in Sicily, 197
Phrygia, plundered by Eumenes of Cardia, 43 sq.; 179

INDEX

Phrygians, in army of Antiochus III, 145
Phrynichus, oligarch, 86 sq.
Piraeus, garrisoned by Demetrius, 58; by Antigonus Gonatas, 66
Pirates, as mercenaries, 53, 59, 67, 262 sq.
Pisidia, 44; a recruiting ground, 261
Pisidians, in army of Alcetas, 44; of Antiochus III, 145; at Aspendus (Ptolemaic), 316
Pisistratus, recruits through Argos, 255
Pissuthnes, Arcadian mercenaries of, 237, 255
Pitos, Thracian settlers at, 119 n. 3
Plataeans, as Athenian περίπολοι? 87 sq.
Polemaeus, officer of Antigonus I, 52
Polyclitus, Cyrenaean, 206 n. 2
Polylaus, officer of Eumenes I, 173, 287
Polyperchon, Macedonian soldiers of, 39, 41, 46; his war with Cassander, 45 sq.; his mercenaries, 45; his relations with Eumenes, 47; 106
Polyrhene, treaty with Philip V of, 70
Pompey (Cn. Pompeius Magnus), 190
Pontus, kingdom of, 166, 176, 181; mercenaries with kings of, 182 sqq.
Potidea, 294 sq.
Prasiae, 6
Priene, an employer, 90
Protarchus, Ptolemaic financial official, 277
Prusias I, of Bithynia, 185
Prusias II, 181 sq., 185
Psammetichus I, of Egypt, 3, 236, 255
Pseudophilippus (Andriscus), 323
Ptolemaeus, an employer? 8
Ptolemaeus, son of Pyrrhus, 64
Ptolemaeus, officer of Ptolemy IV, 122
Ptolemais, Ptolemaic garrison at, 132; 163
Ptolemies, employers, chap. v
Ptolemy I (Soter), Macedonian soldiers of, 41, 52 sqq., 109 sqq., 139, 162; an employer, 109 sqq.; military settlements of, 116 sq.; 133, 142; receives deserters from Perdiccas, 262; his mercenaries desert, 262; importance of Greek soldiers to, 301
Ptolemy II (Philadelphus), 120, 131, 281
Ptolemy III (Euergetes I), 116 sq.
Ptolemy IV (Philopator), 127, 281
Ptolemy VI (Philometor), 121, 133 n. 5
Ptolemy VII (Euergetes II), 121
Ptolemy VIII, 134
Ptolemy Keraunus, 61
Punjaub, 26
Pydna, battle of, 76
Pyrenees, 226, 233
Pyrrhus, 57 sq., 60; an employer, 60 sqq.; recruits Gauls, 63; temperament of, 64; 66 sq., 93, 203, 214, 233

Raphia, battle of, 111 sqq., 117 sq., 137 sq., 140, 142 sq., 153, 161, 165 sqq., 251 sqq., 318, 320
Recruiting, methods of, 254 sqq.
Red Sea, Ptolemaic military stations on, 131 sqq.
Regulus, M. Atilius, 212 sqq., 219
Rhagai, 150
Rhagai-Europos, a military settlement? 150
Rhegium, 196, 198
Rhodes, siege of, 52, 58; treaty with Hierapytna of, 69, 91, 174, 257, 303 sqq., 310; an employer, 90 sqq.
Rhodian slingers, 211, 238; mercenaries (4th century), 239; Ptolemaic, 246
Rhone, 215, 230
Romans, officers and deserters with Mithridates VI, 192 sq.; deserters at Syracuse, 207; a military settler in Egypt, 243; pay of, 290 n. 1
Rome, at war with Pyrrhus, 61 sqq.; with Perseus, 73 sqq.; relations with Crete of, 92; at war with Achaean League, 106; 121; prohibits Seleucid recruiting, 165; 168, 173 sqq.; conquers Crete, 187; at war with Mithridates VI, 188 sqq.; supports Mamertines, 203; relations with Hieron II, 205 sq.; at war with Carthage, 212 sqq., 222 sqq.; an employer, 234 sq.; Cretan mercenaries at, 234
Roxolani, 189
Russia, South, 248

INDEX

Saguntum, 225, 227
Salamis (Cyprus), 110
Samians, mercenaries of Antigonus I, 52 n. 2; in Egypt, 242 n. 4
Samnites, mercenaries of Agathocles, 199
Samos, 268, 299
Sardinians, 209
Sarissa, adopted by Greek soldiers in general? 318
Sarmatians, mercenaries? of Mithridates VI, 189
Scipio, P. Cornelius Africanus, 226, 229
Scopas, Aetolian, 121, 128, 132 n. 7, 242 n. 2, 280, 292, 322
Scutage, 257
Scythia, Mithridates VI in, 190
Scythians, mercenaries? of Mithridates VI, 189 n. 3; archers (5th century), 238
Seleuceia, a dynastic name, 152
Seleucids, the, employers, chap. VI; provenance of their mercenaries, 251 sq.
Seleucus I (Nicator), supports Antigonus against Eumenes, 48 sqq.; his army at Ipsus, 53 sqq.; 60, 142; military settlements of, 149 sqq., Macedonian soldiers of, 162
Seleucus II, 154, 166
Selinus, 209
Sellasia, battle of, 65, 70, 95, 100, 102, 252, 319
Selymbrian, Ptolemaic officer, 136
Sertorius, Q., 192
Seuthes, Thracian prince, his contract with "Cyreians", 266 sq.; his promised bonus, 292
Sicans, 195, 209
Sicels, mercenaries? 195, 198
Sicily, Pyrrhus in, 62; mercenaries in, 194 sqq. *passim*, 234, 239
Sicyon, tyranny at, 89; 99, 105, 110; Ptolemaic garrison at, 131
Side, 22, 27
Sidon, 18, 20, 30
"Silver Shields", the, 40 sqq., 47, 48 n. 2, 50
Sinope, 187 sq., 191, 266
Sitalcas, Thracian name, 180
Sitalces, Odrysian prince, 14, 21 n. 2, 29
Smertorix, Gallic name, 180
Smyrna, relations with Seleucid κάτοικοι of, 151, 154 sqq.; 291; mercenaries receive citizenship at, 315
Solon, 2
Solonian law, 158
Solous, 212
Sosibius, 122, 127
Sotas, of Priene, 90
Spain, a recruiting ground, 208 sqq.; in 2nd Punic War, 222 sqq.; 234, 251
Spaniards, *see* Iberians
Sparta, permits Antigonus I to recruit, 52; 64, 67; an employer, 80, 93 sqq.; connection with Dionysius I of, 197; mercenaries of (4th century), 239; controls recruiting? 255; rate of pay at, 295 sq.; adopts Macedonian style for citizen soldiers, 318
Spendius, Campanian, 220
Spitamenes, 22 sq.
Strombichus, officer of Demetrius, 58
Successors, the, as employers, chap. II
Sunium, Athenian garrisons at, 84, 290
Susa, 20, 22; Seleucid military settlement at, 160 sq.
Susus, Cretan, 74
Syene, 132
Syllus, Cretan, 74
Syracusans, citizen soldiers of Agathocles, 199; mercenaries of Carthage, 201, 211; exiles, 201
Syracuse, an employer, 194 sqq.; Arcadian mercenaries at, 237; 239, 295
Syria, Ptolemaic garrisons in? 127; pirates, etc. of, 130; 132, 142
Syrians? mercenaries of Antigonus Gonatas, 68

Taenarum, Harpalus at, 33; Leosthenes at, 35; Thibron recruits mercenaries at, 43; Aristodemus perhaps recruits at, 52; a recruiting base, 259 sq.
"Tarentines", with Antigonus I, 49 sq.; with Demetrius at Gaza, and at the siege of Athens, 53; at Athens, 86; with Sparta, 94, 96, 98; with Achaean League, 104 sq.; with Antiochus III, 145; summary of, 246 sqq.

INDEX

Tarentum, Pyrrhus at, 61 sqq.; an employer, 61; employs Agathocles, 198; connection with "Tarentines" of? 246 sqq.
Tauromenium, 196
Taurus, Mt., 60, 165, 178
Tegea, 94
Telemnastus, Cretan, 105 n. 4
Telesphorus, officer of Antigonus I, 52
Teleutias, Spartan general, 273
Teuta, Queen, 253
Theangela, an employer, 292 sqq.; mercenaries receive land at, 315
Theangelites, mercenaries at Athens, 240 n. 4
Thebes (Egypt), royal bank at, 278
Theocritus, 2, 131
Theodotus, Aetolian, 322
Thera, Ptolemaic garrisons at, 131
Thermopylae, 11, 66
Thesprotians, levy of Pyrrhus, 62
Thessalians, cavalry (allies) of Alexander, 16 sq., 29, 300; of Pyrrhus, 61 sq.; mercenaries in Ptolemaic army, 134 n. 1, 242 n. 2; mercenaries (5th century), 238; at Athens, 240 n. 2; of Pergamum, 241 n. 2; a *type* of soldier in Egypt? 250; but not in general? 251
Thessalonica, 75
Thessaly, 53; "Tarentines" in, 248
Thibron, commands the mercenaries of Harpalus in Crete, and at Cyrene, 43; recruits mercenaries at Taenarum, 43, 260
Thibron, Spartan general, 295
Thrace, a recruiting ground, 74, 186; Ptolemaic possessions in, 132, 253
Thracians, mercenaries? with Alexander, 13 sqq.; settlers in the Far East, 48 sq.; from Bithynia? 49; mercenaries with Lysimachus, 54; with Philip V, 71 sq.; military settlers? of Perseus, 74; mercenaries with Perseus, 74 sqq.; with Achaean League, 105, 107; military settlers in Egypt, 114, 118 sqq.; Ptolemaic mercenaries, 118 sq., 133, 134 n. 1, 137, 243; Seleucid mercenaries, 144 sqq., 166; Pergamene mercenaries (Trallians), 173 sqq.; with kings of Bithynia, 185; with Mithridates V and VI, 186, 188 sqq.; with Rome, 234 sq.; in 5th century, 238; disappearance in 4th century of, 239; at Athens? 241; a *type* of soldier in Egypt? 250; summary, 253 sqq.; 293; rate of pay of (5th century), 295; its value, 308
Thrasybulus, of Calydon, 87
Thrasybulus, tyrant of Syracuse, 194
Thrasydaeus, tyrant of Himera, 194
Thyatira, κατοικία and πόλις? 153 sq.; 155 sq.
Tigranes, of Armenia, his Greek soldiers, 191 n. 4, 193 n. 3; deports "Greeks" into Armenia, 321
Timo, 98
Timoleon, 197, 209 sq.
Timotheus, financial devices of, 268 sqq., 299
Tios, 185
Tlepolemus, officer of Ptolemy IV and V, 128
Torone, garrisoned by Perseus, 75
Trapezus, 266, 269
Trasymene, Cretans at, 206; 229 n. 1, 230, 233
Trebia, battle of, 205, 229 n. 1, 230
Triballians, mercenaries? with Alexander, 13 sqq.
Tripolis, 168
Tritaeans (Achaea), employers, 101
Tychaeus, 227
Tyre, 131

West, the, a recruiting ground, 240 sqq.

Xanthippus, Spartan, 213 sq., 216, 219, 233, 260, 322
Xenoetas, Arcadian, 143
Xenophilus, ἀρχιπειράτης, 99, 263
Xenophon, *dilettante*, 1; his account of the "Cyreians", 3; his tactical experiment, 5; as a disciplinarian, 25
Xerxes, 237

Zama, battle of, 215, 223, 228 sqq.
Zamaspes, Parthian "stratiarch" of Susa, 160
Zariaspa, 20
Zoilus, Boeotian, 59

Lightning Source UK Ltd.
Milton Keynes UK
UKOW05f0506010814

236166UK00001B/13/P